# Legal Systems and Wind Energy

A Comparative Perspective

**Energy and Environmental Law & Policy Series**
**Legal Systems and Wind Energy**

VOLUME 2

**Editor**

Kurt Deketelaere

*Professor of Law, University of Leuven, Belgium,*
*Honorary Professor of Law, University of Dundee, UK; Chief of Staff,*
*Flemish Minister for Public Works, Energy, Environment and Nature*

**Editorial Board**

The aim of the Editor and the Editorial Board of this series is to publish works of excellent quality that focus on the study of energy and environmental law and policy.

Through this series the Editor and Editorial Board hope:

- to contribute to the improvement of the quality of energy/environmental law and policy in general and environmental quality and energy efficiency in particular;
- to increase the access to environmental and energy information for students, academics, non-governmental organizations, government institutions, and business
- to facilitate cooperation between academic and non-academic communities in the field of energy and environmental law and policy throughout the world.

KLUWER LAW INTERNATIONAL

# Legal Systems and Wind Energy

## A Comparative Perspective

Helle Tegner Anker, Birgitte Egelund Olsen
& Anita Rønne (eds.)

DJØF Publishing Copenhagen
2008

Wolters Kluwer
Law & Business

AUSTIN   BOSTON   CHICAGO   NEW YORK   THE NETHERLANDS

*Legal Systems and Wind Energy*
*– A Comparative Perspective*

1. edition

Published by:
DJØF Publishing
17, Lyngbyvej
P.O.Box 2702
DK 2100 Copenhagen; Denmark.
Phone: +45 3913 55 00
Fax: +45 39135555
Email: fl@djoef.dk
www.djoef.dk-forlag

Published by:
Kluwer Law International
P.O. Box 316, 2400 AH Alphen aan den Rijn
The Netherlands
Email: sales@kluwerlaw.com
www.kluwerlaw. com

ISBN 978-87-574-1817-0 (DJØF-Publishing)
ISBN 13 – 9789041128317 (Kluwer Law International)

Printed in Great Britain.

# Table of Contents

# Preface

This book is the result of a cooperation between legal scholars from University of Aarhus, University of Copenhagen and University of Southern Denmark together with colleagues from University of Oslo (N), University of Auckland (NZ), University of Waikato (NZ), Georgia State University (US), University of Illinois (US), University of Maine (US) and University of New Mexico (US).

The cooperation has been centred mainly around the Danish Masters Programme of Environmental and Energy Law (MEEL), and the book has been designed to fit into the comparative part of the programme.

We would like to thank our colleagues for all their contributions to the MEEL programme and to this book and Donald Zillman for reading through the manuscript. We would also like to thank Lene Munk Rasmussen and David Telyas for assistance in working with the manuscript and for compiling the bibliography. Special thanks are addressed to Steven Harris who has advised on language and also on questions related to consistency in substance.

The publication of this book has been supported generously by the Aarhus University Research Foundation.

Copenhagen and Aarhus, July 2008

*Helle Tegner Anker, Birgitte Egelund Olsen & Anita Rønne*

# Contributors

*Helle Tegner Anker* is Professor of Law at the Faculty of Life Sciences, Copenhagen University. She specialises in planning law, nature protection law, water law and other environmental law issues at EU as well as at national level. Helle Tegner Anker is the coordinator of the Nordic Environmental Law Network (NELN). E-mail: hta@life.ku.dk

*Barry Barton* is Professor in the School of Law, University of Waikato, Hamilton, New Zealand. His main teaching areas are land law, environmental law, natural resources law and (in the graduate programme) resource management law. His field of research is natural resources law, energy law and environmental law. He is New Zealand member and Chairperson of the Academic Advisory Group of the Section of Energy, Environment, Natural Resources and Infrastructure Law of the International Bar Association, director of the Environmental Defence Society, editor of the Australian Energy and Resources Law Journal, and member of the Journal Board of the Journal of Energy and Natural Resources Law. E-mail: barton@waikato.ac.nz

*Ellen Margrethe Basse* is Professor, dr. juris and the Head of the Climate Secretariat at Aarhus University. She was a visiting professor at Georgia State University in 2005 and 2008 and at the University of Florida in 1993, 1996 and 1998. She has been a member of several research policy councils, boards and committees. She was the Director of the Centre on Social Science Research on the Environment at Aarhus University in 1992-2002. She has written several national and international books and articles (see www.basse.dk). E-mails: emb@adm.au.dk and em@basse.dk

*Hans Christian Bugge* has been Professor of Environmental Law at the University of Oslo since 1998. He holds a doctorate in regional planning from Université de Paris II and is dr. juris of the University of Oslo. Before becoming an academic lawyer in 1991 he held senior positions in Norway's Ministry of the Environment, including the post of Director General of the Regional Planning Department, and Director of the Pollution Control Authority. He has also worked extensively with development issues, *inter alia* as deputy minister for development cooperation. He served as personal advisor to Mrs. Gro Harlem Brundtland in her work as chair of the World Commission on Environment and Development. E-mail: h.c.bugge@jus.uio.no

*Jørgen Dalberg-Larsen* is Professor of Sociology of Law and Jurisprudence at the Aarhus University School of Law. He has been a member of a number of research councils and boards, and has written several national and international books and articles including on environmental law. E-mail: jdl@jura.au.dk

*Sanford E. Gaines* is the Director of the Utton Transboundary Resources Center at the University of New Mexico School of Law. He has wide-ranging experience in environmental law, including work for the US Environmental Protection Agency and the chemical industry as well as 20 years as a law professor. He also worked at the Office of the US Trade Representative on trade and environment issues. He has written widely on US and international environmental law and legal institutions and trade-environment questions, including a textbook, Trade and the Environment. E-mail: gaines@law.unm.edu

*David Paul Grinlinton* is an Associate Professor of Law at the Faculty of Law, the University of Auckland, New Zealand. He specializes in land law, natural resources law, and mining and energy law. He has published widely on these topics. He is a founding member of the New Zealand Centre for Environmental Law, and Managing Editor of the New Zealand Journal of Environmental Law. He is also a member of the IUCN Commission on Environmental Law Specialist Group on Sustainable Use of Soils and Desertification. E-mail: d.grinlinton@auckland.ac.nz

*Margaret Rosso Grossman* is Bock Chair and Professor of Agricultural Law in the Department of Agricultural and Consumer Economics, University of Illinois, USA. She teaches courses in agricultural law, environmental law, and veterinary jurisprudence. She is author of numerous US and European law review articles and book chapters on agricultural and environmental law topics. Professor Grossman has received three Fulbright Senior Scholar Awards and a German Marshall Fund Research Award to support her research in Europe. She received the Professional Scholarship Award (2006) and the AALA Distinguished Service Award (1993) from the American Agricultural Law Association, and the Silver Medal (1999) from the European Council for Agricultural Law (CEDR). E-mail: peggyg@illinois.edu

*Ulf Hammer* has been Professor dr. juris at the University of Oslo, Scandinavian Institute of Maritime Law since 2004. He is head of the Institute's Department of Petroleum and Energy Law. Before that he was Senior Executive Officer in the Ministry of Petroleum and Energy (1983-88), Assistant Judge (1988-90), Legal Counsel in Hydro (1990-95), and Research Fellow, Researcher and Associate Professor at the Scandinavian Institute of Maritime Law (1995-2004). His main area of research is energy law. Ulf Hammer wrote his doctoral thesis on the regulation of the Norwegian electricity market. He is co-author of several books on electricity law and petroleum law, and has published several articles on these topics, both nationally and internationally. He is co-editor of the European Energy Law Report. He is a member of the Academic Advisory Group of the International Bar Association, Section on Energy, Environment, Natural Resources and Infrastructure Law. E-mail: ulf.hammer@jus.uio.no

*Julian Conrad Juergensmeyer* is Professor and Ben F. Johnson Jr. Chair in Law and Co-Director of the Center for the Comparative Study of Metropolitan Growth at Georgia State University and Adjunct Professor in City and Regional Planning at the Georgia Institute of Technology. He has taught environmental and land use law in the USA and abroad for over 40 years. His list of publications on these subjects extends to nearly 100 titles. E-mail: jjuergensmeyer@gsu.edu

*Bent Ole Gram Mortensen* is Professor at the Department of Law at the University of Southern Denmark. He specialises in EU and Danish energy and environmental law and Danish marketing law. He has written several books and articles in Danish as well as a number of international articles and book chapters in English and German within these areas. Furthermore, he is Chairman of the Patent Committee at the University of Southern Denmark and a Member of The Danish Energy Board of Appeal. E-mail: bom@sam.sdu.dk

*Birgitte Egelund Olsen* is Professor of EU and Environmental Law at the Department of Law at the Aarhus School of Business. She specialises in environmental law at international, EU and national levels, and she also does research on more general issues of EU and WTO law. She is the Programme Director of the executive Master programme in Environmental and Energy Law (MEEL) and a board member of the Nordic Environmental Law Network (NELN). E-mail: beo@asb.dk

15

*Anita Rønne* is Associate Professor in Energy Law, Faculty of Law, University of Copenhagen where she teaches courses in international energy law and environmental impact. She holds the chairmanship of the Danish Society for Energy Law and is an appointed member of the stakeholder forum of the state-owned Energinet.dk with economic/societal/legal expertise and is the legal expert of the Danish Safety Technology Authority. She is a member and former chairman of the Academic Advisory Group, Section on Energy, Environment, Natural Resources and Infrastructure Law, International Bar Association. She has administrative and consulting experience as a civil servant with the Danish Ministry of Energy and as project coordinator and regulatory consultant to the Energy Restructuring Group, Ministry of Industry and Trade, Poland under EU Commission and World Bank secondment. E-mail: anita.ronne.jur.ku.dk

*Donald N. Zillman* is President of the University of Maine at Presque Isle and Edward Godfrey Professor of Law at the University of Maine Law School. Professor Zillman has been involved in energy law matters for over 30 years in his positions at Arizona State University, the University of Utah, and the University of Maine Law School. His writings in the area include six books, several dozen articles, and an equal number of professional and academic presentations around the world. He is an author-editor of the forthcoming, Beyond the Carbon Economy (Oxford University Press 2008) with Redgwell, Barrera-Hernandez, and Omorogbe. As President of the University of Maine at Presque Isle he is leading a campaign to introduce wind generation to the campus. E-mail: donald.zillman@umpi.edu

CHAPTER 1

# Introduction

*By Helle Tegner Anker, Birgitte Egelund Olsen & Anita Rønne*

## 1. Background

As a renewable energy source, wind energy attracts considerable interest in the climate change debate. Wind energy has become a proven technology that has the potential to partly replace the dominance of fossil fuels. By giving wind energy a greater role, $CO_2$ emissions will be reduced and thereby the negative environmental impact of energy consumption. However, wind energy installations have land use implications and may also have negative effects on the environment – in particular on landscapes and other amenity values. Furthermore, the promotion of wind energy affects market conditions as the development of wind energy often requires the use of economic incentives to attract potential investors. In general, the promotion of wind energy faces certain regulatory challenges, both those embedded in environmental and land use legislation and those in energy legislation. The types of challenges may vary from one country to another and may be related to the availability of natural resources, geographic circumstances, political awareness and the level of development of industry and infrastructure etc. A key question is thus whether the challenges and chosen instruments of regulation are comparable across different countries and different legal traditions, and whether it is possible to identify the potential barriers or constraints in the legal frameworks that need to be addressed – and maybe on this basis to outline potential model solutions for further development.

This book provides an insight into the legal frameworks of selected countries by exploring the role of legal traditions, the particular legal systems as well as more specific environmental and energy legislation which is relevant to the development of wind energy. The analyses of the book thus focus on specific legislation, but they also take into account the general institutional and legal contexts in which the legislation analysed has evolved and is actually applied.

This book has many aims, including research and educational purposes as well as more practical aims directed towards legislators, public and private decision-makers and stakeholders involved in the wind energy sector. The primary aim is to gain knowledge about different measures and legal frameworks which affect the development of wind energy. In this respect a comparative approach can provide a much broader range of solutions and the opportunity of finding better solutions than an analysis which focuses on a single legal system.

However, the primary impetus for this book has been educational. The book and its case study of the installation of wind turbines has been a component of the curriculum in the third semester of the Danish Masters programme in Environmental and Energy Law (MEEL).[1] The third semester of the programme focuses on issues of comparative environmental and energy law in order to enhance the students' understanding of the differences which characterize various countries' regulatory traditions. Furthermore, the aim is to give the students a better understanding of their own legal systems and to provide them with the ability to handle the growing internationalisation of law.

## 2. A Comparative Approach

The topic of analysis in this book is the legal framework relevant to wind energy and the installation of wind turbines in four selected countries – Denmark, New Zealand, Norway and the United States. The case of wind energy is well suited to illustrate both environmental and energy law issues as well as the relationship and interplay between these areas of law.

The approach adopted in this book is a case-based comparative approach, in the sense that the focus is on the regulation of a particular case or topic – wind power and the installation of wind turbines. In order to provide a fuller reference for the comparative analysis of specific rules in the national legal systems, the book also includes a general introduction to the core western legal traditions of common law and civil law. There could be a general presumption that the legal framework for wind energy would to some extent be dependent upon the basic legal system in the country in question. To address

---

1.  The course for the Masters degree in Environmental and Energy Law is a two-year part-time post-graduate programme designed to give professionals working within the environmental and energy areas a thorough introduction to environmental and energy law, and to selected environmental and energy related issues within the fields of economics and political science.

this issue the book compares the legal framework in two countries character-ized by a civil law approach – Denmark and Norway – with two countries characterized by a common law approach – New Zealand and the United States.

Furthermore, the interplay between different regulatory levels, i.e. interna-tional, EU, federal, state and local levels, is emphasized in the book and in the comparative approach. Of the civil law countries chosen, one is an EU Member State (Denmark), and one is affiliated with the EU (Norway – an EEA State). Of the common law countries chosen, one is a federal country (the United States), and one is a non-federal country (New Zealand). The general characteristics of the relationship between different regulatory levels at international, EU and national level are also highlighted. Another impor-tant reference is to the basic elements of selected national legal systems, with a special emphasis on Denmark and the United States.

This book is not intended to be merely a description of the various rules and regulations of the countries selected. It seeks to emphasize the similari-ties and the differences of the different systems and to explain these similari-ties and differences by taking into account the different legal systems and tra-ditions, including aspects such as constitutional basis, historical precondi-tions, accessibility of natural resources, geographic location etc. The macro-comparison however is not an aim in itself and it is not intended to be an in-depth analysis. The actual comparative study is placed in the concluding chapter of the book, whereas the main part of the book contains descriptions and analyses of the different national systems and their various rules, regula-tions and legal solutions relevant to the development of wind energy.

It would be beyond the scope of this book to make exhaustive compari-sons of the case of wind energy. Further study of legislation, case law and the comments and proposals by legislators and academic writers would be neces-sary. Our intention is to give a comparative review of the most central issues addressed by the various contributors and thereby hopefully to be able to identify the main barriers and differences in the legal approaches, and to point out the main trends and possibly better solutions.

## 3. Environmental and Energy Law

Environmental law and energy law comprises a system of complex and inter-locking statutes, case law, treaties, fundamental legal principles, and soft law instruments and policies. In this book the term 'environmental law' is used broadly and includes legislation that regulate external 'environmental effects', e.g. effects on landscape, nature, neighbours etc.[2] Planning law and other elements of land use control are also included within the meaning of 'environmental law' used in this book. The term 'energy law' in this book primarily covers the regulation of and access to energy resources, access to the market – in this case the electricity market, grid connection, price setting etc.

The academic disciplines both of energy law and environmental law are relatively new, but they are already substantial and are quite complex. The discipline of environmental law evolved in the 1960s in response to visible – and sometimes catastrophic – environmental deterioration due to industrial activities. Energy law emerged in the 1970s as a result of the growing concern about security and diversity of supply and the energy crisis of 1973 in particular. Both energy law and environmental law are of enormous importance to society and to achieving sustainable development. Awareness of scientific knowledge is fundamental to both fields of law and inevitably leads to an interdisciplinary approach to environmental and energy problems. Further, both disciplines include other legal disciplines such as constitutional law, administrative law, competition law, tort law, property law etc. Additional elements of unquestionable importance are the irreversibility of environmental harm, the finite availability of fossil fuels and the need to avoid transferring pollution from one medium to another, which leads to a focus on preventive measures rather than traditional legal remedies.

## 4. The Structure

The general structure of the book is divided into an introduction to basic legal traditions and systems of a more general applicability (Chapters 2-4), followed by an analysis of more specific elements of environmental and energy law relevant to wind energy (Chapters 5-10), and finally by a concluding comparative chapter (Chapter 11). In addition a set of case scenarios and questions is included in Appendix I – primarily for educational purposes – together with cases and project examples in Appendices II and III. Further, Appendix IV contains a short account of facts about each country included in the analyses.

Given the differences in the legal systems and legal regimes of each country considered in this book, it is clearly impossible – nor has it been the inten-

---

2.  Not all environmental law aspects have been analysed in the study, but a selection has been made to focus on those aspects most relevant to wind energy development.

tion – to adhere strictly to an identical structure and approach in each of the national descriptions.

The structure of the book is as follows:

Chapter 2 introduces the basic elements and core concepts of the civil law and common law traditions, emphasizing the main similarities and differences. A major difference between the civil law and common law traditions is the priority given in civil law to legal codes over case law, while the opposite is a general characteristic of common law. This difference in priority can be explained by the role of the legislator in both traditions. Generally speaking, in civil law the function of the legislator is to legislate, and the function of the courts is to apply the law. In contrast, in the common law tradition judge-made precedent and the doctrine of *stare decisis* is a core element of the law. However, in common law countries in areas characterised by statutory law the role of the judges may resemble that of the civil law countries, where the judges give effect to the intentions of the legislature.

Chapter 3 highlights general characteristics of international law and EU law with respect to environmental law and energy law. International law generally regulates inter-state relations and imposes obligations on states that are parties to an international agreement. It governs matters such as jurisdiction, use of the sea and state responsibility. In contrast, EU law is characterized as supranational law. It constitutes a new legal order that operates alongside the law of the Member States, but it also overrides national law in areas such as environmental and energy policy. In the EU Member States and the EEA States affiliated with the EU it is thus EU law which to a great extent determines the legal framework for national law.

In Chapter 4, the focus is on more general characteristics of the national legal systems in Denmark and the United States respectively, with comments from New Zealand and Norway. Both descriptions of the legal systems include a brief historical overview of developments and of legal institutions and lawmaking. In addition, the chapter introduces the characteristics of the Scandinavian legal tradition, which takes its starting point in the civil law tradition, but is characterized by considerable pragmatism and a focus on the effects of the law rather than its formal content.

Before going into more detail on environmental and energy legislation Chapter 5 introduces some more general points regarding the power of public decision-makers. This includes the question of jurisdiction – in an international as well as a national context – addressing the important question of who is actually the competent authority. Furthermore, in many ways fundamental rights such as private property rights and rights related to public participation may restrict or restrain public decision-makers either substantively or procedurally. Finally, Chapter 5 outlines the basic rules regarding market conditions which prevent discrimination or distortion of competition, and which are also highly relevant when promoting wind energy production.

As location is a very important element in energy development, Chapter 6 analyses the more detailed planning and land use law rules relevant to wind energy at international, EU and at national level in the selected countries. Planning law instruments include physical or land use planning as well as other types of zoning, such as within coastal or marine areas. Differences with respect to planning instruments and planning authorities regarding on-shore versus offshore installations are emphasized.

Chapter 7 focuses on environmental assessment procedures relevant to wind energy at international, EU and national levels. This includes project-specific environmental impact assessments (EIA) as well as more strategic environmental assessments (SEA) of plans and programmes. Environmental assessment procedures are generally aimed at ensuring thorough consideration of the environmental impact prior to decision-making. The extent to which such requirements apply to the installation of wind turbines may, however, vary from one country to another.

Chapter 8 analyses the role of law for the protection of nature in a broad sense, focusing in particular on the protection of habitats and landscapes, including wetlands and the conservation of species. These aspects are relevant to wind energy development, since the installation of wind turbines may affect larger areas as well as individual species. The interests of nature protection are often reflected in the designation of protected areas or in the listing of protected species. However, a more general protection, for example of the landscape, may also be part of the legal framework.

Chapter 9 deals with specific elements of environmental protection law. Wind turbines do not cause pollution in the traditional sense. However, wind turbines may have other negative effects in particular those resulting from noise, vibration, shadows and reflections. In this respect in most countries there is a certain interplay between public law and private law, e.g. compensation claims based on nuisance or neighbour law. The chapter seeks to clarify this relationship and the extent to which negative effects of wind turbines must be compensated for under private law.

Chapter 10 emphasizes the changes in policy directions from monopoly markets and tight state control towards liberalization and open competition and, more recently, of sustainable development. Within this framework the developments in the regulation of wind energy are discussed in more detail. This covers both the international and the EU levels as well as national law.

The focus is on the instruments that are used to promote renewable energy and more specifically wind energy in generating power.

Finally, Chapter 11 attempts to synthesize the comparison between the selected countries and to draw some conclusions on the role of law and legal traditions for the development of wind energy and the installation of wind turbines. Consequently, it is not the aim to make an extensive analysis of all the possible similarities and differences in the field of wind energy law. One overall question posed is whether there is a correlation between the legal framework for wind energy and the legal tradition which forms the basis for regulation in the country in question. Another question is whether the regulatory challenges are comparable in different countries and different legal traditions, and whether it is in fact possible to identify a common approach to wind energy regulation.

CHAPTER 2

# Civil Law and Common Law Systems

*By Julian Juergensmeyer & Ellen Margrethe Basse*

## 1. Introduction

In this Chapter the two most important western legal traditions – 'civil law'[1] and 'common law'[2] – will be considered so as to provide the contexts for the descriptions of the regulation of wind turbines in the EU, Denmark and Norway (based primarily on civil law), compared with the legal regulation in New Zealand and the USA (based on common law). The civil law tradition also has relevance for international law because it is the legal tradition which was most familiar to the Western European scholars and politicians who were the fathers of international law.[3]

There will be a special emphasis on the significance of the differences – or perhaps one should say the 'alleged differences' – between the two legal traditions.

Traditionally the categorization of legal systems is based on a balancing of a number of criteria, where the historical background, constitution, ideology, way of thinking, legal systems as well as the legal traditions are all important. The following aspects are the most important:

- *The nature and role of law.* For example, rule-fixation is stronger in the culture of the civil law than in the common law; in civil law 'special legislation', e.g. environmental or energy law, refers to laws that have grown

---

1. This system is also referred to as the Roman or Franco-German system, see *Jacob W. F. Sundberg:* 'Civil Law, Common Law and the Scandinavians', in Scandinavian Studies in Law, 1969 pp. 184-205.
2. The 'Anglo-American' system, see *Jacob W.F. Sundberg:* 'Civil Law, Common Law and the Scandinavians', in Scandinavian Studies in Law, 1969 pp. 184-205.
3. *John Henry Merryman, David S. Clark & John O. Haley* (eds.): The Civil Law Tradition: Europe, Latin America, and East Asia, 1994 pp. 3-4.

up around the codes, and they regulate topics that articles of the codes themselves do not specifically cover.

–   *The sources of law.* The differing sources of law reflect and determine many of the distinguishing characteristics of the two traditions. Case law and the concept of precedent or *stare decisis* are very important in common law systems, whereas statutory rules and codes are most important in civil law systems.

–   *Institutional structure and organization.* The differing roles and sources of law influence the institutional structure which is needed to make, administer, and interpret legal rules. In the civil law system judicial supremacy rests with legislative assembly rather than the courts. Another characteristic of civil law is the bureaucratic colouring of the judicial bench. The approach is different in common law, where the attitude of judicial sovereignty and the courtroom perspective are of special importance.

–   *Roles and actors.* Legislative and administrative roles, judicial proceedings, and legal education all reflect and determine the nature of the legal systems. The courts in most *civil law* countries do not have the power to overrule statutes because they conflict with the constitution or with other statutes. All that the judges are empowered to do is to examine whether the administrative or private application of the statutes and the legal principles is correct. The sovereign position of courts in *the common law system* is in contrast to this. Common law judges are not – as is the case in the civil law countries – trained to act as civil servants. [4]

## 2. The Civil and Common Law Traditions

'Tradition' or 'family' are more accurate terms than 'system' to describe those countries which follow the common law or civil law paths because generalizations are difficult, and on some points very different approaches are followed by countries within the common law tradition or civil law tradition. [5] The terms 'legal tradition' or 'legal family' are not used to describe an operating set of legal institutions, procedures, and rules. Instead, they refer to a set

4.   Concerning these important aspects, see *Jacob W.F. Sundberg:* 'Civil Law, Common Law and the Scandinavians', in Scandinavian Studies in Law, 1969 pp. 191-196.
5.   A 'legal system', as the term is often used, covers an operating set of legal institutions, procedures, and rules, see *John Henry Merryman, David S. Clark & John O. Haley* (eds.): The Civil Law Tradition: Europe, Latin America, and East Asia, 1994 p. 3.

of deeply rooted, *historically conditioned attitudes* relating the legal system to the culture of which it is a partial expression.[6]

## 2.1. Historical Background of the Civil Law System

The civil law, the European civil law or the 'Romano-Germanic civil law system' as it is often called,[7] is the older of the two legal traditions.[8] It traces its roots back to Roman law and owes it name and core concepts to the *Corpus Juris Civilis* promulgated in the sixth century by the Byzantine Emperor *Justinian*. The *Corpus Juris Civilis* included four parts – the Institutes, the Digest, the Code and the Novels. In later centuries the Digest and the Code proved to be the most influential on the development of the civil law tradition. The Digest was a treatise summarizing what Justinian's jurists considered to be the best Roman legal writing, particularly in regard to personal status, torts, unjust enrichment, contracts and remedies. The Code was a collection of the most important Roman legislation.

The immediate influence of the *Corpus Juris Civilis* was minimal outside Byzantium, and especially in Western Europe. From the sixth century to the eleventh century the legal systems in most of Western Europe were characterized by Germanic customary law with some Roman canon law influences.[9] Beginning in the mid eleventh century, however, there was a revival of Roman law (as preserved in the *Corpus Juris Civilis*) which spread throughout Europe – with England, Ireland and Wales as exceptions. Roman law had some influence in England and Wales if not in the common-law courts then in other courts, such as those of the church, the Court of Admiralty and the Star Chamber.[10]

The history of law in France and Germany is of particular importance to the civil law tradition. Ninth century France was characterized by the development of feudal institutions. The feudal system was a simple system, where

---

6. *John Henry Merryman, David S. Clark & John O. Haley* (eds.): The Civil Law Tradition: Europe, Latin America, and East Asia, 1994 pp. 3-4.
7. The discussion which follows relies heavily on *Mary Ann Glendon, Michael Gordon & Paolo Carozza:* Comparative Legal Traditions, 1999.
8. See *John Henry Merryman, David S. Clark & John O. Haley* (eds.): The Civil Law Tradition: Europe, Latin America, and East Asia, 1994 p. 5, pp. 228-238 and pp. 333-338.
9. The customary law was based on the customs, usages and practices of the community rather than on the practices of the courts, see *Lester Bernhard Orfield:* The Growth of Scandinavian Law, 1953 p. xii, pp. 14-16, pp. 170-172 and pp. 252-257.
10. *John Henry Merryman, David S. Clark & John O. Haley* (eds.): The Civil Law Tradition: Europe, Latin America, and East Asia, 1994 pp. 348-349.

all land was owned by the King. Feudalism spread from France and by the twelfth century this system was found throughout most of Western Europe.

In the ninth century both Roman and German law was applied in France. The country was divided into two regions: the south of France was a region of written law where the law was basically Roman; and the centre and north France was a region of customary law in which the law was Germanic in origin. In the north the Roman law was in part a supplementary system and in part it superseded the customary law. Judicial decisions were a minor but not unimportant source of law.

In the thirteenth and fourteenth centuries a number of compilations of local French customary law appeared. Prior to the publication of these customs, the courts had the role of confirming the existence and scope of customary rules, and after their publication the courts had the role of interpreting them. The first official measure designed to reduce the general customary law to writing was issued in 1453, when it was directed that the customary law of all the regions of France should be written down. This edict was largely mistreated and ignored. It was, however, repeated by subsequent sovereigns.

By the middle of the sixteenth century the customs of all the important regions in France had been published. Part of the Roman law was declared by court decisions to be accepted as a part of local usage and incorporated in the Customs of Paris. Later, royal Ordinances were published. These were mainly to do with procedural and commercial issues, but they also left permanent marks on French civil law. Henceforth, Roman law could only make inroads into French law by way of interpretation, and only in those parts of the law that were unregulated.

In Germany the history of law in the period from the ninth to the fifteenth centuries is closely linked with the developments in northern France. The universities, which were founded in the fourteenth century, ignored the different German territorial customary laws, and taught only Roman and canon law. In the fifteenth century the formerly purely local character of the customary laws became unsustainable as the growth of trade led to constant commerce between different territorial groups. The replacement of lay judges by educated judges and the re-establishment of the Imperial Court of Justice in 1495 resulted in the acceptance of Roman law. In contrast to France, German jurisprudence became essentially Roman jurisprudence. The construction of the system including both German and Roman elements was carried out by practitioners from the sixteenth to the eighteenth centuries.

It was the legal tradition inspired by Roman law that became known as the *civil law tradition*. When European colonization of much of North America, South America, Asia and Africa flourished in the sixteenth and later centuries, European countries, other than England, carried the Roman law inspired institutions and legal concepts to their new colonies. However, some key parts of the Continental laws have primarily non-Roman roots. For example, this is the case with *land law*, with *marital property law*, and with the major parts of *commercial law.*[11]

At the beginning of the seventeenth century, European countries which were members of the civil law 'family' began to adopt codes as a means of responding to the growth of legal nationalism. The Scandinavian states had national codes, some of which go back to thirteenth century. The first of these is the Danish Code of 1240, known as the Jutland Code. It was in the tradition of national legislation and remained in effect until 1683. There is no Roman law in it.[12]

By the end of the seventeenth and the beginning of the eighteenth centuries the Scandinavian countries adopted new codes. In Denmark, a Code (King Christian V's Danish Code) based on the acceptance of ideas of sovereignty was issued in 1683.[13] Roman law did not play an important part in this Code.

The Danish Code failed to provide a general principle on damages. It was left to judicial practice around the middle of the eighteenth century to establish *the rule of culpa* as the fundamental rule in that respect. The Norwegian Code (King Christian V's Norwegian Code) was issued in 1688 and was based on the Danish Code.[14] Sweden, more than Denmark and Norway, was influenced by learned jurists, from Uppsala University and elsewhere.[15] Accordingly, the Swedish Code – issued in 1734 – was more influenced by Roman law than the Danish and Norwegian codes.

## 2.2. Historical Background of the Common Law System

The common law tradition developed at approximately the same time that Roman law was being 'rediscovered' and propagated on the European continent. Its origin dates back to 1066 – or shortly thereafter – when William,

---

11. *Jacob W.F. Sundberg:* 'Civil Law, Common Law and the Scandinavians', in Scandinavian Studies in Law, 1969 pp. 187-188.
12. *Lester Bernhard Orfield:* The Growth of Scandinavian Law, 1953 p. 15.
13. *Ditlev Tamm:* 'The Danes and Their Heritage', in *Børge Dahl, Torben Melchior & Ditlev Tamm* (eds.): Danish Law in a European Perspective, 2002 pp. 48-50.
14. The reason for this is that the King of Denmark ruled as an absolute monarch over Norway in the period from 1661 to 1814, see *Lester Bernhard Orfield:* The Growth of Scandinavian Law, 1953 p. xiii and p. 255.
15. *Lester Bernhard Orfield:* The Growth of Scandinavian Law, 1953 p. xiii and p. 256.

Duke of Normandy, seized the crown and land of England through his victory at the Battle of Hastings. Even though William and his advisors were, of course, familiar with the feudal system in their native Normandy, this had not then been greatly influenced by the Roman law revival. The challenges presented by his victory and the need to organize and exploit his new lands necessitated the creation of a different land law system that would be applied by the King's judges throughout his kingdom. From this grew a system of law that differed in many ways from the legal traditions on the Continent both before and after the Roman law revival. It came to be known as *common law* because it was 'common' to the King's courts throughout England.

The role that judges, juries and lawyers played in the English King's courts soon extended beyond land law issues and into other areas of law. The common law was established as the safeguard of lawful landholding. Power and prestige were based on land.[16]

## 3. Civil Law and Common Law Systems – Compared and Contrasted

The historical development of the two traditions might lead one to expect vastly different approaches to the regulation of modern society and the resolution of disputes. The reality is that the two traditions often seem more different in theory than they are in practice. There was considerable cross-fertilization of the two at the beginning and this has increased as the centuries have gone by. Nonetheless, in the twenty-first century there are still meaningful differences as well as numerous nuances in their content, practice and application.

There is an important difference between the court's perspective of the legality principle in common law tradition and with the idea of the sovereignty of Parliament which lies behind the perception of this principle in the civil law tradition. In the common law tradition the principle is first and foremost a question of 'due process of law'.[17] In the civil law countries the principle of legality is a matter of the competence of the authorities to ensure that their decisions are based on the wording of the statutory rules and the general principles of law. Lawyers, regulators and business managers involved in energy

---

16. *John Henry Merryman, David S. Clark & John O. Haley* (eds.): The Civil Law Tradition: Europe, Latin America, and East Asia, 1994 p. 348.
17. *Jacob W.F. Sundberg:* 'Civil Law, Common Law and the Scandinavians', in Scandinavian Studies in Law, 1969 p. 195.

and environmental projects, where decision-making has implications based on the legal approaches of either of the two legal traditions, risk adverse consequences if they ignore such differences.

## 3.1. Sources of Law

In any attempt to compare and contrast the common and civil law traditions, the starting point should be the sources of law of the two traditions. Nearly all other characteristics of the respective traditions are determined or influenced by the differing sources of law. A seeming paradox is that the sources of law are virtually identical in civil law and in common law. However, there are significant differences in the restrictions on the courts with respect to the wording of the rules and *hierarchy of the sources* in terms of their importance and status in the respective systems. In this regard, there is considerable difference.

### *3.1.1. Sources of Law in Civil Law Systems*

Civil law theorists make a fundamental distinction between primary sources of law which can give rise directly to binding legal norms, and secondary sources which are sometimes called authorities or legal principles. The primary sources are enacted laws, which are the pre-eminent source of law in a civil law jurisdiction. The history of legislative acts as well as the preparatory works of the acts is very important. Case law and the writings of legal scholars are secondary sources. They are given weight when primary sources are unavailable, incomplete or unclear, but they are not considered binding and they are 'neither necessary nor sufficient as the basis for a judicial decision'.[18]

The various types of enacted law form a hierarchy, with the written constitution at the pinnacle, followed by statutes, then by executive orders, administrative regulations, and local ordinances. Today in most civil law countries parliamentary legislation is the principal source of enacted law, though the special position occupied by codes is still of great importance, as discussed below.

Secondary sources or 'authorities' in the civil law tradition include case law and the writings of legal scholars – also referred to as 'doctrines'. 'Customs' and 'general principles of law' are theoretically considered primary sources, but in most civil law countries today they are used as supplementary

---

18. *Mary Ann Glendon, Michael Gordon, & Paolo Carozza:* Comparative Legal Traditions, 1999 p. 125.

guiding principles. In relation to environmental and energy law the principles of administrative law are of special importance, as the principles limit the competences of the authorities. The most important examples are the legality principle, the proportionality principle, the principles of specialisation (separation of powers) and the principle of equality.

The status of case law in civil law merits special attention because of its huge importance in the common law tradition.

According to civil law theory – going all the way back to Justinian and the *Corpus Juris Civilis* – the role of the judges is limited to deciding the disputes before them and does not extend to 'making law'. Nonetheless, case law plays an important role in the everyday operation of civil law systems, because of the need to interpret and apply the written law.[19] Thus, even though in theory there is no concept of *stare decisis* in the civil law, as a practical matter the importance of judicial decisions to judges, lawyers, professors and litigants is on the increase and it promises to lessen the traditional difference in this regard between the civil and common law traditions. A corresponding increase in the importance of judges as lawmakers would seem inevitable – again lessening the divide between the two legal traditions.

### 3.1.2. Sources of Law in Common Law Systems

From the very beginning of the common law tradition, judge made law – or 'case law' as it is usually labelled – has been a (if not the) major source of law. As explained above, the very name *common law* refers to the law 'common' to the King's courts as developed by the King's judges. Simply stated, the concept of precedent or *stare decisis* is that judicial decisions are binding upon judges deciding future disputes where the legal issues are identical to or conceptually similar to those found in previous judicial decisions. Of course there has always been and continues to be considerable scope for judges and lawyers to distinguish earlier court decisions as being neither identical nor conceptually similar to the issues in the current litigation. However, since it is within the power of a judge to decide whether or not to treat a previous decision as a precedent, the judge's role as lawmaker is even enhanced by this aspect of common law. Law students in most common law countries are trained first and foremost in how judges interpret the law and decide cases. In US they use casebooks which contain edited versions of the decisions of appellate courts rather than textbooks discussing legal rules and principles, as is the

---

19. *Mary Ann Glendon, Michael Gordon, & Paolo Carozza:* Comparative Legal Traditions, 1999 pp. 129-130.

norm in civil law schools. In the UK, textbooks are used alongside case-books. The decisions of common law appellate courts are usually lengthy and contain in depth analyses of the legal issues presented by the dispute and the relevance of or distinctions from previous judicial decisions.

The end result is that judges, and not legislators, lawyers or legal scholars are at the apex of the common law tradition.

The key role given to judges and case law should not obscure the fact that legislation has always been an important source of law in common law countries. Key legislative acts adopted as early as the thirteenth century were instrumental in shaping the development of the common law tradition. In fact many such statutes 'became part of the common law' and are still used as sources of law by judges in England and in former colonies such as the United States.

In those common law countries which have constitutions, such as the United States, constitutional provisions are of transcendent importance and trump legislative enactments and judicial decisions. Administrative rules also have considerable consequences in dispute resolution, just as they do in the civil law. The point that should be emphasized is that even with regard to constitutional provisions, legislation and administrative rules it is the judicial interpretation of these sources of law that becomes the major sources of law on the point, thereby reinforcing the importance of precedent in the common law tradition.

The common law is related to conflicts over land use. There were (and still are) different means applicable to such conflicts. The law of *negligence* provides redress for injury resulting from the actions of persons who fail to take care in the way that a reasonably prudent and careful person would have done in a similar situation. In English the law of negligence is a prime example of judge-made law dating from the 20th century. *Trespass to land* was a form of action brought to recover damages for any injury caused by an unlawful interference with another person's property. In its origins it was a form of action designed to provide compensation for the damage caused by the defendant's actions. The law of *nuisance* deals with unreasonable, unwarranted or unlawful use by a person of their own property, which destroys or damages the property of another or interferes with their lawful use of their property. It was designed to restore ancillary rights associated with land ownership. The purpose of the law of nuisance was, therefore, to settle disputes between neighbours. The law of trespass has been assimilated with negligence, as they overlap in most areas where they are applicable. In both cases it is necessary to establish fault on the part of the defendant. Liability in trespass and nuisance is stricter than in negligence.[20]

The property law differences found in the common law are particularly relevant to many energy and environmental law issues in common law countries. The reason for this is the conflicts between the interests of property owners and the interests of the local community. For example, the property law principles mentioned are relevant to cases concerning environmental damage caused by industrial production.

Other areas of law, which developed differently and are frequently relevant to energy and environmental law issues include criminal law and the law of torts which originated in the common law from a moral basis i.e., from the idea that someone was to blame. The test of foresight in both cases is based on what a reasonably prudent person would have foreseen. The common law system of private liability for the consequences of a person's own acts, for example in trespass, started from the idea of actual intent and actual personal culpability. The basis of *the owner's liability* for damage in common law was ownership of the offending thing and failure to maintain or surrender control of it.[21]

### 3.2. Codes

Codes and the concept of codification on which they are based are of great importance in most civil law countries. Although there are many approaches to code drafting and conceptualisation in the civil law world, codes have become more than just collections of various items of legislation. Most are designed to provide a complete system of positive law in an area of law. A code is not only a collection of the existing statutory law, but also of much of the unwritten law on the given subject. It includes such materials as might be available from all sources and deemed by the codifiers to be necessary for harmonizing and perfecting the existing system.[22] In civil law jurisdictions the Code becomes the starting point for researching or 'finding' the law for judges, lawyers and citizens. The role of judges is largely confined to applying rather than interpreting the Code if there are relevant provisions on the point in dispute.

Common law countries also have codes and codification but with very few exceptions the terms are understood quite differently. In the United States, for

---

20. *Mark Wilde:* Civil Liability for Environmental Damage. A Comparative Analysis of Law and Policy in Europe and the United States, 2002 pp. 24-30 and p. 48.
21. *Oliver Wendell Holmes, Jr.:* The Common Law, reprinted 1991, p. 20.
22. *W. Lile:* Brief Making and the Use of Law Books, 1914 pp. 18-19.

example, most codes are merely collections of statutes enacted by a legislative body organized according to subject matter and codification is only the process (often done by secretarial staff) of organizing and indexing legislative enactments by subject matter. Judges and other participants in the judicial system interpret their provisions using legislative history, common law concepts and – most importantly – case law. In the UK until relatively recently the courts would not look at legislative history or preparatory documentation. Even now the courts are reluctant to do so.

In many civil law countries today Codes play a less important role than in the past because in many fields (environmental regulations in some countries, for example) the key legislative enactments and administrative rules have never been added to or integrated into the basic codes – for example the Civil Code or the Commercial Code. A parallel development is occurring in reverse in some common law countries. In the United States, for example, most states have adopted the Uniform Commercial Code (UCC), which was inspired by the German Commercial Code and intended by its drafters to play a role quite similar to that which a commercial code plays in the civil law world. The judicial use of case law and social policy for interpreting the UCC would probably not be acceptable to many civil law judges, but nonetheless the two traditions seem to be drawing closer together as far as the use of codes is concerned.

# CHAPTER 3

# International and EU Legal Systems

## 1. The International Legal System – by *Sanford Gaines*

All nations and their citizens are subject to international law as well as to domestic (national) law. International law has its own hierarchy of norms. At the broadest level, many scholars make a distinction between 'hard' law and 'soft' law in international law.[1]

### 1.1. Legal Sources and Main Principles

Hard law is international law that nations must follow and to which they can be held accountable – for example, by the International Court of Justice.[2] Hard law has its own hierarchy of sources, as defined in Article 38(1) of the Statute of the International Court of Justice. The most clearly binding international law is that expressed in *international agreements* (variously called treaties, conventions, agreements, etc.). The basic international law rule about agreements is a contract rule: only those nations that have consented to an agreement by becoming a party to it are obliged to comply with its terms.

In addition to written agreements, however, international law also recognizes legally binding obligations under *customary international law*. A special category of customary international law, the *jus cogens,* comprises a small number of extremely important norms that are binding on all nations even without their consent, such as the prohibition of genocide. Other customs or principles become customary international law if they are 1) observed in the conduct of many nations (known as 'state practice', and 2) the

---

1. See, e.g., *Patricia Birnie & Alan Boyle:* International Law and the Environment, 2002 pp. 12-27; and *Hans Chr. Bugge:* 'General Principles of International Law and Environmental Protection – An Overview', in *Ellen Margrethe Basse* (ed.): Environmental Law: From International to National Law, 1997 pp. 53-72.
2. The International Court of Justice is competent to hear a dispute only if the States concerned have accepted its jurisdiction. The website of the Court is www.icj-cij.org.

nations observe them out of a sense of legal obligation (known as *opinio juris*). While a particular customary norm is in the process of becoming established, however, any nation can avoid being bound by the custom by clearly rejecting that particular norm.

A good example of how customary international law comes into being is the norm that each nation has jurisdiction over the resources in or beneath the oceans off its coast to a distance of 200 nautical miles (the exclusive economic zone, or EEZ).

In the 1947, Chile made a unilateral declaration of jurisdiction over marine resources out to 200 miles from its coast (the standard rule had been 12 miles until then). Other nations not only accepted Chile's claim, but over the years they have made similar claims of their own. In 1982, this customary rule was codified in the United Nations Convention on the Law of the Sea (UNCLOS) under the concept of the exclusive economic zone.[3]

To the extent that a particular treaty is understood to codify customary international law, as in the example just given, that legal norm also creates rights and obligations for nations that are not party to the treaty because it is customary international law. Thus, the United States, which is not party to UNCLOS, still can rightfully claim its 200 mile EEZ. By the same token, the United Kingdom, which has not officially claimed a 200 mile EEZ, may nevertheless rightfully take steps to exclude other nations from access to any particular resource within the 200 mile limit, as it has done in Article 84 of its 2004 Energy Act, authorizing the designation of a Renewable Energy Zone in which it will exercise regulatory control over wind farms or other energy facilities.[4] See also Chapter 5, section 2, on jurisdictional issues.

Further down in the hierarchy of international law are *legal principles or ideas* that have been expressed by governments or by international organizations or have been advanced by eminent international law scholars. The boundary between widely shared 'soft' or non-binding principles and 'hard' customary international law is often difficult to draw, and scholars and governments may have differing views. For example, *the precautionary principle* is widely recognized and is even included, in various forms, in a number of international agreements and declarations. Some assert that the precautionary

3.  Of course, where two nations face each other across a body of water less than nautical 400 miles wide, the EEZ cannot extend beyond the maritime boundary – the line of equidistance – between those countries.
4.  See *Karen N. Scott:* 'Tilting at Offshore Windmills: Regulating Wind Farm Development within the Renewable Energy Zone', in Journal of Environmental Law, Vol. 18(1), 2006 p. 89.

principle has thus achieved the status of binding customary international law. Others argue that because there is no clear agreement on the exact meaning of the principle, and as most governments do not feel legally obliged to follow it, it has no binding effect.

It is universally accepted that international law is binding on and between 'states', that is the national governmental authorities. One nation can take legal action against another for alleged breaches of international law. But does international law also apply to private persons or corporations? This raises another issue with respect to the legally binding obligations of international law, namely how international law is reflected or expressed in the national law of the country.

## 1.2. The Relationship between International Law and National Law

There are two basic approaches, depending on the legal tradition of the particular country – 'monism' and 'dualism'.[5] Under the *monist approach*, the obligations of international agreements or customary law are accepted as an inherent part of national law and can be applied directly by the courts in resolving legal disputes. Under the *dualist approach*, international law obligations only become part of national law when the appropriate law-making authorities incorporate them into statutes or other official statements of national law. Until such incorporation, international law cannot be used to define rights and obligations between parties in legal disputes. In general, the dualist approach is applied in Denmark, New Zealand, Norway, and the United States, whereas the European Union inclines to monism.

Increasingly, courts and scholars are coming to the view that individuals are, in some circumstances, also subject to international law itself. The concept of international criminal law follows this approach; individuals can be held accountable and punished for their personal violations of international norms against torture, genocide, and so forth. But it may also operate in broader areas of personal or corporate behaviour, including contracts and investments. But international law is still evolving in this respect, and the legal doctrines are far from clear.

## 1.3. Energy and Environmental Law

In broad terms, international environmental law has a long history and covers many different aspects of the world's environment and its protection. From

---

5. For more about these theories see e.g. *Ian Brownlie:* Principles of International Law, 1998 pp. 31-33; and *Eileen Denza:* 'The relationship between International and National Law', in *Malcolm D. Evans:* International Law, 2006 pp. 435-441.

the end of the 19<sup>th</sup> century until the beginning of the modern environmental era, most international environmental law concerned the protection of animals or the regulation of animal harvesting (e.g., fish, seals and birds). Since about 1970, international environmental agreements have proliferated, covering such diverse issues as air pollution control, disposal of hazardous waste, prevention of desertification, and protection of biological diversity.

With respect to the development of wind energy in coastal areas, three strands of international law are directly relevant to renewable energy development and the protection of the coastal environment. The first is the still very small body of international energy law. The second is the overarching need to develop renewable energy sources, as reflected in international agreements on climate change and the more all-embracing concept of sustainable development. Finally, there are some specific agreements on the protection of the marine environment and coastal areas that may be relevant in particular locations.

### 1.3.1. International Energy Law

For the time being, there is only one multilateral agreement on the subject of energy – the Energy Charter Treaty. The Charter was launched in Europe in the early 1990s to build a balanced and efficient foundation for mutually beneficial cooperation in the energy sector. The Energy Charter Treaty and the associated Energy Charter Protocol on Energy Efficiency and Related Environmental Aspects, both signed in 1994, establish rules to be observed by all participating governments based on principles of open, competitive markets and sustainable development.

### 1.3.2. Climate Change and Sustainable Development

The second strand relevant to wind farm development is the general rules and principles of international environmental law. The international agreements addressing climate change – currently the United Nations Framework Convention on Climate Change of 1992 and the Kyoto Protocol to that convention that came into effect in 2007 – have prompted many governments, especially in Europe, to overhaul their energy policies and aggressively promote renewable energy sources.

The Framework Convention and the Kyoto Protocol are reinforced by many familiar environmental principles and concepts endorsed by governments as a matter of international law, most of which still seem to be in the 'soft law' category. The 1972 Stockholm Declaration on the Human Environment announced certain principles for environmental protection, the most famous and the most ambiguous being Principle 21. In 1992, on the 20<sup>th</sup> anniversary of the Stockholm Declaration, even more world leaders gathered in Rio de Janeiro at the United Nations Conference on Environment and Development. There they adopted the Rio Declaration, which reaffirmed many of the Stockholm principles and expressed some new ones. Rio Principle 2 restates Stockholm Principle 21, modifying it only to include a reference to national choice in development policy:

'States have, in accordance with the Charter of the United Nations and the principles of international law, the sovereign right to exploit their own natural resources pursuant to their own environmental and development policies, and the responsibility to ensure that activities within their jurisdiction or control do not cause damage to the environment of other States or areas beyond the limits of national jurisdiction.'

Both the Rio Declaration and the agenda of action to implement its principles (called Agenda 21) identify *sustainable development* as an overarching goal. This was foreshadowed by the United Nations Economic Commission for Europe (ECE) Ministerial Declaration on Sustainable Development of 15 May 1990, known as the Bergen Declaration. The universal commitment to sustainable development as a guiding principle was reaffirmed by the World Summit on Sustainable Development in Johannesburg, South Africa in 2002.

The concept of sustainable development was first formulated in the 1980s in the work of the World Commission on Environment and Development (known also as the Brundtland Commission, after the Norwegian Prime Minister Gro Harlem Brundtland who was its chair). The report of the Commission, *Our Common Future*, defined sustainable development as follows:

'Sustainable development is development that meets the needs of the present without compromising the ability of future generations to meet their own needs'.[6]

This definition incorporates three key concepts: human needs, intergenerational equity, and intragenerational equity.

The first key area is *human needs*; Principle 1 of the Rio Declaration declared human needs to be 'at the center' of environment and development policy. Meeting demands for energy clearly falls under the rubric of meeting human needs. At the same time, 'development' also means addressing social and spiritual needs, including giving educational and economic opportunity for all persons to achieve their individual potential.

6.   The World Commission on Environment and Development: Our Common Future, 1987 p. 51.

The second key idea is *intergenerational equity*: our duty to future generations is to leave them an environment with a sufficient variety and abundance of resources to meet their own needs. With respect to energy resources, intergenerational equity means that, as the current generation continues to deplete the finite supplies of resources like fossil fuels, at the same time we should be investing in alternative energy sources and technologies that will allow future generations to meet their own energy needs. Moreover, energy should be produced and consumed in a way that does not impair the long-term viability of ecosystems, because future generations will also need the benefits that ecosystems provide.

The third idea embedded in sustainable development is that of *intragenerational equity*. This draws attention to complex issues of the distribution of resources and development opportunities within the present generation. The Brundtland Commission asserted, quite simply, that economic and human development throughout the world is not sustainable if it does not rest on a stable social and political foundation. Intragenerational equity thus underscores the social and political dimensions of sustaining ecological systems, which have been elaborated recently in the United Nation's Millennium Development Goals, and in the work of the related Millennium Ecosystem Assessment. Complex issues of governance at local, national, regional, and global levels are thus involved in achieving sustainable development.

Governments and corporations around the world have embraced sustainable development as a goal. But as one commentator has remarked, sustainable development is not a goal, but a 'permanent process'.[7] The difficult challenge is to implement this process by identifying specific actions to take now that will lead to sustainable development over time. To be effective, implementation plans require specific objectives or decision-making criteria. But the complex relationships between economic, environmental, and social considerations are daunting obstacles. Each nation, each ecological system, each economic sector presents a unique combination of current conditions, future goals, and social, economic, and environmental interactions.

Many academic experts and government policy-makers have tried to formulate policy approaches to sustainable development. The 1990 Bergen Declaration, for example, attempted to identify 'national indicators' of sustainable development. But it is fair to say that there is still no consensus on the decision-making criteria. It is also abundantly clear that the absence of spe-

---

7.  *Howard Mann:* 'Comment on the Paper by Philippe Sands', in *Winfried Lang* (ed.): Sustainable Development and International Law, 1995 p. 71.

cific factors or criteria which are widely accepted as defining elements of sustainable development means that neither governments nor private parties are likely to be held legally accountable in a strict sense for any failure to follow a sustainable development path. Accountability is more likely to be imposed through political, economic, and diplomatic pressure.

Sustainable development lacks concrete legal substance, but it has nevertheless imparted a new sense of direction to important sectors,[8] including energy production and consumption. This is especially true in view of the increasing evidence that global climate change is occurring and that it is being driven in significant part by the combustion of fossil fuels. Climate change brings a new sense of urgency to the quest for renewable sources of energy, together with a cautious examination of the true sustainability of different energy technologies and strategies. In this sense, sustainable development is a significant factor in shaping international, EU and national energy policies.

One example of the potential legal influence of sustainable development is the separate opinion of *Judge Weeramantry*, Vice President of the International Court of Justice, in the dispute between Slovakia and Hungary over the Gabcíkovo-Nagymoros energy project on the River Danube.[9]

The case concerned the efforts of Hungary to withdraw from a joint hydroelectric project on the River Danube where it crosses the border between Slovakia and Hungary. Slovakia wanted the project to supply much-needed electricity; Hungary wanted to terminate the project because of concerns about how changes to the flow of the Danube would affect the environment in Hungary. Judge *Weeramantry* said, about sustainable development:

'I consider it to be more than a mere concept, but as a principle with normative value which is crucial to the determination of this case'.

After reviewing the history of the sustainable development idea and its use in many legal texts, he concluded, with reference to the definition of customary international law:

'The principle of sustainable development is thus a part of modern international law by reason not only of its inescapable logical necessity, but also by reason of its wide and general acceptance by the global community'.

8. See generally, *Ellen Margrethe Basse:* 'Regulatory Chain – Results of an International Development', in *E.M. Basse* (ed.): Environmental Law: From International to National Law, 1997, pp. 9-51.
9. Case Concerning the Gabcíkovo-Nagymoros Project, *Hungary* v *Slovakia*, 1997 I.C.J. 92 (Sept. 25).

The Judge then explored historical practices and cultural norms in various societies that are congruent with sustainable development. He summed up his argument:

'Sustainable development is thus not merely a principle of modern international law. It is one of the most ancient ideas in the human heritage. Fortified by the rich insights that can be gained from millennia of human experience, it has an important part to play in the service of international law'.

### 1.3.3. *Protection of the Marine Environment and Coastal Areas*

The third strand of international energy and environmental law of special relevance to wind farm development in coastal areas is the various agreements for the protection of wetlands, sensitive marine areas, and various species of marine mammals and birds. Some of these agreements are regional, others multilateral, and often their application depends on the location.

For example, the Convention on the Protection of the Marine Environment of the Baltic Sea Area (the Helsinki Convention) clearly affects only the marine areas defined by the treaty; the Convention on Wetlands of International Importance Especially as Waterfowl Habitat (known as the Ramsar Convention) is applicable if the home nation has listed the wetland concerned under the convention.

## 2. The EU Legal System – by *Birgitte Egelund Olsen*

The law of the European Union (EU law) has evolved considerably both in scope and importance within the last 50 years. It is a new kind of law in Europe, a 'new legal order' as stated by the European Court of Justice in its very early case law.[10] EU law has developed quickly and within only a few decades has become a major legal system – also from a global perspective. It includes all the major elements of modern law: treaty law, statute law, fundamental legal principles, instruments of soft law and case law.

The use of the terms 'European Union' and 'European Community' can be confusing. The term 'European Union' was brought in by the Treaty on European Union (also known as the Maastricht Treaty) and describes the extension of the European project into additional policy areas and areas of cooperation.

---

10. Case 26/62, *Van Gend en Loos*.

The European Union is founded on three pillars. The European Community (and the EC Treaty) is the first and the most important pillar, and it remains the primary source of EU law. Supranationalism is strongest in this pillar. The other pillars were introduced with the Maastricht Treaty – and adjusted by the Amsterdam Treaty – and they relate to the Common Foreign and Security Policy (the second pillar) and the Cooperation in the Fields of Justice and Home Affair (the third pillar). Both the second and the third pillars are more intergovernmental in nature. If the Treaty of Lisbon – also known as the Reform Treaty – is ratified by all Member States, the European Community will be fully absorbed into the European Union and the three pillars will be merged into a single structure.[11]

Thus the European Community is not coterminous with the European Union, but is a part of it. In this book references will generally be made to the European Union, EU law, the EU legal system etc., unless reference is specifically made to the European Community.

## 2.1. The EU Legal Tradition

EU law is a complex field of law. It has evolved considerably both in scope and importance since the early days and is characterized by its rapidly changing legal landscape and its supranationalism. Equally, the European Union is not a static organisation, but is continuously evolving and at the time of writing it is awaiting the ratification of the rewritten Constitutional Treaty – the Lisbon Treaty.

### 2.1.1. Clarifying the 'European Union'

The European Union is not a new state that replaces the Member States, nor is it a federal system comparable to the federal system in the United States.[12] In particular, the Member States' *partial* surrender of their *sovereign* rights is an indication that the European Union is a different system, although it is in many respects structured along the lines of a federal state. The European Union (or rather the European Community[13]) is a legal entity with the ability to

---

11. The Treaty of Lisbon was signed on 13 December 2007 at a summit in Lisbon. It amends the existing Treaties of the European Union and is due to come into force in 2009, if ratified by all Member States. It will implement many of the reforms previously proposed in the rejected European Constitutional Treaty.
12. See Chapter 4, section 2.3.2.
13. The European Community has legal personality according to Article 281 of the EC Treaty. The European Union does not *yet* have legal personality but will become a legal entity if the Lisbon Treaty is ratified.

enter into contracts, notably to be a party to international conventions or to be a member of an international organisation (such as the WTO) representing its Member States. However, this view of the European Union as a federal system fails to take into account that the EU institutions only have powers in certain areas to pursue the objectives specified in the Treaties. This means that the EU institutions are not free to choose their objectives in the same way as a sovereign state. The European Union and its institutions have neither the comprehensive jurisdiction enjoyed by sovereign states nor the powers to establish new areas of responsibility.

The European Union also has features in common with international organisations. One such feature is that it too came into being as a result of international treaties. However, the anchoring of the European Union within an organisational structure and with institutions far more powerful than those of conventional international organisations has made the European Union different from traditional kinds of international organisations.

The Treaties establishing the European Community have led to the creation of an independent European Union with its own sovereign rights and responsibilities. Thus, the duality that is typical of international law does not characterize EU law. Unlike traditional international law, EU law does not require acceptance by the individual Member States in order to be valid if its decisions are made in those areas in which the Member States have transferred their sovereign powers to the European Union.

In conclusion, on the one hand the European Union is not an international organisation in the usual sense, and on the other hand it is not an association of states. Rather, it is an autonomous entity, a supranational organisation, and somewhere between the two.

### 2.1.2.   The Nature of the European Union

The tasks of the European Union are very different from those of traditional international organisations. The European Union has responsibility for a long and broad range of areas. Under the EC Treaty, the primary task of the Union is to establish a common market that unites the national markets of the Member States and on which all goods and services etc. can be offered and sold on the same conditions as on an internal market.[14] However, the European Union not has only economic policies with a focus on free trade, open markets and competition; it also aims at protecting the environment, ensuring sufficient energy supplies, promoting social progress etc.

---

14.   Articles 2 and 3 of the EC Treaty.

The scope of EU law has been widened by each successive Treaty, and the EU institutions have also received greater powers through these Treaties. Nevertheless, the Member States still retain the right to act independently in many areas. Basically, the Member States are separate, sovereign entities under international law, though most international environmental agreements are mixed, which means that both the European Community and its Member States are parties to the agreements. The European Union has so far been reluctant to harmonize in areas of national sensitivity such as criminal justice and taxation, and the Member States are in general responsible for enforcement of EU laws. However, in these areas too changes are in the pipeline.[15] This cautiousness does not apply when it comes to regulating other aspects of the environment or energy supply. These areas of EU law – and in particular EU environmental law – are generally characterized by having very comprehensive and detailed EU legislation that leaves little room for independent national initiative.

### 2.1.3. A Common European Law Tradition?

The European Union is an entirely new creation which differs from earlier efforts to unite Europe in that it works, not by means of force or domination, but simply by means of law. As stated above, as a new legal order EU law goes beyond the distinction between national and international law. This has required the elaboration of new legal ideas, instruments and regulatory techniques.

The EU Member States represent both the common law and the civil law traditions. The civil law tradition forms the basis of the law in the majority of the EU Member States, in particular in the continental European countries, whereas the common law tradition is the basis of the legal systems of Ireland and the United Kingdom. The original Member States (the Benelux countries, France, Germany and Italy), which were all signatories to the European Coal and Steel Community, represented strong but differentiated civil law systems,

---

15. In March 2008 the EU Commission put forward a proposal for a directive amending the EU Directive on ship-source pollution and on the introduction penalties for infringements; see COM(2008) 134 final. See also *E. Herlin-Karnell:* 'Commission v Council: Some Reflections on Criminal Law in the First Pillar', in European Public Law, 2007 pp. 69-85; and *R. Pereira:* 'Environmental criminal law in the first pillar: a positive development for environmental protection in the European Union?', in European Environmental Law Review, 2007 pp. 254-269.

which have from the beginning strongly influenced the development of a common European law.[16]

On the one hand EU law is constructed on the civil law model, with the emphasis on codification. The core of EU law consists of written norms, organized in a hierarchy established in the Treaties, and is thus characterized by a strong rule-fixation. Many areas of EU law are regulated in detail and in some areas – including the areas of energy and the environment – there is extensive regulation. EU measures are not restricted to cross-border issues. The competence of the European Union is very wide, and whether or not the European Union should deal with matters of a purely local or national nature is subject to the general principle of subsidiarity; see below in section 2.5.

On the other hand, EU law includes a strong element of case law in the form of the rulings of the European Court of Justice. Case law undoubtedly forms a very important part of EU law. It reflects the fact that the role of the Court of Justice is not limited to deciding the disputes before it. In some instances it even extends to 'making law' and in these cases precedent becomes a major source of law – though only until this judge-made law may be included in the ongoing codification efforts in the EU Treaties or secondary legislation.

Equally, the Court of Justice attempts to follow its own precedents where facts are sufficiently similar. It makes references to former decisions and bases its decisions on principles suggested by earlier cases. However, precedents are only referred to and not stated as being the legal basis of a decision. The Court of Justice does not consider itself bound by its own previous decisions. Rather, it treats such decisions as persuasive. This dynamic approach of the Court of Justice is also reflected in its method of interpretation – a very contextual or teleological approach – which has led to the Court being described as rather political. The Court of Justice thus tries to give the interpretation that best fulfils the purpose of the law in the particular context.

In general, since the 1960s the decisions of the Court of Justice have had an immense influence on the development of European integration. In performing this function, it has frequently favoured the interests and institutions of the European Union over those of Member States, but nevertheless the Member States have complied with even the most far-reaching decisions of the Court.

---

16. The United Kingdom was invited to take part in the ECSC Treaty but declined to do so.

## 2.2. Historical Background

The European Union has accomplished many things in its short existence. Since 1951 the Union has evolved from a relatively small alliance of states with common industrial interests to one of the world's most important economic and political forces. The scope of the Union's common interests and concerns has moved far beyond the economic to include other interests, such as energy and the environment.

The European Union had its origins in the period following the Second World War. The Organisation for European Economic Cooperation was created in 1948 as a multinational agency to assist in the administration of the Marshall Plan for the reconstruction of Western Europe. In 1950, the French Foreign Minister, Robert Schuman, proposed integrating the coal and steel industries of Western Europe.

The evolution of the European Union itself began in 1951 with the Treaty establishing the European Coal and Steel Community (ECSC).[17] The ECSC Treaty did not contain any provisions on the environment or energy law. It provided a 'common market' for the coal and steel industries of the Benelux countries, France, Germany and Italy. The ECSC Treaty proved successful, and in 1957 two additional treaties were agreed: the Treaty of Rome which established the European Economic Community (EEC) and the EURATOM Treaty establishing the European Atomic Energy Community.[18]

The ECSC Treaty, the EEC Treaty and the EURATOM Treaty collectively formed a supranational organisation, the European Community, with Member States ceding a substantial amount of their individual sovereignty to it. The European Parliament was created as the sole deliberative assembly of the European Community. Each of the treaties had its own council and commission. This arrangement continued until the Merger Treaty (signed in 1965) came into effect, creating a single Council and Commission for the whole Community.[19]

In 1960, after the creation of the European Economic Community, a number of countries that either could not or did not wish to take part in it established the European Free Trade Association (EFTA). It was set up under the leadership of the United Kingdom and among others it included Denmark, Norway and Sweden. Later they were joined by the rest of the Nordic coun-

---

17. The power to take decisions about the coal and steel industries was placed in the hands of an independent, supranational body called the High Authority. *Jean Monnet* was its first President.
18. Both these treaties officially entered into force on 1 January 1958.
19. The Merger Treaty entered into force in 1967.

tries – Finland and Iceland. Most of the EFTA countries later joined the European Union – Denmark in 1973, and Sweden and Finland in 1995. Today the European Economic Area (EEA), which was set up jointly by the European Union and EFTA, consists of Iceland, Liechtenstein and Norway and the 27 EU Member States.

From the late 1960s until the mid-1980s, the European Community continued to develop and refine a substantial body of law and procedure. In 1972 – the year of the first United Nations Conference on the Environment – the European Community adopted its first five-year environmental action programme, which was the starting point for the development of EU environmental law setting out the principles and priorities for future policies.[20] Although the European Community evolved out of the European Coal and Steel Community, binding legislation on energy was not adopted until the beginning of the 1990s. Hitherto, EU energy policy had been based on resolutions and recommendations.

An important turning point was the 1987 Treaty known as the Single European Act. The major feature of this Treaty was the completion of the European internal market by the end of 1992. It also introduced an express legal basis for environmental measures. A section on the environment was included in the EC Treaty, which confirmed that one of the Community's tasks is the development of a European environmental policy.

Before the 1987 Single European Act there was not an express legal basis for environmental measures. However, legally binding instruments on environmental issues were adopted from the mid 1970s, under Article 94 and/or Article 308 of the EEC Treaty and referring to the Community's environmental action programmes.

To further the goals of economic and monetary union, and to respond to the new political realities in Europe in the 1990s, the 1991 Treaty on European Union (the Maastricht Treaty) made substantial changes to the Treaty of Rome.[21] The Maastricht Treaty established the three 'pillars' of the European Union referred to above. It also introduced the term *sustainable growth* in Article 2, added energy and trans-European networks to the range of Commu-

---

20. OJ 1973 C 112/1. Between 1973 and today six environmental action programmes have been agreed at Community level. Their main effect has been political. However, the latest environmental action programme from 2001 was adopted in the form of a legally binding decision. This is a significant departure from the five previous action programmes as it may require the Commission to make proposals for specific measures; see Article 175(3) of the EC Treaty.

21. The Maastricht Treaty entered into force on 1 November 1993.

nity tasks, and amended the legislative procedures by introducing majority voting on, among other things, environmental matters. The 1997 Amsterdam Treaty introduced the concept of *sustainable development*, but neither it nor the Nice Treaty in 2000 added any measures of particular importance in relation to energy and the environment.[22]

EU membership was increased dramatically on 1 May 2004, when ten new Member States joined. The expansion was the largest in the history of the European Union. Two further new Member States joined the Union on 1 January 2007, giving the European Union a total of 27 Member States.

On 13 December 2007, the EU leaders signed the Treaty of Lisbon, thus bringing to an end several years of negotiation about institutional issues. Ratification of the new Treaty will mark the end of a phase of controversial political integration which began with the Convention on the Charter of Fundamental Rights in 1999, and which was later developed by the Convention on the Future of Europe (2002-03), the Treaty establishing a Constitution for Europe (2004) and the referendums in France and the Netherlands (2005). The negative referendum results led to a 'period of reflection' that lasted until the spring of 2007, when the negotiations on a revised treaty – the Lisbon Treaty – continued.

The Treaty of Lisbon amends the current EU and EC Treaties, but without replacing them. It will provide new provisions on climate change and energy security, supplementing the environment policy with a reference to combating climate change and strengthening the common energy policy with a view to security and interconnectivity of supply and solidarity, and by providing a specific legal basis for energy measures.

### 2.3. Legal Institutions and Law Making

The European Union has an independent institutional system and the EU institutions have the power to legislate in the shape of regulations, directives and decisions which are binding on the Member States and their citizens.

The EU law-making process involves three main institutions: the *European Parliament*, which represents the Community's citizens and is directly elected by them; the *Council of the European Union*, which represents the individual Member States; and the *European Commission*, which seeks to uphold the interests of the European Union as a whole. The Commission is divided into departments known as Directorates-General (DG). Each DG is re-

---

22. The Amsterdam Treaty came into force on 1 May 1999.

sponsible for a particular policy area. There is a DG for the Environment and one for Transport and Energy.

Proposals for new legislation are put forward by the Commission which, under the EC Treaty, has the right to initiate legislative measures. The Commission also submits general action programmes and action programmes for specific sectors. EU law is generally adopted by the Council and the European Parliament jointly. The procedure used for most EU legislation, including environmental and energy legislation, is the co-decision procedure set out in Article 251 of the EC Treaty, where the Parliament shares legislative power equally with the Council.

EU law comprises the norms that have been laid down in the Treaties and in secondary legislation and which are enforced through the rulings of the European Court of Justice. Like any legal order, that of the European Union provides a self-contained system of legal protection for recourse to and the enforcement of EU law. However, the EU legal order and the national legal orders are interlocked and interdependent.[23] In EU law there is strong reliance upon the Member States, although EU law gives the Member States limited room for manoeuvre in relation to implementation and enforcement.

The enforcement of EU law relies on the Commission and the European courts (the Court of Justice and the Court of First Instance). The Commission has been given the task of supervising how EU law is implemented and enforced in the Member States.[24] It has discretion as to whether or not to bring an action against a Member State for non-compliance with EU law.[25] Moreover, in certain cases (State aid) the Commission has express power to order a Member State to undo measures which do not comply with EU law.

Although, one Member State may bring an action against another Member State for failure to comply with EU law, this rarely happens. When contested, all cases concerning a breach of EU law come before the Court of Justice for a final decision. When a case has been decided by the Court, the Member States must comply with the ruling. Otherwise the Commission may consider bringing the case back before the Court of Justice, which may then impose a

---

23. See further sections 2.4 and 2.5.
24. Article 226 of the EC Treaty.
25. See e.g. Case 416/85, *Commission v United Kingdom*, and Case C-234/91, *Commission v Denmark*.

fine. There have been several instances of fines in cases of 'serious shortcomings' in the implementation of EU environmental law.[26]

### 2.3.1. Legal Sources

The autonomy of the EU legal order is of fundamental importance for the nature of the European Union. By establishing the European Union, the Member States have limited their legislative sovereignty and in so doing they have created a self-sufficient body of law that is binding on them, their citizens and their courts

EU law comprises various types of legal sources. Basically there is a distinction between primary sources – the EU Treaties – and the secondary sources – regulations, directives, decisions etc. listed and defined in Article 249 of the EC Treaty.

The legal acts that encroach furthest on the domestic legal systems are regulations which apply in full in all Member States. EU regulations are directly applicable, which means that the legal acts may not be, transposed into national law, but confer rights or impose duties on Community citizens directly in the same way as national laws.

Alongside EU regulations, EU directives are the most important legislative instrument. A directive is intended to harmonise the national laws of the Member States. Directives are binding on the Member States as regards the objective to be achieved, but they leave it to the national authorities to decide on how the agreed Community objective is to be incorporated into their domestic legal systems. The force of directives has been increased by the case law of the Court of Justice. The Court has held that directives may have direct effect and enable individuals to rely on them, at least in actions against a Member State, and Member States can be liable for damages for non-implementation of a directive.[27]

### 2.3.2. Main Legal Principles

The EU's general principles of law are essential to the structure of EU law – just as in the common law tradition. The general legal principles may be treaty-based, they may be derived from secondary legislation, or from action programmes or developed in the case law of the Court of Justice. Of particular importance in the context of this book are the specific environmental principles laid down in the EC Treaty.

26. Article 228 of the EC Treaty. See e.g. Case C-387/97, *Commission* v *Greece,* and Case C-278/01, *Commission* v *Spain.*
27. See also sections 2.5 and 2.6.

The concept or principle of *sustainable development* in Article 2 of the EC Treaty has been transformed into a form of legal obligation, although the precise definition of the concept remains unclear.[28] The Court of Justice has not explicitly interpreted or developed the understanding of the concept. Most importantly, the principle forms the basis of and is explicitly used in EU action programmes and strategies. It seems that the concept exists at the political level but it does not yet operate as a general principle that can be used as a standard against which the validity of EU law and policies can be measured by the Court.

The *integration principle* is one of the most important principles of EU environmental law. It is laid down in Article 6 of the EC Treaty that environmental protection requirements must be integrated into the other Community policies and activities in order to ensure the promotion of sustainable development. In accordance with the general understanding of the principle this amounts to a general obligation on the EU institutions to reach an integrated and balanced assessment of all relevant environmental aspects when adopting other policies.

Article 174(2) of the EC Treaty sets out the principles on which EU environmental policy is based. The provision includes the *high level of protection principle*, the *precautionary principle*, the *prevention principle*, the *source principle*, the *polluter pays principle* and the *safeguard clause*.[29] These are not legally binding principles but rather general guidelines for EU policy. Only in very exceptional cases would a measure be liable to annulment because the environmental principles of Article 174(2) are not sufficiently taken into account.

### 2.4. The Relationship between EU Law and International Law

The European Community has international legal personality. The international capacity of the EU is governed by public international law. Under international law the EU enjoys the right to be represented, the right to enter into treaties, the right to submit claims or appear before an international court, and the right to be a party to international conventions.[30]

In accordance with Article 300(7) of the EC Treaty, international agreements entered into by the EU are automatically incorporated into EU law and

---

28. The concept is also referred to in the seventh recital of the Treaty on European Union (TEU).
29. See further in *Nicolas de Sadeleer:* Environmental Principles, 2005.
30. See *P. Craig & G. de Búrca:* EU Law, 2008 pp. 167-189.

form an integral part of the EU legal order, ranking above EU secondary legislation.[31]

A related question is whether a rule of international law has direct effect – so that an individual may rely on it as a source of rights in domestic law. Within the European Union, the Court of Justice has laid down specific criteria for determining whether or not a measure is given direct effect.[32] Apart from WTO law, the EU legal system generally gives direct effect to international agreements to which the European Union is a party, even where the international obligations have not specifically been transposed into EU or national law.[33]

This has been stated by the Court of Justice in two cases concerning the discharge of freshwater from a hydropower station to a saltwater marsh area.

The saltwater marsh, Étang de Berre, is linked directly with the Mediterranean Sea through the Caronte Canal. The marsh is consequently governed by the Barcelona Convention and the Athens Protocol for the Protection of the Mediterranean Sea against Pollution from land-based sources.[34] In the first case the Court of Justice gave direct effect to the obligation to strictly limit pollution from land-based sources, and to the requirement for a prior emission permit in the Athens Protocol, see Case C-213/03 *Syndicat professionnel coordination des pêcheurs de l'étang de Berre et de la region.*[35]

In the second case the Court found that France had failed to take all appropriate measures to prevent, abate and combat heavy and prolonged pollution of the Étang de Berre under the Convention and the Protocol, thus giving Article 6(1) of the Protocol direct effect. The Court referred to the emissions from the hydropower station, while not denying the significance of other sources of pollution, such as the industrialisation of the marsh's shores, the rapid increase in the population of the neighbouring communities, the extension

31. *Robert Uerpmann:* International Law as an Element of European Constitutional Law: International Supplementary Constitutions, 2003 p. 27.
32. The concept of 'direct effect' traditionally denotes the relationship between EU law and national law and those provisions of EU law which give rise to rights which individuals may assert before their national courts. The Court of Justice developed the concept of direct effect in the landmark decision, Case 26/72, *Van Gend & Loos.*
33. *Birgitte Egelund Olsen & Michael Steinicke:* 'The WTO and the EU' in *B. Egelund Olsen, M. Steinicke & K. Engsig Sørensen* (eds.): WTO law from a European perspective, 2006 pp. 91-129.
34. The Barcelona Convention for the Protection of the Mediterranean Sea against Pollution, was entered into by the EEC by Council Decision 77/585/EEC (OJ 1977 L 240/1), and the Athens Protocol was approved by Council Decision 83/101/EEC (OJ 1983 L 67/1).
35. Article 6(1) and (3) of the Athens Protocol.

of agricultural activity and the deterioration of the water quality of the rivers which flow into the marsh, see Case C-239/03 *Commission* v *France*.[36]

### 2.5. The Balance of Powers between the EU and the Member States

The relationship between EU law and the laws of the Member States is defined in EU law. Under EU law the Member States must take all appropriate measures to ensure fulfilment of their obligations arising from the EU Treaties and abstain from any measure that could jeopardise the attainment of the objectives of the EU Treaties; see Article 10 of the EC Treaty.

Although, the EU legal order is a self-contained system but relies on the support of the national systems for its operation. All three branches of government – legislative, executive and judicial – therefore have to acknowledge that the EU legal order is not a foreign system and the Member States and the EU institutions have established permanent links between them so as to achieve their common objectives.

Article 5 of the EC Treaty lays down the balance of powers between the EU institutions and the Member States.[37] In the first paragraph of Article 5 it is recognized that the European Union only has competence within the areas in which it has been given powers by the Treaties.[38] Some powers belong exclusively to the European Union, such as the common commercial policy. Most competences – including the competences on environmental and energy issues – are shared between the European Union and the Member States. When competences are shared, both the European Union and the Member States may legislate and adopt legally binding acts. However, the Member States may only exercise their competence to the extent that the European Union has either not exercised or has decided to cease exercising its competence, cf. *the doctrine of pre-emption.*

When the European Union finds a sufficient legal basis to act in the EU Treaties, but not an exclusive competence to act, the next question is whether there is a need for EU action or whether it should be left to the Member States to implement the measures needed. The assessment of the need for EU

---

36. See also *Vanessa Edwards:* 'European Court of Justice – Significant environmental cases 2004', in Journal of Environmental Law, Vol. 17, 2005 p. 132.
37. On the subsidiarity principle see *Birgitte Egelund Olsen:* 'The Principle of Subsidiarity and Its Impact on Regulation', in *Birgitte Egelund Olsen & Karsten Engsig Sørensen* (eds.): Regulation in the EU, 2006 pp. 35-79.
38. *Lenaerts Koen:* 'The Principle of Subsidiarity and the Environment in the European Union: Keeping the Balance of Federalism', in Fordham International Law Journal, Vol.17, 1994 pp. 847-853.

action is based on the principles of *subsidiarity* and *proportionality* and depends on the finding that:

'… the objectives of the proposed action cannot be sufficiently achieved by the Member States and can therefore, by reason of the scale or effects of the proposed action, be better achieved by the Community'.[39]

These principles are important for the Member States in preserving self-determination, legitimacy and the democratic process, and could thus be described as principles of balanced governance by which actions to accomplish legitimate objectives should be taken at the lowest level of government capable of dealing with the underlying problem.[40]

### 2.6. The Role of the Court

The EU legal system started out with many of the limitations and weaknesses that characterize most international legal systems.[41] The transformation of the EU legal system into a supranational legal system was initiated by the Court of Justice in its legal interpretations of the aims of the European Union. The turning point that made EU law more binding was the case which established the *direct effect doctrine,* the *doctrine of state liability* and the *doctrine of supremacy* of EU law over the domestic laws of the Member States.

In 1963, in the landmark judgment of *Van Gend & Loos,* the Court of Justice launched the direct effect doctrine.[42] In its judgment the Court recognised that certain EU legal norms should give rise to rights and obligations directly, without the need for implementation in national law.

At the beginning of the 1990s, with the Court of Justice ruling in the *Francovich* case, the direct effect doctrine was supplemented with the *doctrine of state liability* for damages for non-implementation of a directive.[43] This

---

39. Article 5 of the EC Treaty.
40. *George A. Bermann:* 'Subsidiarity and the European Community', in Hastings International and Comparative Law Review, Vol. 17, 1993 pp. 97-98, and *J.H.H. Weiler:* 'The Transformation of Europe', in Yale Law Journal, Vol. 100, 1991 p. 2403.
41. *Karen J. Alter:* Establishing the Supremacy of European Law – The Making of an International Rule of Law in Europe, 2003 pp. 213-214. For accounts of these developments see also *Hjalte Rasmussen:* 'Remedying the Crumbling EC Judicial System', in Common Market Law Review, Vol. 37, 2000 p. 1071; and *Paul Craig:* 'The Jurisdiction of the Community Courts Reconsidered', in *Gráinne de Búrca & J.H.H. Weiler* (eds.): The European Court of Justice, 2001 p. 177.
42. Case 26/62, *Van Gend en Loos.*
43. Joined Cases C-6 and C-9/90, *Francovich and Boniface v Italy.*

meant that the Member States became answerable to the citizens of the EU for any harm caused by breaches of EU law. The *Francovich* case implied that Member States cannot implement EU law at their discretion. Thus, EU law is one and the same in all Member States and the doctrine holds that Member States are liable for any failure to implement EU law.

Another landmark case which changed the way that EU law was perceived, was the case *Costa v ENEL* from 1964, which laid down the *doctrine of supremacy of EU law*: EU Member States must change their own law so as to conform with EU law.[44] The case strengthened the principle of the unity of EU law by excluding conflicts between the norms of EU directives and the norms of the Member States' laws.

With the judgments in these landmark cases and subsequent developments in its case law, the European Union has *de facto* become an autonomous entity with its own sovereign rights and a legal order independent of the Member States, to which both the Member States themselves and their citizens are subject within the EU's areas of competence. The role of the Court of Justice as a 'law maker' also shows that common law traditions have strongly influenced the making of EU law.

### 2.7. Energy and Environmental Law

The 1972 UN Stockholm Conference was the stimulus for the development of a complex and comprehensive set of rules on environmental law within the European Communities. Since then a large body of environmental legislation has been developed in the form of regulations, directives and non-binding recommendations. Since the end of 1993, environmental action programmes under Article 175(3) of the EC Treaty have been adopted in the form of legally binding decisions and are thus also a source of law.[45]

Today there is EU legislation in almost every conceivable field of environmental policy, although there are still some parts which have not been harmonised, but which are still restricted by EU primary law. The EU environmental assessment requirements for certain plans and projects, and the legislation on nature conservation which has been adopted since 1979, and which to some extent is designed to fulfil obligations under international treaties

---

44. Case 6/64, *Costa v ENEL*.
45. Until now only the latest environmental action programme (the sixth), which covers the period from 22 July 2002 to 21 July 2012, has been adopted under Article 175(3) of the EC Treaty.

such as the 1979 Berne and Bonn Conventions, are of great importance to the issues discussed in this book.[46]

Unlike the environment, energy issues were not regulated in an EU context until much later. The first legislative measure on energy was adopted at the beginning of the 1990s. The reason for this tardiness was the strong opposition of the Member States to harmonisation of this area. This opposition is also reflected in the lack of a special chapter on energy in the EC Treaty. Not until the 1992 Maastricht Treaty were energy measures included among the various Community activities. The principle of subsidiarity thus plays a very important role in the formation of EU energy law in a way which is not comparable to the area of EU environmental law.[47]

If the Treaty of Lisbon is ratified, the competence of the European Union will be extended to include a new section on Energy and a specific provision on climate change under the section on Environment. Another recent turning point in EU energy and climate policy has been the commitment to raise the market share of renewable energy in the European Union to 20 per cent by 2020.[48] See also Chapter 10, section 3.

---

46. See the 1979 Berne Convention on the conservation of European wildlife and natural habitats, (OJ 1982 L 38/3) and the 1979 Bonn Convention on the conservation of migratory species of wild animals (OJ 1982 L 210/10).
47. See section 2.5 on the principle of subsidiarity. See also *Birgitte Egelund Olsen:* 'The principle of subsidiarity, and its impact on regulation' in *B. Egelund Olsen & K. Engsig Sørensen:* Regulation in the EU, 2006 pp. 35-79.
48. COM(2008) 30 final, 20 20 by 2020 – Europe's climate change opportunity.

# CHAPTER 4

# National Legal Systems

## 1. The Danish Legal System – by *Ellen Margrethe Basse & Jørgen Dalberg-Larsen*

The Danish legal tradition forms part of the Scandinavian law tradition, which is characterized by the influence of Continental law and thus takes its starting point in the civil law tradition.[1]

### 1.1. The Scandinavian Legal Tradition

The Scandinavian countries have never developed a case law like that of England and the United States nor comprehensive codes like those of France and Germany.[2] Nevertheless, the legal systems of the Scandinavian countries are placed in the civil law tradition because of the many similarities with that tradition and because in many respects Scandinavian law has been influenced by German civil law.

The Scandinavian countries consist of Denmark, Norway and Sweden – in some contexts Finland and Iceland are included, and they then constitute the Nordic countries.

Since the middle ages it has been possible to view Scandinavian law as an entity. Even today, the Scandinavian countries have a certain degree of commonality based on shared history, including the sharing of kings, wars and treaties. To be able to understand the legal and political structure and culture, it is important to be aware of the Scandinavian pragmatism and the tradition for close cooperation between the regulated sector, the public administration and, to a certain extent, the political parties.

Within the Nordic region contacts between the countries can take place directly through officials and civil servants, without the necessity of going

---

1. *Jacob W.F. Sundberg:* 'Civil Law, Common Law and the Scandinavians', in Scandinavian Studies in Law, 1969 p. 204.
2. *Lester Bernhard Orfield:* The Growth of Scandinavian Law, 1953 p. 14.

through the ministries of foreign affairs, as if the countries were a unified political entity. This is due in part to historical practice and the attitude that it is acceptable to contact an official or one's counterpart in another Nordic country, and there is formal recognition of this practice in Article 38 of the Helsinki Agreement.[3] The countries' delegates and staff work together in international organizations by sharing information and agreeing joint positions for the Nordic region as a whole. This teamwork has also been established in relation to different energy and environmental issues as an effective platform for pursuing common interests.[4] There is also a high degree of formal legal unity and of shared identity among Nordic jurists.

### 1.1.1. Inspiration from Civil Law

As already mentioned, the Scandinavian legal tradition originates from Roman law and is based on the idea that 'personal' and 'real' rights are different in kind: the law of obligations deals with claims for the performance of contracts and is not applicable against third parties, whereas the law of property deals with rights to dispose of real or movable property, which are legally protected against third parties.[5] The importance and influence of the civil law tradition is clear in the administrative law of the Scandinavian countries. Administrative law was established in Scandinavia as a special legal discipline in 1924, based on a doctoral thesis by the Danish Professor *Poul Andersen* who introduced the theories of French and German administrative law.[6]

However, the systematic and theoretical German approach to legal problems has never had much impact on the judge made law. Nor have civil codes – based on the concepts of the German or French civil codes – been part of the Scandinavian legal tradition.[7] In contrast to the Continental codes, the Scandinavian codes have rather unsystematic structures.

---

3. The Treaty of Cooperation between Denmark, Finland, Iceland, Norway and Sweden (the Helsinki Agreement), entered into force 1 July 1962.
4. A striking example is the common Nordic electricity pooling system established to ensure harmonization of the electricity markets.
5. *Jacob W.F. Sundberg:* 'Civil Law, Common Law and the Scandinavians', in Scandinavian Studies in Law, 1969 pp. 198-205; and *Bo von Eyben:* 'Danish Property Law', in *Børge Dahl, Torben Melchior & Ditlev Tamm* (eds.): Danish Law in a European Perspective, 2002 p. 209.
6. *Ole Due:* 'Danish Law in a European Context', in *Børge Dahl, Torben Melchior & Ditlev Tamm* (eds.): Danish Law in a European Perspective, 2002 pp. 18-19.
7. *Jacob W.F. Sundberg:* 'Civil Law, Common Law and the Scandinavians', in Scandinavian Studies in Law, 1969 pp. 202-203.

The Scandinavian countries have made a contribution to the development of law. The principle of participation – including the right of access to information – has a long tradition in Scandinavian planning law – especially in relation to the right of access to administrative proceedings. In public law the ideas of transparency of administrative proceedings, public access to official documents and control of the administration by a Parliamentary Ombudsman have gained ground in countries outside the Nordic region.[8]

There is clearly a very strong influence from the civil law tradition on the Scandinavian courts. The judges view themselves as the servants of the administrative and legislative branches, rather than as a body appointed to act as a check upon their powers. The Scandinavian courts are therefore very reluctant to interfere with the work of the legislatures.

Scandinavian judges share with French judges the fear of trespassing upon the field of the legislature, and tend to allow a considerable margin of discretion to the administrative authorities. Court decisions reflect a general view that the judiciary may not pursue a policy of its own. However, the judges are also pragmatic in the same way as common law judges,[9] though they have a less strict attitude to the importance of precedent than common law judges. Judicial precedent is not an important part of the legal system.

*1.1.2. Historical Background*
From the middle of the nineteenth century the idea took root of Scandinavia being a natural legal community to be preserved and elaborated to the greatest possible extent. However, in some respects the origin of the Scandinavian cooperation was more ideological than practical. It was closely linked to the movement of 'Scandinavianism' which was motivated by the desire to put an end to confrontation, especially to wars between Denmark and Sweden.[10] This movement towards Scandinavian legal unity resulted in the drafting of uniform Scandinavian laws.

---

8.   The first ombudsman was established in Sweden in 1809, in Finland in 1919, in Denmark in 1954 and in Norway in 1962, see *Ellen Margrethe Basse:* 'The Ombudsman as Protector of Environmental Rights', in *Ármann Snævarr, Gudrun Erlendsdottir, Jónatan Pórmundsson, Páll Sigurdsson & Porgeir Örlygsson* (eds.): Afmælisrit Til Heiduira Gunnari G. Schram, 2002 pp. 65-66.

9.   *Ole Due:* 'Danish Law in a European Context', in *Børge Dahl, Torben Melchior & Ditlev Tamm* (eds.): Danish Law in a European Perspective, 2002 p. 21.

10.  *Ole Due:* 'Danish Law in a European Context', in *Børge Dahl, Torben Melchior & Ditlev Tamm* (eds.): Danish Law in a European Perspective, 2002 p. 20.

The background for this orientation towards Scandinavia was twofold. *First*, the idea stemmed from romanticism and historicism spread through the discipline of legal history, i.e. that law should be considered part of a larger comprehensive whole, which is developed slowly and continuously in harmony with the development of other areas of society. According to this thinking, it was meritorious to endeavour to maintain a connection with past laws and to avoid a drastic modernization of the law based on foreign models or new ways of thinking. It was common to see Scandinavia as a natural legal unit, based on an often romanticised common history, a shared language and the idea of an ancient shared legal culture. *Second*, from the middle of the nineteenth century, especially in Denmark, a pronounced anti-German attitude emerged due to the territorial disputes which led in 1864 to the loss of all of Schleswig to the German superpower to the south. This too added to the desire for a community of the Scandinavian countries, including in the area of law.

The Scandinavian idea had a breakthrough with regard to law in about 1870. In 1872 the first big Scandinavian meeting of jurists was held, and ever since then there have been frequent meetings of Scandinavian jurists. Here Scandinavian affairs and the possibilities for strengthening the community were discussed. In the 1870s practical collaboration on the enactment of laws was initiated. The laws should as far as possible be the same in all the countries in order for legal unity to be achieved.[11] Further, from the 1870s the publication of the extensive *Nordisk Retsencyklopædi* (Nordic Legal Encyclopaedia) was commenced. Just a decade later, in 1887, the publication of the periodical, *Tidsskrift for Rettsvitenskap*, began.

The Nordic Council (*Nordisk Råd*) was established in 1952. It operates as the formal organ for cooperation between the Scandinavian countries. The Council was not established by a treaty but by national legislation in each of the member countries, as is customary in cooperation between the Nordic countries. While it is neither a parliament nor a supranational body with authority to make decisions which are binding on member countries, the Nordic Council serves as a forum for discussion and cooperation for resolving the problems facing the region. Although, there was cooperation and uniform legislation prior to the establishment of the Council, and although much of the cross-border cooperation in the Nordic countries takes place outside its framework, the Nordic Council nevertheless plays a significant role through

---

11. *Lester Bernhard Orfield:* The Growth of Scandinavian Law, 1953 p. xvii.

its annual sessions and the ongoing political work of its different committees and party groups.

From the 1960s on, a number of observers have identified one or rather two crises in the Scandinavian legal collaboration – crises that have threatened to bring an end to the Scandinavian legal tradition, regardless of how old it may be.

The relationship to the European Community was *one of crises*. In 1972 Denmark was the only Scandinavian country that chose to join the European Community (EC), which meant entering into a legal unit with a number of other non-Scandinavian countries, while it could not follow Scandinavian solutions which were contrary to Community law. Up to 1995 Denmark was the only Nordic country which was a full member of the European Community (under a special agreement Danish participation excludes the regions of Greenland and the Faeroe Islands from the European Union). Finland and Sweden became members in 1995, while Iceland and Norway are not members. Nordic cooperation continued after these accessions to the European Union and the creation of the European Economic Area (EEA), which includes Iceland and Norway. The EEA cooperation covers environmental law and energy law. See also Chapter 3, section 2.2.

*The other crisis*, according to some, was the fact that the domestic legislation of the Scandinavian countries has increasingly been shaped by domestic politics and a desire to use the law as an instrument of social reform rather than considering Scandinavian legal unity as the highest objective. There is probably some truth in this. Today, especially outside the classic areas of private law, laws are not shaped primarily by the views of legal experts but by political debate. Consequently, the weakening of the jurists' previously dominant position in the legislative process has made it more difficult to achieve formal legal unity between the Scandinavian countries.

The Nordic Environmental Protection Convention (1973) was the result of an initiative taken by the Nordic Council. This Convention was interesting at the time because of its direct impact on national laws. It covers all kinds of activities which are harmful to the environment, but it does not prescribe a single administrative system for each state to adopt. The purpose of the Convention was to secure the rights of citizens in matters relating to environmental protection. It sought to achieve this by giving administrative authorities and individuals the right of access to courts and it put administrative authorities in other Scandinavian countries in the same position as if all parties were under the same jurisdiction. The *consultation principle*, which relates to the notification of states potentially affected by activities that may have significant adverse cross-border effects, was codified by the Convention. In other words, the primary principle of the Convention is that the pollution of a neighbouring country is equivalent to the pollution of one's own country.

The recent trends towards internationalization will almost automatically mean that foreign influences will have an important impact on the legal systems and the common Scandinavian understanding of law. However, throughout the past millennium the Scandinavian legal systems have been constantly subject to influences from abroad. Especially with the rise of modern society in the 19th century there was a trend towards internationalization. In the 19th century a conscious choice was made to rally round the idea of a Scandinavian legal entity. This did not imply a wish to shut Scandinavia off from influences and information from abroad, but rather it led to a debate about how the new influences should be dealt with in a Scandinavian context.

### 1.1.3. Scandinavian Law of Today

Despite the developments discussed above, the common Scandinavian legal tradition has been continued and elaborated. It is a tradition which today must be considered a historical fact.

Legal positivism – as expounded for example by the Danish professor *Alf Ross* – which focuses on a logical methodology, has had a strong impact on legal rationality and legal theory since the 1920s. His views bear a close resemblance to American legal realism.[12] It was (and still is) generally characterized by a liberal attitude, which means that due account should be taken of private economic interests which are particularly affected by the decisions of public authorities.[13]

An attempt to identify some of the important general characteristics of Scandinavian law would point to its pragmatic, practical and realistic conception of law. For example, more importance is attached to the effects of the law than to its formal content. One could refer to this as a new Scandinavian legal tradition, which has been developed in the 20th century in order to use the law as an instrument for political reform. Thus, this new common legal tradition is not founded on the idea that a legal tradition must be based on a shared set of ancient legal customs. Rather, the unity consists of a common perspective of the role of law in society.

---

12. *Lester Bernhard Orfield:* The Growth of Scandinavian Law, 1953 p. 65.
13. *Helle Tegner Anker & Ellen Margrethe Basse:* 'Rationality, Environmental Law, and Biodiversity', in *Suzanne C. Beckmann & Erik Kloppenborg Madsen* (eds.): Environmental Regulation and Rationality, 2001 p. 166.

## 1.2. The Danish Legal Tradition

It is said, that Denmark is one of the oldest kingdom in Europe. There is a reference to Denmark existing as a kingdom dating back to 700. By 800 most of Scandinavia had been colonized from Denmark.[14]

### 1.2.1. Historical Background

From around 1200 a number of Scandinavian provincial codes were enacted.[15] The criminal laws of the thirteenth century are to be found in the Laws of King Valdemar the Victorious (1202-1240).[16] In Denmark a royal committee drafted the Jutland Code. It was passed to the *Landsthing* in Viborg and issued by King Valdemar the Victorious in about 1240. The Jutland Code contained a collection of explanations, decisions, customs, and new rules. In 1326 it was ratified as official law and made applicable to all parts of Denmark. This led to a formalization and stabilization of the legal system, which was largely based on old customary law. A revision of the Jutland Code was introduced in 1590.[17]

At that time the King was a hereditary monarch. In 1660 absolute monarchy was proclaimed with the Code *Lex Regia*, which was not withdrawn until the adoption of the Danish Constitution in 1849. In 1661 King Frederik III directed a commission to prepare a modern code which, after his death, was adopted in 1682 as King Christian V's Danish Code. Its sources were the national laws of the sixteenth and seventeenth centuries. The Code was not systematic or wide in scope, but for a long time it was the most important law in Denmark, and some provisions are still in use today.

### 1.2.2. Legal Institutions and Law Making

### 1.2.2.1. The Constitution

The written Danish constitution dates back to 1849. The constitution was largely based on the Belgian constitution, and was therefore based on the normally accepted Continental principles following the French Revolution. The traditional legal structure of the Constitution was based on a strict sepa-

---

14. *Lester Bernhard Orfield:* The Growth of Scandinavian Law, 1953 p. 1.
15. *Ole Due:* 'Danish Law in a European Context', in *Børge Dahl, Torben Melchior & Ditlev Tamm* (eds.): Danish Law in a European Perspective, 2002 pp. 16-17.
16. *Lester Bernhard Orfield:* The Growth of Scandinavian Law, 1953 p. 44.
17. *Lester Bernhard Orfield:* The Growth of Scandinavian Law, 1953 pp. 15-16.

ration of powers between legislative, executive and judicial institutions.[18] It included certain fundamental rights: personal liberty, property rights, freedom of opinion, freedom of organization and freedom of assembly.[19] It provided for the introduction of the jury system and established a State church and religious freedom.

The public law system – the law and order principles – serves to protect the rights and interests of individuals (e.g. rights of private property) with the concept of legality. Within that framework, the role of the executive bodies which administer environmental and energy laws becomes very clear: once democratically constituted, the national legislature and the municipalities at the local level have the responsibility of formulating laws, bylaws, spatial planning laws etc., which the executive institutions (including the municipalities) then implement, and the judicial system ensures that they are consistently applied.

Article 63 of the Constitution lays down the right of the courts to review all administrative decisions. Article 73 of the Constitution provides that no-one can be deprived of their private property rights, except in accordance with the statutes and unless full compensation is paid. Based on these expropriation rules, legislative acts and administrative decisions may mean that the authorities have to pay full compensation to the owners of property or to other persons who have specific interests in the use of property, if the act or decision reduces their rights.

Historically, the legal status of real estate and land ownership has been very similar in the Nordic countries, but recent administrative and environmental developments have led to differences arising in national legislative measures and procedures. One reason for these differences has been the introduction of measures on land use, planning, pollution control permit systems, the protection of natural resources etc.

### 1.2.2.2. The Parliament

The Danish legislature is based on the concept of representative democracy. The Parliament (*Folketinget*) has 179 members of whom two are elected in Greenland and two in the Faeroe Islands.

Members of Parliament, as well as members of the Government, can propose legislation. No legislation may be passed until it has been read three

18. *Helle Tegner Anker & Ellen Margrethe Basse:* 'Rationality, Environmental Law, and Biodiversity', in *Suzanne C. Beckmann & Erik Kloppenborg Madsen* (eds.): Environmental Regulation and Rationality, 2001 p. 169.
19. Articles 71-79 of the Danish Constitution.

times in Parliament and has received Royal Assent. A minority of the members of Parliament (at least one third of the 179 members) may ask that a bill passed by Parliament should be submitted to a referendum before Royal Assent is given. Royal Assent will be refused if a majority in a referendum votes against the bill and if that majority constitutes not less than 30 per cent of those entitled to vote. Some bills, however, are exempt from this provision, particularly bills on taxation or other financial legislation. With regard to expropriation bills, it is possible to ask for a postponement of the third reading. Parliament, as the legislative power, may delegate its authority to the Government, except where the Constitution specifically requires the legislative assembly to formulate the rules in question.

### 1.2.2.3. The Government and Administrative Bodies

The Danish Government is subordinate to Parliament both with respect to its legislative powers and its executive powers. Any member of Parliament may put questions to ministers during a weekly question time. A number of members of Parliament may collectively request a debate on a particular matter. The fact that ministers are politically answerable to Parliament implies a measure of cohesion between the legislature and the executive. Because of this, the Danish state administration is relatively centralised.[20]

The structural framework of the Danish state administration is that of a hierarchy in which each minister is the top executive in their field. Where traditional state authorities are concerned, the hierarchical relationship implies that the superior authorities have the right to intervene *ex officio*. The most important ministries in respect of environmental and energy laws are the Ministry of the Environment and the Ministry of Climate and Energy. Some of the responsibilities of these ministries have been delegated to agencies. The National Agency for Environmental Protection is part of the Ministry of the Environment. It is responsible for the daily administration of environmental protection at national level.

To a large extent public authority has been decentralised to local authorities. Since 1 January 2007 there have been 99 municipalities and 5 regional bodies. Among their duties the elected local and regional bodies are responsible for the environmental and planning procedures and they must ensure that the local administration acts in conformity with local wishes.

The Danish administrative appeals system is different from that used in the other Nordic countries. The appeal boards in the area of environmental

---

20. *Ellen Margrethe Basse:* Environmental Law – Denmark, 2004 p. 17.

and energy law have several members, and their primary function is the settling of disputes. Such appeal boards are independent of the ordinary administrative hierarchy. They are composed with a view to consideration for legal protection and, *inter alia*, representing special interests and/or political representation.

Conflicts in environmental and energy cases brought before the administrative appeal bodies are resolved on the basis of an open and not very precise framework of rules, technical guidelines and political opinions. The normal limits of an appeals system are transcended and resolutions of conflicts are not decided by legal factors alone.[21] These appeals bodies can make references to the European Court of Justice for preliminary rulings under Article 234 of the EC Treaty, but this has never yet been done.

### 1.2.2.4. The Ombudsman

The Danish Ombudsman is appointed by Parliament under Section 55 of the Constitution. The main task of the Ombudsman is to ensure that the administration complies with current law and administrative principles, and that public bodies behave in a proper manner in their relations with citizens. The Ombudsman has no power to reverse or quash administrative decisions – his only function is to monitor the administration on behalf of Parliament. Therefore, the Ombudsman does not intervene directly in administrative acts, but the institution of the Ombudsman has had considerable influence on the behaviour of the administration.

One of the great advantages of this institution is that, unlike a review by administrative appeal bodies or the courts, a claimant does not have to prove that they have a specific interest and the procedure for handling appeals against administrative decisions is direct, informal, quick and cheap. The Ombudsman may also make investigations on his own initiative.

When the Ombudsman assesses the administrative acts of local authorities he has to take into account that these authorities have a special position as politically elected bodies. If a case concerning an administrative decision is brought to the courts, the assessment by the courts has priority and the Ombudsman will consequently terminate his investigation.

In contrast to the courts and the appeal bodies, the Ombudsman may not make references to the European Court of Justice for preliminary rulings under Article 234 of the EC Treaty in cases concerning the correct implementa-

21. *Helle Tegner Anker & Ellen Margrethe Basse:* 'Rationality, Environmental Law, and Biodiversity', in *Suzanne C. Beckmann & Erik Kloppenborg Madsen* (eds.): Environmental Regulation and Rationality, 2001 p. 168.

tion of EU law. It is therefore not easy for the Ombudsman to assess whether Danish law complies with EU law.

## 1.3.  The Role of the Courts

There are three levels in the Danish court system. The lowest courts of first instance are the district courts. The superior courts of first instance are the High Courts – one for the Eastern circuit (*Østre Landsret*) and one for the Western circuit (*Vestre Landsret*). They also act as courts of appeal from the district courts. The Supreme Court (*Højesteret*) is the highest level.

The courts' independence is based on Section 64 of the Danish Constitution, which provides that in the performance of their duties judges shall be directed solely by the law. Unlike many other Continental European countries (including some of the Nordic countries), there are no special administrative courts for dealing with the judicial review of administrative acts. Such cases come before the ordinary courts. Also, there are no Danish courts which deal specifically with environmental issues, in contrast to the Swedish environmental courts. All the courts are ordinary courts. The same courts deal with all cases – including cases on the administration of environmental and energy law, criminal cases, cases on tortious liability etc.

The judgments of the Danish courts are very short and without the detailed analysis known from the decisions of courts in common law jurisdictions. The judgments are also shorter than those given in other Scandinavian courts, as Danish judges do not like to make long arguments which could establish precedents precedent, and they certainly do not like to make judgments with legal reasoning or statements of principle.

To some extent the civil law approach, as well as the dualistic approach to international law, prevents the Danish courts from taking into account the development of the concept of sustainable development as well as environmental principles. Accordingly, the concept of sustainability and the environmental principles are generally regarded by the Danish courts only as irrelevant political guidelines.

Where a matter of EU law is raised before a national court and the court considers that a decision on that question is necessary to enable it to give judgment, the national court may (and in some case must) request the Court of Justice to give a ruling on the matter in accordance with Article 234 of the EC Treaty. However, the Danish courts do not use this procedure very often.

## 1.4.  Environmental and Energy Law

On the one hand environmental and energy legislation in Denmark is characterized by the traditional principles of administrative law, and on the other hand it is characterized by its close relation to private law, procedural law and criminal law. Rules with retroactive effects are normally not accepted. The rules on environmental and energy issues, therefore, usually only apply to prospective cases. The rules state that they only apply after the date on which they are published or thereafter – and if the rules are not clear on this issue, the courts will not accept retroactive effect.

Except for the law on environmental liability and the neighbour law, environmental and energy legislation is strongly rooted in administrative law. Administrative acts involve a complicated system of objection clauses, rules on competence, rules of procedure, rules on appeals etc. The traditional principles of administrative law – i.e. the legality principle, the principle of specialization and the proportionality principle – form the basis of these acts. They have a special importance in Denmark compared with the other Nordic countries. In administrative and judicial practice, the aim of establishing environmental and energy laws as holistic regulation may be restricted by administrative law principles. The principles of public law, based on the need to protect the rights of individuals, thus have an important role in the decision-making process.

Interference with property rights may be regarded as expropriation, as regulated by the Constitution. The courts use several criteria to assess this question, and their decisions rest on a combination of them. The most important are: generality, intensity and purpose.[22] No compensation will be given if the legislative act is based on important public interests (e.g. environmental protection or energy supply security), and the interference is general and necessary. See also Chapter 5, section 3.1. Water and land use legislation in Denmark (as well as in the other Nordic countries) makes widespread use of full compensation and other guarantees that make it difficult or costly to interfere with the individual's management of their property. Thus, strong protection has traditionally been given to private property and economic interests, rather than environmental values and non-economic interests.[23]

Environmental and planning law is generally aimed at ensuring a sustainable societal development as stated in the first section of the Danish laws as well as in the other laws of the Nordic countries. The implementation of the

22. *Orla Friis Jensen:* 'The Role of Property Rights: Danish Perspective', in *Helle Tegner Anker & Ellen Margrethe Basse* (eds.): Land Use and Nature Protection. Emerging Legal Aspects, 2000 pp. 47-68.
23. *Hans Christian Bugge:* 'Legal Issues in Land Use and Nature Protection', in *Helle Tegner Anker & Ellen Margrethe Basse* (eds.): Land Use and Nature Protection. Emerging Legal Aspects, 2000 p. 26.

objective of sustainability depends to a large extent on the constitutions, the systems for decision-making and the measures which the authorities have to use for realising the aims of statutory rules. In this respect, there is an important difference between the Nordic countries. In the 1990s the constitutions of Finland and Norway were amended and supplemented by specific provisions on the rights and duties of citizens in connection with the environment, stressing the goal of sustainable development. The constitutions of Denmark, Iceland and Sweden do not include similar provisions on sustainable development. See also Chapter 5, section 3.2.

### 1.5. Commentary from a Norwegian Point of View – by *Hans Christian Bugge*

The Norwegian legal tradition and concepts have much in common with the Danish, but there are also important differences.

The first written (regional) Norwegian laws date back to the 10th century. The first Norwegian codes from the second half of the 13th century were enacted at a time when the Catholic Church had a strong influence. Towards the end of the 14th century Norway came under Danish rule. This greatly influenced legal development, although special laws applied to Norway throughout the period, which lasted until 1814.

In 1814 Norway became independent of Denmark and a written constitution – *Grunnloven* – was adopted. Although it has had numerous changes since 1814, the Norwegian Constitution is still in force as the oldest written constitution in Europe. It was very much inspired by the philosophy of the enlightenment, the ideas of Montesquieu and the Constitution of the United States.

Although it was in a Union with Sweden from 1814 to 1905, Norway developed its law rather independently during the 19th century. However, the extensive contacts between Nordic lawyers and legal scholars, the common influence of German jurisprudence, as well as cooperation on legislation, have contributed to there being many similarities in the development of the law in Norway and its Nordic neighbours.

The basic pattern of the division of roles and powers the legislature (*Stortinget*), the executive and the judicial branch is the same in Norway as in Denmark. However there are some differences, and these are relevant not least in the field of environmental law.

First, it is probably correct to state that in one sense the Norwegian courts – and the Supreme Court in particular – have been more restrictive in their interpretation of constitutional and other rules related to the protection of property rights. Through a series of cases – several before the plenary Court –

the Supreme Court has actively developed a restrictive doctrine on compensation for landowners' possible economic losses due to land use regulations governing private land – in particular the effects of restrictions with an environmental objective. The main rule is that a landowner is not entitled to compensation for possible economic loss due to land use, planning and environmental regulations.[24]

Similarly, the prohibition of retroactive legislation which is laid down in the Norwegian Constitution has been interpreted so that it does not prevent stricter regulations being adopted and applied to ongoing activities.[25] The solution to these fundamental issues is very important for the proper management of land, natural resources and the environment.

As in Denmark, environmental law in Norway is dominated by a public law approach. The use of land, activities which may harm the environment, and the exploitation of natural resources are regulated through regulations (executive orders) and individual permits. Norway has a quite detailed and precise Public Administration Act[26] which lays down general rules for administrative procedure. The procedural rights of citizens are well developed, and include recently established rights to environmental information, and to participation in environmental cases.[27] Environmental organisations have quite a broad right of insight, administrative appeal and access to the courts.

On the other hand, many of the *substantive* rules in such legal fields as environmental law, land use law, the exploitation of natural resources etc. are quite broadly formulated. They leave wide discretionary powers to the Norwegian Government or the municipalities to lay down more detailed regulations and to issue concessions and permits. So, the priorities and trade-offs between industrial and economic objectives on the one hand, and environmental considerations on the other, are to a large extent purely political issues rather than legal issues.

One effect of this is that the Norwegian courts play only a limited role in the enforcement and development of environmental law. Briefly, the courts may only review the legality of a decision made by a branch of the executive, and not generally its appropriateness or proportionality. The general court

---

24. An exception applies when an area is protected as nature reserve which is the strictest category of protection. In this case, the landowner is entitled to compensation for his economic loss, pursuant to Nature Protection Act of 19 June 1970, section 20.
25. Article 97 of the Norwegian Constitution.
26. Act of 10 February 1967.
27. A new act in this area is the Environmental Information Act of 9 May 2003 No 39, initiated by the Aarhus Convention and reflecting the EU directives on the issue.

system also deals with public administration cases. There are few special administrative courts in Norway, and none in the field of the environment. However, there is a general right of administrative appeal against all decisions, and it is possible to bring a case before the Norwegian Ombudsman. This partly explains why very few cases on environmental law come before the courts in Norway, compared to other European countries.

Over the last decade, however, a development towards stricter substantive rules may be observed in the field of environmental protection and resource management, laying down clearer rights for citizens as well as obligations for authorities and other actors. This development is to a great extent due to international conventions and to the development of environmental legislation within the European Union. Although Norway is not a member of the European Union, most of its environmentally related legislation applies to Norway through the Agreement on the European Economic Area (EEA). In 1992 Norway's Constitution was amended to include a general Article on the obligation of the State to ensure the right of citizens and of future generations to a healthy environment and the productivity and diversity of nature.[28] See also Chapter 5, section 3.2.

In the field of environmental law authority lies mainly with the State, but some power has been decentralized to the counties and the municipalities. The counties, and even more the municipalities, are the main authorities for spatial and land use planning. On the other hand, development in the energy sector remains fully in the hands of the State. Broadly speaking, the competence of the Ministry of the Environment covers spatial and land use planning, nature conservation, control of pollution and of hazardous products, and protection of the cultural heritage. The energy sector is for the most part the responsibility of the Ministry of Petroleum and Energy.

## 2. The United States Legal System – by *Julian Juergensmeyer & Sanford Gaines*

### 2.1. The US Legal Tradition
In the context of energy and environmental regulation, the United States legal system is best understood as a combination of two important legal traditions.

---

28. Article 110b of the Norwegian Constitution.

*First,* with respect to the structure and authority of the national, state, and local governments and their relationship to each other and to private persons, the main elements of the United States legal system are determined by the United States Constitution and the constitutions of each state. Most of energy and environmental law in the United States is based on federal and state statutes. The powers of the federal and state governments to enact these statutes and the power of federal and state administrative agencies to impose and enforce regulations governing private conduct under those statutes are grounded in constitutional law.

*Second,* with respect to most interactions between private persons, such as contractual relationships or disputes over the use of private property, the United States and each state fundamentally follow the common law tradition in which the primary rules for resolving private disputes are derived from and are continually reshaped by the decisions of courts that are generally bound to follow precedent established by earlier court judgments on the same issue under the principle of *stare decisis*, see Chapter 2, section 3, above. Of course, in the modern era the common law tradition also includes the extensive body of statutory law referred to above. Statutes may modify the rights and obligations of individuals involved in private disputes.

### 2.1.1. The Constitutional Tradition

The United States Constitution, in force since 1789, establishes the national government, creates the basic structure of the national government, and defines the relationships between the national government, the governments of the states, and the rights of individuals. It is based on three corresponding principles that are somewhat in conflict with each other:

- that there should be a unitary central government with extensive powers on issues of national significance;
- that the structure of the national government should include a system of checks and balances to prevent abuses of power; and
- that a government of free individuals and sovereign states should have limited powers.

The first three articles of the Constitution enumerate the powers of three branches of government – the legislative, the executive, and the judicial branches. Each branch has broad powers within its respective sphere, but those powers overlap or intersect in significant ways that provide checks and balances.

The legislative branch is called the Congress and comprises two chambers or houses – the House of Representatives and the Senate. The House now has 435 members; the number of House districts in each state is determined by population, except that even the states with the fewest people – Wyoming and Alaska – get at least one representative. Because House districts are determined by population, the number of districts in a particular state, and therefore the geographic boundaries of those districts, is subject to change after the national census which takes place every ten years. States with growing populations get more districts, and those with stable or declining populations may lose districts. All Representatives stand for election every two years. Under the Constitution, the House has original responsibility for setting taxes and appropriating money for each government agency and programme.

The other part of the Congress is the Senate. Each state has two senators, so the Senate now has 100 members. Senators serve for terms of six years; every two years one-third of the Senate seats are up for election. Under the Constitution, the Senate has special responsibility for confirming the President's appointment of judges and senior government officials. The Senate must also give its consent, by a two-thirds majority, to any new international treaty before the United States can become a party to it. Even so, the United States agrees to many international agreements through executive action only; under prevailing Constitutional law, these lesser agreements are not 'treaties' and therefore are not subject to Senate approval.

The executive branch includes the President and the Vice President (and their staffs) and all the executive or administrative agencies of the government. The heads of the most important departments, including the Department of Defense, the Department of State, the Department of Justice, and the Department of the Treasury, constitute the President's Cabinet, that is, his principal political team. The Executive Office of the President includes some other powerful offices, such as the National Security Council, the Office of Management and Budget, and the Office of the United States Trade Representative. Finally, there are many other agencies, sometimes known as 'independent agencies' that are not part of the major departments. Examples of these include the Environmental Protection Agency, the Federal Energy Regulatory Commission, and the Nuclear Regulatory Commission.

The third branch of government is the judicial branch. The judiciary has the power to decide all 'cases or controversies' under federal law, and to decide disputes between states. As defined in the Constitution, the judicial branch comprises the Supreme Court of the United States and 'such other lesser courts as the Congress may from time to time determine'. The federal court system is described below.

The Constitution's allocation of government power was carefully crafted to create a system of 'checks and balances' so that no one branch of government could become too powerful. For example, enactment of a statute requires not only approval by a majority of the House of Representatives and the Senate, but signature by the President. If the President refuses to sign – vetoes – a bill, it goes back to Congress. The bill can still become law, however, but only if both the House and the Senate override the President's veto by a two-thirds majority. Efforts both by Congress and by the President to change this balance have been ruled unconstitutional by the courts. Congress is not allowed to veto an executive regulation, except by passing a law that is presented to the President in the usual way. On the other hand, if the President signs a law, he may not then decide to follow only part of it.

More generally, the executive branch often proposes new laws, but only the Congress can make the law. It then becomes the responsibility of the executive branch to 'faithfully execute' the law, without any interference from Congress. The executive has substantial discretion in how to administer the law, but it must follow the terms of the statute. The courts can, on request of an affected person, review an executive action to determine whether it conforms to the law and the Constitution, and if the executive has acted in ways contrary to the law, the courts will send the matter back to the executive branch for a new decision under the law as the court has interpreted it. Similarly, a private person can challenge the constitutionality of a statute as it may affect that person. Since the earliest days of the United States, the Supreme Court has asserted its prerogative to say 'what the law is', and to nullify a statute that is unconstitutional or to order the executive, including the President himself, to conform its behaviour to the Constitution.

Finally, there is the *principle of limited government*. Immediately after the Constitution was drafted but before it was ratified by the 13 states then in existence, a set of ten amendments, known as the Bill of Rights, was added. The ten amendments place important limits on the power of the government with respect to individual rights and liberties; for example, the Fifth Amendment declares that no person may be 'deprived of life, liberty, or property without due process of law', and requires the government to pay 'just compensation' if it takes property. Later, under the Fourteenth Amendment, some of these constitutional limits on government power were also applied to the state governments. The Tenth Amendment limits the power of the national government with respect to the individual states. It reserves to the individual states all government power not expressly granted to the federal government in the Constitution.

## 2.1.2. The Legal Tradition – Common Law and Statutory Law

The law in the United States, at the time the Constitution came into effect, was understood to be the common law of England, which was the law at the time the colonies became independent of Great Britain. The English common law was then subject to further developments by the decisions of the state courts, which differed somewhat in each state. Over the years, the question also arose as to whether the federal courts could or should develop a federal common law. As commerce between the states and the movement of people between the states increased, this became a more important issue.

Ultimately the question was resolved by the United States Supreme Court in the case of *Erie Railroad* v *Tompkins* in the 1930s.[29] The *Erie Rule*, put simply, instructs the federal courts to apply the state common law of the state with the closest connection to the particular case and question. The federal courts can formulate federal common law only on those issues which, by their nature, are federal – for example because they arise under a federal statute or concern the conduct of the federal government, or involve some relationship between the states, or a relationship between the citizens of one state and the government of another. For example, when the State of Illinois sued the City of Milwaukee (in the neighbouring state of Wisconsin) in a nuisance action for polluting Lake Michigan, the Supreme Court held that federal common law should apply.[30]

But there is another important limit on federal common law. In the dispute between Illinois and Milwaukee, shortly after the Supreme Court decision in 1972 just mentioned, the federal Clean Water Act was enacted, which included many detailed provisions about the regulation of pollution from various sources, including city-owned sewage treatment plants, and it required all sources to obtain permits for their discharges. How did this statute affect the dispute between Illinois and Milwaukee? In 1981, the United States Supreme Court decided the case of *City of Milwaukee* v *Illinois*,[31] holding that when a federal statute creates a comprehensive system of regulations and procedures on the matter at issue, then the statute determines the law to apply and the federal courts are pre-empted from applying federal common law on those questions.

As the *Milwaukee* case suggests, with respect to energy and environmental issues the many detailed federal and state statutes enacted since 1970 have supplanted most of the role of the common law. Statutes, and the administra-

---

29. *Erie R.R.* v *Tompkins*, 304 U.S. 64 (1938).
30. *Illinois* v *City of Milwaukee*, 406 U.S. 91 (1972).
31. *City of Milwaukee* v *Illinois*, 451 U.S. 304 (1981).

tive regulations promulgated under them by government agencies, have thus become the dominant sources of the law. Nevertheless, the common law remains in the background, and private persons sometimes bring cases or argue legal points based on the common law when the statutory framework does not specifically cover the point in question. For example, in 2006 the State of California filed a common law nuisance action against automobile manufacturers, based on the argument that the failure of those companies to regulate carbon dioxide emissions from automobiles is causing injury and expense to the State because of rising sea levels, changes in mountain snowfall affecting water resources, and other damaging effects of climate change.[32]

## 2.2. Historical Background

Although several European countries launched explorations of North America and established settlements there (the Vikings, the French, the Dutch, the Spanish, and the English), it was the English who rapidly came to dominate and control the eastern coast of America. Under British rule, throughout the 17th and 18th centuries a steady flow of immigrants from various parts of northern Europe established cities and towns and moved inland, effectively displacing or isolating the Native Americans who had previously resided there.

The British monarchs established the basic elements of public administration in each of their colonies, including court systems. Thus, the common law that prevailed in England became the law in the colonies as well. The only exceptions to the prevalence of the common law in what is now the United States are the continuing influence of the Napoleonic Code in French-settled Louisiana and the remnants of Spanish law, especially on issues of family and property law, in the south-western United States, from Texas to California, which was part of Mexico until the 1830s and 1840s.

The 17th and 18th centuries also brought a period of intellectual and political ferment to England and the American colonies. In 1688, England had its Glorious Revolution, in which Parliament gained substantial authority at the expense of the monarchy and enacted a Bill of Rights for citizens with respect to the government. Before and after this, important political philosophers such as Thomas Hobbes and John Locke explored the basis of government and the idea of the consent of the people to be governed. When the colonies came into dispute with the British crown, political leaders in the

---

32. *California v General Motors*, (N.D. Cal., case No C06-05755), complaint filed 20 September 2006. Other automobile companies named in the complaint are Toyota, Ford, Honda, Chrysler, and Nissan.

colonies invoked these British traditions to justify their own struggle. The tensions broke into armed conflict in 1775, and in 1776 leaders from all of the colonies met and issued their famous Declaration of Independence from Britain. After seven years of armed conflict, and with the important assistance of the French (the square in front of the White House is named after the Marquis de Lafayette) the 13 colonies gained their independence from Britain through the Treaty of Paris.

Now came the task of creating a government. Each of the 13 colonies had their own governors and governments, and this tradition of strong state government power continues, including separate and autonomous court systems for legal matters governed by state law. Thus, the common law varies, sometimes quite substantially, from one state to the next. But the colonies, now states, also saw the need for a unifying government structure. After an unsettled period under a framework known as the Articles of Confederation, the 13 states convened a constitutional convention, leading to the drafting of the current Constitution of the United States of America, described below in section 2.3.1. The Constitution was then approved by each of the 13 states, but only after the 10 amendments known as the Bill of Rights were added. All of these documents owe their inspiration to English (and some French) philosophy and political thought. Even so, they have evolved over the last two centuries in ways that reflect the distinctive experience of a rapidly growing frontier country, proud to have avoided the religious and political conflicts of Europe and populated, until recent decades, largely by religious and political refugees from Europe.

### 2.3. Legal Institutions and Law Making

*2.3.1. The Structure and Powers of the Federal Government*

As described in section 2.1.1 above, Article I of the United States' Constitution vests the legislative power of the United States in the Congress. The legislative power includes the power to make laws, to impose taxes, and to appropriate funds to specific government agencies and programmes. For energy and environmental issues, the authority of the Congress, and thus the federal government, extends to interstate and foreign commerce under the Commerce Clause (Article I, Section 8), and to the management of lands and resources owned by the federal government, including offshore submerged lands to the limits of national jurisdiction as defined by international law (Article IV, Section 3). The federal power under the Commerce Clause has been broadly interpreted to include laws protecting wildlife, preventing pollution, and regulating the production and distribution of energy, including electricity, that crosses state boundaries. For offshore wind energy, it should also be noted that the federal government has been held to have full and exclusive authority over navigation, through its inherent sovereignty over the seas and its power over interstate and foreign commerce.

Article II of the Constitution vests the executive power in the President and through him in the many subordinate departments and agencies of government. In addition to his important powers in the area of foreign affairs (Article II, Section 2), the Constitution directs the President (and the executive branch agencies) to 'take care that the laws be faithfully executed' (Article II, Section 3). This means that the agencies have the responsibility for adopting rules and regulations to carry out the laws enacted by Congress, and for the enforcement of those laws through administrative processes or by prosecution by the Attorney General (the head of the Department of Justice).

In the energy and environmental context, there are several federal departments and agencies with important responsibilities. The Department of Energy (DOE) handles energy policy and manages federal energy programmes. The Department of the Interior (DOI) has jurisdiction over most federal land and the mineral resources under that land, and freshwater fish and wildlife on federal land, and endangered species. The Environmental Protection Agency (EPA) administers most pollution control laws, and oversees the implementation of the environmental impact statement requirement of National Environmental Policy Act (NEPA). The United States Army Corps of Engineers has historical responsibility for navigation, and thus has environmental as well as navigation responsibilities in the waters of the United States. The United States Coast Guard, which is now part of the Department of Homeland Security, has operational and enforcement authority over boats and ships, as well as some enforcement authority over fixed installations in the waters of the United States. The roles of these agencies and some of their sub-units in relation to offshore wind farms are described in Chapter 5, sections 2.2 and 2.3 and in Chapter 10, section 6.

Article III of the Constitution vests the judicial power in the Supreme Court and in lower federal courts established by Congress. The lowest level of Article III courts are district courts, which are the courts of first instance for most cases in the federal system. There is at least one district court in each state, but many states are divided into several districts (e.g. the Eastern District of Texas). Most cases are assigned to an individual judge at the district court level. The next level up is the circuit courts of appeal. The judicial districts are grouped into eleven geographic circuits, with a United States Court of Appeals for each circuit. Massachusetts, for example, is in the First Circuit; California is in the Ninth Circuit. In addition, there is a court of appeals for the District of Columbia (the DC Circuit), and one appeals court that hears certain cases involving the federal government directly, including patent cases and trade cases (the Federal Circuit). Each circuit court has many judges, and cases are heard by a three-judge panel, with occasional appeals to the whole court *en banc*.

The judicial power of all the Article III courts extends to all 'cases and controversies' under the Constitution and federal law. This clause has been interpreted as prohibiting the federal courts from issuing advisory opinions. It has also been interpreted as meaning that private citizens or citizens' organizations must have suffered or be threatened by a specific injury in order to have standing (*locus standi*) to bring a case. The federal courts have jurisdiction over all cases involving the federal government as a party or involving the application or enforcement of federal law, and over cases in which the citizen of one state is suing the citizen of another state (called 'diversity jurisdiction'). Many federal cases in the energy and environment area involve disputes between a private party (such as an energy company or an environmental organization) and a federal agency, in which the complaining party invokes the power of the court to review the legality of the government's action. The federal courts also have jurisdiction to hear cases between two private parties in which the parties involved reside in different states, based on their 'diversity of citizenship'. In such cases it is now the rule that the federal court will apply the statutes and the common law of the state with the closest connection to the issues as determined by conflicts of laws principles.

Cases between private parties residing in a single state or governed by state law are heard in state courts. Each state has its own system of courts. Most state systems have a variety of lower courts (e.g. general county or district courts, small claims courts, family courts, juvenile courts etc.) and appellate courts and a supreme court. Even the names of the courts vary from state to state; for example, the lowest courts in New York State are called supreme courts, and the highest court is the Court of Appeals.

### 2.3.2. Federalism – The Allocation of Power between the Federal Government and the States

It is said that the United States Constitution creates a federal government of 'enumerated powers'. That is, the federal government has only those powers expressly or implicitly granted to it by the Constitution. This is confirmed by the Tenth Amendment, which expressly reserves to the individual states all the legal powers not granted to the federal government. This arrangement creates three possibilities for where government power resides:

1) exclusively in the federal government;

2) exclusively in the state governments; or
3) shared or overlapping federal and state power.

The federal government has exclusive power in two situations. First, if the power is one that can only be effectively exercised at the national level it belongs exclusively to the federal government. For example, foreign policy, national defence, foreign commerce, and the management of federal lands are exclusively federal. Second, it is also possible for the Congress to assert, by law, exclusive authority over a certain issue within its enumerated powers, and thus to pre-empt state law. The management of civilian nuclear power generation and other sources of radioactivity is one example where the federal government has pre-empted state authority and created an exclusively federal system of regulation. The rule applied by the courts to determine whether pre-emption exists is that the intention of Congress to pre-empt state power should be expressly stated or clearly implied by the legislation and the surrounding circumstances.

If, on the other hand, the issue is one that has traditionally been controlled by state law, the federal government cannot make laws or regulations unless it has some clear authority to do so in the Constitution. The Supreme Court recently decided, for example, that only state governments, and not the federal government, can define a zone around a public school where it is prohibited to carry a gun, even though the sale of guns can be federally regulated under the Commerce Clause.[33] Moreover, the federal government may not require state governments to enact specific laws and it may not interfere with their management of state government activities.[34]

The lands within the United States that are under the jurisdiction of Native American tribes are of increasing interest for energy development in general, including renewable energy. Generally speaking, the tribes have substantial sovereign authority over their lands and tribal members. The exact extent of that sovereignty, and the interaction of tribal law with state and federal law, is too complex to describe here. Indeed, there is a whole field of law, especially important in the western states, known as Indian Law.

For many issues and for many large private projects, there is often overlapping or shared jurisdiction between the federal, state, and tribal governments. This is particularly true in the energy and environmental contexts. The states have traditionally regulated energy production, distribution, service,

---

33.  *United States* v *Lopez*, 514 U.S. 549 (1995).
34.  E.g. *New York* v *United States*, 505 U.S. 144 (1992) holding that Congress cannot direct a state to arrange for the disposal of low level radioactive waste.

and the pricing of electricity and other forms of energy, even though the energy distribution system is connected with other states by electrical wires or pipelines. For example, a wind farm located in offshore federal waters will require permits from federal agencies for the location and construction of the turbines and submarine cables, but it will also need to be connected through state waters and over state land to the electricity distribution network, and it will therefore also be regulated under various state energy and environmental laws and regulations. It has been a matter of considerable political discussion in recent years whether the federal government should develop a national energy policy and pre-empt state regulation, but so far there has only been pre-emption of certain specific decisions, such as the location of offshore terminals for liquefied natural gas. The United States Congress remains very sensitive to, and legally supportive of, local choices about the location of energy facilities implemented through state government laws and regulations.

Environmental laws often reflect another model of shared federal and state power, called 'cooperative federalism'. Under this model, Congress establishes federal laws and policies to protect an environmental resource (e.g. wetlands) or to control pollution, but the individual states are encouraged to adopt state laws and regulations through which the state government can administer and implement the federal requirements within the state. In most such instances, the states are permitted to establish more protective rules under state law, but they must conform to the minimum requirements of the federal law. For example, under the major pollution control statutes the federal government sets national policy goals, national technology standards for pollution control, and the essential elements of the administrative structure, such as a requirement for individual sources of pollution to have permits for the release of pollution to the air or water. The states have the opportunity or responsibility to determine local goals (such as water quality standards for the waters in the state), for deciding on the specific standards for pollution control in different industrial sectors and individual firms in the state, for the exercise of administrative discretion in applying all the detailed rules and procedures to specific cases, and for enforcement of the law (although the federal government also retains enforcement authority).

Another example of cooperative federalism is the federal Coastal Zone Management Act (CZMA). The CZMA sets forth the basic elements that should be included in a Coastal Zone Management plan, but each state government has the responsibility for drawing up a plan for its state. As long as the state plan has the basic elements described in the Act, the federal government will approve it. The important legal consequence of such approval is that federal activities in that state are then required to conform to the state

CZM plan. Some coastal states (Florida, Georgia and California are leading examples) have their own detailed state CZM laws and regulations that go far beyond the minimum requirements for federal approval under the CZMA. See also Chapter 6, section 6.2.

### 2.4. The Role of the Courts

The courts, whether state courts or federal courts, play two major roles in the United States legal system. One role is the natural role of courts everywhere: to serve as a forum for the resolution of civil disputes between two (or more) private parties and to adjudicate civil enforcement actions or criminal prosecutions brought by the state against individuals. In both civil and criminal litigation the courts will apply statutory law constitutional law, and the common law, as appropriate in each case.

The other role of the courts in the United States, more prominently than in many other countries, is to engage in judicial review of government agency action, which is the central element of the system of administrative law. The Supreme Court established the prerogative of judicial review in the early case *Marbury* v *Madison*, where the holder of a government office challenged the right of the President to remove him from office.[35] With the enormous growth of government agencies and government regulation in the 1930s, legal challenges to the authority of administrators or to the legality of their decisions multiplied. In 1946, following the recommendations of a government commission, Congress enacted the Administrative Procedure Act (APA).[36] The APA clearly confirms the role of judicial review in the statute:

'A person suffering a legal wrong because of agency action, or adversely affected or aggrieved by agency action within the meaning of a relevant statute, is entitled to judicial review thereof'. (Section 702).

In such actions, the court 'shall decide all relevant questions of law, interpret constitutional and statutory provisions, and determine the meaning or applicability of the terms of an agency action' (Section 706). The court has various remedies, including the power to 'compel agency action unlawfully withheld or unreasonably delayed', and to set aside agency action that is, *inter alia*, 'in excess of statutory jurisdiction, authority, or limitations' or 'arbitrary, capricious, an abuse of discretion, or otherwise not in accordance with law'. (Section 706).

35. 1 Cranch 137 (U.S. Supreme Court, 1803).
36. 5 United States Code, SS. 551-706.

Administrative law cases challenging government decisions are especially common in complex areas like environmental law and energy law. Also, every case involving an environmental impact assessment under the federal National Environmental Policy Act (NEPA) is an administrative law case because the legal issue will either be

1) whether the agency is required to make an environmental impact assessment for the particular decision, and whether that assessment should be a full 'environmental impact statement'; or
2) whether the agency has conducted its environmental review at the right point in the decision-making process; or
3) whether the statement which the agency has prepared adequately examines the relevant environmental issues, analyzes alternative actions and takes account of the available scientific evidence.

In most respects, the law governing wind farms and other energy installations is statutory law administered by governmental authorities, and is therefore adjudicated in court cases applying the principles of administrative law. To be sure, in administrative law a court is also generally bound to follow the precedents of that court as well as the decisions of higher courts. Nevertheless, in administrative law the broad legal doctrines to be applied are well established, so that cases tend to be determined by the specific facts of the case and the interpretation of the specific laws and regulations applicable, which may not previously have been interpreted by any court in the same context.

## 2.5. Energy and Environmental Law

Historically, the regulation of energy in the United States has focused on the financial and corporate structure of energy suppliers and on the regulation of prices for such basic energy sources as electricity and natural gas and for their distribution. From the earliest days of electric power generation, there was recognition that it made sense to give the provider of electricity and its transmission a monopoly in a particular region, but that such monopoly market power needed to be publicly regulated to prevent private companies from making monopoly profits.

Publicly owned power generation was never widespread in the United States; only a few large cities established municipal power companies, and in some rural areas cooperatives became involved. But from the days of Thomas Edison, private power companies have been prevalent.

During the 1920s, there was intense financial speculation in public utilities, and great holding companies were formed that owned many different electric power companies. In the 1930s, federal New Deal legislation required the break up of these holding companies. Meanwhile, at the state level, most states established public utilities commissions with the responsibility for overseeing the industry and setting rates for electricity, natural gas, and other public utility products and services. The Federal Power Commission exercised similar regulatory authority over interstate networks such as long-distance transmission lines and natural gas pipelines, and for power generation installations serving interstate regions.

After the energy shock of the Arab oil embargo of the 1970s and the move for the United States to gain energy independence, the executive branch and Congress began to pay closer attention to energy policy. Legislation eventually created a new Department of Energy, and restructured the Federal Power Commission to become the Federal Energy Regulatory Commission. This was followed by a new statute, the Public Utility Regulatory Policy Act, which set forth new approaches to the corporate structures of electricity and other utilities.

In the 1990s, new technologies and a further wave of deregulation led many states to try new approaches to the regulation of electric power generation and distribution. The old monopolies, through which a single company provided power to a city or region, were replaced with a system in which any company could generate electricity and the distribution network was required to carry that power to customers. This led energy companies to reorganize, splitting off the distribution networks as separate corporations (which still had a monopoly within their service areas). Under this system, the state public utilities commissions primarily regulate the distribution of electricity and the cost of distribution, but exercise little or no regulatory or pricing authority over the independent power generators. Prices are determined primarily or exclusively by the market; commercial and residential customers can choose the company from which they buy their electricity. However, some states still have more traditional regulatory systems in place.

One result of these regulatory changes has been to create a more dynamic market for the generation of electric power. Companies that focus exclusively on the generation of electricity from renewable sources, especially wind (the largest such company is Green Mountain Energy), have constructed wind farms and other renewable systems in many different states. These companies can market their power directly to households and other consumers, and the transmission grids are required to carry that power to the customers. More recently, smaller independent companies have been formed just for the purpose of building a single wind farm, which will then sell the electricity generated to an energy wholesaler or distributor.

The history of significant environmental regulation in the United States is generally much shorter, beginning in 1970 (though there are many antecedents, including common law cases). On 1 January 1970, President Nixon signed the National Environmental Policy Act (NEPA), the law that laid down the environmental impact analysis requirement for federal actions. Later that year, Congress passed major amendments to an early air pollution control law; the newly expanded law, amended several times since, is now known as the Clean Air Act. Many other federal pollution control and natural resources management laws were enacted throughout the 1970s. Examples relevant to offshore resource development include the Coastal Zone Management Act (1972), the Marine Protection, Research, and Sanctuaries Act (1972), the Marine Mammal Protection Act (1972), and the Endangered Species Act (1973). For areas and resources historically subject to direct federal control, including offshore waters and migratory birds, laws enacted about 100 years ago still have continuing relevance. The Rivers and Harbors Act of 1899 gives the United States Army Corps of Engineers authority and responsibility for regulating possible hindrances to navigation. The Migratory Bird Treaty Act of 1916 establishes federal protection for migratory birds protected under international agreements between Mexico, Canada and the United States.

United States environmental law does not specifically refer to or base regulation on the principle of sustainable development. The United States, like most countries in the world, signed the Rio Declaration and participated actively in the Johannesburg World Summit on Sustainable Development, but the term 'sustainable development' scarcely appears in federal law or in court decisions in environmental cases. Moreover, as a dualist state, the United States government does not accept sustainable development as an international law principle that guides the law or policy of the United States in any specific respect. On the other hand, the United States does not question sustainable development, and supports various international programmes that seek, in one way or another, to promote sustainable development.

State and local governments in the United States have been more active in adopting sustainable development as a guide to policy and legal development. Several cities have established offices of sustainable development, which work to promote sustainable development in various government actions and decisions. Moreover, thinking about sustainable development has clearly had an influence on certain energy policy decisions at the state level such as the renewable portfolio standards described in Chapter 10, section 6, on energy law.

## 2.6. Commentary from a New Zealand Point of View – by *Barry Barton & David Grinlinton*

The common law tradition in New Zealand can be traced back to the Treaty of Waitangi in 1840, in which Maori (the indigenous peoples) agreed that New Zealand would come under British sovereignty, in exchange for guarantees of tribal rights and the rights of British citizens. For many years Maori custom and English law have co-existed, and aspects of Maori custom remain important in relation to land and environmental management. Through a gradual process, the colonial government developed into self-government and in the first half of the twentieth century New Zealand became entirely independent. History, culture and a similar legal tradition continue to provide links with Britain.

This process of constitutional development has been punctuated by a number of important developments, but none of them has provided New Zealand with a written constitution from which the legal order can be said to flow and from which legality is derived. The Constitution Act 1986 brought together and restated a number of important basic rules, but its own status is simply that of a statute of the New Zealand Parliament. Other statutes establish the rules for the election of members of Parliament, the judiciary and basic human rights. There is a Bill of Rights Act but it is not entrenched, and again it is simply a statute of Parliament. All of these enactments, in theory and in practice, are subject to amendment by Parliament by a simple majority vote.

As New Zealand has a unicameral legislature there are not the constitutional complications that exist with bicameral legislatures, and federal/state jurisdictions. Parliament is sovereign in the sense that it has a general power to make, amend, repeal, and replace laws. It can override the judge-made law that is characteristic of the common law tradition. Although there is room for learned debate about the limits of parliamentary sovereignty, the general picture is that legislation enacted by Parliament cannot be declared unconstitutional for failure to comply with any founding constitutional document.

Parliament has one house or chamber. Elections take place every three years, using a system of proportional voting. There is only one legislature for the nation. Local government exists and exercises substantial powers, but those powers are (or that jurisdiction is) subject to alteration at any time by an Act of Parliament. As well as enacting legislation, Parliament exercises oversight through the Ombudsman and the similar Parliamentary Commissioner for the Environment. New Zealand was the first common law jurisdiction to borrow the ombudsman institution from the Scandinavian tradition.

Following the dualist approach, for international treaties and conventions to become part of New Zealand law, there must be an Act of Parliament to that effect. While New Zealand, like other countries, has entered into many treaties and conventions that in effect confine the sovereignty of Parliament, it is not a member of any institution like the EU that would impose a new legal order on the country.

At the head of the executive is the Cabinet, all of whose members are members of Parliament and are therefore accountable to Parliament. The government or executive is formed from the political party or parties that can command support in Parliament to enact legislation. Cabinet ministers oversee the ministries and departments of government. Most energy law and environmental law has its origins in policy initiatives that come from government departments. Legislation to give effect to government policy will usually be enacted by Parliament.

The courts operate under a long and strong tradition of independence from the legislature and the executive. Judicial independence is secured by statute. As noted above, there is a continuous interplay between judge-made law and statute. Once Parliament enacts energy or environmental law, its interpretation and application is a matter for the courts, but if judges interpret a law in a manner that is inconsistent with the policy intentions of government, then amending legislation will quite possibly follow in order to change the interpretation.

The courts consider themselves bound by the doctrine of precedent, and adhere to previous decisions on a point of law by a court at the same level or a higher one. In some fields of law the courts will refer extensively to judicial decisions from Britain and other countries which have persuasive, but not binding effect. In other fields, where the law has evolved differently in New Zealand there will be no point in using such decisions.

What are the main differences between the common law tradition in New Zealand and its expression in the United States? The overwhelming difference is that constitutional law pervades all aspects of the legal system in the United States in a way that it does not in New Zealand. New Zealand judges and administrators do not have to wrestle with the division of powers between federal and state legislatures. New Zealand judges cannot strike down an enactment for inconsistency with a Constitution or a Bill of Rights. In addition, whole fields of law such as criminal law or civil procedure are not affected by concepts like due process derived from a constitution.

# CHAPTER 5

# Jurisdiction, Fundamental Rights and the Market

*By Helle Tegner Anker, Sanford Gaines & Birgitte Egelund Olsen*

## 1. Introduction

A key question as regards the possibility of establishing a wind farm is the legal authority of public decision-makers. As a general rule, the legal authority of public decision-makers relies upon the allocation of powers to that authority by law. In the case of establishing a wind farm, this normally concerns powers to issue a licence, grant support, monitor etc. according to substantive law. The more specific requirements of substantive law will be analysed below in Chapters 6-9 (environmental and planning law issues) and Chapter 10 (energy law issues).

This Chapter deals with the overall considerations regarding the authority of public decision-makers. This includes questions about jurisdiction in a broad sense, i.e. the sovereignty of nation states. It also includes questions about the distribution of powers within countries, i.e. the relationships between public authorities at federal, state, regional and local levels. Such formal limitations of legal authority are supplemented by more fundamental (substantive) limitations of public authority aimed at the protection of the rights of individuals and ensuring legal certainty. These general substantive limitations ensure that the powers given to public authorities are not abused. Furthermore, a number of procedural requirements, aimed at improving and controlling the exercise of public authority, form part of the general picture of the legal authority of public decision-makers. Finally, rules governing market conditions may impose certain limitations on public authority. This is reflected in rules on non-discrimination, competition or antitrust, subsidies and State aid.

## 2. Jurisdictional issues

Jurisdiction can be defined as the limits of the legal competence of a state or other regulatory authority – such as the European Union – to make, apply, and enforce rules of conduct upon persons.[1] It thus 'concerns essentially the extent of each state's right to regulate conduct or the consequences of events'.[2] In more general terms jurisdiction means that a specific legal or political body/person has the power to deal with a case. In the context of public authority to establish a wind farm, jurisdictional issues primarily address the question: Who is the competent authority?

In the international context, jurisdictional issues may focus on *territorial aspects*, i.e. the territorial sovereignty of nation states. However, in a broader sense jurisdictional issues may also address the question of what law governs the exercise of *regulatory power*, i.e. is the decision solely a national matter or is it subject to limitations under international law? Similar questions may arise within a state as regards the distribution of power between state, regional and local levels of authority. In some cases more than one authority will have the power to make decisions about the same activity, e.g. the establishment of a wind farm, reflecting different regulatory aspects.

### 2.1. International – National Level

International law sets certain limits on the jurisdiction of nation states as regards both territorial matters and regulatory matters.[3]

International law is based on the *territorial sovereignty* of states within their geographic borders. Questions of territorial rights over the sea and the seabed have been resolved through the United Nations Convention on the Law of the Sea (UNCLOS).[4] The European Community, Denmark, New Zealand and Norway are all parties to UNCLOS. This is not the case for the United States. Nevertheless, the United States can still rightfully claim jurisdiction over the resources in or beneath the oceans off its coast in accordance with UNCLOS, as UNCLOS is regarded as being an expression of customary international law. See also Chapter 3, section 1.1.

---

1. *V. Lowe:* 'Jurisdiction', in *Malcolm D. Evans* (ed.): International Law, 2006 p. 335.
2. *L. Oppenheim, R. Jennings & A. Watts* (eds.): Oppenheim's International Law, 1992 p. 456.
3. On international law see Chapter 3, section 1.
4. United Nations Convention on the Law of the Sea of 10 December 1982, see www.un.org/Depts/los.

According to UNCLOS Article 3, coastal states have sovereignty over their territorial sea. The *territorial sea* may extend up to 12 nautical miles from the baseline (Article 4). Waters inside the baseline, such as the Sydney Harbour or the Chesapeake Bay, are internal waters under full national control. Within the *Exclusive Economic Zone* (EEZ), which extends up to 200 nautical miles from the baseline, coastal states have sovereignty for the purpose of exploring and exploiting, conserving and managing the natural resources, whether living or non-living, of the waters superjacent to the seabed and of the seabed and its subsoil, and with regard to other activities for the economic exploitation and exploration of the zone, such as the production of energy from the water, currents and winds (Article 56). The jurisdiction of coastal states in the EEZ with respect to the establishment and use of artificial islands, installations and structures is also stated in Article 56.

Furthermore, UNCLOS defines the *continental shelf* as the seabed and its subsoil that extends beyond the limits of the territorial sea to the outer edge of the continental margin or up to 200 nautical miles from the baseline (Article 76). The continental margin comprises the submerged prolongation of the land mass of the coastal state, and consists of the seabed and subsoil of the shelf, the slope and the rise. It does not include the deep ocean floor with its oceanic ridges or the subsoil thereof (Article 76(3)). Within the area of the continental shelf, the coastal state has sovereign rights for the purpose of exploring it and exploiting its natural resources.

## 2.2. Federal – State Level

Jurisdictional issues in federal states primarily relate to the distribution of power (or jurisdiction) between the federal level and the state level.[5]

The European Union is not a federal state and jurisdictional issues do not exist in the same manner as in federal states. The European Union as such, i.e. the EU institutions, does not have territorial jurisdiction allowing it to make decisions within the territories of the Member States.[6] However, under the EC Treaty the European Union has power to lay down rules and regulations as regards the administration of public authority in the Member States. According to Article 249 of the EC Treaty, EU regulations are directly applicable in the Member States creating rights and duties for individuals, whereas

---

5.  In nations with federal systems, the sub-national units are often called 'states', (though in some cases they are called provinces or prefectures), and the national government level is often called 'federal'.
6.  There are a few exceptions as regards, e.g. the granting of EU subsidies for specific projects, and Commission decisions on competition/antitrust and State aid.

EU directives have to be transposed into national law; see Chapter 3, section 2.3.1.

In the United States, federal power over federal lands and over the seas and the seabed is an inherent aspect of national sovereignty. Over the years, the government has created various categories of public land, including national parks, national forests, national historic sites, national marine sanctuaries, land for military use, and so on. The federal government determines what activities, public or private, can take place on these various categories of public land and the conditions and procedures for allowing such activities.

In Chapter 4, section 2.3, and in particular section 2.3.1, it was briefly explained that the United States federal government has three bases for its authority over offshore energy installations: 1) the federal power to manage federal lands, including the seabed; 2) the federal power to regulate navigation on the seas and inland waters; and 3) the federal power to regulate activities, including energy production and distribution, affecting interstate commerce. The first two powers are exclusively federal; that is, the state governments have no jurisdiction over these issues. The federal power under the Commerce Clause, however, is often exercised in a limited way that allows each state to continue to exercise its own control over those same activities within the state's territorial jurisdiction. In particular, the states exercise significant control over the production, distribution, and sale of energy within their state.

In 1953, in view of new technical capability to exploit the resources of the seas and the seabed, and after the proclamation by President Truman of United States jurisdiction over the continental shelf, Congress enacted the Submerged Lands Act[7] and the Outer Continental Shelf Lands Act[8] to define the geographic reach of federal power over the seabed. The Submerged Lands Act grants to each of the states ownership of and regulatory control over the territorial sea and the seabed beneath it. For most states, the territorial sea is defined by the British maritime tradition as extending outward to three nautical miles. Texas, however, was historically under Spanish control and was later an independent country so that, according to Spanish tradition, it has jurisdiction outward to 3 leagues, or approximately 10 nautical miles. The Outer Continental Shelf Lands Act (OCS Lands Act) specifies that the resources of the seas and seabed beyond the limits of the territorial sea and out to 200 nautical miles or to the limits of the continental shelf are subject to federal jurisdiction.

---

7.  43 United States Code, SS. 1301-1315.
8.  43 United States Code, SS. 1331-1356.

In areas of complex coastal geography, the boundary between state sub-merged lands and the federal Outer Continental Shelf may be difficult to de-marcate precisely.

In the case of the Cape Wind project in Nantucket Sound offshore from Massachusetts, the project developer designed the layout of the wind turbines to be entirely within federal waters as then defined. The federal government subsequently adjusted the state-federal boundary in such a way that 10 of the project's 130 planned wind turbines would be within state waters, and thus subject to the jurisdiction of Massachusetts agencies. This would have been a significant problem for the project, because Massachusetts' Ocean Sanctuaries Act[9] generally prohibits the construction or operation of offshore electric generating stations within the Cape and Islands Ocean Sanctuary which includes the state waters and lands of Nantucket Sound. The project developer therefore redesigned the project to move the 10 turbines into federal waters.

## 2.3. National – Regional – Local Level

At a national level the allocation of legal authority is normally established by law. A decisive element of the territorial allocation of power is normally the level of decision-making, e.g. federal, state, regional or local level, which is most appropriate for dealing with the issue. If an issue is assigned to a specific level of authority, it can be necessary to establish coordination procedures etc. in order to ensure that the interests of other levels of authority are reflected.

In most countries the allocation of power is a key issue with respect to the establishment of wind farms. It is quite clear that the local level has a considerable interest in the siting of a wind farm with respect to physical interference. However, the establishment of wind farms of a significant size may also have physical implications beyond the local level. Furthermore, wind farms may represent significant national interests, e.g. as regards the fulfilment of national environmental and energy objectives, including complying with international obligations.

The siting of wind farms is dependent upon the availability of wind energy. Wind energy is often strongest in coastal areas. Thus, the allocation of legal authority in coastal areas on land and at sea is a key issue.

### 2.3.1. Denmark – Jurisdictional Aspects

In Denmark there is a clear distinction between legal authority on land and at sea. The regulatory system that governs land areas and land-based activities is subject to powers vested in the local authorities, though with certain excep-

9. Massachusetts General Laws, Chapter. 132A, S. 15.

tions as regards the shoreline, where the Ministry for the Environment has powers over land-based activities within a 100-300 metre protection zone. The regulatory system that governs the sea is subject to powers vested in national authorities on the basis of the state supremacy (*statens højhedsret*).[10]

The Danish territorial sea is divided into the inner territorial sea within the baseline and the outer territorial sea which extends 12 nautical miles from the baseline.[11] Any installation within the territorial sea requires a permit from the Ministry of Transport. The permit procedure for wind turbines is administered by the Danish Energy Authority. In the area from the limit of the territorial sea to the limit of the exclusive economic zone the Ministry of Transport also has the power to authorize new installations, including energy installations, under the Exclusive Economic Zones Act.[12] Since the end of 2007 energy installations at sea are authorized by the new Ministry of Climate and Energy according to the Electricity Supply Act[13] and the Energynet.dk Act.[14] See further in Chapter 10, section 4.2 and 4.3 on the Danish licensing system.

### 2.3.2. Norway – Jurisdictional Aspects

The issue of jurisdiction in wind turbine cases has not yet been a problem in Norway. So far all wind turbines have been constructed on land. However, the construction of wind turbines at sea is foreseen in the near future. In the longer term it may become an important part of the solution to Norway's energy needs and climate policy. This will undoubtedly raise new questions of jurisdiction.

Norway's territorial sea extends, like Denmark's, 12 nautical miles from the coastline. The baseline is drawn along the Norwegian coast in such a way that all major fjords and fjord estuaries are included in Norway's internal waters.[15] On land and in internal waters the state and municipalities share jurisdiction. There are no distinctions in this regard between the various zones on land, along or beyond the shore. The common understanding is that the territory of coastal municipalities extends to the baseline.

---

10. The concept of state sovereignty is derived from international law, e.g. as reflected in the Danish Ordinance 259/1963 on the exercise of Danish state sovereignty over the continental shelf. State sovereignty is primarily administered by the Ministry of Transport & Energy.
11. Act No 200 of 7 April 1999. The exact delimitation is laid down in Executive Order No 680 of 18 July 2003.
12. Act No 411 of 22 May 1996.
13. Act No 1115 of 8 November 2006.
14. Act No 1384 of 20 December 2004.
15. See the UN Convention on the Law of the Sea, Article 7 and Article 8.

Whether the state or the municipality or both has authority in a given legal field or in a particular case depends on the law in question. In the energy field, and in particular as regards the construction of wind farms, the state is the main regulator through the Energy Act. But the Planning and Building Act also applies to some extent, so the municipalities also have some authority through the land use planning system described in Chapter 6, section 5.

Outside the baseline it is commonly understood that the state has exclusive jurisdiction, but this is also a question that may be regulated by ordinary legislation. Today, neither the Energy Act nor the Planning and Building Act apply outside the baseline.[16] A new Planning and Building Act will enter into force in 2009. It will improve the instruments for coastal planning and management within the general land use planning system. Its area of application will be extended to one nautical mile beyond the baseline. This will also affect the planning of wind farms at sea.

It is clear that the present legal framework is not adequate for regulating wind power installations in Norway's territorial sea or on its continental shelf.

### 2.3.3.  *The United States – Jurisdictional Aspects*

In the United States, the federal government has control over the Outer Continental Shelf (OCS) – that is, the sea and seabed seaward of the limit of the territorial sea – but this does not tell us which agency or agencies of the federal government exercise that control, or what statutory powers they have been granted. In fact, several agencies have jurisdiction over different activities in this zone.

The US Coast Guard sets the rules for navigation of vessels and manages shipping lanes and navigational aids. A permit is required from the US Army Corps of Engineers (the Corps), under Section 10 of the Rivers and Harbors Act of 1899, for any fixed structures, such as bridges or towers, that may impede navigation. The Corps has asserted that its jurisdiction includes structures on the seabed, such as wind turbines, under the OCS Lands Act. The National Marine Fisheries Service (part of National Oceanic and Atmospheric Administration within the Department of Commerce) regulates marine fishing activity and is responsible for the protection of marine mammals. The Fish and Wildlife Service of the Department of the Interior has responsibility for protection of birds and terrestrial wildlife; the Federal Aviation Administration has authority over air traffic and structures like wind turbines that

---

16.  See Energy Act, S. 1 and Planning and Building Act, S. 1.

may affect aircraft. And the Minerals Management Service (part of the Department of the Interior) regulates mining activities or oil and gas production on the outer continental shelf.

Until recently, federal law said nothing specifically about renewable energy facilities, such as wind turbines, situated on the OCS seabed. In response to the application of Cape Wind Associates for permits to build a wind monitoring tower in Nantucket Sound offshore from Massachusetts, with the expectation that they would later build an array of 130 wind turbine generators, the federal government had to decide which agencies had jurisdiction. Because the wind monitoring tower itself presumably required a Section 10 permit from the Army Corps of Engineers, that agency became the lead agency for the federal government with respect to the entire project. Under the lead agency concept, the Corps becomes responsible for the environmental assessment of the complete project under the National Environmental Policy Act (NEPA). Some years ago, the Supreme Court agreed that, as the lead agency, the Corps had the authority under the NEPA to consider factors other than navigation in deciding whether or not to grant a Section 10 permit for a project.[17] Moreover, the Corps is required, by statutes and regulations, to consult with other agencies, such as the National Marine Fisheries Service, about resource protection and other environmental issues under their jurisdictions.

A couple of years after the determination of agency jurisdiction just described, the United States Congress designated the Minerals Management Service of the Department of the Interior as the agency with the authority to grant leases for renewable energy facilities in the Outer Continental Shelf area and to act as the lead federal agency.[18]

Each state has the power to make laws and regulations governing the production, distribution, and use of energy within its state, as well as for the protection of the state's environment. As noted previously in section 2.2, under the Submerged Lands Act, the federal government has granted to each state title to, and thus regulatory control over, the territorial sea and the seabed, typically up to 3 nautical miles from the shore (for Texas, about 10 nautical miles).

Naturally, the particular laws and regulations on energy and environmental protection vary significantly from state to state. In general, states regulate electricity through an expert agency, often called a utilities regula-

---

17. *U.S.* v *Alaska*, 503 U.S. 569, 583 (1992).
18. The Energy Policy Act of 2005, S. 388.

tory commission or public utilities commission. This commission is given the authority to set prices for residential, commercial, and industrial purchasers of electricity. It may or may not also have the authority to license electricity generating facilities or to engage in other aspects of energy supply and demand planning. In recent years, a number of states have included 'renewable portfolio standards' (RPS) in their regulatory systems. RPS require that, over a period of years, each provider of electricity services (which may, in a deregulated market, be an energy distribution company) must provide a minimum percentage of its electricity from renewable sources. See further in Chapter 10, section 6.1.

Environmental regulation at the state level may have several features which are relevant to wind farm development. There may be state or local land use planning;[19] there may be specific protection for historic sites or environmentally sensitive areas that could affect the location of wind turbines or distribution lines; and there may be a state environmental impact assessment requirement that is separate from the federal environmental impact statements (EIS) under the National Environmental Policy Act (NEPA).[20] As part of the state coastal zone management (CZM) plan, a separate set of state laws and regulations apply to projects along the coast or in a state's offshore area.

### 2.3.4. *New Zealand – Jurisdictional Aspects*

New Zealand is free of many of the jurisdictional complexities that arise in other countries. There is no federal system allocating jurisdiction or sovereignty between federal and state or provincial authorities. And there is no equivalent of the EU. Regional councils exist, but they are merely a form of intermediate local government, usually with several district or city councils (territorial authorities) within their boundaries. The jurisdiction, functions and powers of both regional councils and territorial authorities is laid down by law made by Parliament.

The main law conferring jurisdiction to regulate land use, the use of marine areas, and environmental matters is the Resource Management Act 1991.[21] In Section 30, it confers jurisdiction on each regional council in respect of integrated resource management in its region, the use of water, and pollution of air and water. It also confers jurisdiction on regional councils in relation to the 'coastal marine area' bounded by the mean high water mark and the 12 nautical mile limit, being the limit of the territorial sea. Regional

---

19. See Chapter 6, section 6.1.
20. See further Chapter 7, section 7.1.
21. See further on the Resource Management Act in Chapter 6, section 7.

council jurisdiction in the coastal marine area is to some extent shared with the Minister of Conservation, acting on behalf of the national government. The extent of the Minister's role is governed by the New Zealand Coastal Policy Statement made under Section 57 of the Resource Management Act and regional coastal plans under Section 68, defining activities as restricted coastal activities. An offshore wind farm is therefore sure to come under the jurisdiction of a regional council and very likely under the jurisdiction of the Minister of Conservation.

Beyond the 12 mile limit, but within the exclusive economic zone that New Zealand enjoys as a signatory of UNCLOS, there is no New Zealand environmental legislation in place to assert jurisdiction on behalf of the nation. This is an unfortunate gap in the legal system. However no development of wind farms is currently contemplated offshore, either within or beyond the 12 mile limit.

Onshore, above the mean high water mark, the primary regulatory jurisdiction over wind farms under the Resource Management Act is the territorial local authority (district or city council). Under Section 31 these authorities have jurisdiction over land use and noise. Regional council jurisdiction can be relevant in relation to soil conservation – in New Zealand wind farms are often in hilly country and require substantial earthworks for access and construction. See further on the Resource Management Act in Chapter 6, section 7, and Chapter 10, section 7.2.

## 3. Protection of Fundamental Rights

The establishment of a wind farm involves significant (economic) interests not only on the part of the developer but also on the part of those affected by the wind farm. The legal system sets certain limits on the exercise of public authority on the basis of fundamental rights aimed at protecting the vital interests of landowners and citizens in general. This includes substantive rights such as private property rights and (other) human rights in a broad sense, and procedural rights such as rights of public participation and access to justice.

### 3.1. Private Property Rights
Private property rights are recognized as fundamental rights in most legal systems, either explicitly in constitutional provisions and/or in court rulings.

However, private property rights are not only recognized in national legal systems. In Europe, private property rights are recognized as a human right in the European Convention on Human Rights.[22] Article 1 of the first Protocol of the Convention[23] states that 'every natural or legal person is entitled to the peaceful enjoyment of his possessions. No one shall be deprived of his possessions except in the public interest and subject to the conditions provided for by law and by the general principles of international law.' Thus the text of the Convention stresses both rights of property and the possibility of regulatory restrictions on such rights. Recent rulings of the European Court of Human Rights (ECHR) have emphasized the need to strike a proper balance between private property rights on the one hand and public interests in restricting the use of private property on the other hand.[24]

### 3.1.1. Expropriation and Takings

In traditional legal theory private property rights (personal or individual) are confined to a piece of property (land or goods). However, other more intangible interests may also be characterized as private property. Private property rights may limit the exercise of public authority to the extent that private property cannot be taken or interfered with without proper compensation and the fulfilment of other criteria.

The forced transfer of ownership to the public domain, i.e. the public acquisition of a piece of land, is normally termed *expropriation* and in most countries this is subject to specific substantive and procedural requirements. Other types of public interference that affect the enjoyment of private property through regulation are, in a US context, termed *regulatory takings* or in a Danish context, *expropriative interference*. However, public interference through regulation may not necessarily amount to a regulatory taking or an expropriative interference. A certain level of public interference must gener-

---

22. Convention for the Protection of Human Rights and Fundamental Freedoms. The Convention was adopted under the auspices of the Council of Europe in 1950 to protect human rights and fundamental freedoms.
23. Protocol to the Convention for the Protection of Human Rights and Fundamental Freedoms as amended by Protocol No 11, Paris 20 March 1952.
24. See in particular *Housing Association of war disabled and victims of war of Attica and others* v *Greece*, judgment of 13 July 2006. In this case a general prohibition of building houses on forest land without paying compensation to the landowners who had a legitimate expectation of property development being allowed did not meet the requirement of striking a reasonable balance between the public interest and the protection of the rights of the landowners.

ally be accepted without compensation, as long as the interference is necessary and the intensity of the interference is below a certain threshold.

The Danish Constitution establishes the criteria for expropriation by stating that the right of property is inviolable, except where it is required in the public interest, if it is provided for by statute, and against full compensation.[25] The reference to the public interest does not exclude expropriation on behalf of private development projects. The Danish planning system provides a legal basis for expropriation if it is necessary for the realization of a local plan. However, the necessity requirement is quite strong.

The situation in Norway is quite similar. The Constitution states that if the needs of the state require that someone's property should be taken for public use, they must have full compensation from the state.[26] The Expropriation Act of 1959[27] explicitly allows expropriation for purposes such as wind power, including the installation of power lines.[28] The general conditions are that expropriation must be 'necessary' and that the positive effects of the expropriation must clearly exceed the possible negative effects. Whether these conditions are fulfilled is rarely a matter of dispute. The state is the authority for expropriation decisions, unless otherwise stated in legislation. Pursuant to the Planning and Building Act[29] a municipality may authorize expropriations on the basis of adopted local development plans, as such plans are usually agreed by state authorities. The most difficult and controversial issue in the field of expropriation law in Norway relates to the amount of the compensation paid and the principles to be applied in this regard. The question is regulated in general by the Expropriation Compensation Act,[30] but hard cases are regularly required to be solved by the Supreme Court.

There is similar constitutional protection in the United States. The government may take property for a 'public purpose' as long as it pays full compensation. The Supreme Court recently affirmed that a private development project which was encouraged by a municipality for economic development may be considered a 'public purpose'.[31]

---

25. Article 73(1) of the Danish Constitution; Act No 169 of 5 June 1953.
26. Article 105 of the Norwegian Constitution.
27. Act No 3 of 23 October 1959.
28. Act No 3 of 23 October 1959, S. 2, No 19.
29. Act No 77 of 14 June 1985.
30. Act No 17 of 6 April 1984.
31. *Kelo* v *City of New London*, 545 U.S. 469 (2005).

New Zealand has no explicit constitutional protection of private property rights, and largely follows the English common law tradition.[32] In English common law, private property rights have never been regarded as absolute, but rather as an element of 'that residuum of natural liberty, which is not required by the laws of society to be sacrificed to public convenience'.[33] These qualifications are reflected today in the doctrines of private and public nuisance, and the systems of land, air and water use regulation now incorporated in the Resource Management Act 1991 (RMA).

Land ownership rights are subject to certain overriding state control of minerals and other resources, and have been progressively restricted by legislation on town planning,[34] environmental protection, and the expropriation of land for public purposes. In New Zealand the government and local authorities may take land for public purposes under the Public Works Act 1981. This Act provides procedures for voluntary or compulsory expropriation of private land for purposes such as parks, reserves, and the provision of infrastructure and utilities. The Act provides for compensation, usually based on the market value of the land taken.[35]

Potentially, private landowners may now have their land taken by the private sector for public purposes. Reflecting New Zealand's adherence to free market economic polices since the mid-1980s, the RMA allows private operators to become network utility operators and to compulsorily acquire private land for the provision of services.[36]

The question of expropriation may arise in particular in connection with land-based wind farms. However offshore wind farms may also raise questions of expropriation for ancillary installations on land, such as cables etc. Certain areas may be designated as being suitable for the establishment of

---

32. This is reflected in Blackstone's description of the three basic rights of 'personal security [...] personal liberty, and [...] private property', see *William Blackstone:* Commentaries on the Laws of England, Vol. 1, p. 125. Blackstone relied on the *Magna Carta* and the statute *Confirmatio Cartarum 1297* (25 Edw. I); the *Bill of Rights 1689* (1 W & M, St. 2. c.2); and the *Act of Settlement 1701* (12 & 13 W. III, c.2) as confirmation of these fundamental rights.

33. *William Blackstone:* Commentaries on the Laws of England, Vol. 1, p. 125.

34. See, for example, *Falkner* v *Gisborne District Council* [1995] 3 NZLR 622 at 632; and *Coleman* v *Kingston* Unreported, High Court, Auckland (AP 103-SW00), 3 April 2001, noted (2001) 4 BRMB 59.

35. See *Kenneth Palmer:* 'Compulsory Acquisition and Compensation', in *Tom Bennion, David Brown, Rod Thomas & Elizabeth Toomey* (eds.): Land Law in New Zealand, 2005 pp. 1139-1192.

36. Resource Management Act 1991, Sections 166-186, especially Sections 185-186.

wind farms, e.g. due to the prevalence of high wind and/or landscape considerations. If a private landowner is unwilling to accept the construction of a wind farm it may be deemed necessary to expropriate their land.

The construction of a wind farm on land occupies a certain area but it may have external effects beyond that area, such as noise and visual interference. Furthermore, other environmental interests may be affected, e.g. birds.

### 3.1.2. *Nuisance and Neighbour Law*

Private property rights may also serve as a basis for protection against interference from private (or public) parties. This is reflected in the concepts of *neighbour law*, the law of *nuisance* and *trespass*. Nuisance or neighbour law aims at dealing with the negative effects resulting from an activity on adjoining (or nearby) property, such as from a wind farm. The exact criteria may vary from one country to another.

In Denmark the decisive criterion is whether the effects exceed the 'limit of tolerance' (*tålegrænsen*), i.e. what one must expect under normal circumstances in the area in question. So far, no Danish court case has led to compensation for the negative effects from wind turbines on the basis of neighbour law, since neighbour interests are primarily protected through specific public law requirements as regards distance etc.; see Chapter 9, section 4.1.

In Norwegian law Section 2 of the Neighbour Act[37] states that nobody may carry on activities that negatively affect a neighbouring property 'unreasonably or unnecessarily'. Whether the activity is unreasonable or unnecessary depends on an assessment of several factors which are explicitly mentioned in the Act: to what extent it is technically and economically feasible to avoid the effects, whether the type of activity could be expected in the neighbourhood, and whether the nuisance is particularly serious for a limited group of people. If this rule is violated, the neighbour has a right to corrective measures or compensation based on strict liability; see Chapter 9, section 5.1.

In the US legal system the law affecting energy installations and environmental protection includes, in some circumstances, the application of common law principles.[38] For example, a neighbour of a wind turbine may have a case in nuisance for the noise from the turbine if it interferes with the use and enjoyment of their own property; see Chapter 9, section 6.1.

In New Zealand, private nuisance is widely recognized as the primary environmental tort and it protects the enjoyment of property; see Chapter 9, sec-

---

37. Act No 15 of 16 June 1961.
38. See Chapter 2, section 3.1.2 and Chapter 9, section 6.1 on nuisance.

tion 7.1. An action for public nuisance is available where a number of private nuisances flow from a common cause, or where there is some interference with a public right or with the lawful use of a public place. In this situation an action can be brought by someone who has suffered a particular or special loss over and above that sustained by the public at large.[39]

If a wind turbine or a wind farm causes damage to economic interests or to the environment, the issue of liability in tort may arise. Generally, liability in tort will depend on negligence. The EU Environmental Liability Directive[40] introduces strict liability with regard to occupational activities causing harm to protected habitats or species.[41]

### 3.2. Right to a Good Environment?

International law does not establish a fundamental (human) *right to the environment* as such. However, soft law instruments such as the Stockholm Declaration and the Rio Declaration have expressed such rights in varying terms. See, for example, the idea in the Stockholm Declaration Article 1 of 'a fundamental right to freedom, equity an adequate conditions of life, in an environment of a quality that permits a life of dignity and well-being'.

In Europe, Article 8 of the European Convention on Human Rights establishes that 'Everyone has the right to respect for his private and family life, his home and his correspondence.' Rulings by the European Court of Human Rights (ECHR) have given some support to arguments that negative environmental conditions could interfere with the enjoyment of the rights and freedoms of individuals guaranteed by Article 8 of the Convention. This has particularly been the case as regards hazardous activities, noise etc. A certain level of interference should be met, however.[42]

Article 8 imposes a positive obligation on states to ensure a minimum level of protection, e.g. through the exercise of regulatory powers. According

---

39. *Attorney-General* v *PYA Quarries Ltd* [1957] 2 QB 169 especially at 191 per Denning LJ. The action is usually brought by the Attorney-General on behalf of the class of people affected.
40. Directive 2004/35/EC of the European Parliament and of the Council of 21 April 2004 on environmental liability with regard to the prevention and remedying of environmental damage.
41. In Article 3 a distinction is made between strict liability for certain listed activities (not including wind turbines) and fault-based liability for other activities.
42. In *Fägerskiöld v Sweden*, judgement of 26. February 2008, No. 37664/07 an application regarding noise and reflections from wind turbines was declared inadmissible as being ill-founded since the nuisance in the case was not so serious as to reach the high threshold established in Article 8 cases dealing with environmental iaaues.

to the Court there is a positive duty for states to take reasonable and appropriate measures to secure individuals' rights under Article 8(1) of the Convention.[43] In these circumstances the Court's first task is to assess whether the state could reasonably be expected to act so as to prevent or put an end to an infringement of the individual's rights. However, the states have a certain discretion as regards the determination of the relevant level of protection.[44] The ECHR has also accepted the view that environmental protection for the benefit of a wider community may restrict the exercise of individual rights such as the rights established in Articles 8, 9, 10 and 11 of the Convention.[45]

To varying extents national laws may establish more fundamental environmental rights, e.g. in constitutional provisions. Globally, more than 100 states make some form of provision for environmental protection in their constitutions.[46] This is not the case in Denmark, but the Norwegian Constitution establishes a more fundamental right to a good environment in substantive as well as procedural terms. Article 110b of the Norwegian Constitution, adopted in 1992, stipulates that:

'Every person has a right to an environment that is conducive to health and to natural surroundings whose productivity and diversity are preserved. Natural resources should be made use of on the basis of comprehensive long-term considerations whereby this right will be safeguarded for future generations as well.

In order to safeguard their right in accordance with the foregoing paragraph, citizens are entitled to be informed of the state of the natural environment and of the effects of any encroachments on nature that are planned or commenced.

---

43. See *Powell and Rayner* v *the United Kingdom*, judgment of 21 February 1990, Series A No 172, § 41; and *Guerra* v *Italy*, judgment of 19 February 1998, *Reports of Judgments and Decisions* 1998-I, § 58. See also *López Ostra* v *Spain*, judgment of 9 December 1994, Series A No 303-C, p. 54.
44. In *Hatton* v *the United Kingdom* [GC], No 36022/97, judgment of 8 July 2003 ECHR 2003-VIII this margin of discretion was not exceeded. In *Fadeyeva* v *Russia*, No 55723/00, judgment of 9 June 2005, the Court concluded that, despite the wide margin of discretion, Russia had failed to strike a fair balance between the interests of the community and the applicant's effective enjoyment of her right to respect for her home and her private life. Accordingly Article 8 had been infringed.
45. *Daniel Garcia San José:* Environmental Protection and the European Convention on Human Rights, 2005.
46. *Tim Hayward:* Constitutional Environmental Rights, 2005.

The State authorities shall issue further provisions for the implementation of these principles.'[47]

However, the legal consequences of Article 110b are uncertain and its importance should not be exaggerated. As its third paragraph explicitly states, the more precise content of the right to a healthy environment spelled out in the first and second paragraphs is left to be decided by the state authorities, in particular by Parliament through legislation and by the government through regulations and decisions in individual cases. It appears from the preparatory works to the Article that it is not meant generally to be the basis for specific claims by citizens. Only in extreme cases might a court find a regulation or decision illegal or invalid because it is in breach of Article 110b. The Article has, however, been used by the Supreme Court in several cases as a factor in the interpretation of legislation. And it stands as an ultimate guarantor against a policy of serious and systematic neglect of public health and environmental values by the legislative and executive authorities.

In the US legal tradition, a 'right' to a clean or healthy environment, or a 'right' to a certain condition of the natural environment, would have to be stated in a constitution. The United States Constitution contains no provision on such rights, and there have been no serious attempts to amend the Constitution to add such a provision. In contrast, the constitutions of five of the individual states do contain environmental rights provisions.[48] The five states are Hawaii, Illinois, Massachusetts, Montana and Pennsylvania. There has been little or no effort by private parties to assert those rights, and what court decisions there are tend to construe these rights very narrowly so as to cover only substantial damage to the environment. Nevertheless, there continues to be interest in environmental rights, at least among academics.[49]

A number of US statutes set standards for government conduct that are similar to environmental rights provisions. For example, the US Clean Air Act requires the Environmental Protection Agency (EPA) to set standards for air quality 'requisite to protect the public health' and 'protect the public wel-

---

47. [The Norwegian Constitution, as laid down on 17 May 1814 by the Constitutional Assembly at Eidsvoll (with subsequent amendments, the most recent being that of 23. July 1995).] Official translation.
48. *Anil S. Karia:* 'A Right to a Clean and Healthy Environment: A Proposed Amendment to Oregon's Constitution', in University of Baltimore Journal of Environmental Law, Vol. 14, 2006 p. 37.
49. For example, *Joshua Bruckerhoff:* 'Giving Nature Constitutional Protection: A Less Anthropocentric Interpretation of Environmental Rights', in Texas Law Review, Vol. 86, 2008 p. 615.

fare.' The EPA has determined that the health standard requires the protection of even sensitive groups of individuals from any adverse health effects, and the US Supreme Court has interpreted this language as preventing any consideration of the cost of achieving such an air quality standard.[50] In 2007, the Supreme Court handed down a decision requiring the EPA to explain why it had decided not to regulate carbon dioxide emissions to prevent endangerment of health or welfare under Clean Air Act.[51]

Finally, mention should be made of the American Declaration on Human Rights and the Protocol to the American Convention on Human Rights that declares that 'Everyone shall have the right to live in a healthy environment.'[52] The Inuit people refer to the Declaration on Human Rights and the American Convention in their petition to the Inter-American Commission on Human Rights, in which they argue that the United States greenhouse gas emissions and the resulting change in the climate has violated the legal obligation of the United States not to interfere with their culture and livelihood.[53]

Although there is no constitutionally based right concerning the environment in New Zealand, the country is a signatory to many international conventions and instruments such as the Stockholm Declaration, the Rio Declaration and Agenda 21. The principles of these international instruments are reflected in domestic government policy and legislation. For example, it is implicit in the Resource Management Act 1991 that natural and physical resources must be used sustainably to promote the rights of present and future generations to social, economic, and cultural wellbeing, health and safety, safeguarding the life-supporting capacity of air, water, soil and ecosystems, and minimizing the adverse effects of human activity on the environment; see Chapter 6, section 7.5.[54]

### 3.3. Right to Information and Public Participation

Procedural rights, such as the right to be informed about relevant developments that may affect the environment or individual citizens and the right to participate in public decision-making, set certain limits on the exercise of

---

50. *Whitman v American Trucking Associations*, 531 U.S. 457 (2001).
51. *Massachusetts v EPA*, 127 S.Ct. 1438 (2007).
52. Article 11(1) of the Additional Protocol to the American Convention on Human Rights in the Area of Economic, Social, and Cultural Rights.
53. Petition to the Inter-American Commission on Human Rights Seeking Relief from Violations Resulting from Global Warming Caused by Acts and Omissions of the United States (7 December 2005).
54. Resource Management Act 1991, S. 5.

public authority. Failure to comply with important procedural requirements may lead to the invalidity of public decisions.

Procedural rights of *information* and *public participation* have been laid down in international law, e.g. in the Rio Declaration Principle 10. Primarily at a regional level, the Aarhus Convention firmly establishes a set of procedural environmental rights.[55] The Aarhus Convention obliges the parties to ensure that members of the public have access to information, can participate in decision-making, and have access to judicial review; see below section 3.4 on access to justice.

According to the Convention, the *public in general* must have access to environmental information, whereas the *public concerned* must be allowed to participate in decision-making and have access to justice. The 'public concerned' is defined as 'the public affected or likely to be affected by, or having an interest in, the environmental decision-making; for the purpose of this definition, non-governmental organisations promoting environmental protection shall be deemed to have an interest' (Article 2(5)). The Aarhus Convention prohibits discrimination on the basis of citizenship, nationality or domicile and, in the case of a legal person, the place of its registered office or effective centre; see Article 3(9).

As regards *rights to information*, the Aarhus Convention distinguishes between access to specific information upon request (Article 4) and the general obligation to collect and disseminate environmental information (Article 5). A right to information is an essential precondition for effective participation in environmental decision-making.

As regards *public participation*, the Aarhus Convention distinguishes between participation relating to specific activities (Article 6), plans, programmes and policies (Article 7) and executive regulations and generally applicable rules (Article 8). The Convention underlines the need to ensure early, timely and effective participation and to ensure that, in any decision, due account is taken of the results of public participation.

The Aarhus Convention supplements existing EU legislation, in particular Directive 2003/4/EC on public access to environmental information (repealing Directive 90/313/EC); the EIA Directive 85/337/EEC on environmental

55. Convention on Access to Information, Public Participation in Decision-making and Access to Justice in Environmental Matters, UNECE, 1998. The EU, the EU Member States and other European states, including Norway, are parties to the Convention which is also open to signature by other states having consultative status with the UNECE. Neither the United States nor New Zealand is a party. The Convention entered into force on 30 October 2001.

impact assessment of certain public and private projects;[56] the SEA Directive 2001/42/EC on the assessment of the effects of certain plans and programmes on the environment; and Directive 2003/35/EC providing for public participation in respect of the drawing up of certain plans and programmes relating to the environment, amending Council Directives 85/337/EEC and 96/61/EC.

It is no exaggeration to say that the United States pioneered most of the public participation and public information rights now enshrined in such documents as the Aarhus Convention. The Administrative Procedure Act of 1946[57] established rights of participation in government decisions affecting the interests of individuals. Through decisions of courts in the 1960s, and in many specific acts of Congress in the 1970s, these rights of participation were expanded to include individuals and groups representing broad interests such as environmental protection. At the same time, Congress also passed the Freedom of Information Act, which gives individuals the right to get copies of any government document or collection of data except for confidential or classified information.[58] In 1976, Congress added the 'Government in Sunshine Act', requiring advance notice of government meetings and meetings of advisory committees and the right for the public to attend.[59]

In New Zealand the environmental and resource management reforms of the last two decades have resulted in some significant improvements in the right to information and public participation. Under the Resource Management Act 1991, procedures for policy and plan preparation at all levels require the initiator to undertake an analysis of the need for, costs of, and alternatives to the proposed policy or plan.[60] The analysis is publicly available and *any person* can make submissions on the proposed policy or plan.[61]

Similarly, with applications for specific consent, environmental assessment is an integrated part of the process and is required both in the preparation of policy and planning instruments, and for particular activities where consent is sought.

---

56. As amended by Directive 97/11/EC and Directive 2003/35/EC; see further below in Chapter 7, section 3.1.
57. United States Code, Title 5, SS. 551-559 and 701-706.
58. United States Code, Title 5, S. 552.
59. United States Code, Title 5, S. 552(b).
60. Resource Management Act 1991, S. 32. It has been argued by this writer that this requirement is in the nature of a 'strategic environmental assessment'; see *David Grinlinton:* 'Integrated Environmental Assessment in New Zealand', in Environmental and Planning Law Journal, Vol. 17(3), 2000 pp. 188-191.
61. Resource Management Act 1991, SS. 60, 65(1) and 73(1).

When publicly notified, hearings for applications are open to objections and submissions by *any person* without the need for *locus standi*.[62] Appeals may be brought before the Environment Court by any party.[63] Further appeals may be made to the High Court on points of law.[64]

### 3.4. Access to Justice

Access to justice is another procedural (environmental) right that has been established in international as well as in national law – most explicitly in the 1998 Aarhus Convention. Access to justice concerns the right of individuals (or NGOs) to demand a legal review of a public decision by an independent court or another independent and impartial body. Access to justice includes several elements, i.e. who has standing, in which cases, to which review bodies (courts or other bodies) and what is the scope of review (full or limited review).[65]

As regards the *reviewing bodies*, the Aarhus Convention speaks of 'access to a review procedure before a court of law or another independent and impartial body established by law' (Article 9(1)). This broadens the scope of access to justice to include administrative appeal bodies etc., as long as they can be considered independent and impartial. The Aarhus Convention distinguishes between two situations, namely: where a request for environmental information has been ignored or refused (Article 9(1)), and where the substantive or procedural legality of any decision, act or omission concerning specific activities (as referred to in Article 6) is challenged (Article 9(2)). Furthermore, Article 9(3) obliges the parties to the Convention to ensure that private persons and public authorities have access to administrative or judicial procedures to challenge acts and omissions which contravene provisions of national law relating to the environment.

---

62. Resource Management Act 1991, S. 96(1). However, a local authority has a limited discretion not to notify an application and in such cases the 'standing' rule will effectively apply: Resource Management Act 1991 S. 94. In reality around 95 % of resource consent applications are not notified which makes the ideal of 'open participation' somewhat illusory.
63. Resource Management Act 1991, S. 120. The Environment Court is a specialist judicial body set up to hear appeals and resolve disputes regarding environmental and resource management matters. Appeals are *de novo* and may include consideration of disputed questions of fact or law.
64. Resource Management Act 1991, SS. 299 and 301.
65. See *Jonas Ebbesson* (ed.): Access to Justice in Environmental Matters in the EU, 2002.

Generally, the Aarhus Convention applies a broad standard for *locus standi*, including all members of the public concerned who have a sufficient interest. In the Convention, NGOs are considered to have a sufficient interest; see Article 9(2). However, with respect to Article 9(3) the Convention refers to the *locus standi* requirements of the respective states.

United States law on access to justice in general conforms to the norms of the Aarhus Convention. Under the Administrative Procedure Act, any person who suffers a legal wrong or who is 'adversely affected or aggrieved' by an agency action may seek a remedy against that agency, first through any administrative process that may be available, but ultimately through the courts. The requirement for standing to bring a lawsuit is very broad. There are three basic restrictions. First, the party bringing the case must have suffered an injury, meaning that the individual (or a member of a group such as an NGO) must have been in some way personally affected by the agency's action or inaction. For environmental effects, however, the party does *not* have to show that the environment has been altered, only that it might be altered. Second, the agency action has to be the cause of the claimed injury. Third, the court must be in a position to do something to redress the injury.

As for the courts' scope for review, the Administrative Procedure Act authorizes courts to compel an agency to act if its inaction is unlawful (that is, if the statute requires the agency to act), or to overturn any agency action that is: 1) 'arbitrary, capricious, [or] an abuse of discretion'; 2) outside the agency's jurisdiction or authority; 3) taken without following proper procedures; or 4) unsupported by factual evidence. Many court decisions make it clear that an agency is also required, at the time of its decision, to explain the basis of its decision in terms of both the law and the facts.

As mentioned in section 3.3 above, in New Zealand the resource management reforms of the last two decades have attempted to redress procedural impediments to access to justice. The Resource Management Act 1991 provides that *any person* can make submissions on draft planning instruments.[66] With resource consent applications, again, *any person* can make submissions on a notified application.[67] *Any person* who has made such a submission also has the right to appeal to the Environment Court, and to the High Court on a

---

66. Resource Management Act 1991, SS. 60 (Regional Policy Statements), 64(1) (Regional Coastal Plans), 65(1) (Regional Plans), 73(1) (District Plans) and S. 6 of Part I, First Schedule.
67. Resource Management Act 1991, S. 96(1).

question of law.[68] Further, generally *any person* can apply for a declaration or an enforcement order,[69] and can lay an information for prosecution of the most serious offences under the Act.[70]

Unfortunately the 'open standing' provisions relating to resource consent applications only apply to notified applications, and as approximately 95 per cent of applications are not notified by local authorities, access to justice in this context is sometimes illusory. Recourse is through judicial review in the High Court of a decision not to notify, with all the costs and delays that this entails. Legislation to transfer the review of these decisions to the Environment Court has not yet been proclaimed in force.[71]

# 4. Market Conditions

The general principles of open market conditions are very important with respect to the establishment and operation of wind farms. The principles generally seek to establish open market conditions for developers and operators nationally as well as internationally. This is expressed in rules on non-discrimination, competition or antitrust rules, and rules on subsidies and State aid.

At an international level, the WTO aims at securing open, fair and undistorted competition, as expressed in its rules on non-discrimination and its restrictions on subsidies. While the rules on non-discrimination and state subsidies primarily impose limits on governments in the exercise of their legal authority, antitrust rules also set limits on the conduct of private companies.

### 4.1. Non-discrimination

Rules on non-discrimination express the view that the same treatment should be given to foreign goods and services as is given to domestic goods and services. Thus, there should be no preferential treatment of the nationals of the home state.

---

68. Resource Management Act 1991, SS. 120 (Environment Court), 299 and 301 (High Court).
69. Resource Management Act 1991, SS. 311(1) (declaration) and 316(1) (enforcement order).
70. Resource Management Act 1991, S. 338(4).
71. See *Kenneth Palmer:* 'Resource Management Act 1991', in *Derek Nolan* (ed.): Environmental and Resource Management Law, 2005 para. 4.55.

Rules on non-discrimination are expressed in international law, in particular in the WTO regime. The cornerstones of WTO trade law are the non-discrimination principles of 'national treatment' and 'most-favoured-nation' treatment. The national treatment principle in GATT Article III means that the goods and services of other countries must be treated in the same way as those of your own country, whereas the most-favoured-nation principle in GATT Article I requires that, if special treatment is given to the goods and services of one country, that special treatment must be given to all WTO member countries. There are exceptions for the preferential treatment of developing countries, regional free trade areas and customs unions such as the European Union. Also, hindrances to free trade may be justified under GATT Article XX on General Exceptions if they are 'necessary to protect human, animal or plant life or health' or if the trade measures relate to 'the conservation of exhaustible natural resources'.[72]

The EC Treaty similarly states that the provisions on free movement of goods (Articles 28-30), services (Articles 49-55), capital (Articles 56-60) and persons (Articles 39-48) prohibit not only discriminatory measures but also non-discriminatory measures that potentially hinder free movement across borders within the European Union. However, hindrances on free movement may be justified under specific circumstances. This is reflected in Article 30 of the EC Treaty on the free movement of goods and in the practice of the European Court of Justice.

In Case C-379/98, *PreussenElektra* v *Schleswag*, the Court of Justice assessed a German regulation which imposed an obligation on private electricity supply companies to purchase electricity produced in their supply area from renewable sources of energy at minimum prices which were higher than the real economic value of this type of electricity. Further, the regulation shared the costs of this obligation between the electricity supply undertakings and the private operators of the upstream electricity networks. It was considered that the obligation imposed on the electricity supply companies (as regards electricity produced from wind energy sources) could potentially hinder intra-Community trade. The objective of the German regulation, to promote renewable energy, was taken into account in determining whether that hindrance amounted to a breach of Article 30 of the EC Treaty. This represented a shift in the Court's interpretation of Article 30, allowing the environmental purposes of a measure to influence the application of Article 30. Taking into account the policy and the role of renewable energy in the Community, the Court did not consider the purchase obligation to be incompatible with the rules on free movement of goods.

72. See among others, *Birgitte Egelund Olsen:* 'Trade and the environment', in *B. Egelund Olsen; M. Steinicke & K. Engsig Sørensen* (eds.): WTO law – from a European perspective, 2006.

The principle of non-discrimination has been recognized by the Court of Justice as a fundamental principle of EU law which requires that comparable situations are not treated differently, unless the difference in treatment is objectively justified. The principle also applies to secondary EU legislation, e.g. EU energy law. In Case C-17/03, *Vereniging voor Energie, Milieu en Water, Amsterdam Power Exchange Spotmarket and Eneco v Directeur van de Dienst uitvoering en toezicht energie* a national measure that gave priority to the allocation of the cross-border capacity for electricity transmission to a national company infringed the principle of non-discrimination laid down in Directive 96/92/EC concerning common rules for the internal market in electricity.

United States law has similar doctrines of non-discrimination in state regulation of the market. First, any state law that affects interstate commerce is only allowed if it pursues a legitimate purpose of state regulation. Next, any state measure that is, on the face of it (directly or obviously), discriminatory is presumed to be invalid and is subject to strict scrutiny by the courts. Measures which, on the face of it, are non-discriminatory, but which have or may have some indirect discriminatory effect present a more difficult problem. One test is whether the measure's incidental effect on interstate commerce is clearly excessive in relation to the state's interest. The US Supreme Court has repeatedly ruled that state laws which try to restrict the disposal of out-of-state waste within the state are invalid; on the other hand, it has frequently upheld laws that give preference to state residents for licences for fishing and hunting. Most academic commentators emphasize the lack of clarity and consistency in the Court's application of its doctrines.

## 4.2. Antitrust and Competition Rules

Antitrust and competition rules also share some common elements. Antitrust rules not only set limits on the behaviour of public and private enterprises, but they may also set certain limits on the exercise of legal authority. This may be the case if a monopoly or a dominant position is established by national legislation and this legislation encourages or allows an abuse of a monopoly or a dominant position.

There are no general international agreements on competition policy or restrictive business practices. However, there are fragments of such rules in a number of WTO Agreements.[73]

---

73. See among others GATT Article XVII:1 b), GATS Article VIII and TRIPS Articles 8, 31 and 40.

In the European Union there is comprehensive regulation of competition. The competition rules of the EC Treaty apply to distortion of competition that may affect trade between the Member States. In cases of distortion of competition at national level, only national competition rules apply. In most Member States national competition rules follow the same principles as the competition rules of the EC Treaty.

The EC Treaty prohibits agreements that distort trade (Article 81) and the abuse of a dominant position (Article 82). Under Article 86 of the Treaty undertakings entrusted with the operation of services which are of general economic interest or which have the character of a revenue-producing monopoly are subject to the competition rules of the Treaty in so far as the application of the rules does not obstruct the performance, in law or in fact, of the particular tasks assigned to them. As regards public undertakings and undertakings to which Member States grant special or exclusive rights, Member States must not enact nor maintain in force any measure contrary to the competition rules of the Treaty. Furthermore, under EU competition law, mergers between undertakings are subject to control if they exceed certain thresholds.

The enforcement of competition rules has been reformed by Regulation (EC) No 1/2003 which took effect on 1 May 2004. The Regulation decentralized the enforcement system and required greater cooperation between the European Commission (which had been solely responsible for the enforcement of these rules until 2004) and the competition authorities of the Member States and their national courts.

The United States has a number of statutes and regulations designed to maintain a competitive market and prevent the exercise of dominant or monopoly market power. Although the application of these laws becomes extremely complex and dependent on highly technical economic analysis, there are three basic rules. First, business efforts to acquire monopoly power in the market are subject to regulation – for example, requiring a company to sell part of its business to another company. Second, collusion between two or more companies in the same business sector to set prices or control costs of production or divide markets is illegal. Third, business mergers and acquisitions between major firms in a single market are subject to review and approval or disapproval by the government. Some businesses, of course, including electricity distribution, are understood to be natural monopolies. The typical response in these situations is to subject the prices charged by such firms to state regulation. See also Chapter 10, section 6.4.

Antitrust or competition law in New Zealand is embodied in the Commerce Act 1986. Its general purpose is to promote competition in markets for the long-term benefit of customers in New Zealand (Section 1A), but it certainly does not prohibit every exercise of market power, even by dominant players. The Act can be relevant where the developer of a wind farm engages in commercial negotiations with other companies. There are prohibitions against contracts that substantially lessen competition, and against price fixing. Business acquisitions (takeovers) may be prohibited if they increase market dominance.

Section 36 prohibits a company with a substantial degree of power in a market from taking advantage of that power for the purpose of restricting the entry of another company into that or another market, preventing or deterring a company from engaging in competitive conduct, or eliminating a company from a market. However in practice its scope is relatively limited.

The Commerce Act does not specifically address the question of third party access or access to essential facilities, a question which is important in relation to electricity and natural gas networks in many countries. Questions of that kind have been dealt with by ensuring that Transpower NZ Ltd – the owner of the high-tension national transmission grid – is not in competition with electricity generators, and gives them equal treatment. To some extent local electricity distribution companies (lines companies) are subject to similar constraints under the Electricity Industry Reform Act 1998. In addition, Part 4A of the Commerce Act provides for the imposition of price controls on electricity lines companies (local distribution companies) and on Transpower NZ Ltd. This regulation addresses the monopoly position of these companies. See also Chapter 10, section 7.4.

The Commerce Act is administered by the Commerce Commission, an independent regulatory agency. The Commission cooperates with its Australian counterparts, recognizing the connections between the markets of the two countries. The Commission has certain powers to authorize practices that would otherwise be unlawful, and to enforce the legislation. But a number of important enforcement actions require the Commission to apply to the High Court.

### 4.3. Subsidies and State Aid

Aid or subsidies granted by a state – or by public authorities – may distort competition. At an international level, the WTO Agreement on Subsidies and Countervailing Measures prohibits export subsidies (subsidies directly connected to export activity). Members are allowed to grant domestic subsidies, but subsidies that have an effect on trade are subject to countervailing duties or countermeasures by other countries whose economic interests are affected.

EU law treats State aid as a matter subject to the rules on competition. As with the WTO law on subsidies, EU State aid law takes a strict approach to export aid. Thus, export aid or aid favouring domestic products over imported products cannot be considered *de minimis* under Commission Regulation (EC) No 1998/2006, nor can such aid schemes be exempted under the block exemption regulations for aid for environmental purposes.[74]

According to Article 87 of the EC Treaty 'any aid granted by a Member State or through State resources in any form whatsoever which distorts or threatens to distort competition by favouring certain undertakings or the production of certain goods shall, in so far as it affects trade between Member States, be incompatible with the common market.' Article 87 applies a broad concept of State aid including any form of government aid. The Court of Justice has stated that the concept of State aid not only includes positive benefits, but also includes measures which, in various forms, mitigate the charges to which an undertaking is normally subject.[75]

In the *PreussenElektra* case the Court further stated that state resources must be involved in order for State aid to be deemed to exist.

In Case C-379/98, *PreussenElektra* v *Schleswag*, the obligation imposed on private electricity supply undertakings to purchase electricity produced from wind energy sources at fixed minimum prices was not considered by the Court of Justice to involve any direct or indirect transfer of State resources to the undertakings which produced that type of electricity. The regulatory scheme was thus not State aid within the meaning of Article 87 of the EC Treaty.

In certain circumstances State aid may be deemed compatible with the common market under Article 87(2) and (3). The Commission may authorize State aid; see Article 88 of the EC Treaty. Measures complying with Article 87(2) must be exempted, while an exemption under Article 87(3) is discretionary. On this basis the Commission has issued guidelines for national aid with environmental objectives, which were most recently reviewed in January 2008.[76]

The aim of the Commission guidelines for environmental protection is to address market failures, to promote a higher level of environmental protection and to make the EU policy more transparent. In some cases, State aid may be justified to give private firms an incentive to invest more in environ-

---

74. *Pernille Wegener Jessen:* 'Subsidies', in *Karsten Engsig Sørensen, Birgitte Egelund Olsen & Michael Steinicke* (eds.): WTO law from a European perspective, 2006 pp. 440-442.
75. Case 30/59, *Steenkolenmijnen.*
76. Guidelines for state aid for environmental protection, January 2008. The 2008 guidelines are the third set of guidelines on this subject since 1994.

mental protection or to relieve some firms from a relatively high financial burden in order to enforce a stricter environmental policy overall. At the same time, the guidelines serve as a safeguard, ensuring that it will not be possible to grant badly targeted or excessive State aid which not only distorts competition but also frustrates the very objective of meeting environmental targets. For example, aid for investment in energy savings and the promotion of renewable sources of energy may be authorized up to 60 per cent of the eligible costs.[77] These discretionary decisions of the Commission are subject to judicial review by the Court of Justice.

Under EU law, existing aid is subject to retrospective control by the Commission. Further, all new State aid schemes must be notified to the Commission, so it can review their compatibility with Article 87(1) of the EC Treaty prior to implementation.[78] If an aid scheme is implemented without the Member State having fulfilled its obligations, the aid is considered unlawful and must be recovered from the beneficiary.[79]

---

77. The European Council decided in March 2007 to set a target of 20 % reduction of greenhouse gas emissions and a binding target of a 20 % share of renewable energy in the total EU Energy consumption by 2020. The new Commission State aid guidelines are important in order to provide the right incentives for Member States and for industry to increase their efforts for the environment.
78. Article 88(3) of the EC Treaty and Article 2 of Council Regulation (EC) No 659/1999.
79. Articles 1(f) and 14 of Council Regulation (EC) No 659/1999.

# CHAPTER 6

# Planning Law

## 1. Introduction – by *Helle Tegner Anker and Birgitte Egelund Olsen*

Planning law varies from one country to another. This refers not only to the question of what is characterized as planning law, but also questions regarding the level of the planning authority (state, regional or local level), the control of the planning authority (planning limits and interdependence of plans), as well as the character and legal effect of planning instruments.

For the purposes of this book, planning law includes land use planning and coastal planning, as well as marine zoning or planning. The decisive criterion of planning law is that it is a decision-making process which includes the *ex ante* consideration of a future development project, for example the establishment of wind turbines or a wind farm. In line with this definition, land use planning is generally aimed at controlling future development and at coordinating various land use interests. Similar planning instruments may exist for offshore or marine areas. Planning requirements may include mapping, as well as establishing planning guidelines or directions for the activity or development project in question. However, planning law may also encompass different types of environmental planning, e.g. protection of sensitive areas or natural resources. Safeguarding landscape and nature protection interests are specifically dealt with in Chapters 7 to 9.

In this Chapter the different planning systems will be examined, focusing in particular on the planning requirements for the construction of wind turbines. This may include both general and more specific planning requirements. Furthermore, where specific coastal planning provisions apply in some countries, these will also be described. Other relevant sectoral plans may be described as well. Finally, planning for offshore wind farms will be touched upon.

## 2. International Planning Law – by *Helle Tegner Anker*

Generally, international law does not include planning rules. Planning may, however, be seen as an important element in securing sustainable development. The importance of planning was reflected in Agenda 21, which called for the adoption of flexible and integrative planning approaches that allow the consideration of multiple goals and enable adjustment to changing needs. According to Agenda 21, integrative area approaches at the ecosystem or watershed level can help achieve environmental goals.[1] Planning is also mentioned in the Johannesburg Plan of Implementation, in particular with respect to the adoption of an ecosystem approach in protecting and managing the natural resource base, e.g. with respect to coastal areas.[2]

As regards coastal areas, specific calls have been made at international level for integrated coastal zone management in which planning is normally an important element. A specific call for integrated coastal zone management was made in Agenda 21.[3] The Johannesburg Plan of Implementation calls for implementation of Agenda 21, Chapter 17 to promote integrated and sustainable management of coastal areas.[4] Integrated coastal zone management has also been encouraged by the Council of Europe which has published the Model Law on Sustainable Management of Coastal Zones and the European Code of Conduct for Coastal Zones.[5] The Model Law has no legal effect and must be regarded as an inspiration to countries wishing to adopt a legal framework for coastal zone management.[6]

Different regional initiatives may include specific provisions or recommendations for the protection and management of coastal zones. One example is the Helsinki Convention on the Protection of the Marine Environment of the Baltic Sea Area, under which Recommendation 15/1 on the protection of the coastal strip was adopted in 1994. Another example is the trilateral Wadden Sea cooperation that led to the adoption of a Trilateral Wadden Sea Plan in 1997.[7]

1.   Agenda 21, Chapter 8.
2.   Plan of Implementation of the World Summit on Sustainable Development, 2002 Chapter IV, p. 20.
3.   Agenda 21, Chapter 17.
4.   Plan of Implementation, Chapter IV, p. 16, para. 30.
5.   *Council of Europe:* 'Model law on sustainable management of coastal zones and European code of conduct for coastal zones', Nature and Environment No 101, 2000.
6.   See *John Gibson:* 'Integrated Coastal Zone Management Law in the European Union', in Coastal Management, Vol. 31(2), 2003 p. 132.
7.   See below Chapter 8, section 2 about the Wadden Sea cooperation.

Other international instruments may require or encourage land use or environmental planning in different ways. The European Landscape Convention, adopted by the Council of Europe, calls upon the parties to integrate landscape protection into regional and town planning policies as well as into other policies. The Convention stipulates a duty to define landscape quality objectives and to introduce instruments aimed at protecting and/or planning for the landscape. The Pan-European Biodiversity and Landscape Strategy adopted under the auspices of the Council of Europe (and the United Nations Economic Commission for Europe – UNECE) also encourages the use of planning instruments.[8]

## 3. EU Planning Law – by *Helle Tegner Anker and Birgitte Egelund Olsen*

There is no specific EU land use planning legislation. Land use planning is primarily considered a national matter in accordance with the subsidiarity principle.[9] This is reflected in Article 175(2) of the EC Treaty, which states that measures for town and country planning and land use have to be adopted unanimously by the Council. Community planning initiatives are accordingly subject to the veto power of each Member State and an EU planning measure can only be adopted with the approval of the Member States concerned.[10]

At the beginning of the 1990s the EU Commission issued some communications on town and country planning, urban environment, integrated coastal zone management and wetlands.[11] In addition, in 2002 the European Parliament and the Council adopted a very general recommendation on the implementation of integrated coastal zone management (ICZM).[12] The recommen-

---

8.  About the European Landscape Convention and the Pan-European Biodiversity and Landscape Strategy; see Chapter 8, section 2.
9.  For more about the subsidiarity principle, see *Birgitte Egelund Olsen:* 'The subsidiarity principle and its impact on regulation', in *Birgitte Egelund Olsen & Karsten Engsig Sørensen* (eds.): Regulation in the EU, 2006 pp. 35-79.
10. Measures on environmental impact assessments (EIA) or strategic environmental assessments (SEA) do not come under Article 175(2) as they do not concern planning as such, but the way in which planning may be organised. See also *Ludwig Krämer:* EC Environmental Law, 2003 pp. 148-151.
11. COM(90) 544 final; COM(90) 452 final; COM(90) 218 final; COM(95) 189 final; and COM(97) 197 final.
12. Recommendation 2002/413/EC concerning the implementation of integrated coastal management (OJ 2002 L148/24).

dation encourages the adoption of common principles for ICZM and it advises the Member States to develop national strategies for ICZM.

ICZM is expected to be incorporated as an element in a new EU-wide Maritime Policy. In June 2006 the Commission published a Green Paper on a future maritime policy.[13] The Green Paper stresses the need to manage the interplay between land and sea through integrated coastal zone management. The Green Paper also suggests the development of spatial planning for marine activities or even an overall coastal and marine spatial development plan that could provide a coherent set of policy objectives and principles. It is stated that 'a future maritime policy has to build instruments and methods for ensuring consistency between land and marine systems in order to avoid duplication of regulations, or the transfer of unsolved land-planning problems to the sea. One idea is to associate as closely as possible the same stakeholders in the planning processes of each'.[14] The EU Maritime Policy should be seen in the context of the initiatives for the protection of the marine environment.

In 2005 the Commission proposed a Maritime (Environmental) Strategy Directive[15] aimed at protecting the marine environment through the designation of marine regions for which the relevant Member States, in close cooperation with third countries, will be required to develop marine strategies. A marine environment strategy should contain a detailed assessment of the state of the environment, a definition of 'good environmental status' at regional level and the establishment of clear environmental targets and monitoring programmes.

In 2006 the Commission adopted a communication on a thematic strategy on the urban environment.[16] The urban environment strategy is one of the seven thematic strategies mentioned in the Sixth Environment Action Programme.[17] The main aspect of the strategy is the adoption of environmental management plans and transport plans in order to improve the planning of urban areas.

Community measures for planning and land use are to a great extent based on national planning and land use laws. Accordingly, the existence of national planning law is either directly or indirectly assumed in several EU

13. COM(2006) 275 final p. 34.
14. COM(2006) 275 final p. 34.
15. COM(2005) 505, Proposal for a Directive of the European Parliament and of the Council establishing a Framework for Community Action in the field of Marine Environmental Policy (Marine Strategy Directive). The Directive was adopted 17 June 2008 (OJ 2008 L164/19).
16. COM(2005) 718 final. See the preparations for the sectoral action programme in COM(2004) 60.
17. Article 7(2g) in Decision No 1600/2002/EC (OJ 2002 L242/1).

documents and legislation. In some cases national planning law is regarded as an obstacle to the implementation of EU legislation and policy. There is an example of this in the Commission's 2004 communication on the share of renewable energy in the EU which, among other things, considers the obstacles which national planning rules create to the development of offshore wind energy; and in view of this the Commission may make proposals for legislation if necessary.[18]

## 4. Danish Planning Law – by *Helle Tegner Anker*

Planning law is an important element in Danish environmental law, providing planning guidelines for the administration of environmental legislation. The overall purpose of the Danish Planning Act,[19] according to Section 1 of the Act, is to coordinate different land use interests and ensure sustainable development. More specifically the aim of the Act is to ensure planned development, safeguard urban environments, landscapes and coastal areas, prevent pollution – including noise pollution, and ensure public participation as far as possible.

The Planning Act establishes a land use planning system as well as a rural zone permit system.[20] Generally, the Planning Act only applies to land-based activities. However, the land use planning system also includes certain limited planning requirements for coastal areas; see below section 4.2. Otherwise, there is no general planning system for development activities in marine areas. Regulation of marine areas is embedded in sectoral legislation, for example water law, nature protection law, fishery law, transport law and energy law. There is a general requirement for permits for new construction and other activities in marine areas under the state supremacy rule (*statens højhedsret*). This requirement for permits is generally administered by the Ministry of Transport.

---

18. COM(2004) 366 final.
19. Consolidated Act No 813 of 21 June 2007 on planning.
20. For a more comprehensive description of Danish planning law, see *Ellen Margrethe Basse:* Environmental law. Denmark, 2004 pp. 255-271; and *Helle T. Anker:* 'Planlovgivning', in *Ellen Margrethe Basse* (ed.): Miljøretten, Vol. 2, 2006 pp. 175-335. For a specific analysis of Danish and Swedish planning law with respect to wind power, see *Maria Pettersson:* Legal Preconditions for Wind Power Implementation in Sweden and Denmark, 2006.

### 4.1 Land Use Planning

The planning system in the Planning Act has a significant element of decentralization. The Planning Act establishes a planning hierarchy consisting of national, regional, municipal and local planning. Lower level plans may not conflict with higher level plans.

*National planning* does not include an overall national land use planning document. National planning consists of specific national planning rules explicitly laid down in the Planning Act, including the coastal planning provisions, as well as national planning directives that can be issued on specific matters (Section 3). National planning directives may either lay down planning guidelines of a more general character or of a very specific character.

An example of general national planning guidelines is the 1999 Circular on planning and rural zone permits for wind turbines (Wind Turbine Circular).[21] An example of specific planning guidelines is the 2000 Circular on planning for a wind power testing station.[22] The Wind Turbine Circular lays down specific planning requirements with the aim of safeguarding not only energy policy objectives but also neighbour, nature, landscape, cultural heritage and agricultural interests. It includes specific distance requirements – minimum 4 x the total height to nearest dwelling (Section 2(2)). If a wind turbine is to be located closer than 500 metres from a dwelling, the planning proposal must examine the potential disturbance to the dwelling. Furthermore, the circular imposes a positive obligation on the authorities to *designate wind turbine areas* as part of the land use planning process. Under the 1999 Wind Turbine Circular this requirement applies to the regional planning level, but in future it will apply to the municipal planning level. The regional (or municipal) planning guidelines for wind turbine areas must be based on an assessment of the effects on the interests mentioned above (Section 3). It is only possible to grant a rural zone permit – or issue a local plan – for wind turbines within designated wind turbine areas.[23]

*Regional planning* has undergone significant changes due to the local government reform that replaced 14 county councils with 5 regions, with much

---

21. Circular No 100 of 10 June 1999 regarding planning and zoning for the establishment of wind turbines.
22. Circular No 79 of 25 May 2005 regarding the planning and establishment of a national testing station for large wind turbines at Høvsøre.
23. Certain exemptions apply to small-scale wind turbines.

more limited responsibilities, with effect from 1 January 2007.[24] In the Danish planning system regional planning had a very important role in balancing land use interests, particularly outside urban areas. However, the existing regional plans will be abolished and for the most part incorporated into the municipal plans. A new regional planning instrument will emerge in the form of regional development plans. At a more strategic level, regional development plans must describe the desired development for the region as a whole with respect to nature and the environment, business, employment, education and culture etc. It is unlikely that the regional development plans will play any significant role with respect to the establishment of wind turbines.

After the local government reform, *municipal planning* will result in plans that lay down municipal planning guidelines for various land use interests. This includes not only planning guidelines for the construction of technical installations, such as wind turbines, but also planning guidelines for safeguarding other interests, such as nature protection, landscape, cultural, geological and agricultural interests (Section 11a). The municipal planning guidelines are binding on the municipal authorities in the sense that they must strive to implement the guidelines and that lower level plans may not conflict with higher level plans. The municipal plans must also provide more specific outlines for local plans (Section 11b).

*Local planning* is the detailed planning level. A local plan is required for new activities that may lead to significant changes in the existing environment. In relation to wind turbines, the construction of wind turbines in a new area may thus require a local plan, whereas the construction of additional turbines in an existing wind turbine area may not necessarily require a local plan.[25] However, a local plan may also be produced in such cases. A local plan for a wind turbine must include provisions on their exact location, height etc. (Wind Turbine Circular, Section 5).[26]

.

---

24. Most of the former environmental responsibilities at regional level have been transferred to the municipalities which have been reduced in number from 274 to 98.
25. In a Nature Protection Appeal Board case (MAD1998.1468) the establishment of 8 new turbines in an area with 14 existing turbines was considered a significant change requiring a local plan.
26. In a Supreme Court ruling, failure to comply with the assessment and information requirements was, however, not considered significant in the specific circumstances of the case and a local plan for two wind turbines was not deemed invalid; see UfR 2004.1552H/MAD2004.84H; see also UfR 2005.116H/MAD2005.628H.

Local plans are legally binding with the effect that activities may not be carried on in contravention of a local plan (Section 18). On the other hand activities which are in accordance with the local plan are allowed unless other restrictions or permit requirements apply, for example building permits according to the Building Act.[27] The construction of wind turbines is generally exempt from the building permit requirements if the wind turbine is in accordance with the technical specifications in the certification scheme, but notification is necessary; see Section 3 of the Building Act and Section 1.7 of the Building Regulation 2008.[28]

The *rural zone permit system* in the Planning Act establishes a general permit requirement for new activities in rural zones (Section 35).[29] The purpose of the rural zone provisions is to protect rural areas against unplanned industrial or urban development. The construction of a wind turbine in a rural zone is subject to a rural zone permit requirement, unless a local plan explicitly allows the project (Section 36(1)(5)).

### 4.2 Coastal and Marine Planning

The *coastal planning provisions* of the Planning Act lay down a general requirement that coastal land areas should be kept free of non-coastal dependent constructions and installations (Section 5a). The Planning Act defines a 3 kilometre coastal planning zone landwards from the coastline in rural zones and summer cottage areas. Within the coastal planning zone, urban developments or other installations require specific planning or functional reasons (Section 5b). Furthermore, the coastal planning provisions include specific requirements for visual impact assessments for local plan proposals (Section 16). The coastal planning provisions of the Planning Act focus on land-based activities. However, according to Section 11a of the Planning Act a municipal plan must include an assessment of future development in the coastal planning zone *and in adjacent waters*.

As mentioned above, there is no *marine planning* system in Denmark apart from the planning provisions embedded in sectoral legislation. The designation of offshore wind turbine areas under energy legislation is described in Chapter 10, section 4.1 and 4.3.

---

27. Consolidated Act No 452 of 24 June 1998 on building, with later amendments.
28. Building Regulation 2008 No 45 of 30 January 2008.
29. Rural zones consist of areas that are not designated as urban zones or summer cottage areas (Planning Act, S. 34).

## 4.3 Public Participation and Appeals

The Planning Act provides for extensive public participation in the planning process at regional and local level. When a plan proposal has been adopted it must be subject to public consultation for at least 8 weeks before the final adoption of the plan. During the same period the Minister for the Environment and other state authorities may raise objections to a plan proposal with the effect that the proposal cannot be adopted before agreement has been reached. Neighbouring municipalities may also raise objections to plan proposals.

The adoption of a plan can be appealed to the Nature Protection Appeal Board on the basis of legal merits, such as failure to comply with planning procedures, with higher level plans or with general principles of law. If a rural zone permit or an environmental impact assessment permit has been granted, an appeal can be made on the full merits of the case. A wide right of appeal is accepted in planning cases, including neighbours and other individual citizens, local citizens groups and NGOs. Decisions by the administrative authorities or by the Nature Protection Appeal Board can be appealed to the ordinary courts (the district courts in the first instance).

## 5. Norwegian Planning Law – by *Hans Christian Bugge*

Spatial and land use planning is regarded as an important instrument in Norwegian environmental policy and law. The main act in this field, the Planning and Building Act,[30] is often referred to as 'the most important environmental act' in the country. Mainly through the system and rules of this Act, construction and other use of land is strictly controlled in Norway. The Act applies to land, including watercourses, and to internal coastal waters; activities in other marine areas and on the continental shelf fall outside its scope.

The Planning and Building Act establishes a system of comprehensive social, economic, cultural and spatial planning in the counties and the municipalities, with the active participation of state authorities. The plans are meant to cover all important sectors of society. Hence, the Planning and Building Act applies to, but is not limited to, the planning of land use. The plans serve as guidelines for activities and decisions of municipal, county and state authorities within the plan area. Land use plans at the municipal level are also

---

30.  Act No 77 of 14 June 1985.

legally binding on landowners' future use of their land, and are the basis for decisions on building permits.

The system may be described as a hierarchy of plans. County plans serve as guidelines for sectoral and municipal plans. General municipal plans (*kommuneplan*) provide the framework for sectoral planning and decisions, as well as for more detailed land use plans: local development plans (*reguleringsplan*), and building plans (*bebyggelsesplan*). The system is quite flexible. For example, a new local development plan may deviate from, and replace, the existing municipal master plan for an area. County plans and general municipal plans must be reviewed and may be modified every fourth year.

Planning is the responsibility of the highest political bodies in the counties and the municipalities: the county council and the local (municipal) council. These bodies also formally adopt the plans. Thus, planning is clearly defined as a political task, and an important element in Norwegian local democracy.

Most types of construction and other changes in the use of land need a permit – a building permit – from the municipality. As the main rule, a permit must be issued if the building or construction is fully in accordance with the land use plan for the area, as well as with other rules in the Act or in regulations. If this is not the case, the municipality must refuse permission. In special cases, a permit may nevertheless be granted as an exemption (*dispensasjon*), on the basis of a general exemption clause in Section 7 of the Act.

The Planning and Building Act only partly applies to installations for energy production such as hydropower plants and wind turbines. A system of concessions under energy legislation[31] generally replaces the building permit provisions under the Planning and Building Act.

In addition to the Planning and Building Act, there are a number of sectoral acts of importance for the use of land. A few of these acts are formally linked to the Planning and Building Act in the sense that plans approved in accordance with the Planning and Building Act either replace decisions required under a sectoral act, or serve as basis for such decisions. In other areas, no such link has been formally established. In this case, several acts may apply more or less independently of each other, and even overlap to some extent.

A new Planning and Building Act was adopted by the Parliament in June 2008 and is expected to come into force in late 2009. It maintains the main

---

31. The most important acts are Act No 17 of 14 December 1917 on hydropower development, and the Energy Act, Act No 50 of 29 June 1990, which includes a general concession system for energy production facilities, including wind turbines.

elements in the system as described here, but implies many technical changes and some special rules for the energy sector.

## 5.1. County Plans

A county plan is a flexible instrument within the Norwegian planning system. It is usually a four year, cross-sectoral plan for activities and resource use within a county.[32] It provides policy guidelines for – and seeks to coordinate – decisions by state and county authorities in the various sectors. It is decided by the county council and then formally approved by the government. It usually includes general guidelines for land use planning and development, as a framework for the more detailed land use planning in the municipalities. However, in the Norwegian system a county does not have the authority to give instructions to a municipality. Therefore, the county plans are not legally binding on the municipalities in a strict sense. But a county may object to a municipal plan which conflicts with the county plan, in which case the issue is decided by the government.

County plans may also be developed for one or a few sectors of particular importance, or for an area of the county which needs special attention. Due to the increasing controversy about the development of wind farms along the Norwegian coast, the Ministry of the Environment has recommended that counties should develop county plans for the location of wind turbines. Such plans should indicate areas which are well suited for wind farms, and areas where wind turbines should be avoided for nature conservation or other reasons. The methodology is now being developed. So far (spring 2008) only one county has adopted such a plan. It is expected that county plans for wind turbines will become an important instrument in the development of wind power in Norway.

## 5.2. Land Use Plans at the Municipal Level

The *municipal master plan* draws up the main pattern of future development and land use in the municipality, by using a system of zoning. Areas are designated for specific purposes: housing development, industry, public services, public roads etc., or to be kept as agricultural or uncultivated land, protected from development. An area could be designated as an area for wind farms in such a plan.

Certain supplementary provisions, as listed in the Act, may be adopted to further define the possible future use of areas, or restrictions on their use.

---

32. Norway has 19 counties.

However, there are formal limitations as to what may be decided in a master plan. Many questions of detail have to be decided either in a local development plan (or building plan), which requires a more thorough procedure, or through decisions pursuant to sectoral legislation.

The municipal master plan is legally binding. Any new construction, building or other change in the use of land must not conflict with the plan and its supplementary provisions. This is mainly controlled through the building permit system. As mentioned, a building permit will normally not be issued for a building or other type of construction which is not in accordance with the plan and supplementary provisions. Although a wind turbine that has been licensed pursuant to the Energy Act does not need a building permit pursuant to the Planning and Building Act, it will not be allowed in an area designated for agriculture, nature protection and recreation unless a formal exemption is issued pursuant to Section 7 of the Act.

The *local development plan*[33] is used for more detailed land use planning. It is an essential tool for deciding precisely, and in detail, how various plots of land may legally be used or not used. Similarly to a municipal master plan, a local development plan designates zones for various purposes, but it is much more flexible than the master plan in this respect. Supplementary regulations may be issued, with more detailed rules and regulations related to future construction and other activities in the various zones.

Whether the construction of wind turbines *always* requires a local development plan is a matter of dispute. The Planning and Building Act requires major building and construction works to be based on a local development plan (Section 23). However, since a wind turbine in any case requires a concession under the Energy Act[34] some municipalities may choose to exempt them from this requirement. The national energy authorities often accept and even support this view, which is clearly contrary to the view of the national planning and environment authorities. The new Act explicitly states that a local development plan is not required for energy production installations, which includes wind turbines.

A local development plan is legally binding on landowners in much the same way as a municipal master plan. However, in contrast to the master plan, an approved local development plan provides the legal basis for expro-

---

33. There is a more detailed level, the Building Plan. This is used to decide on land use details within the framework of a master plan or local development plan, such as the location of specific buildings within the plan area.
34. Act No 50 of 29 June 1990.

priation of land. Thus, the plan can be used by the municipality, the county or the state, as the basis for acquiring land for public purposes.

A local development plan may be initiated and proposed by any citizen. If a person (natural or legal) wants to build on or develop their land, they may present a draft plan to the municipal planning authorities. The authorities then decide whether the plan has enough merit to be forwarded for formal adoption, or whether it should be rejected.

In fact, today the large majority of local development plans are private plans. They are initiated by landowners or land developers and presented to the municipality for formal adoption.

In these cases it is not uncommon for the developer and the municipality enter into an agreement about how the project should be carried out and about the development or improvements to the technical infrastructure necessary for the development. Such development agreements (*utbyggingsavtaler*) raise several difficult legal questions, related to their substance, procedure and legal status. Since 2005 the Planning and Building Act has provided a framework for their content and for a procedure which makes it possible for interested parties and the public at large to get information about such negotiations and to influence the outcome.

## 5.3. Coastal or Marine Planning
The Planning and Building Act covers the coastline and internal waters. There are no special planning instruments for these areas; the ordinary spatial plans at county and municipal level are used for the management of the coastal zone, with its many conflicting interests.

Section 17-2 of the Planning and Building Act generally prohibits construction and other development within a 100 metre zone along the coast. This rule was introduced in the 1960s with the objective of protecting natural and recreational values in this zone.

There are, however, many exceptions to this general rule, which in fact only serves as a starting point. A municipal master plan and a local development plan may open up the shore for development. Most types of industry and public services which need to be located along the shore are also exempted. And finally, municipalities may give exemptions in individual cases if there are special reasons for doing so; see Section 7. In fact, many municipalities have been quite liberal, in particular with regard to exemptions for recreational homes, in spite of government requests for maintaining a strict policy.

## 5.4. Public Participation, Appeals and Objections

Public participation is an important goal. At all levels the planning authorities have a duty to actively inform the public about planning activities from an early stage. Individuals and groups with interests in the plan must have the opportunity to participate. There are specific rules on public information and participation for each type of plan. For detailed land use plans, land owners and other rights holders have special rights, and must be directly informed. When a plan is adopted, it has to be made public. The system of environmental impact assessments is integrated into the Act; see Chapter 7, section 5.

In Norwegian administrative law there is a general right to appeal against individual decisions of public authorities for parties to the decision and others with a legal interest.[35] Neither a county plan nor a municipal master plan may be subject to appeal. However, both a local development plan and a building plan – and a building permit – may be appealed,[36] for example by landowners in the plan area or the neighbours to the property in question. The criterion for having a legal interest for an appeal is not entirely clear, but it is usually interpreted rather liberally. For example, environmental organizations usually have a right to appeal.

The state representative in the county – the county governor – is the appeal body. The general rule in Norwegian administrative law is that the appeal body may review all aspects of the case, both issues of law and of fact. This rule also applies in this field of law. However, there is also a rule in the Public Administration Act saying that, when reviewing an appeal of a municipal decision, state authorities must give considerable weight to the discretion exercised by the local authority.

If a municipality does not submit to the views expressed by a county or state authority in respect of a municipal master plan or a local development plan, these may raise a formal objection (*innsigelse*) to the plan. For example, the Directorate for Natural Management may object to a wind farm area in a municipal master plan for reasons of nature protection. In the last resort the issue is decided by the Ministry of the Environment, if necessary after consultation with other ministries. If necessary, the State may itself initiate and carry out planning, and adopt plans.

---

35. Pursuant to the Public Administration Act of 10 February 1967 S. 28.
36. For local development plans and building plans this is stated explicitly in the Planning and Building Act S. 27-3.

# 6. US Federal and State Planning Law – by *Julian Juergensmeyer*

Plans and planning at the federal government level are not part of the American political tradition. The explanation for this lies partly in the unfortunate and inaccurate association by many Americans of plans and planning with socialism. Another explanation is that, since land use regulation is almost entirely a state and local government activity, there is no real scope for land use planning by the federal government. Nonetheless, the increased federal role in environmental regulation has given rise to more planning at the federal level that can be relevant to land development, including the construction of wind farms. However, the only statutory federal planning instrument is embedded in the Coastal Zone Management Act (CZMA) which will be dealt with below in section 6.2.

## 6.1 State and Local Government Land Use Plans

As pointed out above, land use regulation and planning is a state law matter. The issue of land use permits necessary for the construction of a wind farm would involve local government comprehensive plans and their implementation.

The Standard State Zoning Enabling Act (SZEA) from 1926 was the first model act for planning. It expressly stated that zoning should be enacted in accordance with a comprehensive plan. The Act provides that a legislative body is empowered to regulate and restrict, e.g. the height, number of stories, and size of buildings and other structures, as well as the location and use of buildings, structures and land for trade, industry, residence or other purposes.[37]

The Standard City Planning Enabling Act (SPEA) from 1927, calling for a master plan, stated that planning was not mandatory, but optional. The SPEA envisioned a more comprehensive approach to regulating land use and providing municipal services for future growth than zoning could attempt.[38] Even this rudimentary planning requirement had little effect because, although nearly all states eventually enacted all or major parts of the SZEA, no states enacted the SPEA. In 1963 a Model Land Development Code based on the SPEA and the SZEA, and dealing with the physical development of land,

---

37. *Julian C. Juergensmeyer & Thomas E. Roberts:* Land Use Planning and Development Regulation Law, 2003 p. 25 and pp. 72-73.
38. *Julian C. Juergensmeyer & Thomas E. Roberts:* Land Use Planning and Development Regulation Law, 2003 p. 23 and pp. 30-37.

was promulgated by the American Law Institute. In this model act, planning was given considerable emphasis, but very few states have adopted it.

The majority of the states whose legislation enables the preparation of comprehensive plans do not require local governments to prepare plans, and in these states comprehensive plans are principally land use policy documents without the force of law.[39]

The justification frequently given for this lack of legal status is that urban planning has not yet proven itself to be capable of solving urban problems, and there is no consensus among the states over what elements of urban development plans should always address. Furthermore, some commentators believe that a comprehensive plan serves an important 'visionary function', unlike the regulatory function of ordinances and statutes, and that to require a plan to be a painstakingly drafted regulatory document would prevent plans from being inspirational and boldly innovative.

Nonetheless, a recent development in some states which do not mandate comprehensive plans is to give strong encouragement for their adoption by offering incentives to those local governments that do adopt them. The State of Georgia, for example, has used a planning framework that provides for certain incentives and disincentives which are designed to encourage the planning process.[40] Given the funding incentives targeted at them, nearly all of Georgia's counties have 'voluntarily' adopted comprehensive plans.[41]

In 2002, Illinois adopted the Local Planning Technical Assistance Act to encourage its local governments, through funding and other incentives, 'to engage in planning, regulatory, and development approaches that promote and encourage comprehensive planning.'[42]

The traditional position, that individual zoning decisions could be compared to the general zoning code to determine whether they are 'in accordance with a comprehensive plan', had a circularity of reasoning which did not make sense to planning advocates. Many urged reform of the planning enabling statutes so as to clarify the role and status of the comprehensive, or master, plan.[43] It was argued that a plan ought to have some legal signifi-

---

39. *Edward Sullivan:* 'Recent Developments in Comprehensive Planning Law', in Urban Lawyer, Vol. 38, 2006 pp. 685-700, at pp. 686-87.
40. See Official Code of Georgia Annotated S. 50–8–2(a)(18).
41. One of the incentives is the power to adopt certain impact fees.
42. 20 Ill, Comp. Stat. Ann. 662.
43. See *Charles M. Haar:* 'The Master Plan: An Impermanent Constitution', in Law and Contemporary Problems, Vol. 20(3), 1955 pp. 353-366.

cance, and that it ought to be a separate document from zoning ordinances.[44] The states that have adopted this approach, by requiring a separate comprehensive plan, have escaped from the confusion over the role of the comprehensive plan caused by the standard planning and zoning acts. In these jurisdictions, a zoning challenge does not draw the courts into a process of 'discovering' a comprehensive plan inside a general zoning ordinance. As a result, in these states the comprehensive plan is the 'constitution' for the jurisdiction's land use regulations. The legal principle for implementing this recently accepted status for comprehensive plans is the consistency requirement.

The scope of the *consistency doctrine* today is wide, and a number of different forms of the requirement have evolved. As noted above, consistency refers to the relationship between a comprehensive plan and its implementing measures. Not only does this mean that the plan and the regulations promulgated under it must be consistent, it also means, in a growing number of jurisdictions, that any development orders and permits issued must be consistent with the local plan. From a practical standpoint, consistency between a plan and its implementation is probably the most important type of consistency. It is on this basis that the bulk of inconsistency challenges are mounted.

The consistency requirement is also relevant to the implementation of *state comprehensive plans* which are of recent origin and new found importance in the United States.

In 1985, Florida became one of the few states to have a state comprehensive plan, and the only state other than Hawaii with a state comprehensive plan adopted as a statute.[45] By the mid 1990s Florida's growth management programme reached a high level of comprehensiveness and maturity vis-à-vis that of most other states.

The Florida system is often encapsulated in the term 'top-down' consistency and concurrency based comprehensive planning. In essence, the system requires all land development permits to comply with concurrency and consistency requirements. The consistency requirement is especially broad since it means that land development permits must be consistent not only with the mandated local government comprehensive plan, but that the plan must be consistent with regional policy plans and the local and regional plans must be consistent with the state comprehensive plan. In addition, development per-

---

44. *Charles M. Haar:* 'The Master Plan: An Impermanent Constitution', in Law and Contemporary Problems, Vol. 20(3), 1955 p. 367.
45. Laws of Florida Ch. 85–57, codified as Fla. Stat. Ch. 187.

mits for projects in areas of critical state concern or of a type or magnitude which is deemed to be of regional importance are subject to additional procedures designed to recognize state and regional – and not just local – interests and concerns.

Hawaii also has a strong tradition of state-wide land use management. In 1961, only two years after becoming one of the United States, Hawaii passed the nation's first comprehensive state-wide land use classification and regulation, i.e. zoning, system.[46]

Oregon is another state with a state comprehensive plan. In 1973 Oregon's legislature passed the Oregon Land Use Act, which required mandatory local comprehensive planning, mandated state review of local plans, required enforcement of plans, and set up an appeals system.[47] Additionally, this Act created the Land Conservation and Development Commission (LCDC), which is required to determine whether locally prepared plans are consistent with the state's planning goals. The LCDC has adopted 19 goals and guidelines for planning.

### 6.2. Coastal Zone Planning and Management

The National Coastal Zone Management Act of 1972 (CZMA)[48] was the United States' first real attempt to develop a comprehensive coastal zone protection plan. Previously, shoreline regulation had been historically a local concern. However, with the increasing economic and political importance of coastal resources (e.g. offshore petroleum drilling) came a more national outlook on shoreline regulation. The competition for these resources led to federal/state disputes over revenue collection and jurisdictional issues. The CZMA was a congressional response, attempting to diffuse the growing tension between the federal government and the states on these resource management problems. The CZMA thus relies on federal/state cooperation and funding.

The CZMA has a two-tiered process whereby states gain federal financial assistance for coastal zone protection by: (1) developing a comprehensive,

---

46. *Michael McPherson:* 'Vanishing Sands: Comprehensive Planning and The Public Interest In Hawaii', in Ecology Law Quarterly, Vol. 18, 1991 p. 779.
47. *Gerrit Knaap* & *Arthur C. Nelson:* The Regulated Landscape: Lessons on State Land Use Planning from Oregon, 1992 Ch. 1.
48. 16 US Code Annotated S. 1451 et seq. For general discussions of the Act, see The Coastal Zone Management Program, available at www.ocrm.nos.noaa.gov; and *John A. Duff:* 'The Coastal Zone Management Act: Reverse Pre-emption or Contractual Federalism?', in Ocean and Coastal Law Journal, Vol. 6, 2001 p. 109.

long-range coastal management plan meeting federal statutory criteria; and (2) getting approval for that plan followed by state implementation.[49] States which comply with the Act's statutory coastal management programme are granted matching funding from the federal government. By 1990, most of the country's thirty-five coastal states and territories had passed measures to protect coastal areas and, to date, thirty-three states have CZMA-approved programmes.[50] These states and territories make up ninety per cent of the nation's coastline, including the Great Lakes. The range of coastal management plans may vary from one state or one plan to another. Generally, inland areas as well as parts of the territorial sea are included in the plans. The delimitation should be defined more precisely in each plan.

Congress intended that there should be diversity in state coastal management programmes, reflecting individual state concerns. However, while the structure and scope of coastal zone management programmes do vary widely from state to state, each state plan must comply with certain minimum requirements.[51] Perhaps most importantly, each state programme must have meaningful coordination mechanisms with local governments, and must designate a specific state agency to administer the programme.[52] Further, states with approved programmes are given 'federal consistency' authority which assures that federal actions are consistent with state coastal management programmes.[53]

The consistency provision was amended in 1990[54] ensuring that all federal activities affecting the coastal zone, whether taking place in or out of the zone, are covered by the consistency provisions.[55] At the same time, Congress amended the Act to address the problem of coastal 'non-point source

49. *Natural Resource Defense Council:* Land Use Controls in the United States, 1977 Chapter 6, beginning on page 98, is a comprehensive and readable discussion of the history and policies of the Coastal Zone Management Act.
50. See The Coastal Zone Management Program, www.ocm.nos.naaa.gov.
51. See 16 US Code Annotated S. 1455(d)(2).
52. See H.R.Rep.No 97-628, 97th Cong., 2d Sess. 24 (1982).
53. 16 US Code Annotated S. 1456(c).
54. The Coastal Zone Act Reauthorization Amendments (CZARA), see Pub. L. No 101-508 §§ 6203, 6208(a), 104 Stat. 1388 (1990). See California ex rel. *California Coastal Com'n* v *Norton*, 150 F.Supp.2d 1946 (N.D.Cal.2001).
55. See *Jack Archer:* 'Evolution of Major 1990 CZMA Amendments: Restoring Federal Consistency and Protection of Coastal Water Quality', in Territorial Sea Journal, Vol. 1, 1991 p. 191; and *Linda A. Malone:* 'The Coastal Zone Management Act and the Takings Clause in the 1990's: Making the Case for Federal Land Use to Preserve Coastal Areas', in University of Colorado Law Review, Vol. 60, 1991 p. 711.

pollution'.[56] This amendment required states with an approved coastal management programme to 'develop and implement management measures for non-point source pollution to restore and protect coastal waters, working in close conjunction with other State or local authorities.'[57] These State Coastal Non-point Pollution Control Programs were to comply with certain minimum requirements.[58]

To give a few examples of state rules relevant to the establishment of wind farms: the Massachusetts CZM law specifies as Energy Policy #1 that 'coastally dependent energy facilities consider siting in alternative coastal locations', and energy facilities not dependent on the coast must 'consider siting in areas outside of the coastal zone.'[59] New Jersey's CZM rules state that energy facilities must not be sited in specified special areas unless it can be shown that they will have no adverse impacts on those areas. They also state, that 'The scenic and visual qualities of coastal areas shall be maintained as important resources in the siting of energy facilities.'[60] On the other hand, the same rules provide more specifically: 'The construction of electric generating facilities using renewable forms of energy such as ... wind ... is encouraged in the coastal zone provided that the facilities do not detract from scenic or recreational values.'[61] The North Carolina CZM plan includes a comprehensive section titled Coastal Energy Policies. The policies call for impact assessments and cost-benefit analyses for all major energy facilities 'to be located in or affecting any land or water use or natural resource of the North Carolina coastal area.'[62] The policies take account of scenic quality, marine and estuarine resources, wildlife, and 'areas with high biological or recreational value'. For each of these resources, the general policy is to avoid adverse effects. For example, 'Energy development shall be sited and designed to provide maximum protection of views to and along the ocean, sounds and scenic coastal areas, and to minimize the alteration of natural landforms.' Moreover, 'areas of high biological significance, including offshore reefs ... submerged aquatic vegetation beds, [and] shellfish beds' are to be avoided in the siting of energy facilities and related structures.[63]

---

56. Pub. L. No 101-508, Tit. VI; S. 6217, 104 Stat. 1388-314 to 1388-319 (1990).
57. 16 US Code S. 1455b(a)(1).
58. 16 US Code S. 1455b(b).
59. 301 Massachusetts Administrative Code, title 301, S. 21.98(9).
60. New Jersey Administrative Code title 7, S. 7E-7.4(b)(1), (b)(4).
61. New Jersey Administrative Code title 7, S. (r)(1)(v).
62. North Carolina Admin. Code title 15A, r. 7M.0403(b).
63. North Carolina Admin. Code title 15A, r. 7M.0403(e); 0403(f)(10)(A).

The Coastal Barrier Resources Act (CBRA),[64] passed in 1982, provides further federal protection for coastal zones. Coastal barriers are islands or spits consisting mainly of sand that effectively protect landward areas from direct wave action.[65] Even though development was encouraged for years by the federal government's provision of various forms of financial assistance (for example, in the form of subsidies and flood insurance), coastal barriers are particularly ill-suited for development, as they consist of unstable sediments and serve as natural storm protection buffers.[66] The CBRA's purpose is to restrict this type of federal encouragement through the termination of such assistance in undeveloped coastal barriers.[67] Generally, when an area is designated as being within the Coastal Barrier Resource System, no new federal assistance may be authorized, thus requiring any state-approved development to pay its own way.[68]

The CBRA was amended in 1990 by the Coastal Barrier Improvement Act (CBIA).[69] This tripled the area originally covered by the CBRA, and added nearly 820,000 acres to be covered. Most of the newly covered land was made up of aquatic habitats associated with the originally designated coastal barriers.

Coastal zone protection and the regulation of environmentally sensitive lands is a complicated process. Plans, acts, policies and laws at every level of government must be reviewed before coastal development is allowed. It remains to be seen whether the complex web of competing jurisdictions in the United States can achieve the desired goal of comprehensive, cohesive and consistent management.[70]

64. 16 US Code Annotated S. 3501 et seq. See *Elise Jones:* 'The Coastal Barrier Resources Act: A Common Cents Approach to Coastal Protection', in Environmental Law, Vol. 21, 1991 p. 1015.
65. 16 US Code Annotated S. 3502(1)(A). For purposes of the Act, adjacent wetlands are included in the statutory coverage. 16 US Code Annotated S. 3502(1)(B).
66. 16 US Code Annotated S. 3501(a)(3).
67. See *Alexandra D. Dawson:* Wetlands Regulation, Zoning & Planning Law Reports, Vol. 6 No. 9, 1983, at p. 154.
68. See 16 US Code Annotated S. 3503.
69. Pub. L. No 101-591, 104 stat. 2931 (1990).
70. *James G. Titus:* 'Rising Seas, Coastal Erosion, and the Takings Clause: How to Save Wetlands and Beaches without Hurting Property Owners', in Maryland Law Review, Vol. 57, 1998 p. 1279 and p. 1399. See also *Randy Lowell:* 'Private Actions and Marine and Water Resources: Protection, Recovery and Remediation', in South Carolina Environmental Law Journal, Vol. 8, 2000 p. 143 and p. 205.

Federal cutbacks and regulatory changes suggest that future coastal management and protection will continue to be more of a state and local activity. States and localities must respond to this challenge by providing the funding and expertise needed. Without this, the trend toward more localized protection and regulation has the potential to dismantle years of progress in the protection of these sensitive coastal lands.

### 6.3. Public Participation and Appeals

The US Government is not party to or a signatory to the Aarhus Convention. Still, the procedural safeguards laid down in US laws at federal and state level protect more than individual interests.

Comprehensive planning decisions by local government are legislative in nature. The Standard State Zoning Enabling Act had no provisions for reviewing legislative decisions or procedures for challenging the constitutionality of zoning ordinances. Only a few states provide special procedures for reviewing local legislative decisions. In the absence of statutory provisions, parties usually obtain review of such decisions through a *de novo* action for injunctive relief or a declaratory judgment.[71] Provisions for judicial review vary from state to state – as does the status of administrative bodies. Zoning and planning boards of different states in the US may or may not be included in the provisions of state administrative acts for judicial review of administrative decisions.

To bring an action before the courts one must have standing, and the rules on standing may differ depending on the different kinds of action. The courts have evolved essentially consistent rules on the standing issue for several different classes of litigants: those with an interest in the property that is the subject of the dispute, neighbours, taxpayers, competitors, citizens associations, local governments, and extra-territorial litigants. A citizen with no particular interest is unlikely to have standing.[72]

Several federal laws, e.g. the Administrative Procedure Act, the National Environmental Policy Act, the Clean Water Act and the Emergency Planning and Community Right-to-Know Act – impose obligations to actively disseminate information on the environment.[73] With regard to participation in

---

71. *Julian C. Juergensmeyer & Thomas E. Roberts:* Land Use Planning and Development Regulation Law, 2003 p. 260.
72. *Julian C. Juergensmeyer & Thomas E. Roberts:* Land Use Planning and Development Regulation Law, 2003 p. 264.
73. *John E. Bonine, Susan Casey-Lefkowitz, Claudia Saladin & Jennifer Gleason:* Country Report on Public Participation, United States of America. Prepared for the 4th Pan-

the decision-making process, the constitutional guarantee of 'due process of law' is first and foremost of benefit to developers who claim that environmental regulation is taking away their rights. The due process clauses are often of little value to citizens and non-governmental organizations who claim that the granting of a permit is against the law.[74] Under the Administrative Procedure Act, an agency must publish notice of a proposed rule in the Federal Register. Agencies usually have a discreet number of non-governmental organizations and industrial groups that are interested in their activities. They, therefore, typically send notice to such organizations.[75]

## 7. New Zealand Planning Law – by *David Grinlinton*

The Resource Management Act 1991 (RMA) is the primary planning legislation in New Zealand. The Act attempts to integrate into one statute the law relating to the management of land, air and water[76] under the overarching purpose of 'sustainable management of natural and physical resources'.[77]

### 7.1. The RMA – Background and Regulatory Structure
In the late 1980s New Zealand embarked on a comprehensive environmental reform process resulting in a number of institutional and legal reforms including:

- Establishment of a Ministry for the Environment, with broad policy-making, advisory and monitoring roles;
- Establishment of a Parliamentary Commissioner for the Environment (often referred to as the 'Environmental Ombudsman');

European Environmental Ministers Conference, Aarhus, Denmark, 23-25 June 1998, p. 12.

74. *John E. Bonine, Susan Casey-Lefkowitz, Claudia Saladin & Jennifer Gleason:* Country Report on Public Participation, United States of America. Prepared for the 4th Pan-European Environmental Ministers Conference, Aarhus, Denmark, 23-25 June 1998 p. 20.
75. *John E. Bonine, Susan Casey-Lefkowitz, Claudia Saladin & Jennifer Gleason:* Country Report on Public Participation, United States of America. Prepared for the 4th Pan-European Environmental Ministers Conference, Aarhus, Denmark, 23-25 June 1998, p. 22-24.
76. Resource Management Act 1991 (NZ), Preamble.
77. Resource Management Act 1991 (NZ), S. 5.

- Establishment of a Department of Conservation, with a statutory mandate to manage New Zealand's 'conservation estate';[78]
- Extensive reform and rationalization of local government responsibilities for the environment;[79] and
- Rationalization and reform of the environmental and planning legislation culminating in the passage of the RMA in 1991.

These reforms were strongly influenced by the principles of *sustainability* and the *precautionary approach* which were reflected in the new policies, legislation and decision-making processes governing land and resource use.[80]

The RMA[81] provides a policy-making, planning, decision-making and enforcement regime governing the use of land, water and air in New Zealand, including up to the limits of the 12 mile territorial sea.

The RMA has as its central purpose '[the promotion of] the sustainable management[82] of natural and physical resources' (Section 5(1)). The 'sus-

---

78. Conservation Act 1987 (NZ). The 'conservation estate' comprises approximately 30 % of New Zealand's total area and includes unalienated Crown land, reserves, parks, most of the coastline, and other publicly owned land.

79. See *Kenneth Palmer:* Local Government Law in New Zealand, 1993 pp. 564-568; and *David Grinlinton:* 'Contemporary Environmental Law in New Zealand', in *Klaus Bosselmann & David Grinlinton* (eds.): Environmental Law for a Sustainable Society, 2002 pp. 19-20. Regional government is the middle level of government comprising 12 regional councils covering the entire country. City and District councils comprise some 72 municipalities.

80. For a full account of the reform process, see *David Grinlinton:* 'Natural Resources Law Reform in New Zealand – Integrating Law, Policy and Sustainability', in Australasian Journal of Natural Resources Law and Policy, Vol. 2, 1995 pp. 14-23. See also *David Grinlinton:* 'Contemporary Environmental Law in New Zealand', in *Klaus Bosselmann & David Grinlinton* (eds.): Environmental Law for a Sustainable Society, 2002 pp. 19-46.

81. On the Resource Management Act generally, see *Kenneth Palmer:* 'Resource Management Act 1991', in *Derek Nolan* (ed.): Environmental and Resource Management Law, 2005 Ch. 3.

82. 'Sustainable management', is defined in Section 5(2) of the Resource Management Act as follows:
'(2) In this Act, "sustainable management" means managing the use, development, and protection of natural and physical resources in a way, or at a rate, which enables people and communities to provide for their social, economic, and cultural wellbeing and for their health and safety while –
(a) Sustaining the potential of natural and physical resources (excluding minerals) to meet the reasonably foreseeable needs of future generations; and
(b) Safeguarding the life-supporting capacity of air, water, soil, and ecosystems; and

tainable management' purpose provides a 'core' unifying principle by which all environmental and resource management policy-making, planning and decision-making is to be guided.

Under the RMA, strategic planning and operational management of land, air and water is largely devolved to regional councils and municipal authorities (city & district councils). Regional councils have primary responsibility for managing water use and discharges into water, and uses of land which have regional significance. City and district councils (several within each region) have primary responsibility for land use and subdivision, air use and discharges of local significance.

Coastal management policy is primarily the responsibility of central government through the Department of Conservation, with some management of the coastal area delegated to regional councils.

Use of land, air and water is controlled both through the general provisions in the RMA itself, and through a hierarchical system of policies and planning instruments administered by central government agencies, by regional councils, and by municipal authorities.

At the central government level, the Minister of Conservation is required to prepare a *New Zealand Coastal Policy Statement* for management of the coastal environment of New Zealand. Similarly the Minister for the Environment may prepare *National Policy Statements* (NPSs) and *National Environmental Standards* (NESs) on matters of national importance.

Regional councils must prepare *Regional Policy Statements* setting out policies and methods for achieving integrated management of the natural and physical resources of the region. Councils must also prepare *Regional Coastal Plans* for managing the coastal area in conjunction with the Minister of Conservation, and other *Regional Land Use Plans*. As with *Regional Policy Statements*, *Regional Plans* must not be inconsistent with higher level central government policy and planning instruments, or with the *Regional Policy Statement* or other *Regional Plans*.

City and district councils must prepare *District Plans*, mainly to control the effects of land use, e.g. the construction of wind farms. Again, these are vertically integrated as they must not be inconsistent with higher-level policy and planning instruments.

(c) Avoiding, remedying, or mitigating any adverse effects of activities on the environment'.

Horizontal integration is also provided for at both the regional and municipal levels, as Regional and District/City Councils must have regard to neighbouring policies and plans when preparing their own policies and plans.

Strategic environmental assessment of policies and plans is required by their initiators. This involves assessment of the costs and benefits, and alternatives to the proposed policy or plan.[83]

### 7.2. Applying the Regulatory Structure to Wind Energy Development

The RMA itself contains a number of sections that promote renewable energy. On the central purpose of sustainable management, Section 5 of the RMA contains specific reference to promoting resource use efficiency, intergenerational equity, and the protection of the 'life supporting capacity of air, water, soil and ecosystems'. Implicitly these elements have been taken as favouring renewable energy proposals even where such proposals will have some negative effects on other environmental and amenity values.[84] In addition to Section 5, Section 6 of the RMA sets out a number of matters of national importance that must be recognized and provided for in achieving the purpose of the Act. They include matters such as the protection of the natural character of the coastal environment, and the protection of outstanding natural features and landscapes from 'inappropriate' development. However, in recent decisions the courts have stated that more localized landscape and amenity effects will often be subordinate to national and global considerations implicit in the overarching principle of sustainable management contained in Section 5, thus favouring wind energy proposals.[85]

---

83. Resource Management Act, S. 32. See also Chapter 7, section 7.2.
84. See, e.g. *Genesis Power* v *Franklin District Council* [2005] NZRMA 541, at para. 228; *Unison Networks* v *Hastings District Council*, unreported, Environment Court W58/2006, 17 July 2006, para. 82; *Meridian Energy Ltd* v *Wellington City Council*, unreported, Environment Court W31/07, 14 May 2007, para. 448. However, see *Outstanding Landscape Protection Society* v *Hastings District Council*, unreported, Environment Court W24.07, 13 April 2007, especially paras. 115-118, where the Court concluded that the proposed extension to an existing wind farm development did not promote the sustainable management purpose of the Resource Management Act, and indeed local adverse effects outweighed the benefits of renewable energy. See Appendix III for descriptions of, e.g. the *Genesis Power* and the *Unison Networks* cases.
85. *Genesis Power* v *Franklin District Council* [2005] NZRMA 541, paras. 213-219; *Unison Networks* v *Hastings District Council*, unreported, Environment Court W58/2006, 17 July 2006, paras. 75-79; and *Meridian Energy* v *Wellington City Council*, unreported, Environment Court W31/07, 14 May 2007, paras. 447-459.

Further, in Section 7, the RMA requires decision-makers to have particular regard to:

(b)   the efficient use of natural and physical resources; and
(ba)  the efficiency of the end use of energy;
     the effects of climate change; and
     the benefits to be derived from the use and development of renewable energy.

Again these sections have been interpreted as favouring wind energy projects ahead of other land uses.[86]

In terms of higher-level policy, the New Zealand government recently released a draft "Energy Strategy" to 2050.[87] This document, once in final form, will provide a statement of government policy strongly supportive of the development of renewable energy projects, including wind energy. This policy supports the promulgation of NPSs and/or NESs as a means of providing national guidance and encouragement for wind energy development. Once these national level policy instruments and standards are in place, they will provide guidance for *Regional Policy Statements* which will be expected to incorporate similar policies and objectives as such *Statements* are 'not to be inconsistent with' higher level NPSs and NESs. *Regional* and *District Plans* may then be expected to incorporate specific objectives and rules aimed at encouraging development of wind energy projects as such *Plans* are, in turn, 'not to be inconsistent with' the higher level NPSs, NESs and *Regional Policy Statements*.

### 7.3. RMA Resource (Planning) Consents and Decision-making

*Regional* and *District Plans* contain rules. These rules may allow certain permitted activities that do not require formal approval; they may prohibit certain activities absolutely (prohibited activities); and in between these two extremes, they may set out a range of activities that require resource con-

---

86.  *Genesis Power* v *Franklin District Council* [2005] NZRMA 541; paras. 220-224, *Unison Networks* v *Hastings District Council*; unreported, Environment Court W58/2006, 17 July 2006, para. 74; and *Meridian Energy* v *Wellington City Council*, unreported, Environment Court W31/07, 14 May 2007, para. 582.

87.  *Ministry of Economic Development, NZ Govt:* Powering Our Future – Towards a Sustainable Low Emissions Energy System, Dec 2006, www.med.govt.nz/templates/MultipageDocumentTOC__24480.aspx. See also Chapter 10, section 7.1.

sent(s)[88] from the council. Activities that require consent may be allowed by the *Plan*, provided they comply with certain specific criteria (for example, 'controlled' and 'restricted discretionary activities'), or the *Plan* may provide for a higher level of discretionary decision-making on the part of the consenting authority, depending on the nature of the activity ('discretionary activities' or 'non-complying activities').

Only when publicly notified, hearings for applications are open to objections and submissions by any person without any need for *locus standi* ('standing').[89] Appeals may be brought before the Environment Court[90] by any party. Further appeals may be made to the ordinary courts on points of law; see below section 7.5.

Permits will often be required from a number of different consenting authorities. The standardized application, hearing and appeal procedures in the RMA for resource consent applications apply to all consent authorities. Further integration is found in the provisions for joint hearings where two or more consent authorities are involved, or where two or more applications are made in relation to the same proposal.[91] In this way the cumulative and 'cocktail' effects of proposed activities can be considered and decided together and appropriate conditions imposed.

As well as the strategic environmental assessment required when preparing policies and plans, the RMA requires that applications for resource consents must generally be accompanied by an 'assessment of environmental effects' (AEE)[92] and further information may be required by a consent authority;[93] see Chapter 7, section 7.

---

88. 'Resource consent' is a generic term which includes traditional planning permissions such as land use consents and subdivision consents, and also water permits, coastal permits and discharge permits under the Resource Management Act: SS. 2 and 87.
89. Traditionally under the common law, 'standing' requires a litigant to have a property interest or some special interest greater than that of the general community.
90. The Environment Court is a specialist judicial body set up to arbitrate and adjudicate on environmental disputes.
91. Resource Management Act, SS. 102 and 103. For example, a development may require water and discharge permits from the regional council, and a land use permit from the territorial authority. See also S. 269 (hearing matters together in the Environment Court).
92. Resource Management Act, S. 88(2)(b) and Fourth Schedule (lists matters that should be considered or included in an AEE – most are not mandatory).
93. Resource Management Act, S. 92.

### 7.4. Applying the RMA Decision-making Process to Wind Energy Development

A wind energy proposal may require a number of different resource consents; for example:

- permits from the regional council where there is significant land alteration of regional significance;
- land use permits from the district or city council for man-made structures, transmission lines and access roads;
- water use and possibly discharge permits where there is water diversion or concentration through clearance, profiling, tree and bush removal;
- Department of Conservation approval if there is a significant effect on wildlife and natural habitat; and
- coastal permits from the Department of Conservation and/or regional council if the proposed offshore construction is within the coastal marine area.[94]

The resource consent applications will be considered by the consent authority in the first instance, or a hearing committee if more than one consent authority is involved. The decision-makers will be guided by the legislative aims and principles, by any relevant policies, and by the specific rules in the relevant planning instruments.

Currently some *Regional Policy Statements* do contain polices broadly encouraging development of renewable energy, and some *Plans* contain objectives and aims indicating similar support. But more commonly, wind energy developments are treated as industrial activities in rural zones, and are subject to discretionary decision-making by the relevant council.

As illustrated by the *Genesis*, *Unison* and *Meridian* decisions, the consent authority will balance the competing statutory and policy considerations, including negative environmental and amenity effects, and the broader national and international considerations favouring sustainable energy development,

---

94. The outer limit of the Coastal Marine Area is the 12 mile territorial sea limit. Offshore wind farms beyond the 12 mile limit would be subject to, *inter alia*, the offshore regime under the Territorial Sea, Contiguous Zone, and Exclusive Economic Zone Act 1977, the Continental Shelf Act 1964, and the Maritime Transport Act 1994.

and will exercise their discretion accordingly.[95] Currently, consent authorities appear to be leaning strongly in favour of wind energy development.

### 7.5. Public Participation and Appeals

Generally there is open participation by the general public in hearings of publicly notified resource consent applications. Objectors or those who submit views at the consent authority hearing have the right to appeal, or participate in any appeal. For such appeals, New Zealand has established a specialist Environment Court. Environment Court judges are fully sworn judicial officers, but with particular expertise in environmental and planning matters. Often the judge will sit with two environment commissioners, who may be specialist planners, scientists, or have other non-legal expertise. The Environment Court has the power to hear appeals from consent authorities *de novo*, allowing the merits and legal arguments to be argued fully and be determined afresh by the Court, although in practice appeals are usually restricted to specific matters in dispute.

There are opportunities for pre-hearing meetings, conferences and other means of alternative dispute resolution. In particular, the Environment Court can direct the parties to take part in mediation or conciliation, and often the judge or an environment commissioner will take the role of mediator.

Driven by a desire for more open participation in planning and resource use decision-making, the RMA dispensed with the traditional *locus standi* ('standing') requirements for submissions and objections relating to the preparation of policies and plans, or publicly notified applications for resource consents.[96] This reversed the pre-existing situation where those making submissions or objectors to town plans or planning permissions had to have a property right or other special interest that was affected. However, if the consent authority decides not to publicly notify a consent application, there will be no open participation. The only recourse then is to seek judicial review of the decision not to notify. Judicial review requires the applicant for review to show that they are likely to suffer damage to a significantly greater degree than other members of the community, thus effectively reinstating the *locus standi* rule and making it difficult for public interest litigants to challenge proposals. Recent figures indicate that approximately 95 per cent of re-

---

95. See also the fuller discussion by Prof. Barry Barton in Chapter 10, section 7 and in Appendix III.
96. Traditionally objectors have needed some property right or special interest to be able to participate in hearings and appeals.

source consent applications are not notified and therefore in such cases 'open participation' is somewhat of a myth.[97]

Any person who has made a submission also has the right to appeal to the Environment Court, and to the High Court on a question of law. Further, in general any person can apply for a declaration or an enforcement order, and can lay an information for prosecution of the most serious offences under the Act.

There are a number of provisions in the RMA which are aimed at the protection of the interests of Maori, the indigenous people of New Zealand. These provisions ensure that Maori are consulted and have input in relation to any activities that may affect their traditional lands or sacred places. This requirement for consultation applies to the government and local authorities in preparing policies and plans, and in deciding resource consent applications. There are often conflicts between Maori and developers where Maori land or cultural heritage is affected by a proposed development. Maori issues have been considered in a number of recent wind energy decisions and appeals.[98]

### 7.6. Enforcement Mechanisms and Criminal Offences

The RMA contains a comprehensive enforcement regime incorporating both civil enforcement mechanisms, such as enforcement orders and abatement notices, as well as criminal sanctions where prosecution may result in severe financial penalties or even imprisonment. Compared with pre-existing enforcement regimes the RMA provides a graduated range of measures for breach of the duties and responsibilities in the Act itself, of a rule in a plan, or a condition in a resource consent. These measures are generally available to any person and carry a standard range of penalties tailored to different levels of seriousness of the breach.

The maximum penalties that can be imposed for the most serious environmental offences, are up to NZ$ 200,000 for an offence, up to and

---

97. For discussion of this issue, see *David Grinlinton:* 'Access to Environmental Justice in New Zealand', in Acta Juridica, 1999 p. 80.
98. See, e.g. *Genesis Power* v *Franklin District Council* [2005] NZRMA 541, paras. 171-202, 212(v) and 227; *Unison Networks* v *Hastings District Council*, unreported, Environment Court W58/2006, 17 July 2006, paras. 63-68 and 73; *Meridian Energy* v *Wellington City Council*, unreported, Environment Court W31/07, 14 May 2007, para. 367. But see *Outstanding Landscape Protection Society* v *Hastings District Council,* unreported, Environment Court W24.07, 13 April 2007, especially paras. 68-85, 111, 113, and 116, where the impact of the proposal on Maori and cultural interests featured strongly in the Court's decision to reject an extension to an existing wind farm.

NZ$ 10,000 per day for a continuing offence, and up to 2 years imprisonment. To date, fines for offences by corporations and individuals have ranged from NZ$ 10,000 to NZ$ 70,000, and there have only been three instances of the court imposing a prison sentence.[99] There is also the option to impose a sentence of community service, and this was applied in *Smith* v *Auckland City Council*[100] where Smith was sentenced to six months community service for chopping down a historically significant protected tree as a political protest.

The enforcement regime also provides for strict liability for the most serious offences, including corporate liability, and vicarious liability for officers and those involved in the management of corporations that commit offences.[101]

99. In *Franklin District Council* v *McCollum*, unreported, District Court, CRN 3057005960, 14 February 1994, a pig farmer was convicted, fined NZ$5,000 and sentenced to 6 months imprisonment for allowing pollution, but the sentence was suspended; in *R* v *Borrett* [2004] NZRMA 248 the Court of Appeal upheld a sentence of 3 months imprisonment for the construction of an illegal earthworks and the removal of protected native vegetation; and in *R* v *Conway* [2005] NZRMA 274 the Court of Appeal upheld a sentence of 3 months imprisonment for pollution of waterways with oil and fuel. In all cases the offences were at the serious end of the spectrum and involved almost complete disregard for the law.
100. [1996] NZRMA 27 (upheld by Court of Appeal in [1996] NZRMA 276).
101. For a detailed analysis of the enforcement regime, see *Janette Campbell:* 'Statutory remedies: the enforcement provisions of the RMA', in *Derek Nolan* (ed.): Environmental and Resource Management Law, 2005 Ch. 18.

# CHAPTER 7

# Environmental Assessment Procedures

## 1. Introduction – by *Helle Tegner Anker*

Environmental impact assessment (EIA) and strategic environmental assessment (SEA) procedures are important environmental law instruments aimed at providing a better basis for decision-making at project and planning level respectively. This is reflected at international as well as at EU level in the Espoo Convention, the Aarhus Convention and in the EIA and SEA Directives. Environmental impact assessment requirements at project or plan level may be integrated into different parts of environmental or sectoral legislation or may be the subject of separate legislation in themselves. This section focuses on the specific rules relevant to the establishment of wind farms either on land or offshore.

## 2. International Law on EIA and SEA – by *Helle Tegner Anker*

The need to identify and assess the environmental impact of new projects or plans prior to making a decision on such projects or plans has been emphasized in several international documents. The *Brundtland Report* emphasized the integration of economic and ecological considerations in decision-making, i.e. environmental impact assessments, as an important element in securing sustainable development.[1] This was followed by Principle 17 of the *Rio Declaration* stating that 'environmental impact assessment, as a national instrument, shall be undertaken for proposed activities that are likely to have a significant adverse impact on the environment and are subject to a decision

---

1.   The World Commission on Environment and Development: Our Common Future, 1987 pp. 62-65. Prior environmental assessment was included in the proposed legal principles for environmental protection and sustainable development by the World Commission on Environment and Development (WCED) Experts Group on Environmental Law, see Annex I to the Brundtland Report.

of a competent national authority'. The use of environmental assessment was further elaborated in Agenda 21, calling for integration of environmental and development considerations at plan, policy and management levels. More specific international law requirements for EIA and SEA can be found in horizontal instruments such as the Espoo Convention (EIA Convention) as well as in conventions etc. addressing specific environmental issues, such as Article 14 of the Biodiversity Convention.

The 1991 *Convention on Environmental Impact Assessment in a Transboundary Context* (Espoo Convention) was signed under the auspices of the UN Economic Commission for Europe (UNECE). The Convention has been ratified by 37 states, including Denmark and Norway, and entered into force on 10 September 1997. The USA was a signatory to the Convention but has not ratified it.[2]

The Espoo Convention addresses in particular the transboundary effects of certain activities. However, the Convention indirectly establishes a more general framework for national legislation. The Convention stipulates that environmental impact assessments should, as a minimum, be undertaken at the project level of a proposed activity. However, the Parties shall endeavour to apply the principles of environmental impact assessment to policies, plans and programmes as well; see Article 2(7). The need for strategic environmental assessment has further been elaborated in the *Protocol on Strategic Environmental Assessment* (agreed under the auspices of UNECE in Kiev in 2003 – 'the SEA Protocol') requiring SEA for certain plans and programmes.

In its Appendix I, the Espoo Convention lists projects for which an EIA is mandatory in so far as the project is likely to cause significant transboundary impact; see Articles 2(2) and 2(3). Appendix I includes, since the 2004 amendment, 'major installations for the harnessing of wind power for energy production (wind farms)'.[3] In addition, projects other than those listed in Appendix I should, on the agreement of affected Parties, be subject to an EIA if they are likely to cause a significant adverse transboundary impact; see Article 2(5). Appendix III lays down general criteria to assist in the determination of the environmental significance of non-Appendix I projects, including the size, location and effects of the project. If an EIA is needed, the assessment and documentation requirements in Appendix II should be complied with, in-

---

2. Unlike the USA and Canada, New Zealand is not a member of UNECE and is not a signatory to the Convention.
3. However, the 2004 amendment is not yet in force as of June 2008, see www.unece.org/env/eia/amend2ratif.html for ratification status.

cluding a description of the no-action alternative, mitigation measures and, where appropriate, an outline for monitoring and managing programmes.

The Convention establishes *notification and consultation procedures* involving the authorities as well as the general public of states that may be affected by the activity in question. According to Article 2(6), the Party of origin must provide an opportunity for the public in areas likely to be affected to participate and shall ensure that the opportunity provided to the public of the affected Party is equivalent to that provided to the public of the Party of origin.[4] The Party of origin has an obligation to notify any potentially affected Parties of the proposed activity. If a potentially affected Party does not intend to participate in the EIA procedure, or does not respond within the time specified, the specific inter-state consultation provisions will not apply. The consultation procedure set out in Article 5 implies that the involved Parties shall discuss the results of the EIA documentation. The outcome of the consultation, as well as other comments received, should be reflected in the final decision; see Article 6. At the request of any Party it will be determined whether a post-project analysis should be carried out; see Article 7.

The *SEA Protocol* which has not yet entered into force by June 2008[5] sets out a requirement for strategic environmental assessment of certain plans and programmes that are likely to have a significant effect on the environment; see Article 4(1). The Protocol expressly stipulates that health effects should also be taken into consideration. It appears that the obligations of the SEA Protocol are more general in nature than the EIA requirements of the Espoo Convention which focuses on projects with a potential transboundary effect.

The SEA Protocol lays down a general SEA requirement for plans and programmes – sectoral as well as land use plans – which set the framework for development consent for projects listed in Annex I or Annex II; see Article 4(2). Plans or programmes setting the framework for Annex II projects need an SEA if an EIA is required under national legislation. Annex II includes 'installations for the harnessing of wind power for energy production (wind farms)'. Plans or programmes setting the framework for other projects may be subject to an SEA requirement if they are likely to have significant environmental effects, including health effects; see Articles 4(3) and 5. Plans or programmes which determine the use of small areas at local level are only subject to SEA requirements if they may have a significant effect on the environment.

4. Guidance on Public Participation in Environmental Impact Assessment in a Transboundary Context has been issued by the UNECE in 2006.
5. For status of ratification see www.unece.org/env/eia/protocol_status.html.

The SEA Protocol sets out specific requirements regarding the scope and preparation of an environmental report, including public participation and consultation. Where there are potentially significant transboundary effects, specific notification and consultation requirements apply; see Article 10. The Parties must ensure that the public concerned and the environmental and health authorities of the affected Party are informed and given a possibility to put forward their opinion on the draft plan or programme and the environmental report within a reasonable period. Any comments received must be taken into account when adopting the plan or programme. The SEA Protocol also establishes a monitoring requirement; see Article 12. Finally, the Protocol encourages the Parties to ensure that environmental and health concerns are considered and integrated in the preparation of policies and legislation; see Article 13.

The Aarhus Convention (the Convention on access to information, public participation in decision-making and access to justice in environmental matters, agreed under the auspices on UNECE in 1998) indirectly addresses EIA and SEA through the general requirements for public participation, in particular with respect to projects in Article 6 and to some extent with respect to plans and programmes in Article 7. The Aarhus Convention aims at ensuring early, timely and effective participation and at ensuring that in decisions due account is taken of the results of public participation.[6]

## 3. EU Law on EIA and SEA – by *Helle Tegner Anker and Birgitte Egelund Olsen*

Environmental impact assessment and strategic environmental assessment have formed an important part of EU environmental law since the adoption of the EIA Directive[7] in 1985 and the SEA Directive[8] in 2001. The importance of the EIA and the SEA Directives lies in their ability to draw attention to environmental impacts in decision making and to ensure consideration of how such impacts may be reduced. Both Directives contain procedural mechanisms. Although they are intended to prevent environmental harm, there is

---

6. On the Aarhus Convention see Chapter 5, section 3.3.
7. Council Directive 85/337/EEC on the assessment of the effects of certain public and private projects on the environment, as amended by Directive 97/11/EC and Directive 2003/35/EC.
8. Directive 2001/42/EC of the European Parliament and of the Council on the assessment of the effects of certain plans and programs on the environment.

nothing in the Directives that requires decision-makers to reject a project or plan because of negative environmental impacts that may have been identified by the environmental assessment. Neither the EIA Directive nor the SEA Directive distinguish between land-based and sea-based activities, and they cover both types of activities.

## 3.1. The EIA Directive

The EIA Directive requires the competent national authority to carry out an assessment of projects which have a physical effect on the environment before approval can be granted for certain public and private projects. The EIA Directive was adopted in 1985 after many years of negotiations.[9] It was substantially amended in 1999 and again in 2003 in order to align its provisions with those of the Aarhus Convention.

The Directive lists the projects concerned, the information to be provided and the third parties to be consulted in connection with approving such a project. Accordingly, specific procedural requirements are laid down for assessment, such as the requirement for developers to provide information on the project and its likely impact, the participation of administrative bodies dealing with nature protection and environmental protection, the possibility for the public concerned to express an opinion, and the consultation of other Member States if the project is likely to have transboundary effects.

The EIA Directive distinguishes between Annex I projects for which an EIA is mandatory, and Annex II projects which on the basis of an individual screening or in accordance with thresholds established by the Member States require a full EIA; see Article 4 of the Directive. However, all projects that are likely to have a significant impact on the environment should be subject to an EIA; see Article 2 of the Directive.

Wind power installations are listed in Annex II to the EIA directive.[10] An impact assessment of Annex II projects has to be carried out if the project is likely to have significant effects, given the characteristics, nature, size and location of the project. The assessment should cover the cumulative impact of the proposed project.[11] Member States have a certain amount of discretion in

---

9. On the negotiations on the EIA Directive and the objections primarily by the UK and the Danish governments, see *William Sheate:* Environmental Impact Assessment: Law and Policy – Making an Impact II, 1996 pp. 18-22.
10. Annex II, Section 3. Energy Industry, subsection (i) Installations for the harnessing of wind power for energy production (wind farms).
11. See Case C-392/96, *Commission* v *Ireland*. See also the EU Commission's answer to the written question of Laura González Álvarez, E-0550/03.

deciding whether a project has such a significant impact or not. However the scope of discretion has been narrowed considerably by the decisions of the European Court of Justice (ECJ). According to the case law an impact assessment has to be carried out on any project that is likely to have a significant impact on the environment.[12] So far, no ECJ decision has directly involved the question of when wind turbines are or are not likely to have a significant impact on the environment.[13]

### 3.2. The SEA Directive

The SEA Directive introduces a system of prior environmental assessment at the planning stage.[14] The Directive applies to plans and programmes likely to have significant effects on the environment, as well as to their modifications. The plans and programmes must be required by legislative, regulatory or administrative provisions. As regards wind farms, environmental assessment is automatically required for plans and programmes which provide the framework for subsequent consent for specific projects listed in Annexes I and II to the EIA Directive. The Directive thus covers plans for the future development of wind farms. For plans and programmes which involve minor amendments to existing plans and programmes or only involves smaller areas at local level an assessment is only necessary when a Member States determines that the plan or programme is likely to have significant environmental effect. If, according to the criteria laid down in the Habitats Directive Article 6(3), a plan for wind power development could significantly affect an area designated according to the Habitats Directive or the Birds Directive it should be subject to an assessment according to the SEA Directive as well as to the Habitats Directive.[15]

An environmental assessment consists of the preparation of an environmental report that includes the information referred to in Annex I to the Directive.[16] It must include consultations on the environmental report and the draft plan or programme. Affected authorities should also be consulted regarding the scope of the environmental report. Opinions expressed during

---

12. Case C-435/97, *WWF*; Case C-72/95, *Kraaijeveld*; Case C-431/92, *Commission v Germany*; and Case C-392/96, *Commission v Ireland*.
13. In Case C-348/01, *Commission v French Republic*, the ECJ ruled that France had failed to fulfil its obligations under the EIA Directive by not transposing paragraph 3(i) of Annex II on wind farms into national law.
14. Directive 2001/42/EC, (OJ 2001 L 197/30).
15. Council Directive 79/409/EEC on the conservation of wild birds; and Council Directive 92/43/EEC on the conservation of natural habitats and of wild fauna and flora. See Chapter 8, section 3.1 on the Habitats Directive.
16. Article 5 of the SEA Directive.

consultations must be taken into account during the final preparation of the plan or programme and before its adoption or submission to the legislative procedure. Once a decision has been taken, the Member States are responsible for informing all the parties who have been consulted. The SEA Directive includes an obligation to monitor the effects of the plan or programme.

# 4. The Danish EIA and SEA Rules – by *Helle Tegner Anker*

In Denmark the EIA Directive has primarily been implemented in the Planning Act. Since the Planning Act only applies to land-based activities, in respect of sea-based activities the EIA Directive has been implemented in sectoral legislation. The distinction between land-based and sea-based activities is thus very important in a Danish context as regards environmental impact assessment. The SEA Directive has been implemented in a more horizontal manner through the adoption in 2004 of a new Act on the environmental assessment of plans and programmes (the SEA Act).[17] This Act applies to plans and programmes that, in accordance with the SEA Directive, set the framework for future development projects, including plans or programmes prepared for energy purposes. Accordingly, the SEA Act does not distinguish between land-based and sea-based activities.

## 4.1. EIA

The *EIA rules for land-based activities* in the Planning Act operate with mandatory Annex I projects and Annex II projects that, on the basis of an individual screening, may require a full EIA.[18] The Danish Annex I projects are more extensive than Annex I of the EIA Directive. For example, there is a mandatory EIA requirement for wind turbines above 80 metres in height and for groups of more than three turbines.[19] As Annex II projects, other wind power installations must be subjected to an individual screening, taking into account the characteristics and location of the project, including cumulation

---

17. Act No 316 of 5 May 2004 on environmental assessment of plans and programmes (*Lov om miljøvurdering af planer og programmer*).
18. For a more comprehensive description of Danish EIA rules see *Ellen Margrethe Basse:* Environmental law. Denmark, 2004 pp. 261-264; and *Helle T. Anker:* 'Planlovgivning', in *Ellen Margrethe Basse* (ed.): Miljøretten, Vol. 2, 2006 pp. 265-293.
19. Annex I point 37 of Executive Order No 1335 of 6 December 2006 on environmental assessment of certain public and private projects (*Bekendtgørelse om vurdering af visse offentlige og private anlægs virkning på miljøet* (VVM)).

with other projects. All Annex I and Annex II projects must be notified to the municipal council concerned.

If an EIA is required, either mandatorily or as a result of a screening, an assessment must be carried out and municipal planning guidelines for the project must be adopted.[20] The municipal council is normally the competent authority and is responsible for the adoption of municipal planning guidelines. However, for wind turbines of 150 metres in height or more the Ministry for the Environment is the competent authority. The municipal council or the Ministry may request the necessary information from the developer, and the competent authority publishes the final assessment in the form of a statement attached to the municipal planning guidelines. The statement must include, *inter alia*, an assessment of the relevant alternatives examined by the developer or by the authorities, including the zero option.[21] The rules for public participation and appeals follow the general rules of the Planning Act; see Chapter 6, section 4.3.

A specific EIA permit is needed if the project is not otherwise subject to an environmental permit or consent procedure. An EIA permit would normally be required for wind turbines subject to an EIA; see the Planning Act.

The relevant *EIA rules for offshore activities* primarily rely upon the Executive Order on environmental assessment of projects within the territorial sea.[22] The Executive Order directly incorporates the EIA Directive. According to this Order there is no mandatory EIA requirement for wind turbines since wind turbines are not listed in Annex I of the EIA Directive. However, a specific Executive Order lays down rules on EIA for electricity generating installations at sea, i.e. within the territorial sea and the exclusive economic zone (EEZ).[23] All wind or water based installations – including ancillary installations (cables etc.) – that may significantly affect the environment must be subjected to an EIA. A screening is carried out by the Energy Authority.

---

20. For certain major projects the Minister for the Environment is the competent authority. Until 1 January 2007 EIA was embedded in the regional planning process and was the responsibility of the regional authorities (county councils).
21. Specific guidance for EIA of land-based wind turbines has been published in 2002: Vindmøller på land. Drejebog for VVM, Ringkøbing Amt, Møller & Grønborg og Carl Bro, 2002 (Land-based Wind Turbines. EIA Guidance)
22. Executive Order No 809 of 22 August 2005 on environmental assessment of projects within the territorial sea. The Executive Order derives its legal authority from the state supremacy rule.
23. Executive Order No 815 of 28 August 2000 on EIA of offshore electricity producing installations derives its legal basis from the Electricity Supply Act Section 17, see below Chapter 10, section 4.3.

The EIA must be carried out by the developer and must be published for public comments by the Energy Authority.[24]

## 4.2. SEA

The Danish *SEA rules* in the SEA Act[25] apply to plans and programmes for land-based as well as sea-based activities that are prepared by a public authority.[26] A plan or programme which sets the framework for the future development consent of wind turbines must be subjected to an environmental assessment; see Section 3(1) of the SEA Act. However, an exemption is made for plans or programmes which only concern the use of small areas at a local level or minor modifications to plans and programmes; see Section 3(2). In such cases a screening must be carried out to determine whether the plan or programme may have a significant effect on the environment. Plans that can be subject to an environmental assessment according to the SEA Act include plans which designate wind turbine areas on land as well as offshore.[27] Following an environmental assessment, an environmental report must be prepared and made available for public consultation before the plan or programme is adopted. The relevant authority must monitor the environmental effects of the plan or programme.

## 5. Norwegian EIA and SEA Rules – by *Hans Christian Bugge*

The principle of environmental impact assessment is expressed in the environmental section of the Constitution, Article 110b. Detailed rules are spelled out in the Planning and Building Act (section 16-2 and Chapter VIIa) and in

---

24. See e.g. a recent application for a new offshore wind farm at Horns Rev filed in October 2006 with the Energy Authority together with an EIA report, see www.energistyrelsen.dk/sw41528.asp.
25. For a description of the Danish SEA rules see *Ellen Margrethe Basse:* 'Sagsbehandling og beslutningsprocesser', in *Ellen Margrethe Basse* (ed.): Miljøretten, Vol. 1, 2006 pp. 599-603.
26. Plans or programmes prepared by a private undertaking may also be subject to the SEA requirements if the Minister for the Environment so decides.
27. In 2007 an environmental assessment was carried out in connection with a report designating 7 potential offshore wind turbine areas; see *Energistyrelsen:* Fremtidens havmølleplaceringer 2025 – Udvalget for fremtidens havmølleplaceringer, 2007. (Future offshore wind turbine areas 2025 – the Committee for future wind turbine areas).

regulations pursuant to the Act.[28] These were introduced into the Act in 1989 and last revised in 2005. They now implement, through a single set of rules, both EC directives in the field: the EIA Directive and the SEA Directive. Thus, in Norwegian law, the same principles apply to impact assessments for projects and for plans and programmes. The purpose is to elucidate the effects of projects which may have a significant impact on the environment, natural resources or the community in general. The EIA/SEA must ensure that such effects are taken into account during the planning of projects and when a decision is taken pursuant to the relevant sectoral legislation as to whether, and if so on what conditions, a project may be carried out.[29]

The rules apply without exception to county plans and municipal master plans which provide guidelines or a framework for future developments. Furthermore, they apply to local development plans that may have a significant impact on the environment, natural resources or the community in general. They also apply to projects that may have significant impacts and that require a permit or licence from public authorities.

The integration of the EIA into the system for spatial and land use planning in the Planning and Building Act is based on the presumption that most projects that require an EIA will also require a land-use plan, in addition to licences and permits pursuant to sectoral legislation. At the same time, the EIA serves as a basis for decisions made pursuant to such sectoral acts. The combination of several procedures in one simplifies the system as a whole.

However, certain types of projects do not require a land use plan pursuant to the Planning and Building Act. For these, the EIA procedure is linked to the procedure for the permit or concession pursuant to a sectoral Act (Section 33-1 and Regulation Ch. III). This is the case for most energy projects such as hydropower development projects and the installation of wind turbines. The main reason for this is that the concession procedures pursuant to the Hydropower Development Act and the Energy Act are regarded as the most important, and have to be particularly thorough and transparent.

The duty to carry out an EIA lies with the developer, that is the person or company that proposes a plan or project.

The Impact Assessment Regulation defines the types of plans and projects which require an EIA. Generally, the system is in accordance with the two EC directives. The EIA is mandatory for some types of projects and conse-

28. Regulation on Impact Assessments of 1 April 2005 No 276.
29. The new Norwegian rules on EIA/SEA, and how they relate to the EU directives, have recently been analyzed in a doctoral thesis; see *Sigrid Eskeland Schütz:* Miljø-konsekvensutgreiing av planar og tiltak, 2007.

quently also for the local development plan for such projects. These are listed in Appendix I to the Regulation. The mandatory projects include major industrial projects such as oil refineries, extraction of oil and natural gas, hydropower installations with an annual production of more that 40 GWh, thermal power stations with an annual production of more than 150 MW, wind power installations with an effect of more than 10 MW, chemical, metal, and pulp and paper factories, as well as big shopping centres. They also include major infrastructure projects such as motorways and other major roads, and railways. The rules also apply to changes to or extensions of existing projects, if the change or extension itself satisfies these criteria.

For other types projects, and the plans for such projects, an EIA is required only if the plan or project has possible significant effects, based on a case-by-case assessment. In order to simplify the screening procedure the Regulation defines certain relevant criteria. The system is based on a double set of criteria, spelled out in Appendix II to the Regulation combined with section 4 of the Regulation. One set of criteria relates to the type and size of the project. The other set relates to possible environmental effects, particularly if the plan or project may have a detrimental effect on formally protected natural areas, watercourses, valuable outdoor recreation areas, agricultural areas, areas to which certain national policy guidelines pursuant to the Planning and Building Act apply, or if they may cause a significant increase of air or water pollution.

The EIA procedure has several stages. First, the developer must present a draft programme for the planning procedure which includes the assessment of significant effects. The draft is made public, and forwarded to all interested parties, including relevant authorities and organizations, for comments. The final assessment programme (scoping) is then decided by the responsible authority – either the municipality as planning authority, or the relevant sectoral authority, as designated in the Regulation. The Norwegian EIA system is based on the principle of integration, in the sense that the relevant planning authority or sectoral authority is also the responsible authority for the EIA. The environmental authorities take part in the process. If the plan or project could have important national or regional effects, the Ministry of the Environment may intervene. The Ministry of the Environment is also the responsible ministry for the management of the system as a whole, and for coordinating and developing rules and regulations.

For energy production projects and energy transmission lines the responsible sectoral authority is the state directorate – Norway's Water Resources and Energy Directorate (NVE) – regardless of whether the project is subject to a land-use plan pursuant to the Planning and Building Act or not. This reflects the prevailing situation in Norway, that energy production and provision is mainly the responsibility of the state. However, the county or municipality is the responsible authority for an EIA which is carried out as part of the general planning procedure for a county plan or municipal master plan, even if such a plan may also include areas designated for wind power installations.

The completed EIA is part of the final plan proposal or the application for a permit, which again is subject to a public hearing before the final decision is taken – either by the planning authority (normally the municipality) or the responsible sectoral authority. The EIA and the comments on it must be taken into account when the final decision is taken. The decision-making authority also has a duty to comment on the EIA and on how it has been considered in making the decision.

# 6. US Federal and State EIA and SEA Rules – by *Sanford Gaines*

## 6.1. Federal Environmental Impact Assessment – NEPA

The National Environmental Policy Act (NEPA)[30] requires, in section 102(2)(C),[31] that all government proposals for 'major federal actions significantly affecting the quality of the human environment' must include a 'detailed statement' on 5 issues:

1) the environmental impact of the proposed action;
2) unavoidable adverse environmental effects;
3) alternatives;
4) short-term uses compared with long-term environmental productivity; and
5) irreversible and irretrievable commitments of environmental resources.

Such statements have come to be called *environmental impact statements* (EISs). An EIS is subject to the public participation requirements of federal administrative law, including the opportunity for public comment and public availability of the EIS before the agency makes its decision on the action in question.

There are two important limitations to NEPA. First, it should be emphasized that NEPA only requires environmental impact statements for federal government actions. While that includes private projects that require federal

---

30. 42 US Code Annotated SS. 4321-4370a.
31. 42 US Code Annotated S. 4332(2)(C).

approval of some sort, including projects in offshore areas under federal jurisdiction, it excludes most onshore private development projects. The courts have also determined that a proposal for an action must be a specific or definite plan or decision, not a general agency policy or program.[32] Second, NEPA only requires that the agency prepare the EIS before making its decision, and that the EIS fairly and completely describes the likely environmental effects. The EIS does not control the agency's decision.[33] Nevertheless, there is the hope that merely identifying and publicizing the environmental effects will influence government agencies to reject or modify proposals that will have serious or controversial effects.

Numerous federal court decisions in cases, where environmental groups have challenged government actions which they thought did not comply with NEPA's requirements, have led to a body of 'common law' on the interpretation of NEPA. In the late 1970s, the President's Council on Environmental Quality (the CEQ – itself created by another section of NEPA) synthesized these interpretations into a detailed set of regulations defining more precisely for all the federal agencies their obligations under NEPA.[34] The CEQ regulations provided three steps to the impact assessment process. First, government agencies may, by general rulemaking, determine that certain decisions of the agency never have a significant environmental impact and are therefore excluded (categorical exclusion).[35] For example, a government agency's decision to buy an automobile could be excluded. Second, the agency can decide to begin with a short environmental assessment to determine whether or not it needs to prepare a full EIS. If the short environmental assessment leads to a conclusion that the action will not significantly affect the environment, the agency may then issue a 'finding of no significant impact' (FONSI), which it must publish in the Federal Register.[36] A decision to issue a FONSI instead of preparing an EIS is a final decision which is subject to judicial review. Third, if the agency determines that it is required to prepare an EIS, the CEQ regulations spell out the procedures to be followed, including the preparation of a draft EIS that is made available to the public for comment before the final EIS is written.[37]

---

32. *Kleppe* v *Sierra Club*, 427 U.S. 390 (1976).
33. *Strycker's Bay Neighborhood Council, Inc.* v *Karlen*, 444 U.S. 223 (1980).
34. 40 Code of Federal Regulations Parts 1500-1517.
35. 40 Code of Federal Regulations S.1508.4.
36. 40 Code of Federal Regulations S.1501.4.
37. 40 Code of Federal Regulations Part 1502.

A few other aspects of NEPA law may be worth mentioning. In terms of the scope of its analysis, the EIS must include the reasonably predictable and ascertainable indirect effects of the project. For example, an EIS for a project to build a new dock at a seaport should examine the effects of increased road traffic to and from the port if the new dock is built. If the environmental effects are uncertain, they must be discussed with the best evidence available, including evidence that could be easily obtained. Moreover, the analysis should use reasonable suppositions about what the worst case effects might be. Another situation that sometimes arises is that, after the EIS is prepared, the government decision is delayed. If new or additional information comes to light in the time between the 'final' EIS and the agency's decision, the agency may be required to prepare a supplemental EIS, taking the new information into account.

### 6.2. State Environmental Impact Assessment

Because NEPA applies only to federal agency actions, 14 states have adopted their own environmental impact assessment laws, among them large states such as New York, Michigan and California. On the other hand, most states do not have any general environmental assessment requirement. Among the states that do have state EIA laws, each state's system is different, but most share certain common features. They usually cover all actions, government or private, that might have a significant environmental effect, especially land development decisions or land use changes. Second, they require completion of the environmental impact assessment before the project may begin, and before any government approvals are given. Third, they require opportunities to be given for public participation and public comment on the environmental assessment. Finally, at least in some cases the state EIA rules require that a project should be rejected if the assessment predicts significant adverse environmental effects, unless the government agency gives specific reasons for approving the project in spite of its environmental effects.

For example, any project requiring a government permit from a state or local agency in California is subject to the California Environmental Quality Act and the state guidelines implementing that law.[38] The project applicant must prepare an environmental impact report (very similar to a federal EIS) for any project expected to have 'significant effects' on the environment. Section 15042 of the regulations specifically gives the government agency the

---

38. California Public Resources Code, secs. 21000-21177; California Code of Regulations, Title 14, secs. 15000-15387.

right to reject a project that will have significant effects that cannot be miti-gated; section 15043, on the other hand, allows approval in spite of such ef-fects if the agency expressly finds that the benefits of the project outweigh the environmental harms.

In the state of New York, private and public projects are covered by the State Environmental Quality Review,[39] which is administered by the New York Department of Environmental Conservation. Under this law, for all pro-jects requiring government action an Environmental Assessment Form must be completed. For projects classified as Type 1, including those that would affect more than 10 acres (about 4 hectares), a full Environmental Impact Statement has to be prepared. Again, the New York EIS is very similar to a federal EIS under NEPA. Environmental statements for projects in 'critical environmental areas' identified by county or local governments must specifi-cally address the effect of the project on those areas. For example, many bays and wetlands on Long Island, where several wind farms have been proposed, are designated as 'critical environmental areas.'

Wind farms in coastal areas, or even in federal offshore waters, are likely to be subject to both federal and state environmental assessment requirements if approvals are required from both federal and state agencies. The state laws specifically address such overlapping requirements. California, for example, will accept a federal EIS as long as it meets the requirements of the state CEQA; to the extent that it does not, the project applicant will need to sup-plement the federal statement.

## 7. New Zealand's EIA and SEA Rules[40] – by *David Grinlinton*

Environmental assessment[41] has evolved to encompass not only traditional project-specific 'environmental impact assessment' (EIA), but also the 'stra-tegic environmental assessment' (SEA) of policies, plans and programmes

---

39.   New York Code, Rules and Regulations, title 6, Part 617.
40.   For a full discussion of New Zealand's environmental assessment regime, see *Vernon Rive:* 'Environmental Assessment', in *Derek Nolan* (ed.): Environmental and Re-source Management Law, 2005 Ch. 16. See also *David Grinlinton:* 'Integrated Envi-ronmental Assessment in New Zealand', in Environmental and Planning Law Jour-nal, Vol.17(3), 2000 pp. 176-198.
41.   The term 'environmental assessment' is used to refer to the broad spectrum of envi-ronmental assessment processes including traditional EIA, SEA and ESA (see be-low).

and, more recently, the concept of 'environmental and sustainability assessment' (ESA).[42]

In New Zealand project-specific EIA, called 'assessment of environmental effects' (AEE), is integrated into the resource consent approval processes under the Resource Management Act 1991 (RMA).[43] Further, a form of SEA is integrated into the processes in the Act for creating and updating policies and planning instruments (Section 32). The Act also incorporates the principle of 'sustainable management' as a fundamental guiding principle in an integrated system of management of land, air and water in New Zealand (Section 5). As the overarching principle of sustainability applies to the processes for both AEE and SEA under the Act, some measure of ESA is arguably integrated into environmental assessment in New Zealand.

### 7.1. Assessment of Environmental Effects (AEE)

A mandatory environmental assessment process at the local authority decision-making level is an integral part of the integrated resource management philosophy underlying the RMA. Unfortunately, the statutory requirements and guidance for environmental assessments are sparse. The primary obligation is set out in Section 88(2)(b) which requires an application for a resource consent to include:

'an assessment of environmental effects in such detail as corresponds with the scale and significance of the effects that the activity may have on the environment.'

Schedule Four of the Act contains a non-mandatory list of matters that *should be included* in an AEE, and of matters that *should be considered* in its preparation.

There are no special rules that apply to AEE for wind energy developments in New Zealand. They will be treated in the same way as any other development proposal and there will be a requirement for the relevant resource consents to be obtained from the responsible consent authority. Offshore wind energy developments within the 12 mile territorial sea will normally require coastal permits from the Department of Conservation in accordance with the *New Zealand Coastal Policy Statement*, and from the Regional

---

42. See *P.S. Elder:* 'Environmental and Sustainability Assessment', in Journal of Environmental Law & Practice, Vol.2, 1992 pp. 125-148.
43. Resource Management Act 1991, S. 88(2)(b) and (3), and Schedule Four. The integrated environmental and planning regime under the Resource Management Act 1991(NZ) is more fully described above in Chapter 6, section 7.

Council in accordance with the operative *Regional Coastal Plan*. Onshore developments will require consents from the territorial authority (city or district council) under the *District Plan*, and where the development (including construction) will affect water or have land use effects of regional significance, it may also require resource consents from the regional council under its *Regional Plans*.

Local authorities often provide more detailed guidance on AEE through their regional and district planning instruments. A consent authority may also require further information relating to an application generally, or it may commission its own report on the information provided in the assessment.[44]

AEEs are not required to be formally audited or reviewed under the RMA. With *notified* applications public review is intended to be carried out at the hearing itself. This is one of the major failings in the system, as over 95 per cent of all consent applications are not notified and therefore avoid any public review of the AEE. The Parliamentary Commissioner for the Environment may launch an investigation under the Environment Act 1986,[45] or establish an independent review body for a specific proposal.

As AEEs are prepared by proponents, they invariably present a proposal in the most favourable light. Auditing and testing the veracity of the data, analysis and conclusions contained in AEEs therefore relies heavily upon council vigilance and active participation in the hearing and appeals process by submitters and objectors. Often such vigilance is less than vigorous, due to lack of resources or even partisan support for the proposal by the council, and there is often no public participation – again due to lack of resources or the fear of the award of costs against participants.

### 7.2. Strategic Environmental Assessment (SEA)

Section 32(1) of the RMA requires that, before adopting any objective, policy, rule or other method, a local authority, or where the instrument is proposed by central government – the responsible Minister, must carry out an evaluation of the appropriateness of the measure. This evaluation requires consideration of the sustainable management purpose of the Act,[46] and the efficiency and effectiveness of the objective, policy, rule or method. Given the

---

44. Section 92(1); cf. First Schedule, cl. 23; Section 92(2).
45. Environment Act 1986 S. 16(1)(a), (b) and (c) (independent powers of review and investigation); S. 21(1) (right to be heard in proceedings); and S. 22(1) (power of delegation).
46. Resource Management Act, S. 5. See the full discussion of S. 5 above in Chapter 6, section 7.1,

extended definition of 'sustainable management', and the ancillary definitions of 'environment' and 'effects' in the Act, Section 32 clearly requires a broad strategic assessment, integrating principles of sustainability into central and local government policy and planning instruments. Wide consultation is required and a written report must be prepared and made available for public scrutiny and submissions.

In relation to wind energy development, Section 32 does not have the effect of initiating policy and planning changes to facilitate or encourage such developments. However, once policies and plans are proposed which relate to the use of energy resources and to activities connected with energy developments, then Section 32 will require strategic evaluation of these measures in relation to the Part II purpose and principles of the RMA. As already described,[47] these include: protection of the 'life supporting capacity of air, water, soil and ecosystems' (Section 5(2)); the efficient use of natural and physical resources (Section 7(b)); the efficiency of the end use of energy (Section 7(ba)); the effects of climate change (Section 7(i)); and the benefits to be derived from the use and development of renewable energy (Section 7(j)).

### 7.3. Environmental and Sustainability Assessment (ESA)

ESA is perhaps more accurately described as an approach to environmental assessment at both the project and strategic levels which is fundamentally grounded in, and integrates the principles of, sustainability.[48] In New Zealand both project-specific AEE and the Section 32 SEA provisions under the RMA, demonstrate some elements of ESA. For example, the RMA is primarily focussed on managing environmental effects rather than the more traditional zoning approach of earlier planning legislation. As already discussed, the purpose of the RMA is 'to promote the sustainable management of natural and physical resources'.[49] As all persons exercising functions and powers under the Act must promote the Section 5 purpose, the sustainability principle governs the resource management regime at all levels. It is therefore applicable to the requirement that AEEs accompany all applications for resource consent under Section 88(2)(b), and to any SEA undertaken pursuant to Section 32.

---

47. See the discussion in Chapter 6, section 7.
48. See *J.B. Hanebury:* 'Environmental Assessment as Applied to Policies, Plans and Programs', in *S.A. Kennett* (ed.): Law and Process in Environmental Management, 1993 p. 105.
49. Resource Management Act, S. 5. See the full discussion of S. 5 above in Chapter 6, section 7.1.

# CHAPTER 8

# Nature Protection Law

## 1. Introduction – by *Helle Tegner Anker*

This section deals with relevant elements of nature protection law in a broad sense. The protection of sensitive areas, habitats or species is governed by international as well as by EU and national laws. At international level the Biodiversity Convention establishes an overall framework for protecting biodiversity in general. Other elements of international law establish more area-specific or species-specific protection regimes. Similar tendencies of general versus specific nature protection can be found at EU and national levels.

Nature protection interests are often reflected in the designation of protected areas and in various assessment and permit requirements for activities that may affect such areas. Species protection may to some extent be safeguarded through the specific designation of habitats etc. However, species protection goes beyond protected areas. Species may thus be protected, e.g. against destruction of nests or other harmful activities independently of any prior designation.

## 2. International Nature Protection Law – by *Helle Tegner Anker*

International nature protection or conservation law has a long history. However, the reasons behind different international initiatives may vary. *Birnie and Boyle* distinguish between early approaches which address the overexploitation of certain living resources, such as whales, and more recent approaches reflecting a moral dimension in the protection of species, habitats and ecosystems as such.[1] The moral dimension is not necessarily a question of ascribing rights to animals, but of considering and protecting the interests

---

1. *Patricia Birnie & Alan Boyle:* International Law and the Environment, 2002 pp. 554-560.

of nature as such, while safeguarding the interests of both present and future generations in maintaining the life-supporting capacity of the Earth.[2]

International nature protection law includes both hard law and soft law instruments. Among the more important soft law instruments addressing the *general protection of nature and biodiversity* is the 1982 World Charter for Nature[3] which states in Article 1 that 'Nature shall be respected and its essential processes not impaired.' The 1992 Rio Declaration does not specifically address the protection of biodiversity. However, Agenda 21 includes a specific chapter on biological diversity (Chapter 13) and several chapters on the protection and sustainable management of natural resources. As an attempt to encourage the negotiation of an international treaty on sustainable development, the International Union for Conservation of Nature (IUCN) 2000 Draft International Covenant on Environment and Development proposes key elements in the protection of biodiversity as well as cultural and natural heritage, including landscapes.[4]

The 1992 Biodiversity Convention[5] provides a general legal framework for the conservation and sustainable use of biological diversity. Furthermore, the fair and equitable distribution of benefits arising from the utilization of genetic resources is a key objective of the Convention; see Article 1. The relevant provisions of the Biodiversity Convention with regard to the establishment of wind turbines are found in the general requirement for the Parties to adopt national strategies or plans for conservation and sustainable use and to integrate, as far as possible, biodiversity considerations into sectoral plans, programmes or policies; see Article 6. Furthermore, the Parties shall, as far as possible and appropriate, provide for *in situ* biodiversity conservation; see Article 8. *In situ* protection includes: the establishment and management of protected areas; the protection of ecosystems, natural habitats and species;

2.  *Helle T. Anker & E.M. Basse:* 'Rationality, Environmental Law and Biodiversity', in *S.C. Beckmann & E. Kloppenborg Madsen* (eds.): Environmental Regulation and Rationality, 2001 pp. 180-181.

3.  The Charter was adopted as a UN General Assembly Resolution, UNGA Res. 37/7, 1982; see *Patricia Birnie & Alan Boyle:* International Law and the Environment, 2002 pp. 561-562.

4.  See Articles 21 and 22 in *Commission on Environmental Law of IUCN:* The Draft International Covenant on Environment and Development, IUCN Environmental Policy and Law Paper No 31, 3rd ed., 2nd revised text, 2004. Available at: www.iucn.org/law.

5.  The Convention on Biological Diversity (CBD) has 168 signatories, including Denmark, New Zealand, Norway and the USA. However, the USA has not ratified the CBD.

and environmentally sound and sustainable development in areas adjacent to protected areas. In its Article 14 the Biodiversity Convention also calls for the introduction of appropriate procedures for environmental impact assessment, as far as possible and appropriate.

At the European level the 2000 European Landscape Convention[6] could be regarded as a regional instrument aimed at the general protection of landscape values. The Convention stipulates a responsibility to define landscape quality objectives and to introduce instruments aimed at protecting and/or planning the landscape. The 1995 Pan-European Biological and Landscape Diversity Strategy, adopted under the auspices of the Council of Europe (and UNECE), is a regional soft law instrument encouraging environmental cooperation in Europe. The aim is to protect ecosystems, habitats and species through a number of thematic five year action plans. The action plans are intended to stimulate integrated action under the heading of certain action themes. The action themes include conservation of landscapes, and coastal and marine ecosystems.

International law instruments which address the protection of more specific species or habitats include: the 1971 Convention on Wetlands of International Importance (Ramsar Convention); the 1972 Convention Concerning the Protection of World Cultural and Natural Heritage (World Heritage Convention); the 1979 Convention on the Conservation of Migratory Species of Wild Animals (Bonn Convention); and the 1979 Convention on the Conservation of European Wildlife and Natural Habitats (Bern Convention). The last of these is a regional approach confined to Europe. Another regional initiative is the Trilateral Cooperation on the Protection of the Wadden Sea between Denmark, Germany and the Netherlands.

*The Ramsar Convention*[7] has a fairly limited scope. The Convention requires the Parties to designate at least one suitable wetland and to promote the conservation of designated wetlands as well as the wise use of wetlands in their territories; see Article 3. The concept of 'wise use' is not defined in the Convention, but it has been elaborated, e.g. by conferences of the parties and in the Ramsar Convention Secretariat's handbook on wise use.[8] The 2002 Con-

---

6. The European Landscape Convention has been signed by 35 European countries, and has been ratified by 28 signatories, including Denmark and Norway.
7. The Ramsar Convention has been signed and ratified by 157 parties, including Denmark, New Zealand, Norway and the USA.
8. *Ramsar Convention Secretariat:* Wise use of wetlands: A Conceptual Framework for the wise use of wetlands, 3<sup>rd</sup> ed., Vol.1, 2007.

ference of the Parties led to the adoption of new guidelines for management planning for Ramsar sites and other wetlands.[9]

*The World Heritage Convention*[10] imposes an obligation on its parties to conserve and protect the natural heritage. Natural areas that fulfil certain conditions of integrity can be listed as World Heritage sites through a specific procedure. The parties to the Trilateral Wadden Sea cooperation have discussed a proposal for listing the Wadden Sea area as a World Heritage site.[11] However, the proposal only includes the German and Dutch parts since it failed to win the support of the local population in the Danish part.

The *Trilateral Wadden Sea Cooperation* between Denmark, Germany and the Netherlands is an example of a regional area-based soft law instrument based on the 1982 Declaration on the Protection of the Wadden Sea[12] in which the three countries agreed to coordinate their protection efforts in the Wadden Sea.[13] In 1997 the Trilateral Wadden Sea Plan was adopted together with the Stade Declaration. The Wadden Sea Plan is aimed at coordinating policies, measures, projects and actions in the Wadden Sea Area, including coordinating the implementation of international and EU legislation. The Wadden Sea Plan does not provide additional restrictions in the Wadden Sea Area, but seeks to identify potential trilateral projects and actions aimed at the protecting the Wadden Sea.

The *Bonn Convention*[14] is aimed at protecting migratory species, in particular birds but also marine mammals and some fish. The Bonn Convention has two appendices listing protected species. For Appendix I species hunting or taking must be prohibited and the Parties shall endeavour to protect and restore significant habitats. For Appendix II species the Parties should to enter into multilateral or bilateral agreements for the conservation and restoration of habitats which are important for conservation. Furthermore, the Convention

---

9. Adopted by Resolution VIII.14, 2002.
10. 184 states are parties to the World Heritage Convention, including Denmark, New Zealand, Norway and the USA.
11. For further information see http://cwss.www.de/ – the website of the Common Wadden Sea Secretariat.
12. Joint Declaration 1982, adapted in 1991; Ministerial Declaration of the Sixth Trilateral Governmental Wadden Sea Conference (Esbjerg, 1991), for further information see http://cwss.www.de.
13. See *Kees Lambers* et al. (eds.): Trilateral or European Protection of the Wadden Sea?, 2003; and *Kees Siderius & Karel van der Zwiep:* Memorandum. Towards a Trilateral Wadden Sea Convention, 1997.
14. The Bonn Convention has 104 parties, including Denmark, New Zealand and Norway.

encourages other agreements to be made for species other than those listed in Appendix II. A specific agreement on the protection of seals in the Wadden Sea was signed by Denmark, Germany and the Netherlands in 1990. An Agreement on the Conservation of Small Cetaceans (whales) in the Baltic and North Seas (ASCOBANS) was signed in 1991.

The *Bern Convention*[15] has a somewhat broader nature protection perspective than the Bonn Convention, though it is focused on Europe. The Convention urges the conservation of all flora and fauna species as well as their habitats; see Article 1. Particular emphasis is given to endangered and vulnerable species. Article 2 of the Convention contains a general requirement to maintain – or adapt – the population of wild flora and fauna at a level which corresponds to ecological, scientific and cultural requirements, while taking account of, e.g. economic and recreational requirements. More specifically, the Convention requires the Parties to protect in particular the habitats of those species listed in Appendices I and II, and to give special attention to the protection of areas that are of importance to the migratory species specified in Appendices II and III. The *habitat protection requirement* is fairly open, encouraging co-operation between countries on protection measures. The *species protection provisions* of the Bern Convention are formulated as more strict prohibitions. Article 5 prohibits the deliberate picking, collecting, cutting or uprooting of the plant species listed in Appendix I, and Article 6 prohibits, e.g. the deliberate capture and killing, damage to or destruction of breeding or resting sites, and the deliberate disturbance of the wild species listed in Appendix III. Certain exceptions are possible; see Article 9.

## 3. EU Nature Protection Law – by *Helle Tegner Anker*

The protection of species and habitats in the EU is principally laid down in the 1979 Birds Directive and the 1992 Habitats Directive.[16] Both directives

---

15. The Bern Convention was adopted under the auspices of the Council of Europe. It has been ratified by 45 primarily European countries, including Denmark and Norway.
16. Council Directive 79/409/EEC on the conservation of wild birds; and Council Directive 92/43/EEC on the conservation of natural habitats and of wild fauna and flora. EU nature conservation law also includes trade-related species protection as reflected in Council Regulation (EC) No 338/97 of 9 December 1996 on the protection of species of wild fauna and flora by regulating trade therein, which implements the Con-

include a habitat or area protection scheme – known as Natura 2000 sites – as well as a species protection scheme. Safeguarding the most important habitats and species is a key policy area and objective of the EU, as reflected in the proposed EU Action Plan to 2010 and beyond.[17]

### 3.1. Protection of Habitats – Natura 2000

Natura 2000 is the name of the network of sites designated as either Special Protection Areas (SPAs) according to the Birds Directive or as Special Areas of Conservation (SACs) according to the Habitats Directive. The purpose is to establish a coherent ecological network of conservation areas throughout the EU; see Article 3 of the Habitats Directive. The criteria and procedures for designating SPAs and SACs differ significantly between the Birds Directive and the Habitats Directive. The protection of designated sites is primarily governed by the Habitats Directive, Article 6(2) to (4), which replaces the obligations arising under the first sentence of the Birds Directive, Article 4(4); see the Habitats Directive, Article 7. However, the obligation to take action to ensure the favourable status of designated areas relies on the provisions of the Habitats Directive as well as the Birds Directive.[18]

According to the Birds Directive, Member States must designate SPAs (bird protection areas) by classifying the most suitable territories by number and size as special protection areas for the conservation of Annex I bird species; see Article 4(1). Similar measures must be taken for regularly occurring migratory species not listed in Annex I. In a number of rulings the European Court of Justice (ECJ) has narrowed the margin of discretion of the Member States when designating SPAs. Designations shall only be based on ornithological criteria. Economic interests or other interests cannot be taken into consideration.[19] Furthermore, Member States which have manifestly designated fewer sites in number and size than are appropriate on the basis of purely ornithological criteria will have failed to fulfil their obligations under

vention on International Trade in Endangered Species (CITES). Trade-related species protection will not be dealt with in this context.

17. COM(2006) 216 final, Communication from the Commission, Halting the loss of biodiversity by 2010 and beyond, p. 10.

18. On the fairly complex relationship between the Habitats Directive and the Birds Directive see *Nicolas de Sadeleer:* 'Habitats Conservation in EC Law – From Nature Sanctuaries to Ecological Networks', in Yearbook of Environmental Law, Vol.5, 2005 pp. 215-252. See also *Jonathan Verschuuren:* 'Effectiveness of Nature Protection Legislation in the EU and the US: The Birds and Habitats Directives and the Endangered Species Act', in Yearbook of Environmental Law, Vol.3, 2004 pp. 307-328.

19. See Case C-355/90, *Commission v Spain* (Santona Marshes).

Article 4(1).[20] If a Member State fails to designate a site that should have been designated as an SPA, the first sentence of Article 4(4) is directly applicable.[21] Member States are obliged continuously to reconsider the need for new designations.[22] A Member State may not reduce or alter the boundaries of an SPA unless it is no longer the most suitable territory for the conservation of wild bird species.[23] Furthermore, the habitat protection requirements of the Birds Directive are not confined to designated SPAs. According to Article 4(4), second sentence, Member States shall also seek to avoid deterioration of habitats outside protected areas. Also, according to Article 3, Member States shall take the measures necessary to preserve, maintain or re-establish a sufficient diversity and area of habitats for all wild bird species.[24]

According to the Habitats Directive, the designation of SACs (habitat protection areas) is subject to a dialogue between the EU Commission and the Member States; see Article 4 of the Habitats Directive. As a first step the Member States have to submit a list of sites relevant to the conservation of Annex I habitat types and Annex II species. More specific criteria are set out in Annex III. The ECJ has stressed that Member States can only apply scientific criteria and that an exhaustive list of sites of relevant ecological interest must be submitted.[25] The next step is the establishment by the Commission of a draft list of sites of Community importance for each of the five categories of biogeographical regions.[26] The Member States are then obliged to designate such sites as Special Areas of Conservation. By the establishment of the Commission draft list Article 6(2), (3) and (4) apply, whereas Article 6(1) only applies after the final designation by the Member State.

20. See Case C-3/96, Commission v The Netherlands.
21. See Case C-355/90, *Commission* v *Spain*; and Case C-96/98, *Commission* v *France* (Marais Poitevin). See also Case C-418/04, *Commission* v *Ireland.*
22. Case C-209/07, *Commission* v *Austria.*
23. Case C-191/05, *Commission* v *Portugal.*
24. See Case C-355/90, *Commission* v *Spain*; and Case C-117/00, *Commission* v *Ireland.*
25. See, e.g. Case C-220/99, *Commission* v *France*; and Case C-371/98, *First Corporate Shipping.*
26. Such lists have been issued by the Commission from 2001 to 2006. A reservation has been made for further designations in particular marine areas. In May 2007 the Commission issued guidelines for the establishment of the Natura 2000 network in marine areas.

As mentioned above, the *protection regime* for SPAs has been superseded by the protection regime for SACs as laid down in the Habitats Directive Article 6(2), (3) and (4).[27]

Article 6(2) obliges the Member States to take all appropriate steps to avoid the deterioration of habitats and the significant disturbance of the species for which the area has been designated. It has been stated by the ECJ that Article 6(2) obliges the Member States to take action not only against deterioration by ongoing human activities within or outside the designated area, but also to take measures to prevent natural developments that may cause deterioration of the conservation area.[28]

Article 6(3) and (4) apply to new projects or plans that are likely to have a significant effect on a site. In such cases an assessment of the implications must be carried out prior to the decision on the project or plan. According to the ECJ, under the precautionary principle an assessment is required unless it can be shown, on the basis of objective information, that the project or plan may not have a significant effect either individually or in combination with other projects or plans.[29] A project or plan cannot be authorized if it will adversely affect the integrity of the site; see Article 6(3). According to the ruling in Case C-127/02 *Waddenzee*, authorisation shall only be given if there is no reasonable scientific doubt about the absence of such effects. However, under the exemption provision in Article 6(4), a project or a plan can proceed under very specific circumstances, despite a negative effect on the integrity of the site. The conditions are: that no alternative solution exists;[30] that there are imperative reasons of overriding public interest; and that all compensatory measures are taken. In the case of priority habitat types or species, the conditions are even stricter.

### 3.2. EU Species Protection
The species protection provisions of the Birds Directive and the Habitats Directive have certain similarities in providing for both strict as well as less strict species protection.

---

27. Although the Habitats Directive provides a very strict protection regime, as has been stated by the ECJ in a number of cases, the protection regime of the Birds Directive is even stricter with almost no possibilities for exemptions.
28. See, e.g. Case C-117/00, *Commission* v *Ireland*; and Case C-6/04, *Commission* v *United Kingdom*.
29. See Case C-127/07, *Waddenzee*.
30. In Case C-239/04, *Commission* v *Portugal*, the Portuguese authorities had failed to demonstrate the absence of alternative solutions for a new motorway route.

The Birds Directive applies to all wild bird species. In Article 5 there is a general obligation to prohibit, e.g. deliberate killing, deliberate destruction of nests etc. and deliberate disturbance of birds, particularly during the period of breeding and rearing. However, hunting is possible for Annex II species, which provides for a less strict protection regime for these listed species. Article 9 of the Birds Directive lays down specific criteria for exemption from the prohibition in Article 5, including that there is no other satisfactory solution. Only certain reasons may justify derogation, including the interests of public health and safety, the prevention of serious damage to crops, fisheries etc. and the protection of flora and fauna.

The Habitats Directive provides for a strict protection regime for animal species in Article 12 and for plant species in Article 13, which apply to species listed in Annex IV. The strict protection regime in Article 12 requires the prohibition of, e.g. all forms of deliberate capture or killing, deliberate disturbance, as well as the deterioration or destruction of breeding sites or resting places. The latter provision implies the protection of certain areas and not only refers to deliberate deterioration or destruction but also to accidental deterioration or destruction.[31] It has, however, been questioned how strict this provision is in fact, since deterioration of Annex IV breeding or resting sites may occur in a number of cases. In a guidance document the EU Commission accepts the use of mitigation measures that will ensure the continued ecological functionality of a breeding site or resting place.[32] According to the Commission, such measures can be used in cases where a plan or a project may have an impact on a breeding or resting site without applying the derogations stipulated in Article 16. However, they do not encompass compensatory measures for the destruction of a breeding site or resting place.

Article 16 only allows for derogations under specific circumstances which are similar to those referred to in Article 9 of the Birds Directive, i.e. that no satisfactory alternative exists and that the derogation is not detrimental to the maintenance of a favourable conservation status within the natural range of the species in question. Furthermore, a derogation can only be justified by specific reasons, e.g. to prevent serious damage to crops etc., in the interests

---

31. See Case C-98/03, *Commission v Germany*; and Case C-6/04, *Commission v United Kingdom.*
32. EU Commission, 2007: Guidance document on the strict protection of animal species of Community interest under the Habitats Directive 92/43/EEC, pp. 47-48.

of public health and safety, or for other imperative reasons of overriding public interest.[33]

## 4. Danish Nature Protection Law – by *Helle Tegner Anker*

The protection of habitats and species in Denmark primarily relies on the Nature Protection Act.[34] The Nature Protection Act covers both land and sea areas, though with some variation as to the application of various regulatory instruments. The Planning Act provides certain protection for valuable habitats or landscapes through the planning system, including the designation of existing and potential nature areas and corridors, valuable landscapes, cultural heritage areas and areas of geological interest. Since 2007 such designations must be included in new municipal plans, and municipal planning guidelines must be drawn up.

### 4.1. Protection of Habitats etc.

The Planning Act and the Nature Protection Act form the primary legal basis for the implementation of the Birds and Habitats Directives, supplemented by the Forestry Act and various sectoral laws governing offshore areas.

The Executive Order on the designation and administration of international nature protection areas[35] delimits habitat areas (SACs), bird protection areas (SPAs) and Ramsar areas. A total of 16,683 km$^2$ has been designated as Natura 2000 sites in Denmark, extending to 8.3 per cent of the land area and 12.3 per cent of the Danish sea area.[36] The Executive Order restricts planning for new activities in the designated areas. The Executive Order also seeks to implement Article 6(3) of the Habitats Directive. An assessment must be carried out prior to granting a permit for a number of listed activities which require a permit according to several provisions of environmental laws (Sections 7 to 9). A permit cannot be granted if the project will affect the integrity

---

33. According to the ECJ, the construction of installations does not fall within any of the grounds listed in Article 16(1); see Case C-508/04, *Commission v Austria*.
34. Consolidated Act No 749 of 21 June 2007 on Nature Protection (*Lov om naturbeskyttelse*). Furthermore, the Forestry Act provides for certain habitat protection, and the 2007 National Parks Act lays down basic rules on the administration of national parks. The Hunting and Game Management Act also includes species protection rules – primarily restrictions on hunting and certain requirements not to destroy nests etc.
35. Executive Order 408/2007, replaced the previous Executive Order 477/2003 with effect from 16 May 2007.
36. For more detailed information on the designated areas see www.natura2000.dk.

of an area.[37] Similar rules apply to plans for new activities within the designated areas. However, these restrictions primarily apply to land based activities.

As regards offshore activities, the restrictions under the Habitats Directive, Article 6(3), are primarily to be found in sectoral legislation, e.g. in the Raw Materials Act and in the Marine Environment Protection Act. In May 2007 a series of amendments made by the Ministry of Transport to sectoral legislation was adopted by Parliament with the express purpose of ensuring the proper implementation of the Habitats and Birds Directives.[38] It is now explicitly stated, e.g. in the Electricity Supply Act and in the Act on Energinet.dk that offshore wind energy projects that are likely to significantly affect designated areas must be subject to an assessment of their effects. Consent cannot be granted if the project will adversely affect the integrity of a designated area.

The 2003 Act on Environmental Objectives[39] lays down a requirement to draw up a Natura 2000 plan for each Natura 2000 site. The Natura 2000 plans must specify the conservation objectives for the areas and the management initiatives necessary for achieving those objectives. On the basis of the Natura 2000 plans, the authorities, primarily municipal councils, are obliged to ensure the favourable conservation status of species and habitats within Natura 2000 sites. The authorities must enter into agreements or issue orders restricting harmful activities and otherwise take the necessary management steps. If an order is issued, compensation must be paid to landowners for any loss following from the restrictions laid down in the order.

A new Act on National Parks[40] lays down basic rules for the establishment and administration of national parks. Seven areas of outstanding natural interest have so far been proposed as potential national parks, including the Wadden Sea Area.[41] However, the National Parks Act and designation as a national park does not in itself imply further restrictions than the existing restrictions under the Nature Protection Act and other relevant legislation. Ma-

---

37. In addition, the Nature Protection Act and the Forestry Act establish a notification scheme for certain farming or forestry activities that are not subject to a permit procedure.
38. The implementation of the Directives in Denmark had been criticized by the EU Commission in two letters of formal notice in June 2006. Further amendments of the legislation are expected in 2008.
39. Consolidated Act No 1756/2006.
40. Act No 533/2007.
41. However, local opposition may block its designation as a national park.

jor parts of future national parks must be expected to be Natura 2000 sites, subject to nature conservation orders or to the general habitat protection provisions of the Nature Protection Act.

The Nature Protection Act distinguishes between: the general protection of primarily land based habitats, e.g. heaths, bogs, meadows etc., see Section 3; other protection zones including the 300 metre dune or beach protection zone (Sections 8 and 15); and an individual protection scheme through the issue of nature conservation orders.

The *general protection rules for habitats and coastal areas* generally prohibit any alteration of the state of a protected area. However, an exemption may be granted in specific circumstances by municipalities (habitat protection) or the Minister for the Environment (beach protection); see Section 65. In particular the beach protection zone is subject to a very strict exemption practice. Also the Forestry Act provides a general protection of forest areas which prohibits activities other activities than forestry activities. There is only limited scope for granting an exemption.[42] The general protection rules do not entail any compensation to landowners since they only restrict future land use and not existing land use.

*Individual nature conservation orders* may determine the purpose and the specific restrictions in a conservation area on an individual basis. Compensation will be paid to landowners and other users for restrictions on existing activities. An exemption for activities that are not in line with the conservation order may be granted if they do not conflict with the purpose of the conservation order; see Section 50. A nature conservation order is issued by regional conservation boards for land areas and adjacent shallow water areas. The Minister for the Environment issues conservation orders for state-owned areas and for offshore areas within the territorial sea and the fishery territories; see Section 52.[43]

---

42. In a Nature Protection Appeal Board case, MAD2003.723, the establishment of five wind turbines in a forest area was refused. The five wind turbines were part of a wind farm with 25 turbines.
43. An example of a conservation order for an offshore wetland area is Executive Order No 135 of 17 February 1998 on nature conservation and wildlife reserve in the Wadden Sea (*Bekendtgørelse om fredning og vildtreservat i Vadehavet*). The Executive Order restricts public access, hunting and cockle fishery in the conservation area and prohibits the establishment of wind turbines within the territorial sea. Other installations must be negotiated between the Ministry for Transport and Energy and the National Forest and Nature Agency.

There are no specific *wetland protection* rules in Denmark. Wetlands characterized by terrestrial vegetation are normally protected through the general habitat protection of the Nature Protection Act, e.g. as coastal meadows or bogs, or through individual nature conservation orders. In particular, sensitive marine wetlands may be protected through individual nature conservation orders. Many wetlands are designated as Natura 2000 sites[44] and accordingly subject to the Natura 2000 rules. Similarly, there is no additional protection of *coastal areas* as such, except the general habitat and beach protection rules of the Nature Protection Act or individual conservation orders.

### 4.2. Protection of Species

*Species protection* is governed by the Nature Protection Act according to which certain reptiles, fish etc. are given conservation status, prohibiting their killing and collection. However, this does not extend to the protection of resting or nesting places of the protected species. Species that can be hunted, i.e. mammals and birds, are indirectly protected under the Hunting and Game Management Act through the establishment of hunting seasons. The 2007 Executive Order on international nature protection areas establishes general implementation of the species protection provisions of the Birds and Habitats Directives which had not previously been correctly implemented in Denmark. According to the new rules, a permit or plan cannot be issued if it would lead to the deterioration or destruction of breeding sites or resting places (Sections 11-12). More general provisions for species protection are expected to be proposed, aimed at the full implementation of the species protection provisions of the Habitats Directive. According to the Fishery Act,[45] Section 30, certain conservation initiatives and conservation areas that restrict fishing can be established.

## 5. Norwegian Nature Protection Law – by *Hans Christian Bugge*

Nature conservation is an important part of Norway's environmental policy and is based on special legislation for the conservation and protection of species and valuable areas. Here the Nature Conservation Act[46] is a key piece of legislation. However, since most biodiversity is found outside the protected

---

44. All Ramsar areas are also designated as bird protection areas (SPAs) and thus included in the Natura 2000 network.
45. Consolidated Act No 372 of 24 April 2006 on Fishery (*Bekendtgørelse af fiskerilov*).
46. Act of 19 June 1970 No 63.

areas, it is essential that the value of nature and biodiversity is assessed and taken into account in all sectoral policies and legislation, in spatial planning, and in the application of acts that regulate industries and other economic activities which are based on natural resources.

Norwegian environmental policy is based on the principle of integration. All sectoral authorities must take environmental considerations into account when defining goals and applying their legislation. Many of the most important sectoral acts regarding the exploitation of natural resources have environmental protection as one of their objectives,[47] and/or state explicitly that environmental considerations must be taken into account in their application. However, in reality the extent to which this is done varies; this is to a large extent left to the discretion of the authority in question.

In addition, several acts institute legal protection for certain natural resources, or at least provide a legal basis for protection measures. The Planning and Building Act lays down a general prohibition of building within 100 metres from the shore all along the Norwegian coast.[48] In addition, land-use plans pursuant to the Act may designate areas for nature protection, and the new Act will strengthen the planning instruments in this respect. The Wildlife Act[49] lays down a general principle of protection of all wild animals. Hunting is regulated on the basis of the principle of sustainability. The Water Resources Act[50] gives the formal status of Protected Watercourses to those watercourses which the Norwegian Parliament (*Stortinget*) has explicitly excluded from hydropower development.

The EEA Agreement does not include nature conservation in the strict sense, as this is not an issue for the internal market. As a consequence, neither the EC Habitats Directive – and the follow-up work via Natura 2000 – nor the Birds Directive apply to Norway.

### 5.1. The Nature Conservation Act
The Nature Conservation Act[51] provides a legal framework for the protection of four types of protected areas and sites: national parks, protected landscapes, nature reserves and natural monuments. It also includes provisions for

---

47. For example, the Forestry Act of 27 May 2005 No 31 states in its Section 1 that its objective is to promote sustainable forestry in order both to create economic values and protect biodiversity, landscape, etc.
48. However, there are important exemptions, see Chapter 6, section 5.3.
49. Act of 29 May 1981 No 38.
50. Act of 24 November 2000 No 82.
51. Act of 19 June 1970 No 63.

the protection and conservation of species of plants and animals.[52] Furthermore, it regulates the issue of compensation to landowners for economic loss due to conservation measures. The objective of the Act reflects a broad perspective on nature conservation and the main idea of environmentally sustainable development.

The Act itself does not protect anything, but it gives the government the authority to protect areas and species as it deems necessary. Protection is decided by the government in each individual case. The Act provides the legal framework for the different types of protected areas: their purpose, quality, and the legal effects of their protection. It does not itself define the restrictions on land use and other activities within each type of protected area. This has to be decided for each protected area according to what is necessary to achieve the objective of the protection. Major new infrastructure projects, such as roads and energy production installations, will normally be prohibited in all types of protected areas, as well as any significant changes in the way that ongoing activities, such as forestry and agriculture, are carried out.

The restrictions in nature reserves are generally stricter than in national parks and protected landscapes. Restrictions may apply to landowners and other rights-holders in protected areas, as well as to the public at large as regards general access to such areas.

An important issue is the question of compensation for landowners or users for the restrictions imposed in a protected area. The main rule in Norwegian law is that restrictions on the future use of land and other natural resources under legislation, regulations or public plans do not give entitlement to compensation. This is the case with national parks and protected landscapes. However, the rule is different for nature reserves. Pursuant to an amendment to the Act in 1985, the owner of a nature reserve may claim compensation for financial loss on the basis of the same rules and principles as apply in cases of expropriation.[53]

There are some 2000 protected areas in the country, the great majority of which are nature reserves. Altogether, 14 per cent of the area of the Norwe-

---

52. However, as regards animals, a general principle of protection applies pursuant to the Wildlife Act.
53. Article 105 of the Constitution states that the citizen has the right to 'full compensation' in cases of expropriation. What 'full compensation' means in various situations is spelled out in the Act on Compensation for Expropriation of Property of 6 April 1984 No 17. The rules apply *mutatis mutandis* to the situation where an area is protected as a nature reserve while the land remains the property of the landowner.

gian mainland was protected in 2007.[54] However, a large part of this is mountainous areas. For most other categories of nature and landscape the level of protection is far less than 10 per cent nationally, which is the level of protection recommended by IUCN for each of the most important categories of nature and landscape. Some types of landscape, such as river deltas, are seriously threatened in Norway.

The Ministry of the Environment is preparing new legislation on natural diversity which will replace the Nature Conservation Act. This will provide a framework for a better, more holistic protection of biodiversity and Norwegian nature in all its forms.

### 5.2. Species Protection

Although animal species and groups may be protected by the Nature Protection Act (Section 14), its importance is limited in this regard. The reason is that the Wildlife Act[55] lays down a general principle of protection. Without a permit it is prohibited to kill, catch, chase or hurt wild animals, as well as to interfere with their eggs, nests and lairs. A permit may take the form of general hunting regulations which allow hunting of certain species in specific seasons and geographic areas. Also, individual permits may be issued, for example to kill a single bear or wolf which kills livestock or directly threatens a person. The protection of bears, wolves, wolverines and lynx is a highly controversial political issue in Norway.

Plant species and habitats may be protected pursuant to the Nature Protection Act (Section 13).

The special species protection provided by the Nature Protection Act and the Wildlife Act is in fact rather weak. It only protects species against acts of private citizens. The rules do not prevent public authorities from, for example opening up an area for new roads or for the establishment of energy or industrial projects which may harm the species in question, even if the species is threatened. This can only be prevented through the protection of the area by the state pursuant to the Nature Conservation Act or by a municipal plan pursuant to the Planning and Building Act.

---

54. In addition, large parts of Svalbard in the Barents Sea are also protected.
55. Act of 29 May 1981 No 38.

## 6. US Federal and State Nature Protection Law – by *Julian Juergensmeyer*

In the United States of America, a host of state and federal laws attempt in a piecemeal fashion to preserve land or protect particular species. Several federal statutes are species-related, like the Bald Eagle Protection Act,[56] the Wild-Free Roaming Horses and Burros Act,[57] and the Migratory Bird Treaty Act,[58] but have only an incidental effect on protecting the habitat of the species protected. The federal Wilderness Act of 1964[59] is an early example of land preservation, but it is limited to federal public lands. Other examples include the Marine Mammal Protection Act[60] and the Fisheries Conservation Act,[61] which protect fish habitats. The federal law that does the most in terms of habitat protection and ecosystem management is the Endangered Species Act. The states are free to give greater protection to endangered species and ecosystems, but cannot authorize breaches of federal standards.

Wetlands are subject to specific area-based protection regimes in the USA, first and foremost in the Clean Water Act, but also in the Rivers and Harbors Act. Wetlands, in the form of estuarine areas, make up a large percentage of the coastal zone. Many states distinguish between inland and coastal wetlands, affording greater protection to coastal wetlands. The more stringent protection of coastal wetlands, by virtually every coastal state in the United States, comes in the form of coastal zone management programmes or comprehensive plans. The legislative framework for these regulations and plans revolve around two items of federal legislation: the Coastal Zone Management Act, and the Coastal Barrier Resources Act; see Chapter 6, section 6.2.

### 6.1. The Endangered Species Act

The Endangered Species Act (ESA)[62] has proven itself to be a useful control tool in environmentally sensitive areas. The United States Supreme Court has described the ESA as 'the most comprehensive legislation for the preserva-

---

56. 16 US Code S. 668 et seq.
57. 16 US Code S. 1331 et seq.
58. 16 US Code S. 703 et seq.
59. 16 US Code S. 1131(a).
60. 16 US Code Annotated S. 1361.
61. 16 US Code Annotated S. 1801.
62. 16 US Code Annotated SS. 1531-1543.

tion of Endangered Species ever enacted by any Nation.'[63] Enacted 'to provide a means whereby the ecosystems upon which endangered species and threatened species depend may be conserved,'[64] the ESA can halt or require the alteration of development that threatens wild plant or animal species listed by the Secretary of the Interior as threatened or endangered.[65]

The habitat preservation element is found in Section 4 of the ESA. This section reflects ecological reality; there is no use in protecting a plant or wildlife species if that species has no place to live. Section 4 authorizes the Secretary of the Interior to designate areas of 'critical habitat' for specified species.[66]

Section 3 of the ESA defines *critical habitat for a threatened or endangered species* as the 'specific areas within the geographical area occupied by the species, at the time it is listed.'[67] If the designation of the critical habitat is not determinable at the time the species is listed, the Secretary may do so up to one year after the species is listed. Even areas outside the geographical area can be designated as critical habitat if the Secretary determines that such areas are essential for species conservation. A critical habitat is limited, however, and 'shall not include the entire geographical area which can be occupied'[68] by the species.

Section 4 authorizes the Secretary to *list species of plants, fish, and wildlife as threatened or endangered.*[69] Some 1300 species are listed as either threatened or endangered.[70] Section 3 of the ESA defines 'endangered species' as species that are 'in danger of extinction throughout all or a significant portion of its range.'[71] A threatened species is one that 'is likely to become an endangered species within the foreseeable future throughout all or a signifi-

63.  *Tennessee Valley Authority* v *Hill*, 437 U.S. 153, 180, 98 S.Ct. 2279, 57 L.Ed.2d 117 (1978).
64.  *Tennessee Valley Authority* v *Hill*, 437 U.S. 153, 180, 98 S.Ct. 2279, 57 L.Ed.2d 117 (1978).
65.  The process to be followed by the Secretary in adding or removing a species from the Act's domain is found at 16 US Code Annotated S. 1533(a), (b).
66.  16 US Code Annotated S. 1533(a)(3)(A).
67.  16 US Code Annotated S. 1532(5)(A)(i).
68.  16 US Code Annotated S. 1532(5)(C).
69.  16 US Code Annotated S. 1533(a)(1).
70.  567 species of animals and 744 species of plants are listed in the United States as of 15 January 2007. There are also foreign listings. For currently listed plants and animals, see www.fws.gov/endangered/wildlife.html#Species
71.  16 US Code Annotated S. 1532(6).

cant portion of its range.'[72] Whether a particular species falls within one of these categories is determined on 'the basis of the best scientific and commercial data available.'[73] The Act exempts insects that present an overwhelming risk to humans.

*Taking of species*
Section 9 is the triggering mechanism of the ESA. Section 9 *prohibits the taking of any protected species* by government or private parties.[74] Under Section 3 to 'take' includes to 'harass, harm, pursue, hunt, shoot, wound, kill, trap, capture, or collect, or attempt to engage in any such conduct.'[75] The key word for land use issues is 'harm', which the Secretary defines as 'an act which actually kills or injures wildlife, but such act may include significant habitat modification or degradation where it actually kills or injures wildlife by significantly impairing essential behavioral patterns, including breeding, feeding, or sheltering.'[76] The Secretary also defines 'harass' broadly as 'an intentional or negligent act or omission which creates the likelihood of injury to wildlife by annoying it to such an extent as to significantly disrupt normal behavioral patterns.'[77]

*Incidental Takings and Habitat Conservation Plans*
Sections 7(b)(4) and 10(a) of the ESA allow for 'incidental takings' of protected species. An 'incidental taking' is defined as 'a taking [that is] otherwise prohibited, if such taking is incidental to, and not the purpose of, carrying out of an otherwise lawful activity.'[78] The process of obtaining an incidental taking permit differs slightly between a taking involving a federal action and one involving a private action.[79]

---

72. 16 US Code Annotated S. 1532(20).
73. 16 US Code Annotated S. 1533(b)(1)(A).
74. 16 US Code Annotated S. 1538(a)(1). States and their political subdivisions are persons subject to the Act.
75. 16 US Code Annotated S. 1532(19).
76. 50 Code of Federal Regulations 17.3. The Supreme Court upheld the Secretary's definition of 'harm' in *Babbitt* v *Sweet Home Chapter of Communities for a Great Oregon*, 515 U.S. 687, 115 S.Ct. 2407, 132 L.Ed.2d 597 (1995).
77. 50 Code of Federal Regulations 17.3.
78. 50 Code of Federal Regulations 17.3.
79. See, e.g. *Arizona Cattle Growers' Ass'n* v *United States Fish and Wildlife Service*, 273 F.3d 1229 (9th Cir.2001) for a description of the process used for federal requests.

A proposed *federal action*, such as a review for a Clean Water Act Section 404 Dredge and Fill Permit as part of a federal wind farm development project, will trigger the application of Section 7 of the Act.

The proponent federal agency, such as the Corps of Engineers, must first consult with the US Fish and Wildlife Service (FWS) or the National Marine Fisheries Service (NMFS) to determine whether any protected species may be present in the area of the proposed development, to ensure that the action is not likely to jeopardize the continued existence of any such species. The FWS or the NMFS must then issue a written statement detailing how the proposed action would affect the species or its critical habitat.[80] If the service finds that the action will jeopardize a species or its critical habitat, the service will suggest possible 'reasonable and prudent alternatives' to the agency's proposal.[81] The federal agency may then follow the service's suggestions, which may include the right to an incidental taking. If the agency chooses not to follow the alternatives offered or if no alternative is offered and the project will be halted, the agency can apply to the Endangered Species Committee for an exemption based on the argument that the public interest served by its project outweighs the risk to the species or its habitat.[82]

Section 10 applies to *non-federal requests* for incidental taking permits, known as *habitat conservation plans*.[83] Section 10 requires a conservation plan to be submitted to the Secretary showing: the expected effects, the steps that will be taken to minimize and mitigate any taking; that the taking will not appreciably reduce the likelihood of the survival of the species; and what alternative actions have been considered and why they have not been adopted.[84] The Secretary must also be assured that there will be adequate funding for the conservation plan.[85] A permit may be issued subject to terms and conditions that the Secretary deems necessary.[86] Furthermore, the Secretary may revoke a permit if the person holding the permit does not comply with its terms and conditions.[87] Habitat conservation plans, seen as safety valves to prevent Fifth Amendment takings actions, became popular with the Department of the Interior during the 1990s.

---

80. 16 US Code Annotated S. 1536(b)(3)(A).
81. See *Arizona Cattle Grower's Ass'n*, 273 F.3d at 1238.
82. 16 US Code Annotated S. 1536(e).
83. See, e.g. *J.B. Ruhl:* 'How to Kill Endangered Species, Legally: The Nuts and Bolts of Endangered Species Act HCP Permits for Real Estate Development', in Environmental Lawyer, Vol.5, 1999 p. 345.
84. 16 US Code Annotated S. 1536(a).
85. 16 US Code Annotated S. 1539(a)(2)(B)(iii).
86. 16 US Code Annotated S. 1539(a)(2)(B).
87. 16 US Code Annotated S. 1539(a)(2)(C).

Similarly and where the ESA is seen by local governments and their con-
stituent developers as intruding on matters of local control, a 'candidate conservation agreement' may be used.[88] Under these agreements state and local
governments together with private parties agree to provide some protection to
as yet unlisted, candidate species, thereby avoiding the listing process and all
that goes with it.[89]

*Constitutionality as Applied to Development on Private Land*
The United States Supreme Court has not addressed the constitutionality of
applying the ESA to private land. The commerce clause[90] is one source of authority, and perhaps the only source, by which the ESA can regulate private
land. The Property Clause of Article IV of the Constitution confers power on
Congress to regulate activity on public lands. This power extends in some instances to adjacent lands,[91] but not to private land in general. As in the case of
the Property Clause, the treaty-making power may support the extension of
the ESA to private land in narrow circumstances.[92]

## 6.2. Wetlands
With the recognition of the value of wetlands and the need to protect them,
the first hurdle to their sensible management is the question of definition. To
date, there is no standard, all-inclusive definition of 'wetlands' that meets all
needs.[93] In essence, the term 'wetlands' is generic and refers to areas that

88. See Announcement of Final Policy for Candidate Conservation Agreements with
    Assurances, 64 Fed. Reg. 32,726 (17 June 1999); and Safe Harbor Agreements and
    Candidate Conservation Agreements with Assurances, 64 Fed. Reg. 32,706 (17
    June 1999).
89. See *Francesca Ortiz:* 'Candidate Conservation Agreements as a Devolutionary Re-
    sponse to Extinction', in Georgia Law Review, Vol.33, 1999 p. 413.
90. On the commerce clause, see Chapter 4, section 2.3.1.
91. See *Robert B. Keiter:* 'Taking Account of the Ecosystem on the Public Domain:
    Law and Ecology in the Greater Yellowstone Region', in University of Colorado
    Law Review, Vol.60, 1989 p. 923.
92. See *Omar N. White:* 'Comment. The Endangered Species Act's Precarious Perch:
    A Constitutional Analysis Under the Commerce Clause and the Treaty Power', in
    Ecology Law Quarterly, Vol.27, 2000 p. 215; and *Gavin R. Villareal:* 'Note. One
    Leg to Stand On: The Treaty Power and Congressional Authority for the Endan-
    gered Species Act after United States v Lopez', in Texas Law Review, Vol.76(5),
    1998 p. 1125.
93. For examples of definitions see *National Research Council:* Wetlands: Characteris-
    tics and Boundaries, National Academy of Sciences Report, 1995; U.S. Army
    Corps of Engineers, Wetland definition, 33 Code of Federal Regulations § 328.3(b)

support the kinds of vegetation that are capable of withstanding wet conditions. Wetlands generally occur where land elevations are low and ground
water levels are high, and they have been identified by many terms, such as:
marshes, swamps, bogs, some types of hardwood forested areas, sloughs, wet
meadows, natural ponds, potholes and river overflow areas (flood plains).

This section primarily focuses on inland wetlands, whereas the protection
of coastal wetlands is dealt with in the discussion of coastal zones in Chapter
6, section 6.2. However, there is not necessarily a clear distinction between
inland and coastal wetlands in the relevant legislation. At federal level the
Rivers and Harbors Act and the Clean Water Act provide a more general
scheme for protection of inland as well as coastal wetlands.

Wetlands protection is characterized by an ever-increasingly strong federal
and state regulatory presence. The 'do as you please' attitude of the past has
been replaced by an array of state and federal regulations and permit requirements. Also, many states with substantial wetlands acreage have implemented local regulations, attempting to complement and strengthen the
broader federal and state programs.[94] Since permits are required at all levels
before any kind of development (a wind farm for example) may take place in
a wetland area, it is important to understand the regulatory interplay in the
permit process and the federal, state and local jurisdictions involved.

State regulation of wetlands runs the gamut from none to extensive. By
one count, twenty-one states regulate coastal wetlands and seventeen states
directly regulate inland wetlands.[95] Local governments may also regulate
wetlands, usually indirectly through zoning, to protect shorelands or other
sensitive lands. Definitions, scopes and permit processes vary widely.

States that rely on the federal Clean Water Act Section 404 process instead
of enacting their own laws may find themselves under-protected when federal
law is weakened. This occurred in North Carolina, which found itself helpless
to prevent the draining of wetlands when in 1998 a federal court overturned a

---

(1994). See also, *E. Goodman:* 'Defining Wetlands for Regulatory Purposes: A
Case Study in the Role of Science in Policymaking', in Buffalo Environmental
Law Journal, Vol.2, 1994 p. 135; and *W. Rodgers:* Hornbook on Environmental
Law, 1994 § 4.6.

94. 'Wetlands are currently the scene of hard fought legal and political battles about
the proper scope of governmental regulation of land', *F. Bosselman:* 'Limitations
Inherent in the Title to Wetlands at Common Law', in Stanford Environmental Law
Journal, Vol.15, 1996 pp. 247-248.

95. *Linda A. Malone:* Environmental Regulation of Land Use, 2006 § 4:29. See also
*Edward H. Zeigler, Jr.:* Rathkopf's The Law of Zoning and Planning, 2006 S. 7.01
et seq.

Corps of Engineers' regulation dealing with the re-deposit of dredged materials.

## 6.2.1.  The Rivers and Harbors Act

Ironically, the mother of all wetland regulations was not designed to conserve wetlands. When he signed the Rivers and Harbors Act (RHA) in 1899, it was President McKinley's intention to protect navigable waters so that they were safe for shipping.[96] As such, jurisdiction was only provided over 'navigable waters'. It was navigation that was the concern, not water quality. Nevertheless, the Corps of Engineers and the courts have found a basis for protecting both in the RHA Section 10 prohibition of the obstruction or alteration of navigable waters. The construction of a wind farm would therefore come within the purview of Section 10 of the RHA if it had potential effects on navigability or on water quality.

Federal jurisdiction under Section 10 is complicated by changes in water levels. Jurisdiction over tidal waters extends to the mean high water mark.[97] The mean high water mark is calculated by using tidal cycle data. The ordinary high water mark, which defines federal jurisdiction in non-tidal waters, is not so easily determined. As defined by regulation,

'[t]he "ordinary high water mark" on non-tidal rivers is the line on the shore established by the fluctuations of water and indicated by physical characteristics such as a clear, natural line impressed on the bank; shelving; changes in the character of soil; destruction of terrestrial vegetation; the presence of litter and debris; or other appropriate means that consider the characteristics of the surrounding areas.'[98]

Because of the complexity of the definition of Section 10, determining the jurisdiction in non-tidal lakes and rivers (whose shore areas are often classified as wetlands) is accomplished by using eyewitness accounts, photographs, and surveys of biological and physical data.[99]

## 6.2.2.  The Clean Water Act

In 1972, the passage of the Clean Water Act (CWA) introduced some wetland regulation with teeth in its Section 404. The jurisdictional touchstone for Section 404 is the term 'navigable waters', as was the case with the RHA of 1899.

96.  33 US Code Annotated SS. 401–418.
97.  33 Code of Federal Regulations S. 329.12(a)(2).
98.  33 Code of Federal Regulations S. 329.11(a)(1).
99.  See, e.g. *United States* v *Cameron*, 466 F.Supp. 1099, 1111 (M.D.Fla.1978).

However, that term is defined by Section 404 to mean the 'waters of the United States'.[100] With this broad language, Section 404, which prohibits the 'discharge of any dredged or fill material into navigable waters at specific disposal sites'[101] without a permit issued by the Corps of Engineers, covers wetlands. If dredge and fill operations were necessary for the construction of a wind farm, the necessity of obtaining a Section 404 permit would become a key issue.

Initially, the Corps of Engineers (the agency charged with implementing the Act) did not consider wetlands to be covered. This is not surprising, considering the language chosen by the drafter of Section 404.

In 1975 a district court found the Corps's limited view of its own authority to be unlawful and a derogation of its responsibilities under Section 404. That court ordered the Corps to adopt a broader definition.[102] In complying with this ruling, the Corps adopted new regulations expressly regulating wetlands. In 1977 Congress reviewed and had a chance to narrow the Corps's new definition, but refrained from doing so. The Supreme Court, reciting this history, deferred to the Corps's regulations covering wetlands, and emphasized the need to regulate wetlands in order to carry out the purposes of the CWA 'to restore and maintain the chemical, physical, and biological integrity of the Nation's waters.'[103]

Today, the Corps's definition of wetlands reflects earlier judicial mandates and congressional acquiescence. Thus its jurisdiction extends to:

1) all waters which are currently used, or were used in the past, or may be susceptible to use in interstate commerce including waters subject to the ebb and flow of the tide;
2) all interstate wetlands;
3) all other waters such as intrastate lakes, rivers, streams (including intermittent streams), mudflats, sandflats, wetlands, sloughs, prairie potholes, wet meadows, playa lakes, or natural ponds, the use, degradation or destruction of which could affect interstate or foreign commerce;
4) all impoundments of waters otherwise defined as waters of the United States under the definition;
5) tributaries of waters in paragraphs (1) and (4);
6) the territorial seas;
7) wetlands adjacent to waters identified in paragraphs (1) through (6);
8) waters of the United States do not include prior converted cropland.[104]

---

100. 33 US Code Annotated S. 1362 (7).

101. 33 US Code Annotated S. 1144.

102. *Natural Resources Defense Council* v *Callaway*, 392 F.Supp. 685 (D.D.C.1975).

103. 33 US Code S. 1251, as applied in *U.S.* v *Riverside Bayview Homes, Inc.*, 474 U.S. 121, 132, 106 S.Ct. 455, 462, 88 L.Ed.2d 419 (1985).

104. 33 Code of Federal Regulations S. 328.3(a)(3).

The Corps defines wetlands as:

'[T]hose areas that are inundated or saturated by surface or ground water at a frequency and duration sufficient to support, and that under normal circumstances do support, a prevalence of vegetation typically adapted for life in saturated soil conditions. Wetlands generally include swamps, marshes, bogs, and similar areas.'[105]

As one might imagine, these attempts to define jurisdictional reach and wetlands have been the subject of much litigation in the lower courts, as well as three Supreme Court decisions. In *U.S.* v *Riverside Bayview Homes, Inc.*,[106] the Supreme Court supported a broad interpretation of the statute's jurisdictional reach and the Corps's authority. However, in two more recent cases, *Solid Waste Agency of Northern Cook County* v *United States Corps of Engineers*,[107] and *Rapanos* v *United States*,[108] the Court took a narrower view.

*General or individual permits*

The Corps of Engineers issues two types of permits under Section 404 that allow dredge and fill activities that would otherwise be contrary to the CWA. General permits may be issued by the Corps for routine activities that typically have minimal adverse environmental effects.[109] These permits may be issued on a state, regional or nationwide basis and the activities so permitted generally do not require individual permits. The Corps generally reviews these permits every five years for reissuance, modification or termination purposes. For example, in 2000 the Corps reduced the nationwide permit (NWP) that allowed the filling of ten wetland acres to half an acre.[110] While there is public review on the creation of a general permit, once the permit is issued, a landowner need only ask for an authorization to engage in the permitted activity, saving time and paperwork.

General permits, particularly NWPs, are controversial. Since the authorization process is less onerous than with individual permits,[111] landowners and developers like them and want them expanded, while environmental groups dislike them and press for their restriction.

---

105. 33 Code of Federal Regulations S. 328.3(b). This regulation has been construed by the Court in two decisions, *SWANCC* and *Rapanos*, discussed below.
106. 474 U.S. 121, 106 S.Ct. 455, 88 L.Ed.2d 419 (1985).
107. 531 U.S. 159, 121 S.Ct. 675, 148 L.Ed.2d 576 (2001).
108. 126 S.Ct. 2208, 165 L.Ed.2d 159 (2006).
109. 33 US Code Annotated S. 1144(e)(1).
110. *National Ass'n of Home Builders* v *U.S. Army Corps of Engineers*, 453 F.Supp.2d 116 (D.D.C.2006).
111. *Sierra Club* v *Army Corps of Engineers*, 464 F.Supp.2d 1171 (M.D.Fla.2006).

Individual permits are required when discharges are not exempt or are not covered by a general permit. The individual permit process is based on guidelines issued by both the Corps of Engineers and the Environmental Protection Agency.[112] When the Corps receives an application, the proposed activity is initially reviewed to see if it is in the public interest.[113] The factors considered include conservation, economics, aesthetics, fish and wildlife values and general environmental concerns.[114] The regulatory presumption is that wetlands are vital areas that constitute a productive and valuable public resource, and their unnecessary alteration or destruction should be discouraged as being contrary to the public interest.[115] If an activity is determined by the Corps as being not in the public interest, a permit will not be issued.[116]

Even if an activity is found not to be against the public interest, the Corps must still follow certain permit guidelines[117] set out by the Environmental Protection Agency, as authorized by Section 404(b).[118] If the proposed activity would cause or contribute to 'significant degradation' of waters of the United States, no permit may be issued. Effects leading to a finding of significant degradation include:

(1) Significantly adverse effects of the discharge of pollutants on human health or welfare, including but not limited to effects on municipal water supplies, plankton, fish, shellfish, wildlife, and special aquatic sites.
(2) Significantly adverse effects of the discharge of pollutants on life stages of aquatic life and other wildlife dependent on aquatic ecosystems ...
(3) Significantly adverse effects of the discharge of pollutants on aquatic ecosystem diversity, productivity, and stability ...
(4) Significantly adverse effects of discharge of pollutants on recreational, aesthetic, and economic values.[119]

---

112. For the Corps's regulations, see generally 33 Code of Federal Regulations S. 325.
113. 33 Code of Federal Regulations S. 320.4(a)(1).
114. 33 Code of Federal Regulations S. 320.4(a)(2).
115. 33 Code of Federal Regulations S. 320.4(b)(1).
116. The Eleventh Circuit has ruled that neither S. 404 of the Clean Water Act nor the due process clause requires the Corps to give an applicant a trial-type hearing before denying a dredge and fill permit. *Buttrey* v *United States*, 690 F.2d 1170 (5th Cir.1982).
117. The general purpose of the EPA's guidelines is to 'restore and maintain the chemical, physical, and biological integrity of waters of the United States through the control of discharges or dredged or fill material.' 40 Code of Federal Regulations S. 230.1(a).
118. 40 Code of Federal Regulations S. 230.10(b), (c).
119. 40 Code of Federal Regulations S. 230.10(c).

Section 404(b)(1) dictates that the filling of wetlands will not be allowed if there is a practicable alternative available with less adverse effects.[120] An applicant has the burden of showing that there are no practicable alternatives.[121] In evaluating practicable alternatives, availability, cost, logistics and technology are considered. Therefore, practicable alternatives must be both feasible and available.

Section 404(b)(1) also distinguishes activities that are water dependent from those that are not. Non-water dependent activities are those activities that do not have to be located on or around water, such as housing or office facilities. For non-water dependent activities there is a presumption that practicable alternatives are available.[122]

Furthermore, no permit may be issued where the discharge of dredged or fill material breaches any state water quality standard, toxic effluent standard, jeopardizes a threatened or endangered species, or harms a marine sanctuary.[123] When reviewing a permit application which possibly affects a threatened or endangered species, the Corps will consult interested state wildlife agencies as well as the United States Fish and Wildlife Service.[124] If no exemption exists, a finding by the Secretary of the Interior concerning the discharge's impact on a species or its habitat will be considered final by the Corps.[125]

Both state and federal fish and wildlife services can be of considerable importance in dredge and fill permit applications. The Corps must give 'great weight' to these agencies' determinations when wildlife may be affected by development in a wetland area.[126] While the Corps may decide against state or federal wildlife agency recommendations, the Environmental Protection Agency may block any permit authorization by the Corps.[127]

*Mitigation*

A permit may be accompanied by conditions, which may include mitigation. The national goal endorsed by the Corps is that there should be no net loss of

---

120. 40 Code of Federal Regulations S. 230.10(a).
121. Section 404(b)(1). Also see *Bersani* v *United States EPA*, 489 U.S. 1089, 109 S.Ct. 1556, 103 L.Ed.2d 859 (1989).
122. 40 Code of Federal Regulations S. 230.10(a)(3).
123. 40 Code of Federal Regulations S. 230.10(b).
124. 40 Code of Federal Regulations S. 230.10(b)(3).
125. 40 Code of Federal Regulations S. 230.30(c).
126. 33 Code of Federal Regulations S. 230.4(c).
127. 33 US Code Annotated S. 1144(c).

wetlands.[128] Therefore, the Corps may require changes to the plans of a project and will usually require some kind of mitigation to offset or reduce the adverse effects to wetlands.

The Corps considers three methods of mitigation. They are: (1) avoidance, (2) minimization, and (3) compensation. In evaluating the appropriate form of mitigation, the Corps will first determine whether avoiding negative adverse effects to wetlands altogether is possible.[129] If total avoidance is impossible, then the Corps will determine whether the adverse effects can be minimized. This may require alterations to the development plans.[130]

The last resort, and the most controversial, is the use of compensatory mitigation.[131] Compensatory mitigation involves the creation of new wetlands, rehabilitation of degraded wetlands, or the conservation of existing functional wetlands. Generally, compensatory mitigation must take place within the watershed where the adverse effects are caused. The amount of mitigation depends upon the nature of the mitigation. Generally, one to one ratios are the minimum. For example, for each acre of wetlands destroyed, another acre of wetlands must be created, rehabilitated or preserved. The ratios differ according to the type of mitigation used. In cases where wetlands are created, it may be required that two or three acres be created for every acre destroyed. However, developers are only required to monitor and maintain these sites for two years after creation. As a result, many of them ultimately fail.

Mitigation banking is another approach to mitigating adverse effects to wetlands. Under this system, third parties create, restore, or acquire functional wetlands. The third party then sells mitigation credits to developers who need them in order to compensate for adversely affecting wetlands by their developments. Generally, as in compensatory mitigation, the mitigation bank must be located within the watershed where the adverse effects occur. The advan-

---

128. See Memorandum of Agreement Between EPA and Dept. of Army Concerning the Determination of Mitigation Under the Clean Water Action Section 404(b)(1), Guidelines, 55 Fed. Reg. 9210, 9211 (12 March 1990).

129. 40 Code of Federal Regulations S. 230.10(a) and S. 230.10(d). Also see Memorandum of Agreement Between EPA and Dept. of Army Concerning the Determination of Mitigation Under the Clean Water Act Section 404(b)(1), Guidelines, 55 Fed. Reg. 9210, 9211 (12 March 1990).

130. *J.B. Ruhl & James Salzman:* 'The Effects of Wetland Mitigation Banking on People', in National Wetlands Newsletter, Vol.28(2), 2006.

131. *Norman* v *United States*, 63 Fed.Cl. 231 (2004) (requiring a landowner to set aside acreage as mitigation wetlands in consideration of obtaining a permit to fill other wetlands was not a physical or regulatory taking of the set aside land).

tage of this form of mitigation is that the third party is usually more knowledgeable about wetland creation and preservation than most developers, and this leads to more successful mitigation projects.[132]


## 7. New Zealand Nature Protection Law – by *David Grinlinton*

The legislation protecting habitat and species in New Zealand is considerable. It may be roughly divided into generic regulation that is not primarily aimed at nature protection, but which has an ancillary nature protection effect; legislation that sets aside areas of New Zealand for conservation or protection; and legislation that is primarily aimed at protecting species. New Zealand is a signatory to a number of international instruments impacting upon nature and species protection.[133] Even where these international obligations have not been the subject of specific domestic legislation, they can be taken into consideration in decision-making under other natural resources and species protection legislation – such as the Resource Management Act 1991 (RMA) and the Conservation Act (CA) – where those Acts directly refer to such obligations, or where there is ambiguity in the regulatory measures in question.

### 7.1. The Role of the Resource Management Act 1991 in Nature Protection

The general planning legislation in New Zealand, the RMA, provides for the sustainable management of land, air and water.[134] Through *National* and *Regional Policy Statements*, and regional and territorial authority[135] planning

---

132. See Environmental Law Institute, Preliminary Findings of the Environmental Law Institute's Wetland Mitigation Banking Study (2001) available at www.eli.org/wmb/wmbinterim.pdf; *William Haynes & Royal Gardner:* 'The Value of Wetlands as Wetlands: The Case for Mitigation Banking', in Environmental Law Reporter, Vol. 23(5), 1993 p. 10261; *Institute for Water Resources, U.S. Army Corps of Engineers:* Existing Wetland Mitigation Bank Inventory, 2000; *J. Nicholas, J. Juergensmeyer & E. Basse:* 'Perspectives Concerning the Use of Environmental Mitigation Fees as Incentives In Environmental Protection', Part I in Environmental Liability, Vol. 7, 1999 p. 27, and Part II in Environmental Liability, Vol. 7, 1999 p. 71.
133. See *Prue Taylor:* 'International Law and the New Zealand Environment', in *Rob Harris* (ed.): Handbook of Environmental Law, 2004 Ch. 23.
134. For detailed discussion of the Resource Management Act, see Chapter 6, section 7.
135. 'Territorial authority' means a city council or a district council under the RMA: RMA, S. 2, and Local Government Act 2002 (NZ), S. 5.

instruments, central and local government is able to exert significant control over the use of natural resources and environmental protection. For example, *Regional Policy Statements* can provide for green belt areas or other protection for landscape and habitats against urban encroachment. These policy statements must be reflected in regional and district rules controlling development.[136] Further, when considering the preparation of policy and planning instruments, and indeed when deciding on specific resource consent applications, the guiding purpose and principles of the RMA include considerations that promote nature protection. For example, Section 5 of the RMA requires consideration of the 'foreseeable needs of future generations', 'safeguarding the life-supporting capacity of air, water, soil, and ecosystems', and preventing adverse effects to the environment. Also, Sections 6, 7 and 8 of the RMA require protection of the natural character of coastal and wetland environments, natural features and landscapes, areas of significant indigenous vegetation and habitats, and the intrinsic values of ecosystems, and historic and cultural heritage.

As a signatory to the UN Convention on Biological Diversity, the New Zealand government (including local government) is bound to implement its obligations under the Convention in policy-making and decision-making in acts such as the RMA. It is envisaged that there will soon be a *National Policy Statement* on biological diversity which will also have a direct influence on policy-making, plans and decision-making on resource consents under the RMA.

### 7.2. General Legislation Protecting Habitats

The CA established the Department of Conservation (DoC) with a positive obligation to manage land and water areas under its control,[137] and to conserve natural and historic heritage, habitat and conservation values.[138] It also

---

136. See for example, *Auckland Regional Council v North Shore City Council* [1995] NZRMA 424 (CA) (regional policies can limit expansion of urban development by territorial authorities) and *North Shore City Council v Auckland Regional Council* [1997] NZRMA 59 (regional polices can limit urban growth to protect water catchment and landscape values). District plans give effect to higher level policy statements, and must not be inconsistent with regional plans: Resource Management Act, S. 75(3) & (4).

137. This includes 30 % of New Zealand's land area, the 12 mile territorial sea, and New Zealand's Antarctic Territory.

138. See generally, *Kenneth Palmer:* 'Resource Management Act 1991', *Derek Nolan & Claire Kirman:* 'The Coastal Environment', *Veron Rive:* 'Forests, trees and native plants', and *Kenneth Palmer:* 'Heritage', all in *Derek Nolan* (ed.): Environmental and

has an obligation to advocate and educate in relation to conservation values. Lands held under the CA are in a number of different categories, each of which provides different levels of protection for flora, fauna and habitat. These include conservation parks, wilderness areas, ecological areas, sanctuary areas and wildlife areas. General conservation areas and stewardship lands provide for multi-use arrangements and even some agriculture and commercial uses.

The CA includes a policy-making and planning structure for conservation land similar to the RMA but based on a positive obligation to protect and enhance conservation values.[139] Wind energy development is predominantly in rural and coastal areas, so the DoC is invariably involved in the application and permit process. If a development is proposed on conservation land, the DoC may refuse permission, or may allow the development but subject to very stringent conditions to protect the natural environment and species. Freshwater fisheries are also closely controlled under the Act, including restrictions on the ability to translocate species from one area to another, and to introduce new species.

The National Parks Act 1980 provides for the establishment and protection of areas as national parks. As well as giving a higher level of general protection from development under *National Park Management Plans*, some areas can be designated *Specially Protected Areas*. Entry into such areas may require a permit because of the presence of rare or endangered species. Some national parks in New Zealand also have *World Heritage* site status. While commercial activities may be undertaken in national parks, any development that would permanently and significantly alter the landscape or ecosystem would be unlikely to be allowed.

The Reserves Act 1977 provides specific protection of smaller areas for public use for nature and habitat protection. The primary aims of the Act are: to protect and manage areas of particular value for their wildlife, indigenous flora and fauna and special features; to preserve representative samples of natural ecosystems; and to ensure the survival of indigenous species. As with the CA, the Reserves Act provides for a range of different categories of reserve. Again, commercial development that would have a significant permanent impact on the environment would be unlikely to be allowed.

Resource Management Law, 2005; and *Rob Harris* (ed.): Handbook of Environmental Law, 2004 Chapters 18 (Protected Public Land), 20 (Protecting the Landscape), and 21 (Protecting Historic Heritage).
139. CA, Preamble and S. 6.

### 7.3. Species Protection

As well as the species protection mechanisms under the general legislation described above, New Zealand has a number of measures aimed at specific protection for wildlife and plants.[140]

The Wildlife Act 1953 is administered by the DoC, and provides for protected areas for wildlife as well as specific protection for listed species wherever found in New Zealand. The Act provides for the establishment of wildlife sanctuaries, wildlife refuges and wildlife management areas, as well as for the implementation of formal wildlife population management plans. Generally all species within such areas are protected. Most indigenous species of wildlife, including birds, invertebrates and freshwater species, are protected to a high level. Some seasonal hunting of exotic bird species is allowed, and very limited customary hunting of some native species by Maori.

The Wildlife Act provides for the imposition of very stringent penalties for the illegal destruction of protected species, or of species within protected areas. These are generally strict liability offences with very limited defences, and with penalties of imprisonment for up to 6 months, or fines of up to NZ$250,000.

The Trade in Endangered Species Act 1989 complements the WA, and implements New Zealand's obligations under the Convention on the International Trade in Endangered Species. The Act allows the control or prohibition of the import and export of live species and parts of dead specimens listed under the Convention. Search and seizure powers are found under the Customs and Excise Act 1996 and border controls implemented by the Ministry of Agriculture and Forestry (MAF), with significant input in policy and practice by the DoC.

The Biosecurity Act 1993 provides for further species management and control, with options to prepare pest management strategies at local and central government levels, eradication powers and import controls to prevent the import of unwanted species into New Zealand. Again the Act is administered

---

140. See generally, *Derek Nolan & Claire Kirman:* 'The Coastal Environment', *Vernon Rive:* 'Forests, trees and native plants', *Simon Berry & Hannah Hamling:* 'Hazardous Substances', and *Mark Christensen:* 'New Organisms', all in *Derek Nolan* (ed.): Environmental and Resource Management Law, 2005. See also *Neil Deans:* 'The Law and Freshwater, *Rob Harris:* 'Legislation Covering Coastal Marine Areas', *Stephen Christensen:* 'The Law and Forestry', *Jen Crawford:* 'Hazardous Substances and New Organisms', *Rachel Garthwaite & Jen Crawford:* 'Laws Pertaining to Biosecurity', and *Mark Bellingham:* 'Biodiversity and Sustainability', all in *Rob Harris* (ed.): Handbook of Environmental Law, 2004.

primarily by the MAF, but with significant input by the DoC, the Ministry of Health and the Ministry of Fisheries. Hand in hand with the Biosecurity Act 1993 is the Hazardous Substances and New Organisms Act 1996. This Act is intended to control the introduction of new and hazardous substances and organisms into New Zealand, and sets up the Environmental Risk Management Authority which makes decisions on applications for importation. Heavy penalties, including strict liability, are imposed for breaches of these measures.

The Wild Animal Control Act 1978 is aimed at managing and controlling the effects of wild animals – usually introduced non-native species – to protect indigenous habitats and species, vegetation, soil and water. Among other things, the Act provides for control plans, including if necessary the eradication of certain wild animal species that pose a serious threat to habitats and indigenous species.

Fish species, both freshwater and saltwater, are protected at a number of levels. The general Acts already discussed, including the RMA, CA, NPA, RA, WA, TIESA and BA, all provide for protection for marine species at some level. Coastal and open sea species are specifically dealt with under the Fisheries Act 1996 which provides a very comprehensive quota management system limiting the annual take for most commercial fish species, and providing absolute protection for some threatened species. The Act implements New Zealand's obligations under the United Nations Convention on the Law of the Sea. It applies to New Zealand's 200 mile Exclusive Economic Zone, and there are heavy penalties[141] for breaches of the legislation.

Inshore and freshwater aquaculture is provided for under some of the provisions in the FA, through the general coastal and water permit provisions of the RMA, and under the Aquaculture Reform (Repeals and Transitional Provisions) Act 2004. Customary access to fisheries and aquaculture for Maori is generally protected under all of these measures.

141. Including imprisonment, confiscation of catch and vessels, and large fines.

CHAPTER 9

# Environmental Protection Law

## 1. Introduction – by *Bent Ole Gram Mortensen*

Wind turbines are large constructions as well as large machines. As such they affect their surroundings in different ways during construction, operation or dismantling. The topics of this section are the immediate environmental consequences of established wind turbines, i.e. the noise and vibration from the blades, main gearbox and generator, and the shadows and reflections from the rotor blades and the tower.

Noise (also referred to as noise emission) can affect both humans and animals and can be stressful. In relation to underwater noise, there has been discussion of whether the noise emitted from wind turbines could potentially have an effect on the navigation and behaviour of fish.[1]

In operation, a wind turbine causes both *mechanical and aerodynamic noise*.[2] Improved technology has reduced mechanical noise so much that it is no longer considered a problem for a properly designed wind turbine. Some aerodynamic noise seems unavoidable. It depends on the design of the tower and blades and on the speed of the blades. Noise will have different impacts in different locations. Elements such as vegetation, buildings, wind shear, temperature and the form of the landscape can have an impact on the noise level. The clarity of a noise and the likelihood of it being stressful depends not only on its loudness but also, and maybe even especially, on how it compares with the background noise. A special issue is low frequency noise which may be audible to some people.[3]

---

1. *EWEA:* Wind Energy – The Facts – An Analysis of Wind Energy in the EU-25, Vol.4, part 5.2. Available at: www.ewea.org.
2. See in general *National Research Council (US):* Environmental Impacts of Wind-Energy Projects, 2007 pp. 108-109.
3. See *Miljøstyrelsen:* Lavfrekvent støj, infralyd og vibrationer i eksternt miljø, Vol.9, 1997 (Danish guidelines on low frequency noise, infrasound and vibration in the environment). See also section 4.5.

*Visual disturbance* may also be caused by *flickering shadows* cast on the ground or on buildings by the moving blades, and this has even been considered to be a potential public safety hazard.[4]

The extent to which protection from noise, visual effects etc. is safeguarded by public law requirements, i.e. permits, standards etc., varies from one country to another. In most countries neighbour law or nuisance law may also be relevant.


## 2. International Rules on Noise and Related Issues – by *Bent Ole Gram Mortensen*

Noise and other nuisances from wind turbines have not been regulated by international conventions.

In international law, however, it is a generally accepted principle that a nation state cannot exercise its sovereignty in a way which does harm to other states.[5] This may also apply to noise and other nuisances from a wind farm sited close to a national border. In its 53rd session in 2001, the International Law Commission drafted a recommendation to the UN General Assembly on the Prevention of Transboundary Harms from Hazardous Activities. According to Article 3, 'The State of origin shall take all appropriate measures to prevent significant transboundary harm or at any event to minimize the risk thereof.' 'Harm' means harm caused to persons, property or the environment. Nevertheless, it is doubtful whether normal noise from a wind turbine is covered by the term 'harm'.

As a general rule, noise and other nuisances are regulated by national law. However, at the international level certain standardisation bodies deal with particular noise issues.

International standardization bodies have taken up the challenge of ensuring a private form of 'regulation'. The main rule-making body for wind turbines is the International Electrotechnical Commission (IEC). All major industrial countries are members of the IEC.[6]

---

4.  See *National Research Council (US):* Environmental Impacts of Wind-Energy Projects, 2007 pp. 110-111 and pp. 120-121. See also *Bureau of Land Management (BLM), U.S. Department of the Interior:* Wind Energy Final Programmatic Environmental Impact Statement, Vol.1, 2005 Ch. 5, pp. 92-93. Available at: http://windeis.anl.gov/documents/fpeis/index.cfm.
5.  On the no-harm principle, see Chapter 3, section 1.3.2.
6.  See www.iec.ch.

Generally speaking, all over the world wind turbines are subject to the IEC 61400 series of technical standards for wind turbines.[7] A related set of rules (IEC WT 01) has been issued to ensure mutual international recognition.

The IEC 61400 series contains no standards on the maximum permitted noise from wind turbines. Only noise measurement techniques are regulated (IEC 61400-11:1998, Wind turbine generator systems. Acoustic noise measurement techniques). The IEC WT System is based on the principle of mutual recognition of test results and certificates. The US Institute of Electrical and Electronics Engineers (IEEE) has led the development of a consensus on a standard for interconnection, resulting in IEEE 1547: Standard for Interconnecting Distributed Resources with Electric Power Systems.[8]

Regarding the measurement of noise, two different systems are generally applied: either limits based on measurements and calculations of the exact noise emission from the wind turbine at specific wind speeds and distances; or the total noise level, including background noise, is taken into consideration.

## 3. EU Rules on Noise and Related Issues – by *Bent Ole Gram Mortensen*

Under EU law, noise and similar pollution issues related to wind turbines are mainly left to be regulated by national law. National regulations in the various Member States can vary widely. Neighbour law or nuisance law will be applied in most countries. Planning law combined with environmental impact assessment (EIA) is another approach used. A wind turbine can also be seen either as a machine or as a building, or even as a building with a machine on top, and will be regulated by the applicable laws.

For a number of years noise emission has been a topic of interest to the EU. The noise emissions of certain categories of equipment have been regulated.

Examples of this include: Directive 70/157/EEC of 6 February 1970 on the approximation of the laws of the Member States relating to the permissible sound level and the exhaust system of motor vehicles; Directive 77/311/EEC of 29 March 1977 on the approximation of the laws of the Member States relating to the driver-perceived noise level of wheeled

7.   Issued by the International Electrotechnical Commission, www.iec.ch.
8.   See *Hans Larsen & Leif Sønderberg Petersen* (eds.): The Future Energy System – Distributed Production and Use, Risø Energy Report 4, 2005 p. 28.

agricultural or forestry tractors; Directive 80/51/EEC of 20 December 1979 on the limitation of noise emissions from subsonic aircraft; and Directive 92/61/EEC of 30 June 1992 relating to the type-approval of two or three-wheel motor vehicles.

More general rules are found in the Directive 2000/14/EC on noise emission in the environment by equipment for use outdoors, discussed below in section 3.1. When it comes to the assessment of the impact of noise emission, rules are found in both Directive 85/337/EEC on the assessment of the effects of certain public and private projects on the environment (the EIA Directive) and in the Directive 2002/49/EC relating to the assessment and management of environmental noise.

### 3.1. EU Noise Rules for Outdoor Equipment
The main EU rules regarding outdoor noise are in Directive 2000/14/EC of the European Parliament and of the Council of 8 May 2000 on the approximation of the laws of the Member States relating to the noise emission in the environment by equipment for use outdoors. However, the Directive only applies to equipment listed in its Annex I. Among the equipment listed in Annex I is power generators, which are defined as: 'Any device comprising an internal combustion engine driving a rotary electrical generator producing a continuous supply of electrical power'. Wind turbines are not included in the Annex.

### 3.2. EIA Directive
Requirements for environmental impact assessments are laid down in Council Directive 85/337/EEC of 27 June 1985 on the assessment of the effects of certain public and private projects on the environment (the EIA Directive), see above Chapter 7, section 3. Wind turbines are listed in Annex II of the EIA Directive, indicating that whether or not a project is to be subject to an environmental impact assessment in accordance with Articles 5 to 10 is determined either on a case-by-case examination or according to thresholds or criteria set by the Member States. If an EIA is to be carried out, a project description must be elaborated. According to Annex IV, among other things a description of the project must in particular include an estimate, by type and quantity, of expected residues and emissions (water, air and soil pollution, noise, vibration, light, heat, radiation, etc.) resulting from the operation of the proposed project. As such, noise as well as blade glint, shadow flicker and vibration from a wind turbine must be included in the EIA.

### 3.3. Directive Relating to the Assessment and Management of Environmental Noise

Directive 2002/49/EC of the European Parliament and of the Council of 25 June 2002 relating to the assessment and management of environmental noise is intended to 'provide a basis for developing and completing the existing set of Community measures concerning noise emitted by the major sources, in particular road and rail vehicles and infrastructure, aircraft, outdoor and industrial equipment and mobile machinery, and for developing additional measures, in the short, medium and long term'. This includes noise from wind turbines.

The main obligation for each Member State is to ensure that, by 30 June 2007, *strategic noise maps* had been made showing the situation in the preceding calendar year and, where relevant, approved by the competent authorities, for

– all agglomerations with more than 250,000 inhabitants,
– all major roads which have more than six million vehicle passages a year,
– all major railways which have more than 60,000 train passages per year, and
– all major airports within the territory of the Member State.

For the above mentioned areas each Member States was required, no later than 18 July 2008, to draw up action plans designed to manage noise and its effects, including noise reduction if necessary. Furthermore, the Member States must ensure that the strategic noise maps they have made, and where appropriate adopted, and the action plans they have drawn up are made public in accordance with relevant Community legislation.[9]

## 4. Danish Rules on Noise and Related Issues– by *Bent Ole Gram Mortensen*

Under Danish law, noise and similar pollution issues related to wind turbines are mainly regulated by *public law*. However, such issues are also subject to *private law*, i.e. neighbour law.

---

9. In particular Council Directive 90/313/EEC of 7 June 1990 on the freedom of access to information on the environment.

## 4.1. Private Law and Public Law

No general Danish act has been issued on neighbour law. It is the courts that have developed the legal doctrine of general neighbour law. However, public law, especially environmental law, to some extent safeguards neighbour concerns and specific requirements have been established in some areas of public law. Such requirements work in parallel with neighbour law in a rather complex way, establishing permit requirements or setting limits to the permitted level of disturbance from activities, including wind turbines. Even where a permit has been granted or fixed limits for emissions, e.g. noise levels, may have been complied with, it is still up to the courts to decide whether an activity should be prohibited or compensation paid on the basis of an individual assessment of the level of disturbance.[10] Under neighbour law the decisive criterion is whether the 'tolerance limit' (*tålegrænsen*) has been exceeded. If the tolerance limit has been exceeded, the courts may either issue an order to bring the interference below the tolerance limit – or prohibiting the activity if necessary – and/or award the neighbour compensation. Neighbours include not only adjoining properties, but others within a certain geographical proximity to the activity in question, depending on the character of the disturbance.[11]

In determining whether the tolerance limit has been exceeded, in some cases the courts have awarded compensation for significant disturbance from construction and activities which cannot reasonably be considered as being usual in the area concerned. In these cases compensation has been awarded even if all the public law requirements have been fulfilled.

In a Supreme Court decision from 1995[12] a major extension to a sewage disposal plant in territorial waters was not found to be within the bounds of what could reasonably be expected from the point of view of neighbouring private homes. The visual interference was so significant that the owners were awarded compensation under neighbour law, even though compensation for expropriation had already been given. The risk of annoyance due to obnoxious smells was included in the court's evaluation. In another court case compensation for the erection of a telecommunications pole 23 metres from a residential home was awarded under neighbour law, even though the necessary building permit had been granted.[13] In a case concerning the construction of high voltage power lines as close as 33

10. On Danish law relating to neighbouring properties, see *Orla Friis Jensen:* 'Ejendomsret og miljøret', in *Ellen Margrethe Basse* (ed.): Miljøretten, Vol. 1, 2006, pp. 95-105.
11. *Orla Friis Jensen:* 'Ejendomsret og miljøret', in *Ellen Margrethe Basse* (ed.): Miljøretten, Vol. 1, 2006, p. 97.
12. UfR 1995.466 H.
13. UfR 2006.1290 H.

metres from neighbouring residential areas, compensation was awarded on the basis of neighbour law. According to the court, the public debate about the health risks of living close to high voltage power lines had affected the property value and the owner should be compensated accordingly.[14] Similarly, compensation has been given under neighbour law following the erection of a transformer station.[15] Noise from motorways which has exceeded the acceptable limit has led to compensation in several court cases.[16] However, the planned or actual use of an area may affect the tolerance limit and neighbours must accept somewhat higher noise levels.[17]

However, it appears that the situation is somewhat different with respect to wind turbines. Local planning requirements and the planning requirements in the Wind Turbine Circular have been seen as a way of balancing the rights of wind turbine owners and their neighbours. If current noise regulations have been adhered to and if reflection from the blades has been limited, compensation has not so far been given.[18] If a wind turbine operates within the fixed limits for noise and the required distance from neighbours, it will be difficult to get any compensation based on neighbour law.[19]

In a High Court ruling from 2001, the court found that the local plan had taken neighbour concerns into account and that a claim for compensation under neighbour law had to be based on very special circumstances. At the same time, the court rejected the idea that rulings on neighbour law regarding road noise and the establishment of high voltage power lines could be applied to wind turbines.[20] In another 2007 High Court ruling[21] on a challenge to the proposed establishment of two large-scale wind turbines, the court found that it had not been substantiated that the establishment should be prohibited on the basis of neighbour law.

As part of a 2008 Energy Agreement it has been proposed to establish a compensation scheme for neighbours to wind turbines. Such a compensation

---

14. UfR 1998.1515 H (also published as MAD 1998.866 H). See also UfR 1996.540 H.
15. MAD 2006.609 Ø.
16. UfR 2002.1 H. See also UfR 1999.353 H and UfR 1999.360 H.
17. See UfR 2007.559 V about a driving training facility in an area which had previously been designated as an airfield according to planning law.
18. See FED 1997.1617 V, MAD 1997.890 V (also published as FED 1997.1722 V) and MAD 1997.875 V.
19. MAD 2001.112 and KFE 1995.211.
20. UfR 2001.929 V (also published as MAD 2001.112 and FED 2001.121). See also KFE 1995.211 and MAD 2006.609 Ø.
21. Eastern High Court 12 October 2007, 4. afd. B-1854-06, see Annex I for a case description.

scheme is controversial from a legal point of view since it is likely to undermine neighbour law.

The Danish *public law regulation* of noise and similar pollution issues related to wind turbines is mainly to be found in planning law and in environmental protection law[22] under the Ministry of the Environment. Regulation is based on notification of the construction of wind turbines in accordance with an executive order on wind turbine noise issued under the Environmental Protection Act. There is no environmental licensing requirement for wind turbines, see further below section 4.2 regarding noise standards.

Land use aspects are regulated under the Planning Act; see Chapter 5, section 4.1. Section 35 sets out a requirement for a rural zone permit for changes to land use, e.g. the construction of a wind turbine. The rural zone permit requirement may, however, be replaced by a detailed local plan explicitly allowing the construction of wind turbines. A circular on planning and zoning for the construction of wind turbines[23] has been issued in accordance with the Planning Act.

Wind turbines are also governed by the Danish Electricity Supply Act.[24] In accordance with this Act, the Minister of Transport and Energy has issued an Executive Order on a technical certification scheme for the design, manufacture and installation of wind turbines.[25]

The Executive Order's requirements and procedures for the issue of type and project certificates are based on the international regulation IEC WT01 referred to in section 2. All Danish wind turbines (on land, in territorial waters and in the exclusive economic zone) must comply with the technical criteria of the Danish Wind Turbine Certification Scheme. The scheme has been in place since the beginning of the 1980s. It regulates safety, energy and quality in relation to wind turbines and their foundations.

The Danish Energy Authority has contracted out the administration of the approval scheme to the Department for Wind Energy and Atmospheric Physics at Risø National Laboratory. Certification itself is done by a registered body accredited by either the Danish Accreditation and Metrology Fund (DANAK) or some other recognized international accreditation body which must be a

---

22. Consolidated Planning Act No 813 of 21 June 2007 with later amendments; and Consolidated Environmental Protection Act No 1757 of 22 December 2006. On Danish planning law in general, see Chapter 6, section 4.
23. Circular No 100 of 10 June 1999, see Chapter 5, section 4.1.
24. Consolidated Electricity Supply Act No 1115 of 8 November 2006 with amendments.
25. Executive Order No 1268 of 10 December 2004.

signatory to the European cooperation for Accreditation's multilateral agreement on mutual recognition.

In the following, four different kinds of pollution from wind turbines will be discussed, primarily on the basis of public law.

## 4.2. Noise Standards

Noise regulation relates to two areas: the location of the wind turbine, and type certification. Noise related to the location of wind turbines is regulated under the auspices of the Ministry of the Environment. The regulation of type certification is the responsibility of the Ministry of Transport and Energy.

The main rules regarding *noise* are to be found in the Executive Order on wind turbine noise[26] issued in accordance with the Environmental Protection Act. This regulation expresses neighbour law concerns. The Executive Order calls for notification of new wind turbines prior to their construction. The authorities (the municipality) may raise objections to the establishment of a wind turbine within 4 weeks from its notification.

According to Section 2 of the Executive Order, the maximum noise level from wind turbines in outdoor areas at 15 metres from residences (except the private residence of the wind turbine owner) in rural areas may not exceed 44 dB(A) at a wind speed of 8 m/s and 42 dB(A) at a wind speed of 6 m/s. In the outdoor areas most affected by the noise, such as residential areas, institutions, summer cottages, allotments, recreational areas and other areas sensitive to noise, the noise level may not exceed 39 dB(A) at a wind speed of 8 m/s and 37 dB(A) at a wind speed of 6 m/s.[27] These limits are based on measurements and calculations of the exact noise emission from the wind turbine. The background noise is not taken into consideration. In connection with the construction of a wind turbine, the owner is obliged to give notice of the construction to the municipality. The owner must prove that the noise level will be within the above mentioned limits. The documentation must include measurements of the noise level from one or more of the same type of wind turbine and maps of the specific location for their construction. Furthermore, noise measurement can be demanded by the municipality at the cost of the owner when:

1) a notified wind turbine is being put into use,

---

26. The Ministry of the Environment's Executive Order No 1518 of 14 December 2006 on Wind Turbine Noise. Executive Order No 304 of 14 May 1991 on Wind Turbine Noise applies to wind turbines established or notified before 1 January 2007.
27. The measurement methods are defined in an annex to the Executive Order.

2) in connection with an ordinary control, at a maximum of once a year, or

3) in connection with complaints by neighbours regarding the noise.

As regards *type certification*, the guidelines[28] for classes A to C require Type Characteristic Measurements, which must include noise measurement. The guidelines also state that noise emission measurements must be included in the documentation enclosed in the application for type certification according to the Executive Order on the technical certification scheme for the design, manufacture and installation of wind turbines (Section 5).

The guidelines for the technical certification scheme for the design, manufacture and installation of wind turbines in Denmark give further indications for measurements in relation to wind speed, height and sound frequency spectrum.

According to the Executive Order on the technical certification scheme for the design, manufacture and installation of wind turbines, Appendix 2, section 6, the measurement of noise emission or sound output level (source strength) must be performed according to the specifications contained in the Executive Order on wind turbine noise. The noise measurement must be performed and documented as accredited technical testing by accredited laboratories or certified persons; see the Executive Order on quality requirements for environmental measurements carried out by accredited laboratories, certified persons, etc.[29]

### 4.3. Reflection (light)

There are no fixed limits for reflection (*blade glint*) from a wind turbine. Blade glint is not regulated under the Environmental Protection Act. Nuisance from blade glint must be considered as being governed by neighbour law, but according to the Planning Act it should also be considered as part of an EIA.[30]

However, certain standards apply to the type certifications of a wind turbine. According to Appendix 2 of the Executive Order on the technical certi-

---

28. Guidelines for the technical certification scheme for the design, manufacture and installation of wind turbines in Denmark.

29. The Executive Order on the technical certification scheme for the design, manufacture and installation of wind turbines states that the determination of wind speed can be usefully performed as described in standard DS/EN 61400-11 based on the power produced (item 27), and the specifications for placement of the reference position and measurement board in DS/EN 61400-11 can be used. These standards are voluntary.

30. See Chapter 7, section 4.1.

fication scheme for the design, manufacture and installation of wind turbines, the assumed reflection conditions for the rotor blades of a wind turbine must be specified in the wind turbine documentation; see DS/ISO 2813.[31]

### 4.4. Shadows and Visual Impact

Shadows from wind turbines on neighbouring areas and the general visual impact are regulated by neighbour law and by planning law (the Circular on planning and zoning for the establishment of wind turbines). So far, shadows from wind turbines have not been considered a problem according to neighbour law. The Environmental Protection Act does not apply to shadows from wind turbines.

According to the Circular on planning and zoning for the establishment of wind turbines, Section 4, a wind turbine more than 25 metres high, measured with a blade in its highest position, must not be placed closer to a neighbouring house than four times its height. If a wind turbine is placed closer than 500 metres from neighbouring dwellings, the potential negative effects must be described in the local plan which allows the establishment of wind turbines. As old and small wind turbines are replaced by new and larger turbines, the latter must also comply with these limits, even though they are placed on exactly the same spot as the old turbine.

In general, when granting a rural zone permit for the establishment of a wind turbine in accordance with the Planning Act, Section 35, the effects on neighbours must be considered alongside the impact on landscape etc.

### 4.5. Vibration

No fixed limits for vibration have been laid down under the Environmental Protection Act or the type certification scheme. Nuisance from vibration must be considered as being governed by neighbour law. However, according to Section 42 in the Environmental Protection Act, a municipality can demand a reduction in extensive pollution from energy producing facilities, including wind turbines.

The Danish Environmental Protection Agency has issued guidelines on low frequency noise, infrasound and vibration in the environment (1997).[32] When setting the limits for environmentally acceptable vibration levels, the

---

31. See Table 2 in the Guidelines for the technical certification scheme for the design, manufacture and installation of wind turbines in Denmark.

32. *Miljøstyrelsen:* Lavfrekvent støj, infralyd og vibrationer i eksternt miljø, Vol. 9, 1997 (Danish guidelines on low frequency noise, infrasound and vibration in the environment).

guidelines only consider tactile vibration. Re-radiated noise that often accompanies vibration is assessed as low frequency noise. Phenomena such as the rattling of windows or shaking of furniture are not considered as vibration or noise. Damage to buildings and other property is not explicitly regulated by environmental law. Claims are dealt with by the courts in accordance with neighbour or tort law.

Vibration is measured in the room in which the occupants experience it to be strongest. The energy average of the maximum levels that occur simultaneously at the (2 or more) measuring points is calculated and is compared to the recommended vibration limits. These limits are fixed at between 75 and 85 dB depending on the type of area in question.

## 5. Norwegian Rules on Noise and Related Issues – by *Hans Christian Bugge*

### 5.1. Private Law and Public Law

The roots of Norway's pollution control law are found mainly in two traditional private law instruments: neighbour law for air pollution and noise, and water law for water pollution.[33] Neighbour law still plays a certain role, as the Neighbour Act[34] lays down general rules for prohibiting and compensating for 'unreasonable or unnecessary' neighbour nuisance (mainly pursuant to Sections 2 and 9). This continues to be the most important legal basis for claims for damages from noise disturbance from roads, airports and other installations. Noise from wind turbines may also lead to awards of compensation pursuant to the Neighbour Act.

In 1991, the Supreme Court restricted the use of a wind turbine on the basis of the Neighbour Act.[35] Today, compensation is more relevant. In a recent case a district court found that 10 neighbours to a wind farm at the southern tip of Norway were entitled to compensation pursuant to the Neighbour Act for noise nuisance, as the outdoor noise level exceeded 40 dBA.[36]

---

33. Both the first Neighbour Act and the first Watercourse Act were adopted in 1887.
34. Act of 16 June 1961 No 15.
35. Norsk Retstidende 1991 p. 1289.
36. Decision by Kristiansand tingrett, 13 December 2007 in case 07-029945SKJ-KISA/08. The amounts varied between NOK 20,000 and 90,000 (corresponding to USD 4,000 and 18,000).

Since the late 1960s the private law regime has gradually been replaced by public law regulation which has laid down general prohibitions and permit systems for air and water pollution. Since 1981 there has been the integrated Pollution Control Act[37] covering all types of pollution from stationary sources, including noise and waste management.

However, private law pursuant to the Neighbour Act still applies to pollution from ordinary households and other day-to-day activities that fall below the threshold of the regulations or pollution permit requirements. And even if an activity has a permit pursuant to the Pollution Control Act, the neighbours may still be compensated for their economic loss due to pollution and other nuisance from an activity.

## 5.2. Integrated Pollution Control

Norway has quite integrated pollution control legislation. The Pollution Control Act covers air, water and soil pollution, as well as noise and solid waste management.[38] For the most part, however, it only applies to pollution from stationary sources. Pollution from transport is controlled by other legislation, more specifically on road traffic,[39] sea transport[40] and air transport.[41] Chemical and other hazardous products are controlled pursuant to the Product Control Act.[42]

As regards *the energy sector*, the Pollution Control Act applies fully to pollution from power production, such as $CO_2$ emissions from gas-fired power plants, noise from wind turbines (if it exceeds a certain level, see below), and increased water pollution as a result of changes in water flow due to hydropower development. The Act also applies to regular discharges and emissions from offshore oil production. However, these activities are more generally regulated by special legislation: the Energy Act,[43] the Hydropower Development Act,[44] and the Petroleum Act[45] respectively. A new Act on

37. Act of 13 March 1981 No 6.
38. It also applies to vibration and radiation to the extent this is explicitly regulated. However, radiation is mainly covered by a special Act on Radiation Protection.
39. Road Traffic Act of 18 June 1965 No 4.
40. There are several acts related to sea transport which, among other things, implement the international maritime conventions.
41. Air Transport Act of 11 June 1993 No 101.
42. Act of 11 June 1976 No 79.
43. Act of 29 June 1990 No 50.
44. Act of 14 December 1917 No 17.
45. Act of 29 December 1996 No 72.

Greenhouse Gas Emissions Trading[46] has established a system which is linked to the pollution permit system pursuant to the Pollution Control Act.

The Pollution Control Act and the Greenhouse Gas Emissions Trading Act are the responsibility of the Ministry of the Environment. A directorate under the Ministry, the Pollution Control Authority, is the main implementing agency with a broad field of competence as regards the implementation of and decisions pursuant to both Acts.

The Pollution Control Act lays down a general prohibition of pollution, and even of creating a risk of pollution. However, this is just a starting point. There are important exceptions to the prohibition. First, the Act itself states that 'ordinary' pollution from the day-to-day activities of households, offices, shops, schools, hotels etc., and pollution from ordinary agriculture, forestry and fishery, is permitted, unless specific regulations have been issued. Second, pollution from many sources is allowed under regulations made pursuant to the Act. For example, such regulations may lay down technical requirements and/or emissions limits for various types of activities. These may include noise emission limits and other technical requirements related to wind turbines.

Third, pollution may be permitted by an individual pollution permit. Section 11 of the Act states that the pollution control authorities may issue a permit to pollute. Noise from a wind turbine could require a permit if it will clearly be harmful to the neighbourhood or if it is expected to exceed certain noise limits. When deciding on an application, the authorities must make a broad assessment of the effects of the pollution from the project on the one hand, and the possible other advantages and disadvantages of the project on the other hand. This is a good example of an Act that gives the executive authorities wide discretionary power. The Act itself lays down few, if any, further guidelines on the weighting between environmental and other concerns.

Most often, the authorities will issue a permit with strict conditions as to emissions limits and control systems, as well as requiring regular reporting to the authorities, not least if there is an accidental discharge or if the conditions are not fulfilled for any reason.

Applications for pollution permits are always made public and are subject to a hearing. In the case of more important projects, the rules on environ-

46. Act of 17 December 2004 No 99.

mental impact assessments pursuant to the Planning and Building Act[47] apply.

### 5.3. Noise

As stated, a number of regulations have been issued under the Pollution Control Act. Most of them are now included in a main Regulation on Control of Pollution.[48] This includes rules on environmental quality standards (local air quality) and noise. The rules on local air quality implement the relevant EC directives. It lays down environmental quality norms for sulphur dioxide, nitrogen oxides, lead, benzene, carbon monoxide and suspended particles.

As regards noise, the regulation lays down limits for acceptable noise from transport and industrial plants in residential areas and nursery schools, and in education and health institutions. The general limit is 40 dBA. It prescribes certain procedures which must be followed if the limits are exceeded, with a view to reducing them. The main responsibility for monitoring and for taking the necessary measures lies with the owner of the transport infrastructure or the industrial plant.

More generally, the problem of noise is subject to national guidelines, in particular the Guidelines for the Treatment of Noise in Land Use Planning.[49] These also apply to wind turbines. They recommend a maximum outdoor noise limit of 45 dB (Lden) from wind turbines in residential areas and areas with recreational homes. This is a recommendation in the form of a guideline, and is not a legally binding limit. It is used as a starting point and a basis for assessing whether the noise level is acceptable in each situation. In practice, most wind turbines are located in isolated areas where noise does not pose a significant problem. If, however, this is not the case – and in particular if the 45 dB (Lden) level is exceeded – a permit is required pursuant to the Pollution Control Act. Here again, the very open formulation of the relevant provisions gives the authorities a wide margin of discretion when making the decision.

The Pollution Control Act also lays down the general system for the disposal of all types of *waste* in Norway. This is also a field which is regulated

---

47. The Pollution Control Act has its own rules on environmental impact assessments, but in practice these have now been replaced by the general system under the Planning and Building Act.
48. Regulation of 1 June 2004 No 931.
49. Rundskriv T-1442.

in detail through a comprehensive and quite complex regulation,[50] which to a large extent mirrors the main EC directives in this field.

### 5.4. Compensation

One chapter in the Pollution Control Act deals with compensation for pollution damage. As the general rule it lays down strict liability for harm caused by pollution. The owner of an installation or activity that causes harm is the person liable, unless some other person has used or occupied the installation or carried out the activity which has caused the harm. This chapter also applies to noise, including the noise from wind turbines. However, wind turbines are subject to a permit system, and if a permit has been given the pollution or noise will be regarded as legal. If the pollution or noise that is regarded as legal has caused harm or loss, the general private law rules of the Neighbour Act[51] apply; see above section 5.1. If the nuisance exceeds the general tolerance limit in neighbour relations, i.e. if it is unreasonable and unnecessary, the neighbour may claim compensation for damage on the basis of strict liability.

## 6. US Rules on Noise and Related Issues – by *Margaret Rosso Grossman*[52]

The construction and operation of an industrial-scale wind farm raises a number of environmental concerns, and even a single wind turbine may trigger complaints from neighbours. In the United States, environmental protection is governed by federal and state statutes and regulations, state common law and local ordinances. Control of noise pollution is primarily a matter of state and local, rather than federal, control.[53] Indeed, as an April 2007 National Research Council report notes, '[f]ederal regulation of wind-energy facilities is minimal if the facility does not have a federal nexus (that is, receive

---

50. Regulation of 1 June 2004 No 930.
51. Act of 16 June 1961 No 15.
52. This contribution is based on work supported by the Cooperative State Research, Education and Extension Service, US Department of Agriculture, under Project No ILLU-470-309. The author thanks Ryan Finley for his research assistance.
53. *Bureau of Land Management (BLM), U.S. Department of the Interior:* Final Programmatic Environmental Impact Statement on Wind Energy Development on BLM-Administered Lands in the Western United States, 2005, pp. 4-10 to 4-11, June 2005. Available at: http://windeis.anl.gov/documents/fpeis/index.cfm.

federal funding or require a federal permit).'[54] This section will therefore discuss the applicability of nuisance law to wind farms, briefly consider the relevant federal noise regulations and guidelines, and then discuss a few prominent examples of state noise control.[55]

## 6.1. Nuisance

To the extent that wind farms create unreasonable or excessive noise or other interference with neighbouring property, the construction and operation of wind farms may give rise to a cause of action under the state common law of nuisance.[56] Because federal and state regulatory control of noise emissions from wind turbines is limited, nuisance litigation is likely to be a major enforcement mechanism in the event of excessive noise or vibration.

Nuisance offers a remedy when a defendant's activities interfere unreasonably with a plaintiff's use and enjoyment of land, injure life or health, or interfere with public rights.[57] Indeed, in the years before the enactment of zoning (planning) laws, 'the common law doctrine of nuisance served as an all-purpose tool of land use regulation.'[58] Nuisance raises issues of reasonable use of land in light of the circumstances. Both plaintiff and defendant have the right to reasonable use and enjoyment of their property. The defendant cannot cause unreasonable harm to the plaintiff, and the plaintiff may have to endure some inconvenience to accommodate the defendant's legitimate land uses. In part because of the required balance of competing interests, the doctrine of nuisance has suffered from 'confusions, contingencies and lack of principle.'[59]

---

54. *National Research Council:* Environmental Impacts of Wind-Energy Projects, 2007 p. 2. Moreover, 'little dispassionate analysis' has focused on 'the human impacts of wind-energy projects.' Ibid. at p. 6.

55. A June 2007 publication provides extensive information. *Jessica A. Shoemaker, Farmers' Legal Action Group, Inc.:* Farmers' Guide to Wind Energy: Legal Issues in Farming the Wind, 2007. Available at: www.flaginc.org/topics/pubs/wind/FGWE complete.pdf.

56. *Alois Valerian Gross:* 'Windmill as Nuisance', in American Law Reports 4th, Vol.36, 1985 p. 1159.

57. This brief explanation of nuisance is adapted from *Margaret Rosso Grossman:* 'Genetically Modified Crops in the United States: Federal Regulation and State Tort Liability', in Environmental Law Review, Vol.5, 2003 p. 86, at pp. 99-101.

58. *Louise A. Halper:* 'Untangling the Nuisance Knot', in Boston College Environmental Affairs Law Review, Vol.26, 1998 p. 89, at p.101.

59. *Louise A. Halper:* 'Untangling the Nuisance Knot', in Boston College Environmental Affairs Law Review, Vol.26, 1998 p. 91.

*Private nuisance* results from interference with the plaintiff's use and enjoyment of land; it has been defined as 'a nontrespassory invasion of another's interest in the private use and enjoyment of land.'[60] A private nuisance claim often results from activity on a defendant's land that interferes unreasonably with the use of plaintiff's neighbouring land. In contrast, *public nuisance* arises from activities that interfere with the land use of a large number of plaintiffs or with public rights. It is therefore 'an unreasonable interference with a right common to the general public.'[61] In adjudicating a public nuisance claim, the court may be asked to balance the value of the defendant's conduct against the seriousness of the harm to the public right. Public nuisance cases are normally brought by a government official or, less often, by a private plaintiff who has suffered an injury different in kind (a 'special injury') from that of members of the general public.

Nuisance can be an *intentional tort*, which requires that defendant's use of land caused plaintiff to suffer substantial and unreasonable interference with use of property and that defendant have knowledge (called 'civil intent') that its activities were substantially certain to injure plaintiffs. In contrast, *negligent nuisance* requires proof that defendant's activities on its own land (instead of the interference with plaintiff) were unreasonable.[62] Intentional nuisance is often easier to prove, because it does not require proof that the defendant's behaviour is unreasonable. Remedies for successful nuisance claims include injunctions against specific activities and damage awards.

As of the time of writing, several reported decisions have applied nuisance law to wind turbines. In two early cases (North Dakota in 1992, New Jersey in 1982)[63] the defendant had erected a wind turbine in a single-family residential neighbourhood on residential property; the plaintiff and the defendant were neighbours; and the noise produced by the wind turbine exceeded the emission level of the average modern windmill.[64]

---

60. Restatement (Second) of Torts S. 821D (1979).
61. Restatement (Second) of Torts S. 821B (1979).
62. *Zygmunt J.B. Plater et al:* Environmental Law and Policy: Nature, Law, and Society, 3rd ed., 2004 pp. 106-107, 111.
63. *Rassier* v *Houim*, 488 N.W.2d 635, 636 (N.D. 1992; and *Rose* v *Chaikin*, 453 A.2d 1378, 1384 (N.J. Super. Ct. Ch. Div. 1982). See also *Rankin* v *FPL Energy*, 2008 WL 3864829 (Tex. App.).
64. *Rassier* v *Houim*, 488 N.W.2d 635, 636 (N.D. 1992); and *Rose* v *Chaikin*, 453 A.2d 1378, 1384 (N.J. Super. Ct. Ch. Div. 1982). Noise from a modern wind turbine may be 35-45 decibels (dB(A)) at 350 metres. The term dB(A) refers to A-weighted decibels, a measure that assesses human response to environmental noise. See generally

In one case, the New Jersey Superior Court held that the wind turbine was a nuisance. The noise, produced in a residential area, was 'difficult to ignore and almost impossible to escape' and 'offensive because of its character, volume and duration.' In addition, the wind turbine noise, ranging from 56 to 61 decibels (dB(A)), exceeded the 50 dB(A) noise limit for windmills established in the local zoning ordinance.[65] In the other case, the Supreme Court of North Dakota affirmed a trial court finding that there was no nuisance. No local noise ordinance applied, and plaintiff 'came to the nuisance' two years after the turbine was built.[66] A strong dissent, however, characterized the noise from the wind turbine as 'incompatible with a residential neighborhood.'[67] In a case involving a wind farm with 421 turbines in an area of more than 73 square miles, a Texas appellate court held that the aesthetic impact of the wind turbines does not support a claim of nuisance.[68]

The New Jersey and North Dakota decisions involved single turbines. In June 2007, the Supreme Court of Appeals of West Virginia decided a nuisance case involving a large facility.[69] A proposed wind power electricity-generating facility would have up to 200 wind turbines on a site about 14 miles (22.5 km) long and about half a mile (0.8 km) wide. The state Public Service Commission had issued the siting certificate required to authorize construction and operation of the facility. Seven plaintiffs, with homes located between half a mile and two miles (3.2 km) from the proposed turbines, sought a permanent injunction to prevent construction of the facility, alleging that it would create a private nuisance. They asserted that they would be harmed by noise, the flicker effect, and danger from 'broken blades, ice throws, and collapsing towers'; they alleged that the facility would reduce the value of their property.[70] The trial court dismissed the suit, reasoning that it had no jurisdiction to enjoin construction of a project approved by the Public Service Commission. The West Virginia Supreme Court of Appeals reversed the circuit court's order. The Supreme Court of Appeals held that the siting certificate granted by the Public Service Commission did not abrogate the right of plaintiffs to bring a common law nuisance claim to enjoin construction or operation of the wind power facility. Moreover, the court held that the

---

*Anthony L. Rogers, James F. Manwell, & Sally Wright:* Wind Turbine Acoustic Noise, 2002 (revised 2006) pp. 6-7.

65. *Rose* v *Chaikin*, 453 A.2d 1378, 1380, 1382, 1384 (N.J. Super. Ct. Ch. Div. 1982).
66. *Rassier* v *Houim*, 488 N.W.2d 635, 636 (N.D. 1992).
67. *Rassier* v *Houim*, 488 N.W.2d 635, 641 (N.D. 1992).
68. *Rankin* v *FPL Energy*, 2008 WL 3864829 (Tex. App.). At trial, the judge did not allow the jury to consider aesthetic effects of the wind farm and the jury, which heard testimony on noise levels and land values, decided in favour of FPL Energy.
69. *Burch* v *Nedpower Mount Storm, LLC*, 647 S.E.2d 879 (W. Va. 2007).
70. *Burch* v *Nedpower Mount Storm, LLC*, 647 S.E.2d 879, 885 (W. Va. 2007).

plaintiffs' complaints were sufficient to state a claim to enjoin a nuisance prospectively (that is, before the facility was constructed). If their claims were proved at trial, the proper remedy would be abatement of the nuisance.[71] As guidance for the trial court, the Supreme Court of Appeals indicated that the trial court had latitude to create an appropriate remedy – either to enjoin construction of the wind power facility or to devise a less stringent equitable remedy. The court also noted that, although the Public Service Commission's siting certificate did not prevent the nuisance claim (and the plaintiffs should have their day in court), the certificate was 'persuasive evidence of the reasonableness and social utility' of the use of property for the wind facility.[72]

The outcome of a common law nuisance case often turns on the level of interference to the plaintiff,[73] and the applicability of local noise standards may influence the outcome. It is therefore difficult to identify any general principle of nuisance liability for wind farms. It does seem, however, that where wind farm developers use quieter modern wind turbine technology and locate their facilities in sparsely populated areas, nuisance law poses little threat of liability.

### 6.2. Noise and Vibration

Noise control in the United States is primarily a matter of state and local concern.[74] The major federal laws in the area of noise control are the Federal Noise Control Act of 1972[75] and the Quiet Communities Act of 1978.[76] The Environmental Protection Agency (EPA) or another agency enforces regulations for transport equipment, motor carriers, low noise-emission products, and construction equipment. The EPA's Office of Noise Abatement and Control, which was once responsible for enforcing the Noise Control Act, has been closed since 1982, and most noise regulation responsibilities have been

---

71. *Burch v Nedpower Mount Storm, LLC*, 647 S.E.2d 879, 889, 893-894 (W. Va. 2007).
72. *Burch v Nedpower Mount Storm, LLC*, 647 S.E.2d 879, 895 (W. Va. 2007).
73. Interference other than noise may lead to a nuisance cause of action. For example, if a newly constructed wind farm prevents a neighbouring farmer's practice of aerial spraying of pesticides, the decision in the case may turn on whether such interference is reasonable.
74. *Bureau of Land Management, U.S. Department of the Interior:* Final Programmatic Environmental Impact Statement on Wind Energy Development on BLM-Administered Lands in the Western United States, 2005 pp. 4-10 to 4-11.
75. 42 US Code SS. 4901-4918.
76. 42 US Code S. 4913.

shifted to state and local governments.[77] Although the EPA does maintain guidelines for safe noise levels (45 dB(A) indoors and 55 dB(A) outdoors, set out in its 1974 'Levels' document), these guidelines are advisory and have no binding authority.[78]

### 6.2.1. Federal

Although state or local law will generally govern noise arising from the construction or operation of wind farms, federal law applies if a wind farm is located on federally managed lands or in offshore areas.[79] The developer must apply for a right-of-way authorization from the Bureau of Land Management (BLM) for a proposed development on federal lands.[80] Documents that govern the development of wind energy projects address the issue of noise.

The National Environmental Policy Act[81] requires preparation of an Environmental Impact Statement (EIS) for 'major Federal actions significantly affecting the quality of the human environment' (Section 4332(2)(C)).[82] To satisfy this requirement for wind energy developments, in June 2005, the BLM issued a detailed final programmatic EIS for wind farm construction and operation.[83] Among other environmental effects, the programmatic EIS discusses noise impacts from activities associated with development and operation of wind turbines.[84] Wind turbines produce both mechanical and aerodynamic noise. Improved equipment has reduced mechanical noise, which now

---

77. See *United States Environmental Protection Agency:* Frequent Questions: Does the EPA regulate noise? Available at: http://publicaccess.custhelp.com/cgi-bin/publicaccess. cfg/php/enduser/std_ adp.php?p_faqid=1765.

78. *United States Environmental Protection Agency*, Information on Levels of Environmental Noise Requisite to Protect Public Health and Welfare with an Adequate Margin of Safety, 1974 p. 22.

79. See 43 US Code SS. 1761-1770. The Department of the Interior reviews offshore wind energy projects. *National Research Council:* Environmental Impacts of Wind Energy Projects, 2007 p. 131.

80. *Bureau of Land Management, U.S. Department of the Interior:* Instruction Memorandum No 2006-216, 2006. Available at: http://www.blm.gov/nhp/efoia/wo/fy06/im 2006-216.htm. An application for a development on the outer continental shelf (i.e., more than three miles offshore) goes to the Department of the Interior.

81. 42 US Code SS. 4321-4370f.

82. See above Chapter 7, section 6.1.

83. *Bureau of Land Management, U.S. Department of the Interior:* Final Programmatic Environmental Impact Statement on Wind Energy Development, 2005.

84. *Bureau of Land Management, U.S. Department of the Interior:* Final Programmatic Environmental Impact Statement on Wind Energy Development, 2005 pp. 5-20 to 5-27.

'must, to some extent, be viewed as an indication of poor design.'[85] Aerodynamic noise, which may be unavoidable, varies with turbine design and speed. Typical noise from wind turbine rotation may be 58 to 62 dB(A) at a distance of 50 metres from the turbine (about the level of conversation heard from 1 metre) and 36 to 40 dB(A) at a distance of 600 metres.[86] Noise from electrical substations and transmission lines may also occur. The programmatic EIS indicates, however, that construction of a wind farm causes more significant noise disturbance than its ongoing operation.[87] The EIS recommends common sense mitigation measures, such as measuring background noise levels to compare with the expected noise from the proposed wind farm. Other recommended measures focus on minimizing disruptions from construction noise, rather than on eliminating noise from operation of the completed wind energy project.[88]

### 6.2.2. States

State statutes and regulations and county or municipal ordinances govern noise from wind turbines built on private land. Some states have measures that guide the location of wind farms and often require separation from property boundaries, residences and other structures.[89] Typically, the development of a wind farm will require a government permit, and noise is one of the impacts that the permitting agency may consider. A publication by the National Wind Coordinating Committee summarizes the types of approaches to noise from wind turbines:

'Strategies employed by some [state and local] agencies in addressing potential noise concerns have included predicting and measuring noise levels, establishing noise standards, requiring noise setbacks, establishing zoning restrictions, and making turbine modifica-

85. *Bureau of Land Management, U.S. Department of the Interior:* Final Programmatic Environmental Impact Statement on Wind Energy Development, 2005 p. 5-23.
86. *Bureau of Land Management, U.S. Department of the Interior:* Final Programmatic Environmental Impact Statement on Wind Energy Development, 2005 p. 5-24.
87. *Bureau of Land Management, U.S. Department of the Interior:* Final Programmatic Environmental Impact Statement on Wind Energy Development, 2005 p. 5-22.
88. *Bureau of Land Management, U.S. Department of the Interior:* Final Programmatic Environmental Impact Statement on Wind Energy Development, 2005 p. 5-27.
89. For a discussion of setback provisions, which stipulate how far wind power turbines must be from other structures such as roads and residences, and state siting procedures for wind power facilities, see *National Wind Coordinating Committee and National Conference of State Legislatures:* State Siting and Permitting of Wind Energy Facilities, 2006. This publication collects representative approaches to inform other states that may enact legislation.

tions. To effectively handle noise concerns that may arise after permitting, some agencies have implemented a noise complaint and investigation process.'[90]

The discussion below gives brief examples of state approaches to noise control.[91]

California is a leading state, both in construction of wind farms and in state-wide noise control legislation. California's 1973 Noise Control Act[92] established the Office of Noise Control, which studies and monitors noise, assists local agencies in the enactment and enforcement of noise control ordinances, and coordinates noise control activities of state and federal agencies. Under the Act, local communities bear primary responsibility for noise regulation (Section 46060). Local noise standards for wind turbines vary. For example, the city of Sacramento has an exterior noise standard (not specifically for wind turbines) of 55 dB(A) from 7 a.m. to 10 p.m. and 50 dB(A) from 10 p.m. to 7 a.m. Intrusive sounds of 5 dB above ambient levels are permitted for 15 minutes per hour, but sounds of 20 dB above the ambient baseline are not permitted.[93] In more rural areas, such as Kern County (which includes Tehachapi Pass wind resource area, with over 5,000 turbines), the local zoning ordinance establishes setback distances for wind generators. In addition, it limits wind farm noise. Audible noise from wind turbines, measured at 50 feet from a residence or other public building, may not cause exterior noise levels exceeding 45 dB(A) for more than 5 minutes per hour or 50 dB(A) for any time period.[94] Wind farms established in other jurisdictions will be subject to the applicable local requirements, which may include setback distances and maximum noise levels.

Minnesota, too, has a wind farm industry. State law in Minnesota gives the Pollution Control Agency the authority to adopt noise standards.[95] Minnesota rules subdivide all areas into one of three noise area classifications. Noise Area Classification 1 is mostly residential; Classification 2 includes commer-

---

90. *National Wind Coordinating Committee:* Permitting of Wind Energy Facilities, revised ed., 2002 p. 23.
91. For more information on regulation, with focus on various state laws, see *National Research Council:* Environmental Impacts of Wind Energy Projects, 2007 Ch. 5.
92. California Health & Safety Code SS. 46000-46080.
93. City of Sacramento Noise Ordinances (Calif.) S. 8.68.060 (2006). Sounds +10 dB(A) are permitted for 5 minutes per hour; +15 dB(A), for 1 minute per hour.
94. Kern County, CA, County Zoning Ordinance, §19.64.140. The other public buildings are schools, hospitals, churches and public libraries. The allowable dB(A) level is reduced by 5 in the case of a 'steady pure tone.'
95. Minnesota Statutes S. 116.07(2).

cial and transport activities with intermediate noise levels; and Classification 3 includes heavy manufacturing activities.[96] Permitted noise levels depend on the classification. In Classification 1, with the strictest standards, daytime noise levels may not exceed 60 dB(A) for 50 per cent of a one-hour survey or 65 dB(A) for 10 per cent of a one hour survey; night levels are 50 dB(A) and 55 dB(A), respectively. Noise levels in Classifications 2 and 3 may be somewhat higher. Noise levels are measured from the receiving property.[97] The Minnesota Model Wind Ordinance, drafted to provide a model for effective local ordinances, incorporates the state-wide noise control rules.[98]

As another example, the Massachusetts Department of Environmental Regulation governs noise under its regulatory framework for Air Pollution Control. Its noise regulation allows new sources of sound to increase noise levels no more than 10 dB(A) over the ambient baseline, as measured from the receiving property.[99] It seems unlikely that remotely located wind farms (e.g. offshore facilities such as the proposed wind farm in Nantucket Sound) that use modern wind turbine technology will exceed this standard.

A statute enacted in Illinois takes another approach. That law, in force in August 2007, added a section to the Municipal Code and to the Counties Code. Municipalities may now regulate wind farms and electricity generating wind devices within and 1.5 miles beyond their zoning jurisdictions. A public hearing must precede siting decisions. Counties have specific authority to establish standards, including height and density, for wind farms and electricity generating wind devices. After a public hearing, counties may also regulate siting in areas outside the regulatory jurisdiction of municipalities.[100]

### 6.3. Shadows and Visual Effects
Because of the nature of wind turbines and their location in rural landscapes, wind farms are highly visible.[101] Federal legislation in the USA does not regulate the visual impact of wind farms, though lighting on towers is subject

96. Minnesota Rules 7030.0050.
97. Minnesota Rules 7030.0040.
98. *The Minnesota Project:* Minnesota Model Wind Ordinance – 2005 p. 10. See also *The Minnesota Project:* Companion Document to the Minnesota Model Wind Energy Conversion Ordinance – 2005.
    Both available at: www.mnproject.org/e-windresources-tech.html.
99. Massachusetts Regulations, Air Pollution Control, Reg. 310 CMR 7.10: Noise.
100. Public Act 095-0203, 16 August 2007, codified at 55 ILCS 5/5-12020 & 65 ILCS 5/11-13-26.
101. *Bureau of Land Management, U.S. Department of the Interior:* Final Programmatic Environmental Impact Statement on Wind Energy Development, 2005 p. 5-92.

to requirements of the Federal Aviation Administration.[102] Current FAA guidelines, in force in January 2007, require lighting (preferably red flashing lights) to define the periphery of a turbine installation. Daytime lighting is no longer required if turbines are painted bright white or a light off-white colour. These requirements may be tailored to individual installations.[103] Warning lights and other security lighting are likely to emit light to nearby property.[104]

The BLM Programmatic EIS, mentioned above, considers the visual impact of wind turbines on the landscape and other visual effects.[105] For example, during operation, 'shadow flicker' (the 'strobe-like effect from flickering shadows cast by the moving rotors onto the ground and objects') may create a visual disturbance, as well as a potential public safety hazard.[106] Shadow flicker may affect those living or working near turbines, and it may distract drivers on nearby highways.[107] In the USA, however, shadow flicker seems less significant than in Northern Europe.[108] Blade glint from 'reflection of the sun off rotating turbine blades' may also occur.[109] The EIS recommends that visual interference be mitigated by careful site design, including setting turbines back from occupied buildings. Turbine colours should be chosen to reduce visual impact, and non-reflective paints should be applied to reduce reflection.[110]

102. See *The Minnesota Project:* Minnesota Model Wind Ordinance – 2005 p. 9.
103. *National Research Council:* Environmental Impacts of Wind Energy Projects, 2007 p. 129. Requirements for wind turbine farms are listed in *Federal Aviation Administration:* Obstruction Marking and Lighting, 2007 pp. 33-34 (AC 70/7460-1K).
104. *Bureau of Land Management, U.S. Department of the Interior:* Final Programmatic Environmental Impact Statement on Wind Energy Development, 2005 pp. 5-94 to 5-95.
105. *Bureau of Land Management, U.S. Department of the Interior:* Final Programmatic Environmental Impact Statement on Wind Energy Development, 2005 pp. 5-91 to 5-99.
106. *Bureau of Land Management, U.S. Department of the Interior:* Final Programmatic Environmental Impact Statement on Wind Energy Development, 2005 pp. 5-33 and pp. 5-92.
107. *National Research Council:* Environmental Impacts of Wind Energy Projects, 2007 p. 110.
108. *National Research Council:* Environmental Impacts of Wind Energy Projects, 2007 pp. 120-121.
109. *Bureau of Land Management, U.S. Department of the Interior:* Final Programmatic Environmental Impact Statement on Wind Energy Development, 2005 p. 5-94.
110. *Bureau of Land Management, U.S. Department of the Interior:* Final Programmatic Environmental Impact Statement on Wind Energy Development, 2005 pp. 5-34 and pp. 5-97.

In general shadow flicker is not regulated, perhaps because it occurs only for limited periods.[111] State or local regulation may help to mitigate the visual impact of turbines. County or local zoning ordinances may contain provisions that govern the appearance of wind turbines; for example, an ordinance might require colours to be non-obtrusive and finishes to be non-reflective.[112]

Visual impacts that interfere with the use or enjoyment of neighbouring land might be addressed by a claim under the law of nuisance.[113] A nuisance claim may be difficult to prove, however, because to be actionable the effects of a nuisance must be substantial, unreasonable and tangible.[114] Indeed, one commentator has argued that aesthetic objections to wind farms are misguided because of the role played by windmills in seventeenth century Dutch landscape painting and the ability of wind energy to preserve natural beauty by reducing consumption of fossil fuels.[115]

## 7. New Zealand Rules on Noise and Related Issues – by *David Grinlinton*

New Zealand, as a common law jurisdiction, provides remedies against noise, vibration and other polluting 'amenity' issues through civil actions in the courts; in particular the law of nuisance. These matters are also very closely regulated under modern planning and resource management laws.

### 7.1. Common Law Remedies
Historically the law of nuisance has provided the most potent environmental remedy in the courts. Nuisance can be divided into *public* or *private* nuisance. The former provides recourse where there has been an unreasonable interference with the health, convenience or comfort of the public generally; the lat-

---

111. *National Research Council:* Environmental Impacts of Wind Energy Projects, 2007 p. 129.
112. *The Minnesota Project:* Minnesota Model Wind Ordinance – 2005 p. 9.
113. See above Chapter 9, section 6.1 on nuisance.
114. *Gregory H. Birne:* 'Tower or Antenna as Constituting Nuisance', American Law Reports 5th, Vol.88, 2006 p. 641. See also *Rankin v FPL Energy*, 2008 WL 3864829 (Tex. App.), in which the appellate court held that the visual impacts (aesthetic effects) of windmills do not support a claim in nuisance under Texas law.
115. *Avi Brisman:* 'The Aesthetics of Wind Energy Systems', in New York University Environmental Law Journal, Vol.13, 2005 pp. 1-133.

ter applies where there has been a substantial and unreasonable interference with the use and enjoyment of an interest in land.[116]

Cases where nuisance has been successfully pleaded include those arising from excessive noise, vibration, pollution, reflection[117] and interference with visual amenity. Clearly the law of nuisance is applicable to wind energy developments where some or all of these effects occur. However the public interest in an activity such as a wind turbine or wind farm which causes a nuisance may override the private inconvenience or injury suffered by an individual.[118] Further, planning consent generally provides a defence, as long as the nuisance is the unavoidable consequence of the authorized activity and there has been no negligence.[119]

Another cause of action is strict liability, also called the Rule in *Rylands* v *Fletcher* from the early decision in the case of that name.[120] The essence of this doctrine is that a person who collects or keeps something dangerous on their land will be liable if that thing escapes and causes damage to neighbouring land.[121] The doctrine has been widely invoked in pollution cases, although in New Zealand it is now considered a category of private nuisance.[122]

The law of negligence also has potential application as an environmental remedy, particularly where damage arises through ultra-hazardous activities.[123]

The application of these remedies is, however, very limited where the damage arises from activities which have been authorized under relevant

---

116. See generally, *Claire Kirman & Christian Whata:* 'Environmental Litigation and Dispute Resolution', in *Derek Nolan* (ed.): Environmental and Resource Management Law, 2005 Ch. 17, para. 17.42.

117. *Bank of New Zealand* v *Greenwood* [1984] 1 NZLR 525; and see Chapter 9, section 7.3.

118. See, for example, the approval of wind farm developments over private landowner objections in: *Genesis Power Ltd* v *Franklin District Council* [2005] NZRMA 541; and *Meridian Energy Ltd* v *Wellington City* Council (unreported, Environment Court W31/07, 14 May 2007, noted (2007) 7 BRMB 71. See also: *Bamford* v *Turnley* [1861-73] All ER Rep 706; *Kraemers* v *Attorney-General for Tasmania* [1966] TasSR 113 at 125 per Burbury CJ (natural use).

119. *Allen* v *Gulf Oil Refining Ltd* [1981] AC 1001 at 1011 per Lord Wilberforce.

120. *Rylands* v *Fletcher* (1866) LR 1 Ex 265, pp. 279-280 per Blackburn J.

121. *Kirman & Whata:* 'Environmental Litigation and Dispute Resolution', in *Derek Nolan* (ed.): Environmental and Resource Management Law, 2005 Ch. 17, para. 17.52.

122. Hamilton v Papakura District Council [2000] 1 NZLR 265.

123. See, e.g. *Burnie Port Authority* v *General Jones Pty Ltd* (1994) 68 ALJR 331; and *Attorney-General v Geothermal Produce NZ Ltd* [1987] 2 NZLR 348.

planning regulations. Where this is the case, the activity is generally immune from an action in nuisance[124] provided it is conducted within the conditions imposed and does not breach any other legal requirements or obligations.[125]

### 7.2. Regulation of Noise and Vibration

The general planning legislation in New Zealand – the Resource Management Act 1991 (RMA) – deals with noise and vibration in two main ways.[126]

First, noise emissions for activities which affect land, air or water (including the coastal marine area) can be regulated by the inclusion of specific limits in the policy and planning instruments of central and local government. For example, activities in the coastal marine area[127] are the subject of policies in the *New Zealand Coastal Policy Statement* (NZCPS) prepared by the Minister of Conservation, and rules in the *Regional Coastal Plan* prepared by the Regional Council. While there is nothing specific covering noise in respect of wind energy generation in the NZCPS, there are general statements on preserving the natural character of, and limiting the adverse effects of activities on, the coastal environment. Some *Regional Coastal Plans* do contain rules relating to noise levels for certain activities.

For land-based activities, noise is generally the subject of specific regulation and noise level standards contained in *District Plans* prepared by territorial authorities. These often rely upon, or incorporate, New Zealand Standards, of which NZS6808:1998 deals specifically with the 'Assessment and measurement of Sound from Wind Turbine Generators'. Generally the target is an inside residential night-time sound level of less than 30-35 dB.

When applying for resource consents for wind energy developments, and in subsequent hearings and appeals, considerable expert evidence is usually given to establish the likely noise and vibration effects of the proposal. Such effects will depend on the particular characteristics of the chosen turbine design when placed in the specific location with its unique combination of ter-

---

124. *Allen* v *Gulf Oil Refining Ltd* [1981] AC 1001.
125. Cases where the immunity argument has not been accepted include: *JW Birnie Ltd* v *Taupo Borough Council* [1978] 2 NZLR 1975; *Wheeler* v *JJ Saunders Ltd* [1995] 2 All ER 697; *Ports of Auckland* v *Auckland City Council* [1999] 1 NZLR 601 at 611; and *Varnier* v *Vector Energy Ltd* [2004] NZRMA 193.
126. Noise and vibration are dealt with together in the Resource Management Act, as the definition of 'noise' specifically includes 'vibration'. Resource Management Act, S. 2(1), 'Interpretation'.
127. From the high water mark to the 12 mile limit.

rain, climate and wind conditions, and proximity to residential and commercial buildings.[128]

While noise may be intrusive at some times and in some conditions, this will not necessarily mean that consent for a wind energy development will be withheld. The consent authority (or the court on appeal) may well decide that the environmental positives from wind energy (such as reductions in national and global $CO_2$ and other gas emissions) will override the localized negative impact on amenity values.[129]

Where consent is granted, it will usually be subject to stringent noise measurement and auditing requirements, normally funded by the developer and provided to the consent authority. Any later prosecution over a breach of noise standards will require a very high level of independent scientific analysis of the data, and the use of expert witnesses to interpret such data and advise the Court.

The second main way that noise and vibration are dealt with under the RMA is through general and direct enforcement provisions that apply to unlawful or excessive noise. As part of the general planning regime, land-based and coastal activities are unlawful if they contravene the RMA, a rule in a *Plan*, or the terms of a resource consent. Therefore if there are noise standards set out in a *Plan*, contravention of these will constitute an offence under the Act. Further, Section 16 of the RMA contains a general duty to avoid unreasonable noise, and Section 17 a general duty to 'avoid, remedy, or mitigate adverse effects'. In most cases where a wind energy development is conducted lawfully, pursuant to resource consents and in accordance with any conditions, these provisions will not apply. However, if the required resource consents have not been given, or have been given and are not complied with, then there may be a breach of the RMA and enforcement actions may ensue.

There are a number of options for enforcement in such circumstances. The local council may issue an abatement notice under Section 322 of the RMA, requiring the recipient to do, or cease doing, some act. The council may issue an excessive noise direction under Section 327, although that remedy is nor-

---

128. See, e.g. *Genesis Power Ltd* v *Franklin District Council* [2005] NZRMA 541, paras. 112- 128; and *Meridian Energy Ltd* v *Wellington City Council*, unreported, Environment Court W31/07, 14 May 2007, paras. 25-66.
129. This was the case in *Genesis Power Ltd* v *Franklin District Council* [2005] NZRMA 541, para. 228; *Unison Networks Ltd* v *Hastings District Council* , unreported, Environment Court W58/2006, 17 July 2006, para. 82; and *Meridian Energy Ltd* v *Wellington City Council*, unreported, Environment Court W31/07, 14 May 2007, para. 448.

mally used for occasional or intermittent noise pollution such as loud music at parties. Non-compliance with either of these measures constitutes an offence under the Act, with the risk of significant fines on conviction. A further option is the issue of an enforcement order under Section 316 by the Environment Court. An application may be made by the consent authority or 'any person'. An order may require some action to be taken or terminated in order to comply with the RMA. Failure to comply constitutes an offence, again with the risk of high financial penalties. Where there is a serious breach of the RMA, a *Plan* or a resource consent, a council or private person can proceed immediately to lay a charge under the offences provisions for breach of the RMA.

Under the RMA it is possible for the Minister for the Environment to issue a *National Policy Statement* or a *National Environmental Standard* covering noise emissions generally, or noise emissions in a specific context such as wind energy developments. Such national policy instruments and standards are binding on lower level *Regional* and *District Plans* and provide more certainty for wind energy proposals. However, such national level instruments have not yet been issued, nor have there been any clear indications when they may be introduced.

### 7.3. Light Reflection, Shadows and Visual Effects

There is no specific provision in the RMA covering these matters, although there are rules in *District Plans* and the *Building Code* on the location, standards and performance of buildings.[130] The breach of such rules can be rectified by the various enforcement measures under the RMA already mentioned, or under the very similar enforcement regime under the Building Act 2004, as appropriate.

Apart from these measures, the common law still provides a remedy through an action in nuisance as illustrated in *Bank of New Zealand* v *Greenwood*.[131]

In that case a building was constructed in such a way that a glass veranda reflected bright sunlight on to a neighbouring building, to such an extent that people working in the other building suffered headaches and found it difficult to work. The Court held that even though the building complied with local planning requirements and building standards, nevertheless there was an actionable nuisance as the dazzling glare was beyond what was a normal

---

130. Building Act 2004, and see the *Building Code* contained in Schedule One of the Building Regulations 1992.
131. Bank of New Zealand v Greenwood [1984] 1 NZLR 525.

or reasonable consequence of the building construction in this location. The Court required the owners of the offending building to pay for the installation of blinds in the windows of the other building to mitigate the nuisance.

The case is clear authority in New Zealand that reflections, shadows and visual effects of a building or structure may justify an action for nuisance, if they are beyond what might be considered normal or reasonable.

# CHAPTER 10

# Energy Law & Regulation
# of Wind Energy

## 1. Introduction – by *Anita Rønne*

Government intervention in the energy industry is a relatively recent phenomenon. The oil crises of the 1970s were the turning point for the new political and regulatory era. It became evident that the energy sector could not be left to unrestricted market forces. For about 25 years, the regulation of energy supply has thus been characterized by the high degree to which this sector has been subject to public intervention, detailed planning and control by the state. However, in this relatively short period the energy policies of most countries have seen several major changes of direction which have all had major legal implications. The prospects for the energy sector at the beginning of the 21st century have been more turbulent than ever, influenced by the wave of liberalization, deregulation, privatization and globalization. Recent years have brought fundamental changes to the way in which energy is bought, sold, produced, transported and regulated at the local, regional and global levels.[1] Simultaneously, the international energy markets have assumed new forms and energy company ownership and alliances have undergone major changes. The global developments brought about by the introduction of competition to energy markets, increasing transboundary cooperation and trade, major concerns about energy security and global warming have

---

1. See also *Barry Barton, Lila K. Barrera-Hernández, Alastair R. Lucas & Anita Rønne* (eds): Regulating Energy and Natural Resources, 2006, Chapters 1 and 21; *Martha M. Roggenkamp, Catherine Redgwell, Iñigo del Guayo & Anita Rønne* (eds.): Energy Law in Europe: National, EU and International Regulation, 2007, Chapters 1 and 16; and *Aileen McHarg & Anita Rønne:* 'Reducing Carbon-based Electricity Generation: Is the Answer Blowing in the Wind?', in *Don Zillman, Catherine Redgwell, Yinka Omorogbe & Lila K. Barrera-Hernández* (eds.): Beyond the Carbon Economy – Energy Law in Transition, 2008.

created a need for a new foundation for energy policy to ensure that the environment is safeguarded under the new market conditions and that renewable energy is further developed.

Thus it is commonly agreed that there is a need to replace the reliance on fossil fuels with alternatives, particularly renewables. At the World Summit on Sustainable Development (WSSD) held in Johannesburg in August 2002 it was not possible to agree on a global target for renewable energy. A target of 10 per cent of total primary energy supply by 2010 was proposed, but despite intense negotiations no agreement was reached on the proposed target. The WSSD agreed, however, to:

'With a sense of urgency, substantially increase the global share of renewable energy sources with the objective of increasing its contribution to total energy supply'.[2]

In its 2007 Statement, the World Energy Council emphasized:

'If we are to keep the world economy humming along and improve living standards for all, we face a triple challenge:
To provide every household with access to affordable modern energy services, to make energy services available to meet a sharply rising demand and to rein in greenhouse gas emissions at the same time'.[3]

The need for urgent action to achieve more secure, lower carbon energy systems, and the role which energy efficiency, conservation, nuclear power and renewables can play in lowering emissions is also pointed out in the International Energy Agency's most recent World Energy Outlook 2007.[4]

At the regional level, several concrete actions have been taken by the European Union by the adoption of specific targets for increasing the share of renewables of overall energy consumption. New policy action plans and legislative frameworks have supported these developments, together with individual initiatives at Member State level.

In the following sections the development of energy policy and in particular the regulation of wind energy will be discussed. First, there will be an in-

---

2. *World Energy Council:* WEC Statement 2003 – Renewable Energy Targets at: www.worldenergy.org/documents/stat2003en.pdf. See also *Rosemary Lyster & Adrian Bradbrook:* Energy Law and the Environment, 2006.
3. *World Energy Council:* WEC Statement 2007 – The Energy Industry Unveils its Blueprint for Tackling Climate Change at: www.worldenergy.org/documents/stat2007.pdf.
4. *International Energy Agency:* World Energy Outlook 2007, p. 41 and p. 50.

troduction to energy law and wind energy law in general. Then a brief account will be given of the international law relating to the generation of energy from wind and the right to construct wind turbines offshore. Following the discussion of the situation at the international level, the focus will turn to developments in the EU and the action plans and regulation adopted to promote renewable energy in power production. Finally, national reviews are provided for Denmark, Norway, the USA and New Zealand and their policies and regulation of wind energy. Among the regulatory instruments considered, there is a focus on access to sites and wind resources, licensing requirements and permit procedures, regulation of access to the electricity system and the economic conditions in terms of price controls and subsidies.

## 1.1.  Energy Law – by *Barry Barton*

Energy law is as diverse as the sources of energy that we humans use. Globally speaking, oil and natural gas are the central energy resources.[5] They involve legal questions concerning access to geological resources, exploration, development and production. Coal raises similar questions although transport requirements are important for costs. Hydroelectric, geothermal and wind energy sources, mainly for electricity generation, raise questions about access to sites. Nuclear energy raises questions about security. Electricity and natural gas are substantially bound by networks of pipes and wires, which require legal measures for coordination of the system, and for the control of monopoly power. Energy production patterns change, two examples being the emergence of wind energy and the growing carriage by sea of liquefied natural gas. At the same time, in poor parts of the world firewood and dung remain the main energy sources, as they have been for thousands of years.

### *1.1.1.  Energy Security*

Concerns about the security of energy supply are often reflected in the legal system.[6] Access to energy resources is often competitive, and mature bodies of national and international law apply to relations between competing companies, competing states, and investor companies and their host states. States are often anxious to protect their endowment of natural resources from for-

---

5.  Together oil and gas provided 55 % of total primary energy supply in 2003, and coal another 25 %; see *International Energy Agency:* Key World Energy Statistics, 2005 p. 6. For another authoritative source of data on energy, see *International Energy Agency:* World Energy Outlook, 2006.

6.  See *Barry Barton, Catherine Redgwell, Anita Rønne & Don Zillman* (eds.): Energy Security: Managing Risk in a Dynamic Legal and Regulatory Environment, 2004.

eign ownership and control. Producers seek to protect their markets, and consumers seek certainty of supply. Energy security looms large as a concern of energy law and policy. The energy security question shows itself in concerns about the politics of the Middle East, about new resource nationalism in Latin America, and about gas supplies from Russia. Energy security is sometimes discussed in terms of the 'peak oil' debate, although the more immediate pressures stem from the rate of production in relation to the much more rapidly climbing demand in countries like India and China. Energy security is often also discussed in relation to the adequacy of energy plant and infrastructure, for example the adequacy of an electricity transmission network to give dependable supply and freedom from blackouts.

### 1.1.2. Energy Efficiency

Energy use and energy efficiency are the other side of the same coin as energy supply. While all energy use must involve some waste, there are often extraordinary opportunities to reduce waste, and get more useful heat, light, transport, or the like from each petajoule of energy consumed.[7] Energy efficiency can involve legal measures concerning house insulation, appliance standards, industrial motive force and heating systems, electricity cogeneration, motor vehicle fuel standards, public transport systems, and forms of urban settlement. Energy efficiency occurs naturally in many spheres of activity, but if it is pushed in a determined fashion by good law and policy it can result in a decoupling of energy use and economic performance. A better standard of living need not mean a higher level of energy consumption.

### 1.1.3. Energy Industry Structure and Regulation

The legal, institutional and commercial arrangements for the supply of energy vary considerably. In many countries the national oil company has a monopoly or near monopoly on production and even sale of products. State agencies, state-owned enterprises and local government often dominate the supply of natural gas and electricity as well. At the same time, in many countries a substantial role is played by the private sector. A number of developed countries have seen a transition of their energy industries away from state ownership towards private ownership, and a transition to the operation of market forces. This has entailed enormous changes in the legal arrangements of the energy industry. For example, an electricity system that is run by a single

7.   *Paul Roberts:* The End of Oil: The Decline of the Petroleum Economy and the Rise of a New Energy Order, 2004 Ch. 9; and *Rosemary Lyster & Adrian Bradbrook:* Energy Law and the Environment, 2006.

government department makes all the relevant decisions (generation capacity, transmission investment, system operation, price, customer relations) internally – within the department. But after market reform the same system is likely to be run by a number of different companies or agencies operating at arm's length from each other, competing for instance over generation and retail supply, and connected to each other by elaborate contractual and regulatory arrangements for the wholesale market and system operation. In this context, regulation of the industry has grown and changed considerably.[8]

### 1.1.4. Energy Law, Climate Change, and the Environment

The last major piece of the legal framework for energy law is the law concerning the environmental effects of energy development and energy use. Some adverse effects have long been controlled by law; in common law, for example, smoke is subject to the law of nuisance, and it is also commonly controlled by public regulation. Energy development in oil and gas fields, coal mining, and hydroelectric dams has a major impact on soil, water, air and natural habitats. Major installations such as oil refineries, pipelines, power stations and transmission lines have major impacts of their own. Nuclear fuels and nuclear waste present their own special problems. Installations for newer technologies, such as wind and solar energy, pose new problems.

Climate change reflects a whole new level of adverse effects on the environment, most of them caused by the supply and use of energy. While the basic factors of climate change science have been understood for some time,[9] it was perhaps only in 2006 and early 2007 that a tipping-point came in the debate in the developed countries, so that widespread action on climate change has become all but inevitable, even in countries like the United States and Australia where government leaders have held out against substantial action. A number of countries (many in Europe, including the EU Member States, but also Russia, Canada and New Zealand) have accepted assigned quantitative restrictions under the Kyoto Protocol. They have put in place legal measures to give effect to the Protocol, or are seeking to do so, for the first commitment period from 2008 to 2012.

Nowhere is it an easy task. Energy use is such a pervasive part of the economy of the developed world that it is difficult to find a suite of policy measures that will not do overall harm economically, and (perhaps even more

---

8. See *Barry Barton, Lila K. Barrera-Hernández, Alastair R. Lucas & Anita Rønne* (eds.): Regulating Energy and Natural Resources, 2006.
9. *Timothy Flannery:* The Weather Makers: The History and Future Impact of Climate Change, 2005.

difficult) survive the political attacks of the interests and industries which have something to lose from change. Some of the policies in play are price signals; they put a price on carbon dioxide and other emissions, whether by a cap-and-trade system or by a carbon charge or tax, so that economic decisions about energy take into account the environmental costs of emissions. However, price signals are by no means sufficient. Other policies are necessary to promote energy efficiency or to develop renewable energy generation capabilities possible, and to make them understandable and attractive. For example, solar water heating will not be adopted if local bylaws make it difficult to install, or if potential buyers are confused by the lack of reliable information. Similarly, wind or solar electricity generation can be hampered by rules governing wholesale markets that were devised to meet the needs of conventional power plants such as gas and coal-fired generation. Not all climate-change environmentalists realize the extent to which it is necessary to understand the intricacies of energy law. It is practical considerations of this kind that will shape the negotiations for a successor to the Kyoto Protocol that will include a wider range of nations.

Some policymakers approach climate change with the assumption that climate change policies threaten the security of energy supply, such as when measures are enacted to restrict the consumption of oil, gas, and coal. However that approach overlooks the fact that an emphasis on fossil fuels does not guarantee energy security. Where a consumer country imports fossil fuels (or where its fuel prices are affected by world prices), it may still have reason to be concerned about its energy security. It may feel vulnerable to disruption at any point in its chain of supply. That vulnerability can be reduced, and energy security increased, through energy efficiency measures. It can also be reduced by increasing the use of renewable energy resources, and it can be reduced by increasing the local sources of energy. Such steps increase energy security and at the same time improve performance in climate change terms. They may, however, create new questions for the evaluation and comparison of different kinds of impacts on the environment.

### 1.2. Wind Energy Law – by *Anita Rønne*

The higher priority being given to renewable sources can be attributed to an unstable energy market and the prospect of increasing energy prices. Societies everywhere want to save fuel and money and to ensure security of supply. Today, however, environmental concerns – wind energy is basically $CO_2$ neutral – and the renewable energy sector's suitability for small communities have supplemented the security and price aspects and have even become the main reason for giving priority to renewable energy sources. In this context the development of renewable energy technology is not only of domestic value; in the global perspective, local renewable energy technology may prove an environmentally positive alternative to traditional energy production.

Programmes and policies have been designed to accelerate and secure the development and use of renewable energy. To help advance technological development as much as possible, generally sizeable public subsidies have been provided, resulting in reduced prices for installations and improved efficiency of individual technologies. Over the last 25 years the cost of producing 1 kWh from wind has been reduced by 80 per cent, and it has now approached competitive levels. Because of this, governments have already reduced grants for wind turbines. This is the case for example in Denmark. While it is still more economical to construct wind turbines on land, it has become harder to find space on land. Consequently, offshore wind turbines have attracted much attention and the wind conditions at sea are also considerably better than at sites on land.[10]

Increased local electricity production from wind turbines makes special demands on the strength of networks that need to be in balance. During periods with no wind, a back up system based on conventional power generation is needed. Along with the liberalization of the electricity market, this has presented new challenges to the electricity companies that are responsible for the quality and security of electricity supply. Moreover, the expansion of wind energy needs to be balanced against the environmental impacts on the landscape, flora, fauna and neighbours in order to find sustainable solutions. Finally, wind power is still more costly than conventional power systems and consequently needs to be supported by subsidies and access to the liberalized electricity sector. However, if the external environmental costs of the use of carbon-based fuels were fully reflected in electricity prices, the economics might look different.[11]

The establishment of a wind turbine or a wind farm is not only subject to requirements laid down in environmental legislation, e.g. on planning and the

---

10. For more details see *Aileen McHarg & Anita Rønne:* 'Reducing Carbon-based Electricity Generation: Is the Answer Blowing in the Wind?', in *Don Zillman, Catherine Redgwell, Yinka Omorogbe & Lila K. Barrera-Hernández* (eds.): Beyond the Carbon Economy – Energy Law in Transition, 2008.

11. See *Richard L. Ottinger with Lily Mathews and Nadia Elizabeth Czachor:* 'Renewable energy in national legislation: challenges and opportunities', in *Don Zillman, Catherine Redgwell, Yinka Omorogbe & Lila K. Barrera-Hernández* (eds.): Beyond the Carbon Economy – Energy Law in Transition, 2008.

protection of nature and other interests; see further in Chapters 6 to 8. To a large extent specific energy legislation has been adopted. Long-range planning along with pricing policies, guaranteed grid access and purchase obligations have been important elements, combined with tax exemptions and generous state funding for research. Along with the increased focus on market liberalization and competition, market-based instruments have also been introduced in the regulation of renewable energy. The extent of this regulation depends considerably on whether the intended location of the wind turbine is on land or offshore. Although some special requirements have been adopted for the installation of wind turbines on land, it is especially with respect to the installation of wind turbines or wind farms offshore that new regulations have been developed in energy law.

## 2. International Regulation of Wind Turbines – by *Anita Rønne*

### 2.1. Introduction

Traditionally the regulation of energy has been regarded as a matter of national rather than international law. However, a legal regime governing the rights of coastal states to exploit the oceans and the air space above them was adopted already in 1958. Two decades later focus was put on international trade and energy security, and more recently it has been environmental issues that have been at the forefront of attention.

Much of the international law focusing on the development of renewable energy is of a non-binding nature, starting with the 1972 Stockholm Declaration. On the application of the sustainability principle, see further above in Chapter 3, section 1.3.[12] However, some treaties with binding obligations are also relevant in this connection. The Espoo Convention and Aarhus Convention have already been discussed above in Chapter 5, section 3 and Chapter 6, section 2 together with other international environmental treaties; see also Chapter 7 and Chapter 8, section 2. In the following the focus is on three treaties that are of particular importance to the development of wind energy: the UN Convention of the Law of the Sea (UNCLOS), the UN Framework Convention on Climate Change, and the Energy Charter Treaty. However, only the main features of these will be discussed.

---

12. See also *Adrian J. Bradbrook:* 'The Development of Renewable Energy Technologies and Energy Efficiency Measures Through Public International Law', in *Don Zillman, Catherine Redgwell, Yinka Omorogbe & Lila K. Barrera-Hernández* (eds.): Beyond the Carbon Economy – Energy Law in Transition, 2008.

## 2.2. The UN Convention on the Law of the Sea

International law determines the jurisdiction and controls which states exercise over energy resource activities at sea;[13] see further above in Chapter 3, section 1.2 and Chapter 5, section 2.1. In UNCLOS it is recognized that states have sovereignty over their territorial sea,[14] and that they may exercise sovereign rights over the living and non-living resources within the exclusive economic zone (EEZ), which is the area which extends 200 nautical miles beyond the baselines from which the territorial sea is measured.[15] UNCLOS vests jurisdiction and control over activities in this area.

Consequently, a coastal state has sovereign rights over the economic exploitation and exploration of the EEZ which clearly includes the production of energy from wind.[16] Moreover, a coastal state has the exclusive right to construct, to authorize and regulate the construction, operation and use of artificial islands, installations and structures for the economic exploitation of the zone. In other words, a coastal state has the exclusive right to construct etc. wind turbines in the EEZ.[17]

Due notice must be given of the construction of such structures, and permanent means for giving warning of their presence must be maintained. The coastal state may, where necessary, establish reasonable safety zones around such installations etc. All ships must respect these safety zones and must comply with generally accepted international standards for navigation in the vicinity of the installations. However, installations and structures and the safety zones around them may not be established if this would interfere with the use of recognized sea lanes which are essential to international navigation.

13. For more details see *Catherine Redgwell:* 'International Regulation of Energy Activities', in *Martha M. Roggenkamp, Catherine Redgwell, Iñigo del Guayo & Anita Rønne* (eds.): Energy Law in Europe: National, EU and International Regulation, 2007 Ch.2.
14. UNCLOS Article 2. This sovereignty extends to the air space over the territorial sea as well as to its bed and subsoil. The same principles may be found in the Geneva Convention on the Continental Shelf of 29 April 1958, Article 1.
15. 12 + 188 nautical miles. UNCLOS, Articles 55 and 57.
16. See also *Martha M. Roggenkamp, Catherine Redgwell, Iñigo del Guayo & Anita Rønne* (eds.): Energy Law in Europe: National, EU and International Regulation, 2007 p.1344, para. 16.224; and *Catherine Redgwell:* 'International Responses to the Challenges of a Lower Carbon Future: Climate Change, Carbon Capture and Storage, and Biofuels', in *Don Zillman, Catherine Redgwell, Yinka Omorogbe & Lila K. Barrera-Hernández* (eds.): Beyond the Carbon Economy – Energy Law in Transition, 2008.
17. UNCLOS, Articles 56 and 60.

Under UNCLOS the freedoms of the high seas – fishing, laying pipelines and cables, overflight and navigation – within the EEZ are retained. Coastal states must have due regard to these rights.[18]

Any installations or structures which are abandoned must be removed to ensure the safety of navigation, taking into account generally accepted international standards.[19] Such removal must also have due regard to fisheries, the protection of the marine environment and the rights and duties of other states. Appropriate publicity must be given about the depth, position and dimensions of any installations or structures not entirely removed. These obligations include wind turbines that have been established offshore.

### 2.3. The Climate Change Convention and the Kyoto Protocol

It has been increasingly recognized that energy production and consumption is the biggest contributor to the release of $CO_2$ emissions into the atmosphere. Climate change has therefore become a very important argument for the further development of renewables. At the 1992 Rio Conference on Environment and Development the UN Framework Convention on Climate Change (UNFCCC)[20] was adopted, and it came into force on 21 March 1994. All par-

---

18. UNCLOS, Articles 58, 79, 87 and 112.
19. UNCLOS, Article 60 (3).
20. As at 1 November 2007 it had 192 parties, including the EC. The Convention divides countries into three main groups according to differing commitments, see www.unfccc.int:

    *Annex I Parties* include the industrialized countries that were members of the OECD (Organisation for Economic Co-operation and Development) in 1992, plus countries with economies in transition (the EIT Parties), including the Russian Federation, the Baltic States, and several Central and Eastern European States.

    *Annex II Parties* consist of the OECD Annex I members, but not the EIT Parties. They are required to provide financial resources to enable developing countries to undertake emissions reduction activities under the Convention and to help them adapt to adverse effects of climate change. In addition, they have to take all practicable steps to promote the development and transfer of environmentally friendly technologies to EIT Parties and developing countries. Funding provided by Annex II Parties is channelled mostly through the Convention's financial mechanism.

    *Non-Annex I Parties* are mostly developing countries. Certain groups of developing countries are recognized by the Convention as being especially vulnerable to the adverse impacts of climate change, including countries with low-lying coastal areas and those prone to desertification and drought. Others (such as countries that rely heavily on income from fossil fuel production and commerce) feel more vulnerable to the potential economic impacts of climate change response measures. The Convention emphasizes activities that promise to answer the special needs and concerns of these vulnerable countries, such as investment, insurance and technology transfer.

ties are obliged to produce inventories of greenhouse gas sources, to formulate and implement national and regional programmes to reduce global warming, to enact effective legislation, and to take climate change into account when undertaking environmental impact assessments (Article 4). The aim is to return to the 1990 levels of carbon dioxide and other greenhouse gas emissions, to increase cooperation and to promote scientific research. Moreover, developed states must provide new and additional financial resources to developing states to enable them to comply with their Convention obligations.

The UNFCCC provided the legislative framework, but it was not until the adoption of the 1997 Kyoto Protocol that developed states committed themselves to more explicit obligations. The most important feature of the Protocol is that for the first time it establishes specific individual targets and timetables for the reduction of greenhouse gas emissions by Annex I parties. Overall emissions are to be reduced by at least 5 per cent below 1990 levels in the commitment period 2008–2012 (Article 3). To achieve these targets a range of measures are specified, including adopting energy efficiency measures and research on renewable energy and environmentally sound technologies (Article 2). New mechanisms are also provided for achieving emissions reduction targets – flexibility mechanisms, including: joint implementation (Article 6), the clean development mechanism (Article 12) and emissions trading (Article 17). With Australia and the United States not participating, for a while the Protocol was at risk of failing, but it entered into force on 16 February 2005 following ratification by Russia.

The next challenge will be the negotiations on commitments for the period following 2012.

### 2.4. The Energy Charter Treaty

The Energy Charter Treaty and the Energy Charter Protocol on Energy Efficiency and Related Environmental Aspects provides a multilateral framework for energy cooperation that is unique in international law.[21] It was signed in December 1994 and entered into force in April 1998. The origin of these documents was the political, non-binding European Energy Charter of 1991 between a number of Western European states and other developed countries, on the one hand, and Eastern European states and states which were formerly part of the Soviet Union on the other hand. The purpose of the Charter was to encourage investment and trade in energy markets of Eastern Europe after the collapse of communism in the late 1980s.

---

21.  See further: www.encharter.org

The Energy Charter Treaty is designed to promote energy security through the operation of more open and competitive energy markets, while respecting the principles of sustainable development and national sovereignty over energy resources. Most of the provisions of the Treaty relate to issues of international energy investment and trade. However, environmental issues, including renewable energy and energy efficiency are also addressed. Thus it is emphasized that energy markets should more fully reflect environmental costs and benefits (Article 1(2)(b)). It is also required that, in the pursuit of sustainable development and minimizing environmental degradation, among other things each state should have particular regard to improving energy efficiency, to developing and using renewable energy sources, to promoting the use of cleaner fuels and to employing technologies and technological means that reduce pollution (Article 19). The obligations are, however, not very strict or concrete and they may be hard to enforce.

Moreover, the Energy Charter Treaty and Protocol on Energy Efficiency only have some 50 signatories. The only non-European parties are Japan and Australia. Many of the major energy consuming and producing nations, such as the United States, China and India have not signed.

## 3. EU Regulation of Wind Turbines – by *Anita Rønne*

### 3.1. The EC Treaty

The lack of a special chapter on energy in the EC Treaty has not hindered the publication of several Community Green and White Papers on energy policy or the adoption of a wide range of energy legislation in recent years. Legally this has been based on the establishment of the internal market.[22] The Treaty on European Union (the 1992 Maastricht Treaty) added energy measures to the list of the Community's activities[23] and the promotion of trans-European networks in the areas of energy infrastructures to the text of the EC Treaty.[24] The legal basis for Community action on the environment was introduced already in 1987, with the provision of the basis for legislation and programmes on energy efficiency and the requirement that general environmental protection issues must be integrated into the elaboration and implementation of all

---

22. EC Treaty, Article 14.
23. EC Treaty, Article 3(u): 'the activities of the Community shall include ... measures in the spheres of energy, civil protection and tourism.'
24. EC Treaty Article 154 (earlier Article 129b).

Community policies and activities.[25] Much more vigorous enforcement of the competition and free movement rules is also observable, indicating significant changes in the organization of energy activities and the balance of regulatory initiatives between the Commission and the Member States.

Although the Member States have retained their sovereignty over primary energy sources[26] and choice of energy mix, Community rules require notification of certain investment projects in the petroleum, natural gas and electricity sectors, including major power stations and transmission lines.[27] In general, the Commission has no powers to impose on Member States detailed instructions about the choice of the siting of wind farms or any other energy projects, but some national environmental protection legislation may infringe Community law, e.g. the Habitats Directive (Council Directive 92/43/EEC on the Conservation of natural habitats and of wild fauna and flora) and lead to action by the Commission when it is notified of a proposed installation. Of particular importance are Directive 85/337/EEC on environmental impact assessments (the EIA Directive), which was amended in 1997 to include wind turbines in the list of projects, and Directive 2001/42/EC on strategic environmental assessments (the SEA Directive). Both directives are applicable on land and offshore. On the siting of wind farms, see Chapter 6, section 3 and Chapter 7, section 3.

The Treaty of Lisbon amends the Treaty on European Union and the Treaty establishing the European Community.[28] It emphasises the need for sustainable development and for promoting measures at international level to deal with regional or global environmental problems, and in particular combating climate change; see Articles 2 and 174. A special Chapter on Energy is included as Title XX and as a new Article 176 A. Thus, in a spirit of solidarity between Member States and in the context of the establishment and func-

---

25. EC Treaty, now referred to in Article 6 (earlier Article 130r).
26. See the Preamble to Directive 94/22/EC of the European Parliament and of the Council of 30 May 1994 on the conditions for granting and using authorizations for the prospection, exploration and production of hydrocarbons; and the Lisbon Treaty, Article 176A (2).
27. Council Regulation (EC) No 736/96 of 22 April 1996 on notifying the Commission of investment projects of interest to the Community in the petroleum, natural gas and electricity sectors. This includes power stations with a capacity of 200 MW or more, and transmission lines of 345 kV if in the air and 100 kV if underground and constituting an essential link.
28. See Conference of The Representatives of The Governments of The Member States, Brussels, 3 December 2007, CIG 14/07, www.consilium.europa.eu/cms3_fo/showPage.asp?id=1317&lang=da&mode=g.

tioning of the internal market, and with regard for the need to preserve and improve the environment, the EU policy on energy must aim to: (a) ensure the functioning of the energy market; (b) ensure security of energy supply in the Union; (c) promote energy efficiency and energy saving and the development of new and renewable forms of energy; and (d) promote the interconnection of energy networks.

### 3.2. Policy Development

As a landmark decision, on 8 and 9 March 2007 the European Council[29] committed itself for the first time to a binding Europe-wide environmental target: a 20 per cent reduction in greenhouse gas emissions by 2020 compared with 1990. The Council also agreed on a binding commitment that renewable energy will comprise 20 per cent of the EU's total energy consumption by 2020. This is a follow up of the most recent European energy strategy published by the Commission as a Green Paper in March 2006.[30] The energy strategy seeks to provide solutions for the three core objectives of EU energy policy: sustainable development, competitiveness and security of supply. Renewables play a significant role in this context.[31]

On 19 September 2007, the Commission published a third package of legislative proposals to improve liberalization, market transparency and crossborder trade. On 23 January 2008 there followed a major legislative package on climate and energy which includes proposals for new directives on the promotion of renewables and emissions trading and new guidelines for State

---

29. The Presidency Conclusions of the Brussels European Council, 8-9 March 2007 – 7224/07. See also: An energy policy for Europe (COM(2007) 1 final); Renewable energy road map – Renewable energies in the 21st century: building a more sustainable future (COM(2006) 848 final); Limiting Global Climate Change to 2 degrees Celsius – The way ahead for 2020 and beyond (COM(2007) 2 final); Towards a future Maritime Policy for the Union: A European vision for the oceans and Seas (COM(2006) 275 final); and A European Strategy for Sustainable, Competitive and Secure Energy (COM(2006) 105 final). For more details on renewable energy within EU see the Climate Action Network Europe website at: www.climnet.org/EUenergy/renewables.html: the Commission's Sustainable Energy Europe Campaign at www.sustenergy.org/tpl/page.cfm?pageName=home; and The European Renewable Energy Council (EREC) at: www.erec-renewables.org/.
30. Green Paper on a European Strategy for Sustainable, Competitive and Secure Energy (COM(2006) 105 final).
31. For earlier policy documents and reports see also: Energy for the Future: Renewable Sources of Energy (COM(97) 599 final); the White Paper for a Community Strategy and Action Plan; The Share of Renewable Energy in the EU (COM(2004) 366 final); and The Support of Electricity from Renewable Sources (COM(2005) 627 final).

aid. The legislative initiatives include harmonizing the allocation of national targets for increased use of renewables and biofuels.

The new proposal on renewables is aimed at establishing national renewable energy targets that will result in an overall binding target of a 20 per cent share of renewable energy of total energy consumption in 2020, and a binding 10 per cent minimum target for the use of biofuels in transport to be achieved by each Member State. The draft directive is also intended to remove unnecessary barriers to the growth of renewable energy – for example by simplifying the administrative procedures for new renewable energy developments. The emissions trading proposal calls for a reduction in EU emissions of at least 20 per cent by 2020 compared with 1990 levels, and by 30 per cent, provided that other industrialized countries commit to comparable efforts within the framework of a global agreement to combat climate change post-2012. The main changes are that there will be one EU-wide cap on the amount of emissions allowances instead of 27 national caps, that a much larger share of allowances will be auctioned instead of allocated free of charge, and that the rules governing free allocation will be harmonized.

### 3.3. Instruments to Promote Wind Energy

Over the years the EU has adopted and implemented financial support programmes for research and development of renewable energy technologies, e.g. the ALTERNER programme, the Intelligent Energy-Europe programme and, most recently, the EU's Seventh Framework Programme for Research and Technological Development (FP7), (running from 2007 to 2013).[32]

Both the first and the second Electricity Directive[33] authorize the Member States to impose public service obligations (Article 3) which may relate to security, including security of supply, regularity, quality and price of supply, as well as environmental protection. Moreover, the rules for tendering for new capacity ensures that Member States may take into account the interests of environmental protection and the promotion of new technologies (Article 7). With respect to dispatching (Articles 11(3) and 14(4)), the system operator may be required to give priority to generators which use renewable energy. Finally, the regulator is allowed to take full account of the costs and benefits of the various renewable energy technologies (Article 23).

---

32. See http://ec.europa.eu/energy/res/altener/index_en.htm;
    http://ec.europa.eu/energy/intelligent/index_en.html and
    http://ec.europa.eu/dgs/energy_transport/rtd/index_en.htm.
33. Directive 2003/54/EC of 26 June 2003 concerning common rules for the internal market in electricity.

Taxation and possible tax exemptions[34] and the EC guidelines for State aid to protect the environment[35] are also relevant to the promotion of renewables together with the EU Emissions Trading Scheme for greenhouse gas emissions. Since 1 January 2005, (under Directive 2003/87/EC establishing a scheme for greenhouse gas emission allowance trading within the Community) combustion installations with a rated thermal input exceeding 20 MW as well as other listed sectors have been allocated $CO_2$ allowances or must buy these allowances in the EU market in order to be permitted to emit $CO_2$ (Articles 4 and 9). It is assumed that the price of $CO_2$ allowances will be included in the electricity price. In this way electricity which is based on renewable energy obtains a competitive benefit, as it will be $CO_2$ neutral and consequently not bear the costs of $CO_2$ allowance purchases.[36]

It is, however, the Directive on the promotion of electricity produced from renewable energy sources in the internal electricity market of 27 September 2001 that has the biggest impact.[37] Member States are required to take appropriate steps to encourage greater consumption of renewable energy and must periodically publish a report setting national indicative targets for future consumption and on planned actions. The Commission must evaluate the progress made by each Member State according to these national objectives (Article 4). Since 27 October 2003, Member States must also ensure that the origin of electricity produced from renewable energy sources can be guaranteed in response to a request (Article 5). Such a guarantee of origin makes it possible for generators to verify that the electricity generated is based on renewable resources. Guarantees of origin must be mutually recognized by the Member States. Member States are also obliged to evaluate the existing legislative and regulatory framework for production plants using renewable energy sources, with a view to reducing regulatory and non-regulatory barriers, expediting administrative procedures, and ensuring that the rules are objective (Article 6).

Member States must take the necessary measures to ensure that system operators guarantee the transmission and distribution of electricity produced

---

34. Directive 2003/96/EC of 27 October 2003 restructuring the Community framework for the taxation of energy products and electricity.
35. Guidelines 2001/C37/03. See the *Preussen-Electra* Case where financial support of renewable energy was not considered State aid, discussed in Chapter 5, section 4.3.
36. Directive 2003/87/EC of the European Parliament and of the Council of 13 October 2003 establishing a scheme for greenhouse gas emission allowance trading within the Community.
37. Directive 2001/77/EC of 27 September 2001.

from renewable energy sources. They may also provide for priority access to the grid system. When dispatching, system operators must give priority to generating installations using renewable energy sources insofar as the operation of the national electricity system permits (Article 7).

## 4. Danish Regulation of Wind Turbines – by *Anita Rønne*

### 4.1. Policy Development and Expansion of Wind Energy

Denmark has been a pioneer and maintains its position as one of the leading countries in the development and use of renewable energy and especially of wind energy. Since the energy crisis of the 1970s there has been consensus on giving green energy priority and in 2003 the goal of providing 20 per cent of Danish electricity consumption from renewable resources was achieved, compared to an average of 2.4 per cent for Europe as a whole. This is a world record.[38] In 2005 renewables accounted for 15.5 per cent of total Danish energy consumption and 28.8 per cent of electricity was supplied from renewable sources. Wind power contributes the largest share (around 18.5 per cent) compared with other renewable energy sources. Moreover, approximately half the installed wind energy capacity globally is based on turbines produced by Danish manufacturers.[39] Further developments are foreseen, most of which are expected to come from offshore wind turbines due to the difficulties in finding new and suitable land sites.

On 21 February 2008, the Danish Government entered into a comprehensive new energy agreement with the parliamentary parties.[40] The parties agreed that renewable energy should cover 20 per cent of total Danish energy consumption in 2011 and includes better terms for wind turbines. Aside from significantly raising the transfer rate for electricity from land wind turbines, the parties agreed to install 400 MW from new offshore wind turbines by 2012. Moreover, a compensation scheme for neighbours of wind turbines is proposed but it has been criticised as it probably conflicts with the law of nuisance. To create greater transparency about the legislative framework for the use of renewable energy, it has been proposed that all relevant legislation should be collected in a new Act on renewable energy. It has also been agreed to establish a 'green fund' to be used to strengthen the protection of

---

38. Danish Wind Industry Association, www.windpower.org.
39. Danish Wind Industry Association, www.windpower.org.
40. See www.ens.dk/sw67323.asp?usepf=true.

landscape in local areas and a guarantee fund of DKK 10 million to support local wind turbine cooperatives' preliminary surveys, etc.

As mentioned above Danish production of renewable energy amounted to about 15.5 per cent of total energy consumption in 2005. This number may be contrasted with 6.4 per cent in 1990 and 3.4 per cent in 1980.[41] By the end of 2004, installed wind capacity had increased to around 3,124 MW[42] compared to 1,129 MW[43] in 1997. At the time the biggest offshore wind farm in the world, Nysted Offshore Wind Farm was completed in 2003. This large wind farm is located about 10 km south of Nysted and 13 km west of Gedser in the Femer Belt. It has 72 turbines and a total capacity of 166 MW.[44] Moreover, an essential element of a political agreement between the parliamentary parties in March 2004 was the further expansion of the wind turbine network and the installation of two more offshore wind farms, each of 200 MW.[45] In combination with the continued repowering of older turbines, this will increase the share of wind power to more than 25 per cent.

Until recently there were about 6,400 wind turbines in Denmark. This the number has decreased to around 5,234.[46] The older wind turbines (less 175 MW) are being gradually phased out, using public subsidies and according to agreed dismantling schemes, by the end of 2009.[47] This will contribute to improving the landscape while increasing overall capacity because the new wind turbines that are replacing the older have bigger capacities (350 MW).[48] As one of the most important prerequisites of the scheme is the designation of areas for the location of the replacement turbines, the Danish Energy Authority and the Danish National Forest and Nature Agency are in constant dialogue with the planning authorities in order to ensure sites for all the new wind turbines.[49]

---

41. *Danish Energy Authority:* Energy in Denmark 2002, 2003 p. 15 and *Danish Energy Authority:* Energy Statistics 2005.
42. *Danish Energy Authority:* Energy Statistics 2005.
43. *Danish Energy Agency:* Wind Power in Denmark – Technology, Policies and Results, 1998 p. 5.
44. See www.nystedhavmoellepark.dk.
45. It was subsequently agreed to locate the two wind farms at Horns Rev and Rødsand.
46. See Master data register for wind turbines available at: www.ens.dk/sw34512.asp.
47. Annual report of Danish Wind Industry Association, www.windpower.org, 2004.
48. Political Agreement of 29 March 2004 on wind energy, decentralised power and heat, etc (follow-up to the agreement of 19 June 2002), Ministry of Economic and Business Affairs.
49. Energy Policy Statement 2005.

Following the recent administrative reform, responsibility for the designation of land areas is vested solely in the municipalities, whereas the authority for wind turbines in offshore areas is the central Energy Authority. In 2005, the Government initiated a comprehensive task of developing overall planning of the further development of wind energy in Denmark. The task was assigned to two committees which included representation of different interests. The committees have recently published their reports. One committee has examined the consequences of constructing higher wind turbines (up to 150 metres) on land. It has recommended some general principles on the future siting of wind turbines, including the concentration of wind turbines in groups when possible, so that some areas can be kept open without further construction of wind turbines. However, it is still the local municipalities that play the central role in the planning process on land, taking into consideration the protection of regional interests and the advice of the central authorities. Recommendations include a proposal that municipalities should designate areas in a coherent plan in connection with the revision of the municipal plans in 2009. At the same time locations have been designated for test turbines on land.[50] The other committee assessed the future expansion of offshore wind farms and designated seven offshore areas as being suitable for the further development of a capacity of 4,600 MW while balancing the various maritime interests.[51]

From the very first policies in the late 1970s, different forms of direct subsidies and regulatory incentives have been provided to help develop the technology and expand wind turbine usage. First, the Danish Government entered into several political agreements with parliamentary parties and agreements with the electricity utilities on the development of wind energy. This has been combined with the regulation of grid connections and buy-back arrangements, as well as with information programmes, spatial planning procedures, R&D programmes, test stations for wind turbines, an approval and certification scheme and standardization.

---

50. See Report from the Government's Planning Committee for Wind Turbines on Land available in Danish at:
    www.skovognatur.dk/Udgivelser/2007/Vindmoellerapport.htm; and *The Energy Authority:* Report of the Committee on Test Turbines on Land, 2007 available at: www.ens.dk/graphics/Publikationer/Forsyning/Forsoegsmoeller_paa_land/index.htm.
51. *Danish Energy Authority:* Future Offshore Wind Power Sites – 2025, 2007 available at: http://www.ens.netboghandel.dk/english/PUBL.asp?page=pub&objno=16304090. The report is an update of the Offshore Wind Turbine Action Plan of 1997.

In the late 1980s and early 1990s, the political focus gradually shifted from supply security considerations, minimization of costs and local environmental effects to wider environmental considerations, notably the goal of achieving long-term sustainable development.[52] The development of the integration of energy markets within the European Union brought a need for a new foundation for energy policy to ensure that overall environmental objectives could be maintained under the new open market conditions.[53] The strategy 'Energy 21', from 1996, states that the Danish Government should aim for an average annual increase in the use of renewable energy of one per cent per annum until 2030, constituting approximately 35 per cent of the gross energy consumption and 50 per cent of electricity production.[54]

A series of political agreements between the parliamentary parties between 1999 and 2002 resulted in a consensus on giving green energy top priority. On 11 September 2002, the new Liberal-Conservative government announced a new policy direction focusing on increased competition and efficiency.[55] With efforts to strengthen the use of market-based instruments, renewable energy technologies are increasingly sold on market terms, including an environmental bonus or other regulation that capitalizes on the benefits to society of producing energy from renewables.[56] A policy agreement in 2003[57] increased the funds of the Energy Research Programme for the development and demonstration of renewable energy and energy efficiency in the five-year period 2004-08. As mentioned above, in the energy policy agreement of spring 2004 the parties agreed to ensure the basis for the construction of two further offshore wind farms, and in their most recent agreement the political

---

52. This change in priorities is reflected in a plan of action called 'Energy 2000'; see *Danish Ministry of Energy:* Energy 2000: A Plan of Action for Sustainable Development, 1990.
53. These challenges were reflected in the fourth of the energy strategies – *Danish Ministry of Environment and Energy:* Energy 21: The Danish Government's Action Plan for Energy, 1996.
54. *Danish Ministry of Environment and Energy:* Energy 21: The Danish Government's Action Plan for Energy, 1996 p. 39.
55. *Ministry of Economic and Business Affairs:* Liberalisation of the energy market (Report of 11 September 2002 and Background Report).
56. *Danish Energy Authority:* Renewable Energy – Danish Solutions, Background – Technology – Projects, 2003.
57. Political Agreement of 9 May 2003 regarding the development of the Danish energy market and measures to improve the development of new energy technologies.

parties agree to install new capacity for 400 MW from offshore wind turbines by 2012.[58]

The climate issue has been closely related to the development of renewables. Denmark has some of the highest per capita carbon dioxide emissions in the world, and the prospect of climate change is the main reason for the current focus on wind energy use. The Kyoto Protocol obliges the signatory industrialized countries to limit their emissions of greenhouse gases in the period between 2008 and 2012, see above under section 2.3. As part of the allocation of obligations within the EU, Denmark must reduce its emissions by 21 per cent compared to 1990.[59] In 2004 the Danish Parliament passed an Act on $CO_2$ Allowances, which implements Directive 2003/87/EC on trading in $CO_2$ quotas in the energy sector and energy-intensive industry. The scheme entered into force on 1 January 2005 and comprises more than 10,000 production units at EU level and thus about half of all $CO_2$ emissions in the Member States. About 380 production units are covered by the scheme in Denmark.

The most recent long-term Danish strategy on energy policy, *Energy Strategy 2025* from 2005, confirms the Danish Government's intention to use the market as a basis for the continued increased in the use of renewable energy. The strategy was followed up in January 2007 in the Danish Government's draft energy policy vision which set the target of doubling the share of renewable energy to 30 per cent of energy consumption by 2025.[60] In fact the target goes further and includes a long term a vision of total independence from fossil fuels, and the replacement of all coal, oil and natural gas by the renewable energy.

Long-range planning, together with pricing policies and purchase obligations at fixed prices have been important tools, combined with tax exemptions, heavy state funding for research, technical standardization and promotion of local ownership. Since 1 January 2005 the electricity supply market has been fully liberalized. It was thus decided that subsequent offshore wind farm projects should be subject to open invitations to submit tenders and that

---

58. Political Agreement of 29 March 2004 on wind energy, decentralised power and heat, etc (follow-up to the agreement of 19 June 2002).
59. Denmark ratified the Climate Convention on 21 December 1993 and the Kyoto Protocol on 31 May 2002 together with the EU. See also *Anita Rønne:* 'The Danish Way of Combating Greenhouse Gas Emissions', in *Peter D. Cameron & Don Zillman* (eds.): Kyoto: From Principles to Practice, 2001.
60. A Visionary Danish Energy Policy which describes Danish energy policy objectives up until 2025, 19 January 2007.

production should be on market terms. Today, renewable energy is promoted directly by production subsidies and exemptions from energy taxes, as well as indirectly by means of $CO_2$ allowances and $CO_2$ taxes on other forms of energy. In addition, increased use of wind energy is supported by the necessary strengthening and development of the electricity grid.

## 4.2. Establishment of Wind Turbines

Wind turbines may be constructed on land or offshore, and the regulations differ according to their location. Whereas the construction of wind turbines on land is primarily subject to the general planning requirements on the location of new buildings in the landscape, a special licensing system has been introduced for the construction of wind turbines offshore, as set out in the Electricity Supply Act.[61] However, there are also some common rules that apply to all wind turbines.

Among the common rules for wind turbines on land and offshore is the requirement that the design, manufacture and foundations used for wind turbines must be approved in accordance with the technical requirements set out in the Certification Scheme Order, in order to fulfil certain safety and quality standards.[62] The scheme includes type approval (concerning the manufacturer) and project approval (concerning the owner). The owner of a wind turbine has the responsibility for ensuring that a valid project certificate exists before operations start. However, project approval does not replace the special building permit.[63] The administrative regulations include a list of issues that must be taken into consideration before a project may be approved.[64]

---

61. Consolidated Electricity Supply Act No 115 of 8 November 2006, S. 13-18. For more information on the development of wind energy in Denmark, see *Anita Rønne:* 'Renewable Energy on the Market – a Danish Perspective', in Journal of Energy & Natural Resources Law, Vol. 23(2), 2005 pp. 156-172; and *Danish Energy Authority:* Offshore Wind Power, Danish Experiences and Solutions, 2005.
62. See the Electricity Supply Act, S. 68; and on the Technical Certification Scheme for the Design, Manufacture and Installation of Wind Turbines see Executive Order No 1268 of 10 December 2004. The Executive Order is further elaborated in a set of Guidelines of 4 October 2005. All documents related to the approval scheme can be found on the website: www.vindmoellegodkendelse.dk. For a description of the different types of approval, see also *Danish Energy Agency:* Wind Power in Denmark – Technology, Policies and Results, 1998.
63. The Certification Scheme Order S. 6. See Chapter 6, section 4.1 regarding building permits.
64. The Certification Scheme Order, Appendix 3.

There is no question that the approval system has supported the development of the mass production of wind turbines in Denmark, and has resulted in the establishment of an important industry. Today, a countrywide register of all onshore and offshore wind turbines has also been set up. The register is updated every month and includes information on wind-turbine production, power, height, positioning etc.[65]

Moreover, an Act on Environmental Assessment of Plans and Programmes,[66] implementing the SEA Directive, has been adopted and applies to plans or programmes for the establishment of wind turbines both on land and offshore; see Chapter 7, section 4.

If a wind turbine has a height of 100 metres or more, the Act on Air Navigation requires it to be notified to the Civil Aviation Administration. Construction must not be begun before the Civil Aviation Administration has certified that the obstacle is not considered hazardous to aviation safety.[67] Certification may be made conditional, e.g. that a wind turbine must be marked.[68]

Under the aviation regulations on obstruction marking, constructions less than 100 metres high are not usually marked, whereas constructions higher than 150 metres must always be marked. For constructions between 100 and 150 metres high, the Civil Aviation Administration assesses on a case-by-case basis whether, and if so how, a construction must be marked.

As mentioned above, wind turbines on land are subject to the general planning requirements on the location of buildings, and pursuant to the Planning Act[69] a permit is thus required for the installation of a wind turbine together with an environmental impact assessment (EIA). Further rules are set out in the special administrative Wind Turbine Circular;[70] see Chapter 6, Section 4.1 for more details. These rules include a requirement for there to be a certain distance from neighbours, which supplements a specific Executive Order on Noise[71] issued under the Environmental Protection Act. The Executive

---

65. See the website of the Danish Energy Authority: www.ens.dk – Master data register for wind turbines available at: www.ens.dk/sw34512.asp and of the Danish Wind Turbine Owners' Association: www.dk.vind.dk.
66. Act No 316 of 5 May 2004.
67. Consolidated Act on Air Navigation No 1484 of 19 December 2005, S. 67a.
68. Regulations for Civil Aviation BL 3-10 on Obstructions to Air Navigation, section 4 – 4.1.1 and 4.1.2.
69. Consolidated Planning Act No 813 of 21 June 2007, S. 35 (1), see above Chapter 6, section 4.1.
70. Circular No 100 of 10 June 1999 as further elaborated in Guidelines No 39 of 7 March 2001.
71. Executive Order No 717 of 13 June 2006.

Order sets specific limits to noise levels and requires the owner of a wind turbine to notify the municipal authorities, with attached documentation, to verify that the noise level is within the maximum permitted level; see Chapter 9, section 4.2.

The Act on Nature Conservation and the Building Act may also be relevant to the location of a wind turbine. This is discussed above in Chapter 8, section 4 and Chapter 6, section 4.1.

Electricity generation with a capacity of more than 25 MW is subject to a general licence requirement for electricity generation pursuant to the Electricity Supply Act (Section 10). So far, wind turbines installed on land have not exceeded this limit and offshore developments have only been undertaken by electric utilities which already hold an electricity generation licence. Moreover, new electricity production plants may only be established if the Minister issues a permit.[72] Wind turbines on land with production of less than 10 MW are, however, exempted from this requirement (Section 21).[73] Finally, new transmission grids may only be established with the prior permission of the Minister responsible for energy.[74] Such constructions are carried out by the appointed grid and transmission company.[75]

The regulation of tariffs, access to the grid and connection issues are all governed by the Electricity Supply Act; see further below in section 4.4.

### 4.3. Regulation of Wind Turbines Offshore

The exclusive right to utilise the wind offshore is vested in the Danish state but combined with a special licensing system so that this right may be vested with other parties as set out in the Electricity Supply Act.[76] The offshore area comprises Danish territorial waters and the exclusive economic zone (EEZ). The Energy Authority is responsible for the designation of prospective areas for the construction of wind farms and has recently prioritized seven offshore areas; see above under section 4.1. The Act merely lays down the framework

---

72. The Electricity Supply Act S. 11 (1). Pursuant to S. 11 (3), the Minister of Transport and Energy sets rules on the conditions and procedures for the issuing of permits. This has been done by Executive Order No 493 of 12 June 2003.
73. Executive Order No 493 of 12 June 2003, S. 1(2)(2).
74. See also Act on Energinet Danmark No 1384 of 20 December 2004 S. 4. Until the parliamentary election on 13 November 2007 the minister responsible was the Minister for Transport and Energy but a new Ministry has been established – the Ministry for Climate and Energy – the first of its kind.
75. See Section 21 and 22 a, respectively and the Act on Energinet Danmark S. 4 and 4a.
76. The Electricity Supply Act, S. 13-18. See also *Danish Energy Authority:* Offshore Wind Power, Danish Experiences and Solutions, 2005.

for the licensing system; the more specific terms are included in the licences issued and these have only recently been published in advance in the form of model licences included in the general tendering documentation.[77]

The licensing system includes three different licences:

- A licence to carry out preliminary surveys (Section 13)
- A licence to establish a wind turbine (Section 16)
- A licence to use wind energy (Section 13).

This means that the commencement of the most essential stages of operations requires separate public consents to which special conditions may be attached. The first two licences may be granted separately or in combination.

The procedure for establishing offshore wind farms has been gradually developed as experience has been gained.

First, there are limitations with respect to area and time (Section 13(2)). The licensee normally has one year to carry out preliminary investigations, to prepare an EIA and to submit the formal application to establish the wind turbines (Section 13). Surveys must be carried out rationally and must not interfere unreasonably with other activities.[78] A more detailed description of the area, including any special conditions applying to it, is given in the tender material.

A licence is needed for the actual establishment of the production plant and connecting cables (Section 16). The Energy Authority may stipulate terms for the approval of a production plant, including requirements as to construction, design, installation, location, operations, dismantling and the provision of a guarantee for the dismantling of plant, as well as technical and safety matters in connection with establishment and operations (Section 16(2)).

If the activity may be assumed to have a significant impact on the environment, the licence may only be granted on the basis of an environmental impact assessment (EIA) (Section 17).[79] The topics assessed may cover a

---

77. See Conditions for Negotiated Tender on Offshore Wind Turbine Concession at Rød-sand, 13 October 2005.
78. The Model Licence Annex 1, on Conditions on Negotiated Tenders for an Offshore Wind Turbine Concession (only available in Danish).
79. The rules governing EIA reports are described in Executive Order No 815 of 28 August 2000 on assessment of the environmental impact of offshore electricity generating installations.

wide range of environmental matters,[80] and the EIA will also contain suggestions for limiting or neutralising the potential negative effects on the environment (Section 17); see further in Chapter 7, section 4.1.[81]

Once the EIA procedure has been completed, and a public hearing has taken place, the Danish Energy Authority may either withdraw the licence without issuing further licences or prepare the next licence for the establishment of the offshore wind farm in question. The further licences are issued subject to detailed conditions that reflect both the EIA report's conclusions and the consultation responses from the general public and the authorities concerned.

The licence issued by the Energy Authority is made public and any party with a justified and individual interest in the decision has the right to register a complaint with the Energy Appeal Board regarding the decision's environmental aspects (Section 89a). The licence may not be acted upon before the appeal deadline has expired. Once authorized to carry out a project, the licensee must provide the authorities with documentation proving that the conditions in the licence have been fulfilled. This must be done by submitting a detailed project for the installation works. The licensee may only begin to install the offshore wind farm after the Energy Authority has determined that the documentation submitted is sufficient.

When an installation is ready to generate electricity for the grid, the licensee must apply to the Energy Authority for a licence to exploit the wind energy (Section 13(2)). Production may not begin before the licence has been issued and it will then include a sole right to exploit the wind energy within a specific area normally for 25 years. The licensee must first submit documentation showing that all conditions in the installation licence have either been fulfilled or will be fulfilled.

Licences may be granted in two ways:

– following a public tendering procedure; or
– after an application has been made public and other interested parties have been given the opportunity to apply.

The latter procedure is known as an 'open-door procedure' (Section 14).

---

80. Sea bed conditions, raw materials, hydrography, water quality and fauna and vegetation, fish, birds, marine mammals, landscape and visual impact, marine archaeology, emissions, noise, recreation and planning, and the impact on sailing and fishing in the area.
81. See also *Danish Energy Authority:* Wind Energy in Denmark, 2002 p. 8.

A public tender is issued as an EU tender. As a step in the tendering process, the Energy Authority invites interested applicants to request to be pre-qualified. A notice on offshore wind farm concessions describes what documentation and information interested candidates are required to submit. On the basis of an assessment of the applicants' financial, legal and technical qualifications, pre-qualified applicants are asked to submit tenders on the basis of the Energy Authority's tender conditions.

The licence is awarded after a negotiation procedure, and only one licence is awarded for each designated area. The award criteria relate to an evaluation of the legal, economic, financial and technical information provided, and the most crucial criterion is the amount of the feed-in price per kWh of electricity produced that applicants request in order to carry out a project. The specific location proposed for the wind farm and a credible schedule for its establishment are other criteria used in selecting the successful applicant. The winner of the tendering process is given the right to undertake preliminary studies, establish a generating installation and exploit offshore wind energy, but they must also comply with the same planning process as applies to all offshore wind power projects, including EIA procedures.

The licence does not exempt the licensee from obtaining any other licences/approvals[82] required pursuant to other legislation or the notification of relevant authorities.[83] In addition to the special licences for establishing and using an offshore wind power installation, if a wind farm owner does not already hold such a licence they must also obtain a general licence to generate electricity (Section 10); see above section 4.2.

### 4.4. Market Access and Connection to Networks

Under the Electricity Supply Act, renewable energy has priority access to the grid (Section 27c(5)). In practice, this means that wind power has access to grid capacity before all other forms of electricity generation. The system operator, Energinet.dk, has the task of coordinating the prioritized access with general system operation, by which production and consumption are constantly adapted to market conditions. The principle applies to electricity produced both by land based and offshore wind turbines.[84]

---

82. E.g. from the Danish Maritime Safety Administration.
83. E.g. the Danish Maritime Safety Administration; the Danish Maritime Authority; and the Danish Directorate of Fisheries.
84. However, special rules apply to the two planned offshore wind farms at Horns Rev and Rødsand since, in the event of grid limitations, their production may be reduced with financial compensation.

Wind turbines must satisfy the connection rules set by the transmission system operator Energinet.dk. and the Energy Authority must be kept informed of these rules. The rules cover, among other things, the technical requirements that a wind turbine must meet for connection. These requirements deal with control capabilities, the output of reactive power, the ability to remain operational and to continue production when there is a grid outage, gradient limitation and the contents of operation agreements. The grid and transmission companies are obliged to connect wind turbines when these conditions are met (Section 68).[85]

The grid and transmission companies are responsible for carrying out any necessary reinforcement of the underlying grid. These responsibilities are divided so as to promote wind power by making the necessary grid available without cost to the producer.[86]

### 4.5. Price Regulation and Subsidies

The main incentive for the development of renewable energy was previously the obligation for the Danish transmission system operator and consumers to receive and pay for this energy from private producers at prices fixed by the government (feed-in prices). The Danish Government's climate strategy of February 2003 sets the framework for a new direction and a new Act on $CO_2$ allowances implements this new direction. In a market which is subject to $CO_2$ allowances (and taxes), owing to their exemption from $CO_2$ tax wind energy and other renewable sources will have a competitive advantage over installations which generate electricity using fossil fuels. There is a right to have such production labelled as 'green electricity' and the electricity is therefore freely sold on the market (Electricity Supply Act Section 63a). The green certificate is issued by the system operator Energinet.dk which is required to keep a register of issued certificates.

Since 2005, the obligation to purchase production from wind turbines has been replaced by a subsidy scheme that secures owners of wind turbines unchanged prices in accordance with transitional schemes (Section 56). These schemes have given private owners a reasonable safety net for their investments originally made on the strength of the expectation that prices for wind

---

85. See also the Executive Order on grid connection of wind turbines and subsidies for electricity produced by wind turbines etc. No 1365 of 15 December 2004, S. 2.
86. Executive Order on grid connection SS. 3 and 5. The Danish Transmission System Operator's rules for the connection of offshore wind farms (Technical Guidelines TG 3.2.5: Connected wind turbines with a voltage of more than 100 kW) can be found at www.energinet.dk (only available in Danish).

power would remain fixed throughout the expected lifetime of their wind turbines.

Plant owners are now responsible for the sale of their production on the electricity market and for related costs (Section 59(2)). The market price is defined as the spot market price at Nord Pool in the area where the turbine is connected. The subsidy depends on when the turbine was connected to the grid and its age; ownership has no influence on the subsidy paid. All subsidies are passed on to consumers as an equal public service obligation tariff on their total consumption (Section 8).[87]

Generally speaking, for wind turbines connected to the grid as of 1 January 2005, a feed-in tariff of 10 øre/kWh (EUR 0.013/kWh) is paid for 20 years, as well as a rebate of 2.3 øre/kWh (EUR 0.003/kWh) for equalization costs, etc. Offshore wind farms may only be established subject to a tender where the feed-in tariff is one of the bidding parameters.

Special rules apply to offshore turbines financed by the electricity utilities.[88]

### 4.6. Public Authorities and System Operators

The planning of wind turbines on land is under the auspices of municipal authorities, but the Ministry of the Environment may influence the location of wind turbines in the landscape. In November 2007 a new ministry was established – The Ministry of Climate and Energy.

The Danish Energy Authority acts as the central administrative authority in relation to the many, often opposing, interests connected with the establishment of offshore wind power projects. In practice, this means that inves-

---

87. See also Executive Order No 1 of 20 April 2004, which implements Directive 2001/77/EC of 27 September 2001 on the promotion of electricity produced from renewable energy sources in the internal electricity market.

88. With respect to wind turbines connected to the grid after 1 January 2000, plant owners are responsible for the sale of production on the electricity market and for related costs. They are eligible for subsidies which, combined with the market price, comprise 45.3 øre/kWh. The subsidy is payable for 42,000 full load hours. If production is subject to a grid tariff, it is eligible for compensation of up to 0.7 øre/kWh. After all full load hours are used up, a premium of up to 10 øre/kWh is available until the turbine is 20 years old. The premium is regulated in accordance with the market price, as the total of the two must not exceed 36 øre/kWh. If the turbine is located on land, it is eligible for a subsidy which, combined with the market price, comprises 43 øre/kWh. The subsidy is payable for 10 years from connection. Thereafter, a premium of up to 10 øre/kWh is available until the turbine is 20 years old.

tors only need authorization from the Energy Authority for offshore wind power projects.

The Energy Authority is likewise responsible for the administration of the approval scheme for the installation of wind turbines in Denmark, but a group at Risø National Laboratory acts as the secretariat and information centre on behalf of the Energy Authority. The Energy Authority is also responsible for the administration of the Energy Research Programme, which covers both conventional energy and renewable energy. In addition to government research and development (R&D) programmes, the system operators have R&D programmes supported by public service obligation subsidies for non-commercial projects for new and environmentally friendly energy technologies.[89]

System operation is vested in an independent public enterprise – *Energi-net.dk* – owned by the Danish state.[90] The main responsibilities of Energinet.dk are:

- transmission system operation, including responsibility for safe supply and a competitive energy market,
- development of both the natural gas and the electricity infrastructures, and
- equal access for all users of the grid. Energinet.dk has also taken over responsibility for paying the support for renewables in electricity production.

Tasks related to environmental impact assessments (EIA) on land are governed by the Planning Act and are primarily vested in the municipal authorities; see Chapter 6, section 4.1. Planning for offshore wind turbines, including EIAs, is the responsibility formerly of the Ministry for Transport and Energy – now the Ministry of Climate and Energy and its agency, the Danish Energy Authority.

The *Energy Regulatory Authority* is an independent body which fulfils the sector-specific supervisory and complaints functions in relation to the energy sector. The Energy Regulatory Authority has a secretariat which is located in the Competition Authority. Among its main tasks are the regulation of the prices and terms of supply fixed by monopolistic companies — including the

---

89. Danish Energy Authority: Renewable Energy – Danish Solutions, Background – Technology – projects, 2003; and Danish Energy Authority: Wind Energy in Denmark, 2002 p. 12.
90. Act on Energinet Danmark No 1384 of 20 December 2004.

terms applying to access to networks. The Authority also supports structural development and improvements to the efficiency of the energy sector.[91]

The *Energy Appeal Board* is an independent appeal board under the Ministry of Climate and Energy. The Energy Appeal Board is the final administrative appeal body for decisions made by public authorities under various laws governing the energy sector. It deals with complaints that any party with a justified and individual interest in a decision has the right to register, e.g. regarding the environmental aspects of a decision.

# 5. Norwegian Regulation of Wind Turbines – by *Ulf Hammer*

### 5.1. Policy Development and Expansion of Wind Energy

Norwegian electricity production is 99 per cent based on hydropower. Due to variations in precipitation and temperature, there are significant seasonal variances in hydropower production. In a normal year Power generation is estimated to be 121 TWh.[92] There are also significant variations in electricity consumption, as household heating in Norway is largely based on electricity. Electricity consumption is steadily increasing, and Norway is developing from being a net exporter to a net importer of electricity.

There is great potential for wind energy along the Norwegian coast, both onshore and offshore. Wind energy can improve the Norwegian electricity balance. Furthermore, wind energy is a renewable form of energy, without $CO_2$ emissions. By the end of 2006, approximately 1 TWh of wind energy had been developed in Norway, comprising 155 wind turbines onshore. The current political goal is to develop 3 TWh by 2010.[93] The Norwegian Water Resources and Energy Directorate (NVE), the regulator, is now handling several projects.[94] It is expected that Norwegian wind power production will increase considerably in the years to come. This still refers to onshore development, and the Energy Act does not apply beyond internal waters. But in the future it is envisaged that there will be offshore development as well, and in its latest budget submitted to Parliament the Government has indicated that it will take regulatory steps to facilitate offshore wind power development.[95] As

---

91. Its tasks are more closely defined by various provisions in the three energy acts: the Electricity Supply Act, the Natural Gas Supply Act, and the Heat Supply Act.
92. Facts 2006, Energy and water resources in Norway, p. 15.
93. St meld No 29 (1998-99).
94. See section 5.5 below regarding public authorities.
95. St. prp. No 1 (2007-2008).

the outcome of this regulatory process is uncertain, this review is confined to onshore projects.

### 5.2. Establishment of Wind Turbines

The Energy Act (EA),[96] which only applies onshore and in internal waters, requires a licence to be obtained for electricity installations, including generators, switching stations, transformers, electricity lines and cables; see Section 3-1. The term 'electricity installation' also includes buildings and constructions for such installations.[97]

A wind turbine consists of a tower, rotor and blades, and a turbine head containing a generator and a control system. A wind turbine is subject to a licence for electrical installations pursuant to the EA Section 3-1, provided the turbine contains electrical installations with a voltage of 1 kV or more.[98] Turbines with a voltage of less than 1 kV are subject to a building permit, pursuant to the general provisions of the Planning and Building Act.[99]

A licence pursuant to the EA Section 3-1 covers a specific project. A specific project may be for one or several wind turbines (constituting a wind farm). A project licence will cover the wind turbine and the line between the wind turbine and the electricity network. A licence to build and operate a wind turbine is granted for a period of 25 years.[100]

The licence deals with the building and technical operation of the electrical installation. Commercial operations (trading in electricity) require a trade licence pursuant to the EA Section 4-1.[101]

The general purpose of the licence is to ensure that electrical installations are constructed and operated on the basis of uniform standards, which take into account socio-economic criteria and the public and private interests affected; see the EA Section 1-2, which states the objectives of the Act. Specific issues arise with regard to wind turbines. They are often located in open and thinly populated areas near the coast, where wind conditions are best. In these areas, the introduction of wind power often necessitates extensions to

96. Act No 50 of 29 June 1990.
97. The term is defined in the EA Section 1-3, first paragraph.
98. The voltage requirement is stipulated in the Energy Act Regulations (EAR), Section 3-1.
99. In other words, such small installations do not require licences under the EA. Above this threshold, a licence under the EA replaces a building permit under the Planning and Building Act. On building permits, see Chapter 6, section 5.
100. This is the practice of the NVE. According to the EA Section 2-2, the maximum period of a licence can be 30 years.
101. See section 5.3 below.

and reinforcements of the electricity network. Furthermore, wind power development usually involves changes to land use and environmental impacts. The environmental impacts primarily relate to visual effects, animal life (birds) and flora. In Norway, the best conditions for wind turbines are in the northernmost county, Finmark. Here, wind turbines also affect the activities relating to reindeer of the indigenous Sami population, and the activities (air space) of the Norwegian defence forces.

The EA Section 2-1, supplemented by the Energy Act Regulations (EAR) Section 3-2, regulates the contents of the application. The application has to provide technical and financial information about the project, and about the applicant. In addition, the application has to describe how the wind turbine will be integrated into existing energy plans. All licensees pursuant to the EA are under an obligation to carry out energy planning, and to coordinate their planning with the plans of other licensees. The energy plans are then notified to the licensing authority, the Norwegian Water Resources and Energy Directorate (NVE), providing an important input for NVE's handling of applications for electricity installations. If the project has significant environmental impacts, an environmental impact assessment has to be made in accordance with the new Planning and Building Act, Chapter 14, and the assessment has to be included in the application for the electricity installation; see the EA section 2-1.[102]

The NVE conducts a public hearing on the application. The application must be available to the NVE and to the affected municipalities. The public must be informed of this through an announcement and invited to comment. Public bodies and persons/entities which are affected by the project must be directly informed and invited to comment.[103]

The NVE's handling of an application must be based on a socio-economic evaluation of the project, taking into account the public and private interests affected; see the EA Section 1-2 (referred to above). Furthermore, the award of a licence must be based on objective, transparent and non-discriminatory criteria; see the EAR Section 2-2. The latter provision reflects Article 6 (1) of the second Electricity Directive.[104] This is important due to the increased competition between applicants for licences for generating wind energy.

---

102. On environmental impact assessment requirements according to the Planning and Building Act, see Chapter 7, section 5.
103. See the EA, Section 2-1 fifth to seventh paragraphs.
104. Directive 2003/54/EC concerning common rules for the internal market in electricity. Under the European Economic Area Agreement (EEA), Norway has an obligation to implement directives that have been included in the EEA in national legislation.

Several standard licence conditions are stated in the EAR Section 3-4. The NVE can also stipulate conditions which are adapted to each individual project. The standard licence conditions include obligations on maintenance and safety, and obligations to avoid or limit damage to the environment. The establishment of wind turbines is a reversible process. Consequently, licensees are under an obligation to remove installations which are no longer in operation.

The planning system in the present Planning and Building Act (see Chapter 6.5) applies to wind power projects. When a new Planning and Building Act enters into force (expected in late 2009) a local development plan will not be required for wind power projects. However, the Ministry of Petroleum and Energy may decide that a licence pursuant to the EA shall have the same effect as a state local development plan. Affected local and regional municipalities, and the Sami Council, may submit objections or file a complaint to the licensing decision.

The wind power project may also require licences under other legislation, including the Pollution Act and the Cultural Heritage Act.[105] These acts will not be discussed here.

### 5.3. Market Access and Connection to Networks

Network companies operating a distribution network with a voltage of up to 22 kV are subject to an area licence pursuant to the EA Section 3-2.[106] This licence is not limited to individual projects. It is a general licence entitling the licensee to build electricity installations within a defined area. But the licence is restricted to installations for the transmission of electricity. It does not include production units, including wind turbines.

A network company, as area licensee, has an obligation to connect new end consumers to the network; see the EA, Section 3-3. In other words, they must provide physical network access to end consumers, and make the necessary investment. However, this obligation does not apply to producers wanting to be connected to the distribution network. Wind power producers belong to the latter category.

Normally, network companies recover their investments through tariffs, but under Section 17-5 of the Tariff Regulations they may also recover investments by requiring new customers to make a capital contribution. This

---

105. Noise from the rotor blades of the wind turbine may be classified as pollution under the Pollution Act, Section 6. A pollution licence is then required; see the Pollution Act, Section 8. The pollution authority may award a licence pursuant to Section 11.
106. The voltage requirement is stipulated in the EAR Section 3-3.

financing mechanism will apply to wind power producers. The capital contribution is confined to the capital costs related to the new connection.[107] Connecting to wind turbines may also require reinforcement of the network. Wind power producers may be required to pay a share of the capital costs related to reinforcing the distribution network, but they will not be required to pay capital costs related to the reinforcement of the regional and central networks, unless extraordinary circumstances apply.

Network companies at all levels are required to have a trade licence; see the EAR, Section 4-2 second paragraph. As trade licensees, they are obliged to offer market access to all network customers by means of non-discriminatory and objective point tariffs; see the EAR, Section 4-4 d) first paragraph. This provision does not impose an investment obligation on the trade licensee, but it introduces the point tariff system which is fundamental for efficient market access for all kinds of network customers.

The point tariff is based on vertical cooperation between network companies; network costs are reported from the central network via regional networks to the local networks. The result is a tariff that reflects the accumulated costs of transmitting electricity at all network levels. The point tariff refers to the point where the network customer is connected to the network (connection point). Thus, electricity customers and producers, as network customers, pay one point tariff to gain access to the national network (covering the market).

The network company allocates accumulated costs (relating to the connection point) between network customers in accordance with detailed regulations in the Tariff Regulations, Chapter V. These regulations provide for various concerns, including the efficient use of the network, security of supply, non-discrimination between network customers etc. They are not specifically designed to accommodate producers of wind energy.[108]

The physical characteristics of the electricity system demand the central coordination of electricity flows in order to maintain a physical balance in the system between production and consumption. This central coordination is the task of the system operator, Statnett SF. Statnett is under an obligation to use market mechanisms as far as possible in system operations; see the EAR, Section 5A-1 fourth paragraph. Statnett's system operation is based on a series of markets. The spot market, operated by Nord Pool Spot AS, clears the initial balance each day between production and consumption. Unplanned

---

107. Return on capital and operating costs are recovered through the ordinary tariffs.
108. For a short presentation in English, see the summary in *Ulf Hammer:* Tilrettelegging av kraftmarkedet, 1999 pp. 443-445.

imbalances between production and consumption which occur within the 24 hour period of the spot market are handled on the balancing market. Since 2004, the Nordic transmission system operators have operated a balancing market for their respective parts of the Nordic spot market.[109] As far as the Norwegian markets are concerned, i.e. the Norwegian part of the spot market and Statnett's balancing market, wind power producers enjoy no priority for market access.

**5.4. Price Regulation and Subsidies**

According to the Norwegian market reform, a basic distinction is made between production/trade in electricity which can be open to competition, and transmission/distribution of electricity which is a natural monopoly. There is free price formation in the electricity markets where electricity is traded as a commodity. In contrast, the network monopoly is regulated in detail, especially as regards tariffs.[110] Consequently, support mechanisms for wind power are connected to the network tariff.

The distribution network companies are required to add an extra charge to the tariff. This extra charge can be characterized as a feed-in tariff.[111] The distribution network companies transfer the income from the extra charge to the Energy Fund, managed by Enova SF.[112] The Energy Fund provides financial support for renewable energy production, including wind power. Financial support is allocated according to the rules of the Energy Fund, as laid down by the Ministry of Petroleum and Energy.

The EFTA Surveillance Authority has investigated and has accepted the Norwegian support scheme, subject to certain conditions.[113] For renewable energy production, support may be granted to compensate for the high investment costs which are often associated with such production. Assuming a

---

109. For a short presentation of the market chain, see *Ulf Hammer:* 'From self-regulation to public regulation', in *Barry Barton, Lila K. Barrera-Hernández, Alastair R. Lucas & Anita Rønne* (eds.): Regulating Energy and Natural Resources, 2006 pp. 179-181.

110. *Ulf Hammer:* 'Norway: Security of Supply in Liberalized Energy Sectors', in *Barry Barton, Catherine Redgwell, Anita Rønne & Donald N. Zillman* (eds.): Energy Security, 2004 pp. 318-321.

111. The Energy Fund Regulations, Section 3.

112. The extra charge is NOK 0.01/kWh. The Energy Fund received NOK 680 million in 2006. See Facts 2006 p. 50.

113. Norway is a party to the European Economic Area Agreement (EEA) between EFTA states and the EC. According to Article 108(1) EEA, the EFTA states must establish an independent surveillance authority to ensure the fulfilment and control of their obligations under the EEA Agreement.

fair return on capital, the aid may never exceed what is necessary for a project to break even or at any rate may not exceed the costs of the project's investment.[114]

### 5.5. Public Authorities and System Operators

An important aspect of the Norwegian market reform – as in several other countries – is the organization of the state administration. A distinction can be made between: (1) institutional organs of the state, and (2) functional organs of the state. As for the institutional organs, under the EA public authority generally rests with the Ministry of Petroleum and Energy (see the EA, Section 2-2), which has delegated substantial parts of its authority to the NVE (the regulator).[115] As for the functional organs, public authority has been outsourced to the system operator, Statnett SF, and the manager of the Energy Fund, Enova SF. Both entities are organized as state enterprises under the State Enterprise Act. They are not part of the state hierarchy,[116] but they execute public authority pursuant to the Energy Act and its regulations, and according to licences awarded and regulations issued under the Energy Act. However, these authorities are restricted to making individual decisions. General regulation is still the exclusive task of the regulator.

# 6. US Regulation of Wind Turbines – by *Sanford Gaines*

### 6.1. Policy Development and Expansion of Wind Energy

In the United States, neither the federal government nor the state governments have any general regulations specifically for the licensing or location of wind turbines. Therefore, a wind farm, whether on land or offshore, will be regulated in the same way as any other electricity generating or energy producing facility. Nevertheless, private developers of wind energy have received favourable treatment over the years, so the development of wind energy has been increasing rapidly. In 2006 alone, the industry installed 1,546 new turbines with a capacity of 2,454 MW. At the end of 2006, installed electricity generating capacity from wind was 11,600 MW. About half of that ca-

---

114. ESA Decision of 3 May 2006 regarding the Norwegian Energy Fund.
115. See the Ministry of Petroleum and Energy's decision of 23 August 2006, which replaced the former decision of 14 December 2001.
116. Act of 30 August 1991. According to the State Enterprise Act Section 1, the State is sole owner of the enterprise. Consequently, it can instruct the company as an owner.

pacity was located in just two states – Texas and California.[117] Another 5200 MW of wind capacity was installed in 2007. Virtually all development in the United States to date has been onshore, though there are a number of proposed offshore projects.

At various times, the federal government has carried out research or funded efforts to develop new energy technologies. At one time the emphasis was on nuclear power. In recent decades, the interest has shifted to other new technologies – solar energy, biofuels, and fluidized bed coal combustion, among others – but these initiatives have rarely been sustained for more than a few years. In the 1970s and again in the early 2000s, federal government policy has strongly emphasized and supported domestic production of oil and gas for the express purpose of reducing dependence on imported energy. Over the years producers of fossil fuels, especially oil and coal, have also benefited from special tax benefits or other subsidies, but not as part of any coherent or long-term energy policy. Recently, there has been strong government subsidization of corn-based ethanol, due primarily to political support for corn farmers and the strong lobbying efforts of the largest ethanol producer, and not because of any careful consideration of the role of ethanol as an energy source.

The United States has used two basic incentive systems to stimulate an increase in the production of renewable energy, including wind energy. One is a federal tax credit for producers of renewable energy, which is described in section 6.4 below. The other way in which public authorities are encouraging the development of wind power is through state rules known as renewable energy portfolio standards (RPS), which require sellers of electric power in the state to offer for sale a certain percentage of power from renewable sources, including wind. This requirement is usually coupled with a system of renewable energy credits, where the producers of renewable energy sell a credit for each kilowatt hour they provide. The sale of the credit is separate from the sale of the energy itself. Thus, a wind energy producer has renewable energy credits equal to 100 per cent of the energy it produces, but it needs only a smaller percentage to meet the state RPS standard. It can sell the extra credits to energy producers with no renewable energy sources, and these

---

117. There are several general sources of information about wind energy in the United States. Two that are particularly helpful are: 1) The Office of Energy Efficiency and Renewable Energy of the U.S. Department of Energy, www.eere.energy.gov/windandhydro/windpoweringamerica/ and 2) The American Wind Energy Association, www.awea.org. The data cited here are also reported by the Global Wind Energy Council, www.gwec.net.

credits allow those producers to meet their RPS requirement for the particular year. By 2007, this system of minimum renewable energy requirements and renewable energy credits had been adopted by 20 states, including California, Texas and Massachusetts. The basic system is the same in each state, but the states vary noticeably in the amount of renewable energy they will require to be available for sale in the coming years. California has the most ambitious RPS program, calling for an increase in renewable energy of 2 per cent each year, with 20 per cent of the electricity in the state to come from renewable sources by 2010. By contrast, the Texas RPS calls for 5 per cent renewable energy by 2015, and the Massachusetts programme requires 4 per cent by 2009. To give an idea of the amount of renewable energy involved, the Texas RPS is stated in terms of megawatts of electricity; the requirement is for at least 5,880 megawatts of renewable energy capacity to be available by 2015, with a further goal of 10,000 megawatts by 2025.[118]

### 6.2. Establishment of Wind Turbines

The United States has no systematic or legally binding energy programmes or plans, nor does it have any structure for creating such plans; see Chapter 6, section 6 on US federal and state planning law. At the federal and state levels there are many studies, analyses and projections of energy use and sources of supply, such as those published by the Energy Information Administration of the US Department of Energy; but these reports do not lead directly to any government decisions or programmes.

At the state level, some states have modest planning mechanisms, such as boards or commissions that have policies on the need for and location of energy facilities. Many states, for example, use electricity demand projections as a basis for state-level approval or disapproval of new electricity generating stations.

However, there is essentially no regulation, either state or federal, of the amount of electricity to be generated in any particular state or region. Decisions about how much electricity generating capacity to build and about networks for the distribution of electricity are made by the states. The federal government plays only a coordinating role; it has no central planning function. The federal government nevertheless becomes involved, case-by-case, in granting permits for certain energy facilities such as nuclear power plants, offshore oil, gas, or wind energy development, and hydroelectric facilities.

---

118. This description of state programmes comes from the Database of State Incentives for Renewables and Efficiency, www.dsireusa.org.

The Federal Energy Regulatory Commission has jurisdiction over the inter-state natural gas distribution system and the interstate electricity distribution and sales. Especially in the Western states, the large amount of land owned by the federal government means that it has control over, and issues permits for, rights of way for energy distribution facilities such as electricity trans-mission lines.

In the de-regulatory era of the 1980s, most states de-coupled the owner-ship and regulation of generating facilities from the ownership and regulation of distribution systems. Most energy generators, including developers of wind farms, became independent operators with the sole business of provid-ing supplies of electricity to buyers (users) at a competitive price. In some states, the energy generators can sell directly to retail customers. The retail distributors are regulated in the sense that they are required to carry the elec-tricity offered for sale by the generators within the capacity of their distribu-tion system. See section 6.3 below for issues relating to connection to the network.

The two basic licensing and tendering systems for wind farms in use in the United States are illustrated by two offshore wind farm proposals: Cape Wind (Massachusetts) and Long Island Power Authority (New York).

Cape Wind Associates is an independent company with the sole objective of generating electricity from a planned offshore wind farm in Nantucket Sound, south of Cape Cod. Cape Wind is applying for a permit to connect its wind farm with the existing onshore electricity utility grid. It then plans to sell the power it generates either to local electricity utility retail service companies or directly to end-user consumers. There is no separate en-ergy licensing by the state or the federal government. The federal government may charge a leasing fee for the installation of the wind turbines on the outer continental shelf. As of 2008 there is no system through which the federal government solicits tenders for specific sites thought favourable for wind energy development, but the Minerals Management Ser-vice of the Department of the Interior, under a 2007 'Interim Policy', has identified several offshore areas open for leasing for 5 years for private parties to assess renewable energy resources or to test technology. Instead, the federal government simply receives and de-cides on unsolicited applications from businesses such as Cape Wind Associates.

Long Island Power Authority (LIPA) is a publicly-owned power generator and dis-tributor on Long Island, east of New York City. In the case of LIPA's proposed wind farm off the southern shore of Long Island, LIPA identified the preferred site and defined the basic scale of the wind farm (40 turbines), and then issued a 'request for proposals' from private companies to build the wind farm system to LIPA's specifications. The private builder with the winning proposal will then enter into a contract with LIPA. In this situa-tion, the construction of the turbines is separate from the selling of the energy that they will produce.

For land-based projects, there is case-by-case land use and environmental regulation of wind farms at the state level in the United States under the general laws and regulations for energy or industrial facilities, but there is no specific set of energy regulations for the electricity generated by such installations. Federal environmental law may play a role in facility location if the facility is to be located on federal land or if the turbines are expected to have an effect on federally protected birds or animals, especially endangered species.

For offshore projects, the regulation of location and environmental protection is more complex. The allocation of jurisdiction in the United States between federal and state environmental regulation of offshore wind turbines has been described in Chapter 4, section 2.3. For example, in the case of the Cape Wind project in Nantucket Sound offshore from Massachusetts, the project developer designed the layout of the wind turbines to be entirely within federal waters as then defined. The federal government subsequently adjusted the state-federal boundary in such a way that 10 of the project's 130 planned wind turbines would be within state waters, and thus subject to the jurisdiction of Massachusetts agencies. This would have been a significant problem for the project, because Massachusetts's Ocean Sanctuaries Act[119] generally prohibits the construction or operation of offshore electricity generating stations within the Cape and Islands Ocean Sanctuary that includes the state waters and lands of Nantucket Sound. The project developer therefore redesigned the project to move the 10 turbines into federal waters.

Under the allocation of jurisdiction, a number of specific issues arise about the roles of various federal agencies and the interplay of federal and state regulation.

The U.S. Coast Guard sets rules for the navigation of vessels and manages shipping lanes and navigational aids. The US Army Corps of Engineers (the Corps), whose permits are required, under Section 10 of the Rivers and Harbors Act of 1899, for any fixed structures such as bridges or towers that may impede navigation, has asserted that under the Outer Continental Shelf Lands Act its jurisdiction includes structures on the seabed, such as wind turbines. The National Marine Fisheries Service (NMFS, part of National Oceanic and Atmospheric Administration within the Department of Commerce) regulates marine fishing activity and is responsible for the protection of marine mammals. The Fish and Wildlife Service (FWS) of the Department of the Interior has responsibility for protection of birds and terrestrial wildlife. The Federal

---

119. M.G.L. c. 132A, S. 15

Aviation Administration has authority over air traffic and structures such as wind turbines that may affect aircraft. And the Minerals Management Service (MMS, part of the Department of the Interior) regulates mining activities or oil and gas production on the outer continental shelf.

Until recently, federal law said nothing specifically about renewable energy facilities such as wind turbines situated on the outer continental shelf seabed. In response to the application of Cape Wind Associates for permits to build a wind monitoring tower in Nantucket Sound offshore from Massachusetts, in the expectation that they would later build an array of 130 wind turbine generators, the federal government had to decide which agencies had jurisdiction. Because the wind monitoring tower itself presumably required a Section 10 permit from the Army Corps of Engineers, that agency became the lead agency for the federal government for the entire project. Under the lead agency concept, the Corps becomes responsible for the environmental assessment of the whole project under the National Environmental Policy Act (NEPA). Some years ago the Supreme Court agreed that, as the lead agency, the Corps had the authority under NEPA to consider factors other than navigation when deciding whether or not to grant a Section 10 permit for a project.[120] Moreover, the Corps is required, by statutes and regulations, to consult with other agencies, such as NMFS, about resource protection and other environmental issues under their jurisdiction.

In the Energy Policy Act of 2005, Congress decided to resolve the 'lead agency' question by giving primary responsibility over renewable energy activities on the Outer Continental Shelf to the Minerals Management Service. For all offshore projects needing federal approval after 2005, including further federal action on the Cape Wind project, the Minerals Management Service will be the lead agency. The Service has been directed to develop general regulations for the permitting of renewable energy facilities. In November, 2007, the Service announced an 'Interim Policy', but as of mid-2008, no final regulations have been promulgated.

In addition to possible federal regulation, environmental regulation at the state level may have several features that are relevant to wind farm development. There may be state or local land use planning regulations;[121] there may be specific protection for historic sites or environmentally sensitive areas that could affect the location of wind turbines or distribution lines; and there may

---

120. *U.S.* v *Alaska*, 503 U.S. 569, 583 (1992).
121. See Chapter 6, section 6.

be a state environmental impact assessment requirement (EIS) that is separate from the federal EIS under NEPA.[122]

The state coastal zone management (CZM) plan is a separate set of state laws and regulations that will apply to projects along the coast or in a state's offshore area.[123]

### 6.3. Market Access and Connection to Networks

Because most states in the United States have separated energy production from energy distribution, there have been no significant issues with respect to market access for wind energy. Indeed, 20 states have adopted renewable portfolio standards which require energy distributors to obtain and distribute renewably-generated electricity, so there is substantial demand for wind power and there has been a rapid expansion in wind generating capacity since 2005.

Connecting wind farms to the distribution network is a complex problem for two major reasons. First, many of the best sites for wind farms are in remote rural or mountain areas, far from existing networks and from end-use customers. Second, there are technical challenges in feeding an intermittent and variable power source like wind energy into the network without causing undesirable fluctuations in the network.

On the issue of ensuring or developing the necessary connections to the network from remote locations, one interesting development that illustrates the complexity of the issues involved is the recent approval by the Federal Energy Regulatory Commission (FERC) of a financing mechanism proposed for California by the California Independent System Operators (CAISO). The problem addressed by the CAISO proposal is that power generators are normally required to be located as near as possible to existing transmission systems (the default rule). But areas of high wind are often far from existing transmission lines. The idea behind the CAISO proposal is to finance the construction of transmission lines to high wind areas that are planned for wind farm development. CAISO would build the transmission lines and charge a fee to all users of the CAISO system to cover the cost until individual users of the new transmission lines – new wind farms, for example – pay the standard costs for transmission access. Because some of the power that CAISO carries is generated outside California, this fee required the approval of FERC. FERC gave its approval on 19 April 2007.[124] FERC's approval of

---

122. See Chapter 7, section 6.2.
123. See Chapter 6, section 6.2.
124. 119 FERC ¶ 61,061.

the CAISO programme also serves as federal approval of similar transmission expansion programmes of other states which are rapidly developing their wind resources, including Minnesota and Texas. On a more general level, an interesting set of recommendations about transmission was put forward in 2006 by the Clean and Diversified Energy Advisory Committee of the Western Governors Association.[125]

The technical aspects of feeding wind power into the transmission network are highly complex and beyond the scope of this book. What is relevant here is that these technical aspects relate to various tariff rules for network connection, such as penalties for system disruption and costs for the interconnection of certain kinds of power. Managing these technical and tariff aspects in a way that does not penalize wind power requires a multitude of adjustments to be made to existing access and pricing regulations. FERC has established general rules for interconnection access and pricing: one set of rules for large generators (20 MW or more), and another set for small generators.[126] On 12 December 2005 FERC issued an amended order, No 661-A, setting out specific interconnection procedures for wind energy that are designed to improve and facilitate the connection of wind farms to the network.

### 6.4. Price Regulation and Subsidies

In the United States, electricity prices are determined or regulated at the state level. The recent trend has been for states to establish market-based pricing, in which each independent power producer offers its electricity for sale to the distribution system at a price of its choosing, and the distributor buys the lowest priced electricity first, then the next higher priced electricity, and so on until it has enough power coming into the system to meet the demand. In this system, pricing will vary according to time of day and time of year. Large generating companies market their electricity directly to consumers; the price per KWh varies from one company to the next, and the consumer has the option of changing from one provider to another.

Wind power has no fuel costs and low operating costs, but it has high initial capital costs per MW compared to fossil fuel power plants. To promote the development of wind energy and other renewable sources, the United

---

125. See Clean Energy, A Strong Economy and a Healthy Environment, June 2006, available at: www.westgov.org/wga/publicat/CDEAC06.pdf.
126. See generally, FERC Open Access Transmission Tariffs, Order No. 2003, 104 FERC ¶ 61,103 (2003); Large Generator Interconnection Procedures, Order 661, 2 June 2005; Small Generator Interconnection Procedures, Order No 2006, 70 Fed.Reg. 34190.

States Congress adopted a federal Renewable Energy Production Tax Credit (PTC) in 1992.[127] The PTC provides any producer of renewable energy, such as a wind energy company, with an income tax credit of 1.5 cents per kilowatt hour of electricity produced for the first ten years of production. The amount of 1.5 cents is adjusted for inflation, and is currently 1.9 cents per kilowatt hour. The PTC seeks to make the price of wind-generated energy competitive with fossil fuel and nuclear energy. There has been a significant problem with the implementation of this tax credit system, however. When Congress first enacted the PTC, it did so as a temporary measure with an expiry date two years later. It then failed to renew the tax credit before the end of the two-year period; when it did finally renew the credit, it made the renewal retroactive to the original expiry date, but the uncertainty about whether it would be renewed caused a sharp drop in private investment in wind energy. The United States has been through several such cycles of renewal, expiry and retroactive renewal. In the Energy Policy Act of 2005, for the first time in the history of the PTC, the credit was extended for more than two years, keeping the credit in effect until 31 December 2007.[128] There is a comparable incentive system, called the Renewable Energy Production Incentive, for public power authorities which do not generate business income and therefore do not benefit from the income tax credit.

### 6.5. Public Authorities and System Operators

The sections above make repeated references to a variety of public authorities and system operators. At the federal level, the key authority is the Federal Energy Regulatory Commission (FERC), which approves tariffs and regulations for the interstate transmission of electricity and natural gas, among other things. FERC thus has regulatory authority over the network, but not over energy producers.

Each state has its own regulatory authorities for both electric power generation and for electricity transmission and pricing. Because of the many inter-state transmission connections and the frequent situation where power generated in one state is shipped to and used in another state, there is increasing coordination and collaboration. In most regions, the network is operated by a private regional entity involving producers and transmission lines in several states. In some regions, especially the Northeastern USA and the Western states, there is a high degree of coordination and collaboration. For exam-

---

127. 26 US Code § 45
128. Energy Policy Act of 2005, S. 1301

ple, there is reference in section 6.3 above to the renewable energy policy recommendations made jointly by the 11 state governors of the Western Governors Association.

Finally, there are many private organizations that participate in the development of policy at the state and federal levels. For example, the wind generating companies have a trade association, the American Wind Energy Association.[129]

## 7. New Zealand Regulation of Wind Turbines – by *Barry Barton*

### 7.1. Policy Development and Expansion of Wind Energy

New Zealand lies across the path of the westerly winds that blow in the thirties and forties latitudes of the southern oceans. It has high terrain, and it has a low population density. It therefore has high quality wind resources. The best locations are in the mountain ranges of the south of the North Island, the east coast of the Wairarapa; and the far north. Less attractive because of high altitude and distance from load centres are the Kaikoura Ranges and mountains of Canterbury and Otago, Fiordland, and Stewart Island. In addition, the country has a high proportion of hydroelectric generation, which complements wind by being able to store water for generation during calm periods when wind generation is unavailable.

In spite of these advantages, wind energy was slow in coming to New Zealand. One reason was that natural gas from the Maui field was available at a low price. Another was that there were no policy measures to promote renewables. But gas is now less plentiful and less cheap, and greenhouse gas reduction measures are gradually becoming more prevalent, so power companies have turned more actively to wind generation.[130] Geothermal energy is also the focus of a lot of activity. The first wind farm in New Zealand opened in 1996; Hau Nui, which means 'great wind' in the Maori language. By the end of 2006, there were 7 wind farms with a total installed capacity of 170.8 MW. Another two farms, with 151.0 MW capacity, were under construction. Resource consents (environmental permits) have been applied for or obtained

---

129. See www.awea.org.
130. Generally see *Barry Barton:* 'Renewable Energy in New Zealand', in Journal of Energy and Natural Resources Law, Vol.23, 2005 p. 141; and *Parliamentary Commissioner for the Environment:* Wind, Power, People, and Place, 2006.

for another ten farms, with 1,518 MW capacity,[131] although to be realistic it is likely that many of the projects on this list will be withdrawn or scaled back.

Even with this growth, wind supplies only 1 or 2 per cent of the country's total electricity generation at present. In 2005 wind supplied 610 GWh; an official analysis suggests that there is an economic potential for 9,200 GWh/yr, at a cost of less than 9 c/kWh.[132] (For comparison, in the year ending March 2005, total electricity generation was 40,988 GWh.)[133] So one must not overstate the role that wind power will play in New Zealand's energy future.

In 2005 it was noted that the encouragement being given to renewables was only modest, but that it might be enough to stimulate an increase in a country that is well endowed with renewable energy sources.[134] This appears to be so in relation to wind and geothermal energy; the only question is whether the increase will be swift enough and extensive enough in relation to coal and gas, to meet the demands of energy security and climate security.

Offshore wind development is not envisaged at the present. There are many good sites onshore yet to be investigated and developed. Offshore, New Zealand does not have much shallow water and the sea conditions are often very rough. Any development within the territorial sea would be regulated under the Resource Management Act 1991, as noted earlier, and there is little need seen at the present to re-evaluate this statutory framework.

New Zealand has recently concluded a phase of developing a new energy policy. One reason for this spurt of activity has been the need to put a climate change policy in place. For some years after signing and ratifying the Kyoto Protocol New Zealand did very little, and it now finds itself poorly equipped to meet its obligations. Another reason is the continuing uncertainty about security of supply of energy. A third reason is the realization that basic human needs, like warm housing, are not being met properly.

In September and October 2007 this process of policy-making came to a head with the issue of several related policy documents.[135] The New Zealand

---

131. *New Zealand Wind Energy Association:*
   Current Wind Farms, www.windenergy.org.nz.
132. *Ministry of Economic Development:* Energy Outlook to 2030, 2006.
133. *International Energy Agency:* Energy Policies of IEA Countries: New Zealand 2006 Review, 2006 p. 129.
134. *Barry Barton:* 'Renewable Energy in New Zealand', in Journal of Energy and Natural Resources Law, Vol.23, 2005 p. 141.
135. The main documents for these purposes are: *Ministry of Economic Development:* New Zealand Energy Strategy to 2050, Powering Our Future, October 2007; *Ministry for the Environment and The Treasury:* The Framework of a New Zealand Emissions

Energy Strategy sets a target to increase the proportion of electricity generated from renewable sources to 90 per cent by 2025. The present proportion is about 65 per cent, mostly hydroelectricity. The target is challenging, in that most new generation capacity in the last twenty years has been thermal, mainly fuelled by natural gas. The target requires an abrupt end to this reliance on natural gas. There are few hydroelectric sites readily available for development. Wind and geothermal energy are therefore the most likely sources for new generating capacity. In order to hasten action, the government has decided to impose a moratorium or prohibition of the construction of new baseload fossil fuel generation over the next ten years, except to the extent necessary to ensure the security of electricity supply. A bill has been introduced in Parliament to put this moratorium in place in the Electricity Act.[136]

The Energy Strategy includes work by the Electricity Commission to make sure that wind and other intermittent renewable generation sources can be managed in the overall electricity system. Market arrangements and transmission management need to be improved to ensure that frequency, voltage and reliability are maintained notwithstanding unforeseeable fluctuations in wind energy.

The Energy Strategy also includes the development of a National Policy Statement under the Resource Management Act 1991 (RMA) in order to ensure that the national benefits of renewable energy projects are properly considered in planning and resource consent decisions under the RMA, along with any adverse effects of those projects on the environment. A further policy under the Strategy in relation to the RMA is the increased the use of the power of the Minister for the Environment to 'call in' renewable energy projects for referral to a special board of inquiry or directly to the Environment Court. Late in 2007 the Minister exercised this power in relation to a wind farm project and a geothermal project.[137] Whether such call-ins will actually produce better or faster procedures is a matter for conjecture.

In relation to climate change in general, the new policy documents announced that a New Zealand emissions trading system will be established. Although over time it will apply to all major sectors and all greenhouse gases, stationary energy (mainly thermal electricity generation) will be made subject

Trading Scheme, 2007; and *Energy Efficiency and Conservation Authority:* New Zealand Energy Efficiency and Conservation Strategy, 2007.

136. Climate Change (Emissions Trading and Renewable Preference) Bill, Bill 187-1, introduced 4 December 2007.
137. Otago Daily Times, 21 December 2007.

to it at an early stage, in January 2010. If this system works as intended, it will apply price pressure to the thermal generation of electricity, and will therefore improve the economic attractiveness of wind and other renewable energy resources.

## 7.2. Establishment of Wind Turbines

The starting point for the development of a project like a wind farm is ownership of the land concerned. Most of the developments have been on privately owned land, typically on isolated hill farms where sheep and cattle graze. Until the wind prospectors came along, this sort of land was not particularly valuable, but farmers and power companies have made various kinds of arrangements for development. Such arrangements require commercial agreements and land access rights that will last for the life of the project, even if ownership of the project or the land changes. Shared rights may be possible through a joint venture agreement, joint or several ownership of land, leases or easements. Quite often it is possible for much of the land to be returned to pastoral farming after construction is completed. The use of public land is less straightforward; the use of parks or reserves would need to be considered against management plans under the Reserves Act 1977 and the Conservation Act 1987.

If offshore development were to commence, land access and the environmental impact within the twelve mile limit (about 22 km) would, as noted above, be dealt with under the RMA by the relevant regional council as an activity in the coastal marine area. Beyond the twelve-mile limit the RMA does not apply. The Foreshore and Seabed Act 2004 may also be relevant; it extinguished Maori customary rights in lands covered by the sea, and provided modest rights for statutory equivalents to be claimed.

No licence is required to generate or sell electricity, or to build a power station.

The RMA deals with most of the environmental impact matters that are raised by wind energy developments; land use, landscape, visual amenity, earthworks, noise, shadow and birds. The Act is described elsewhere in this work.[138] Its integration of different environmental issues and its emphasis, in

138. See Chapter 6, section 7. See also *Imke Sagemüller:* 'Legislative and Policy Regime Governing the Generation of Wind Energy in New Zealand', in Journal of Energy and Natural Resources Law, Vol.24, 2006 p. 165.

section 7(j), on the benefits of renewable energy are particularly significant.[139]

In Appendix III an account is given of the two significant decisions of the Environment Court to date under the RMA on wind energy development. One concerns a wind farm in a relatively settled area, and the other in a more isolated one.[140]

Other legislation establishes regulations that are relevant to the development of wind energy. The Building Act 2004 ensures that structures, including wind turbine towers, are safe. It is administered by city and district councils. The Health and Safety in Employment Act 1992 controls the process of construction and the design of certain structures. The Historic Places Act 1993 contains requirements to protect archaeological sites.

### 7.3. Market Access and Connection to Networks

In the last twenty years lawmakers in New Zealand have preferred to encourage market forces in the electricity industry (and many other industries like it) rather than to issue detailed regulations for it. There has been considerable faith in the ability of market forces to shape supply and demand for electricity without much regulation; and until 2001 there was very little state regulation at all. A structural separation was imposed under the Electricity Industry Reform Act 1998, preventing transmission and distribution companies from taking any substantial role in the competitive fields of generation and supply to consumers. There was significant industry self-regulation in the wholesale market and aspects of the retail market, but other fields which in most countries are closely controlled (such as transmission pricing) were completely unregulated. In 2003 the Electricity Commission was established to control

---

139. For general comparisons of environmental laws, see, *Guy Salmon, Matilda Sundström & Kim Zilliacus:* Environmental Management and Natural Resource Allocation Frameworks of New Zealand, Sweden and Finland: A Comparative Description (Nelson: Ecologic Foundation, Research Report No 1, 2005), available at: www.ecologic.org.nz; and *I Carlman:* The Resource Management Act – RMA – Through External Eyes, unpublished paper, Mid Sweden University, Östersund, 2006.

140. Three recent cases on wind farm developments are: *Outstanding Landscape Protection Soc v Hastings District Council*, Environment Court W024/07, Judge Thompson, Comsrs Howie & Edmonds, 13 April 2007 (consents declined); *Meridian Energy Ltd v Wellington City Council*, Environment Court decision W031/07, Judges Kenderdine & Thompson, Comsrs Howie & McConachy, 14 May 2007 (consents granted with modifications); and *Unison Networks Ltd v Hawke's Bay Wind Farm Ltd* [2007] NZRMA 340 (HC) (appeal against consents dismissed).

and exercise oversight over the wholesale market, transmission pricing methodology, and transmission capital expenditure. It was also charged with improving security of supply. Price controls under Part 4A of the Commerce Act 1986 were introduced in 2001, but they only apply to electricity transmission and distribution; wholesale and retail pricing of electricity itself is controlled by market competition alone.

The present legal arrangements for the regulation and management of the electricity industry can be summarized as follows:

- No industry licensing; no licence required to generate or sell electricity, or to build a power station.
- Distribution and transmission companies prevented by the Electricity Industry Reform Act 1998 from generating or selling electricity except under certain conditions.
- Wholesale market, including market access, managed under the Electricity Governance Rules made by the Electricity Commission under the Electricity Act 1992.
- No regulation of wholesale or retail electricity prices.
- Regulation of transmission and distribution prices by the Commerce Commission under the Commerce Act 1986.
- Energy security and transmission system requirements regulated by the Electricity Commission.

There are no specific or preferential provisions for market access or connection to the transmission network for wind energy.

The Electricity Commission is currently assessing the likely impact of wind development on the electricity system as a whole over the next ten years[141] and, as noted above, the work is continuing as a priority. An earlier review of the matter was carried out by Transpower, the sole electricity transmission company.[142] The intermittent nature of wind energy has implications for grid reliability; sudden large changes in output (50 MW or more in 5 minutes) can cause problems in maintaining frequency and stability in the transmission network. Some adaptation is therefore required as the proportion of wind generation increases. One measure that can help is the improvement of wind forecasts over two-hour, six-hour and twelve-hour periods.

141. *Ministry of Economic Development:* New Zealand Energy Strategy to 2050: Powering Our Future, October 2007, p. 68.
142. *International Energy Agency:* Energy Policies of IEA Countries: New Zealand 2006 Review, 2006 p. 97.

**7.4. Price Regulation and Subsidies**

Within the legal framework of the electricity system of New Zealand, there is very little specific preference given to wind energy or renewables generally. There are no mandatory measures to support renewables such as subsidies, preferential tariffs, preferential market access or green certificates. The only financial incentive that has been given to renewables has been carbon dioxide credits granted to some projects under the 'Projects to Reduce Emissions' programme for sale on the international market.[143] The only other preference for renewables is that expressed in section 7(j) of the RMA for environmental regulation, as noted above, and more recently the restrictions on the construction of new thermal generation capacity and the restrictions on the emission of greenhouse gases under the proposed emissions trading system. The IEA speaks highly of New Zealand's light-handed approach to the promotion of renewables.[144] However it must be questioned whether the approach is sufficient to signal the merits of renewables and the true environmental costs of non-renewables.

The Electricity Commission has general objectives under Section 172N of the Electricity Act 1992 (inserted in 2003, amended in 2004) to ensure that electricity is produced and delivered to all classes of consumers in an efficient, fair, reliable and environmentally sustainable manner; and to promote and facilitate the efficient use of electricity. One of the more specific requirements that the section then goes on to identify is that the sector should contribute to achieving climate change objectives by, among other things, removing barriers to investment in new generation technologies, renewables and distributed generation. But this must be considered alongside other objectives in the same section for security of supply, efficiency in the use of resources and downward pressure on prices. The objectives therefore only provide weak and general directions to promote renewables such as wind energy.

Another preference for wind and certain other renewables that is to be found in the legislation is in the Electricity Industry Reform Act 1998, section 46A, which allows a distribution or transmission company to generate and market electricity from new renewable energy sources, provided the renewable source is not a hydroelectric or geothermal plant of over 5 MW capacity. This encourages distribution companies to consider small scale hydroelectric and geothermal plants and wind projects of any scale. Some distribution companies are exploring wind possibilities.

---

143. IEA Country Report p. 92.
144. IEA Country Report p. 98.

## 7.5. Public Authorities and System Operators

The operator of the national electricity transmission system is Transpower New Zealand Ltd, a state-owned enterprise. It is regulated by the Electricity Commission under the Electricity Act 1992. The Commission also regulates the wholesale market. The Commission is subject to the general oversight and control of the Minister of Energy. The Ministry of Economic Development is responsible for policy evaluation and development in the energy field, and for giving policy advice to the Minister of Economic Development and the Minister of Energy.

CHAPTER 11

# Comparisons and Conclusions

*By Helle Tegner Anker, Birgitte Egelund Olsen & Anita Rønne*

## 1. The Development of Wind Energy

In a historical context, the high priority placed on renewable sources can be attributed to the unstable energy market of the 1970s with the prospect of increasing energy prices. Society had a desire to save fuel and money and to develop new technology in order to reduce dependence on imported energy and become less dependent on oil. Energy security was thus the first reason for promoting the development of renewable energy. Since then the environmental impact of energy has increasingly come into focus, and was highlighted in the late 1980s by the World Commission on Environment and Development (the Brundtland Commission) in its report 'Our Common Future'. However, at the same time there was another policy focus – the widespread moves towards of liberalization, deregulation and privatization.

In the 1980s and 1990s the global introduction of competition into energy markets and increasing transboundary trade, with major concerns about energy security and sustainable development, brought a need for a new basis for energy policy to ensure that the environment was also safeguarded under the new market conditions and that renewable energy was further developed.

Today the world relies heavily on fossil fuels – oil, gas and coal. Energy production and consumption is the biggest contributor to the release of $CO_2$ into the atmosphere, and it is commonly agreed that there is a need to replace the reliance on fossil fuels with alternative sources of energy. Therefore the development of renewables is closely related to the climate change initiatives to reduce greenhouse gas emissions. Increasing oil prices have added yet another argument. However, market liberalization on the one hand and climate change policy and the development of wind resources on the other hand appear to pull in different directions.

As one of the most common sources of renewable energy, wind energy is rapidly growing but even so, wind power poses a number of environmental challenges such as visual interference, noise etc. The environmental challenges associated with wind energy development may vary from one country to another, depending on the natural characteristics, population density etc. For example, in more densely populated countries noise and neighbour concerns, as well as negative effects on landscape and nature, may pose important challenges. For countries with lower population densities the challenge may be that wind farms are placed far from existing networks and from end-use customers, which may cause technical and financial problems.

Although wind power has no fuel costs and low operating costs, it does have high initial capital costs per MW compared to fossil fuel power plants. Offshore wind energy is still a relatively new development and more expensive than onshore development. There is still a lack of experience of constructing and operating wind turbines in deeper water and with longer distances to the shore. Although wind energy is approaching competitive price levels, it is still more expensive to produce than conventional energy.

Denmark has been a pioneer in the use of wind power and has maintained its position as one of the leading countries in development and use of renewable energy sources, especially wind energy. It was one of the first countries to move offshore in the early 1990s and to establish wind farms in the territorial sea. Further offshore development is expected as sites on land have become scarce, with offshore development planned even further from land within the Exclusive Economic Zone (EEZ). In Denmark the first offshore test plants were established at the beginning of the 1990s. Today the industry has developed 8 offshore wind farms and further projects are planned. The long term vision of Danish energy policy is to be entirely independent of fossil fuels.

In the United States the use of wind energy has also grown rapidly in several of the 50 states. However, about half the wind energy capacity in the United States is located in just two states – Texas and California. Virtually all development in the United States to date has been onshore, though there are a number of offshore projects in the pipeline. Currently, there are proposals for two offshore wind farms: Cape Wind (Massachusetts) and Long Island (New York).

In both New Zealand and Norway wind energy activities have been confined to onshore sites. The exploitation of offshore wind energy is not yet planned. In Norway there is a political debate on the issue, but the outcome of the debate is uncertain. However, in Norway it is generally expected that wind power production will be increased considerably in the coming years. The use of wind energy is only slowly increasing in New Zealand and offshore wind development is not envisaged presently because there are many good sites on land yet to be developed. Moreover, New Zealand does not have much shallow water and the sea conditions are often very rough.

There are many reasons for this diversity in the use of wind energy in the four countries selected for review. These differences partly stem from differences in the accessibility of indigenous fossil fuels, the availability of other renewable sources, and differences in geographical conditions. Norway is rich in many natural resources like hydropower, oil and gas. Likewise in New Zealand natural gas has been available at a low price and there is a high proportion of hydroelectric generation. Although Denmark has been self sufficient in oil and gas resources and energy as such for more than a decade, this has not hampered the development of wind energy. A political focus on this new technology has been combined with the benefits of developing a whole industry that has provided considerable exports.

The general policy trend in all the countries is to set specific targets for increasing the share of renewables of the overall energy consumption. New policy action plans and legislative frameworks are then framed in order to support the proposed developments. To achieve these new targets a range of measures have been introduced in the different countries. At various times Denmark and the United States has supported research on renewable energy and environmentally sound technologies. Developers of wind energy have received favourable treatment over the years, and incentive systems have been used to stimulate the production of renewable energy, including wind energy, though with its 50 different state regimes the United States lacks many of the elements of a general energy policy. In contrast, until very recently, little specific preference has been given by the government in New Zealand to wind energy or to renewables in general. Norway has established a financial support scheme for the construction of wind turbines. Although the recent development in Norway has been rather slow, several projects have been realized and many more are presently being considered for permits pursuant to the Energy Act.

## 2. The Legal Framework for Wind Energy – A Comparison

Even though the development of wind energy may vary from one country to another due to the availability of other energy sources, geographical conditions and policy initiatives etc., the law plays an important role in the promotion of wind energy. Wind energy may face certain legal or regulatory challenges that need to be addressed. In the following these legal or regulatory challenges will be identified and there will be an analysis of the extent to which these challenges are comparable across the different jurisdictions. A comparison of these legal challenges may involve the basic characteristics of the legal systems as well as the detailed rules specifically addressing wind energy development.

## 2.1. The Legal Traditions

A common feature of comparative studies is to reflect on the role of different regulatory traditions and how they influence modes of legal thought. One of the general questions posed in this book is whether the differences and similarities in the laws governing wind energy are to some extent dependent upon the legal traditions in the country in question. The question is thus whether the civil law approach, which is the dominant tradition in Denmark and Norway, and the common law approach, which is the basis of the legal systems of New Zealand and the United States, can explain the different legal approaches to the regulation of wind energy.

Generally speaking, the special feature of common law is that it is judge-made law. When possible, judges try to be consistent and to base their decisions on the principles established in earlier cases. This principle of *stare decisis* – deciding cases by reference to former decisions, or precedents – is the traditional cornerstone of the common law. Nevertheless, the common law only covers areas that are not covered by statutory law. In the common law countries analysed in this book, environmental law and energy law are characterized by being governed by a substantial body of statutory law. If a statute regulates a practice or procedure, the statute will apply rather than the common law doctrine that may have applied prior to the enactment of the statute. This is not to say that common law is of no importance in areas such as environmental law and energy law. Even in areas largely governed by statutory law there is an important interplay between statutory law and common law. On the one hand statutes may codify existing common law rules, and on the other hand the courts will often rely on common law as a guide to the interpretation of a statute.

In contrast, the civil law tradition is characterized by a stronger rule-fixation. Statutory law is the core of civil law, and precedent only plays a secondary role. In the civil law systems statutory law is supposedly more exhaustive. It makes extensive use of definitions and classifications, and it offers a highly systematic and exhaustive view of the law. Traditionally, codes have played an important role in the civil law tradition. However, codes are not used in the regulation of environmental and energy issues in the legal systems based on the civil law tradition which are reviewed in this book; the key legislative enactments have never been added to or integrated in basic codes.

Thus, one of the key characteristics of the civil law tradition is not reflected in the environmental and energy legislation.

The Danish legislation and the Norwegian legislation regulating wind energy onshore are very similar. This is the case not only with regard to the constitutional basis and traditional administrative law principles, but also with regard to the more modern regulation of energy and environmental matters, which may be due to the close historical and cultural ties between them. However, the fact that these countries belong to the same branch of the civil law tradition, namely the Scandinavian law tradition characterized by its pragmatic and realistic conception of law, undoubtedly has an impact. Yet another reason is that Denmark (in full as a Member State) and Norway (in part as an EEA member) are obliged to comply with European Union law. Some of the EU requirements are laid down in the EIA Directive[1] and the SEA Directive,[2] and to some extent the overall policy framework on wind energy is harmonized at EU level.

Given that the general characteristics of the common law and the civil law traditions are not dominant with regard to the regulation of wind energy, environmental law or energy law, these characteristics are not the focal points when analyzing the differences between the approaches of the different countries. The legal approaches to wind energy regulation and the requirements for, e.g. environmental impact assessment, nature protection and noise regulation are surprisingly similar. Although case law and the doctrine of *stare decisis* obviously play an important role in the regulation of energy and the environment in the common law countries reviewed in this book, their energy laws and environmental laws are still characterized by statutory regulation that generally reflects the same regulatory approaches as those found in the Scandinavian countries.

## 2.2. Jurisdictional Issues

A key element in the legal framework for wind energy is the question of jurisdiction – who has the power to exercise legal authority and thus the competence to deal with a case. This includes more traditional territorial aspects as well as regulatory aspects, i.e. which regulatory regime governs the case

1.  Directive 85/337/EEC of 27 June 1985 on the assessment of the effects of certain public and private projects on the environment.
2.  Directive 2001/42/EC of 27 June 2001 on the assessment of the effects of certain plans and programmes on the environment.

and at what level of authority – is it a state or federal matter or is it subject to local, regional or national authorities.[3]

Internationally, territorial jurisdiction is particularly relevant for offshore activities which are governed by the United Nations Convention on the Law of the Sea (UNCLOS). From a legal perspective it is also important to distinguish between the development of wind farms within or outside the territorial sea (12 nautical miles from the baseline). In federal countries like the United States there is a somewhat complex interplay between federal and state powers, especially in coastal areas. In general, federal jurisdiction applies to federal lands and offshore areas outside the territorial sea. In non-federal countries there appears to be some variation as to whether state or local authorities have jurisdiction in offshore areas. In Denmark the shoreline is generally the boundary, as land areas primarily fall within the jurisdiction of local authorities whereas sea areas fall within the exclusive jurisdiction of the state. In Norway it appears to be the baseline that is the boundary, since the common understanding is that the territory of local authorities extends to the baseline, including internal waters. Outside the baseline it is commonly understood that the state has exclusive jurisdiction, but there is no legislation on this. In New Zealand the local authorities (regional councils) have jurisdiction within the territorial sea, but it is to a certain extent shared with the state.

Even though specific authorities may have exclusive territorial jurisdiction, the exercise of powers may nevertheless be subject to other regimes, e.g. international law or EU law. Many of the regulatory requirements laid down in EU environmental law apply equally to offshore and onshore activities, e.g. the EIA Directive and SEA Directive.[4] This also appears to be the case as regards federal legislation in the United States. In non-federal countries like Denmark, New Zealand and Norway there appears to be a regulatory division based on territorial jurisdiction, with much less intense regulation for areas governed exclusively by the state than for areas primarily governed by local authorities. This is perhaps not surprising, but it is important in relation to offshore wind turbines, since they may to some extent fall into a regulatory gap. Another important element regarding jurisdictional issues is the question of coordination where several authorities may share jurisdiction. In such cases it is important for there to be some coordination mechanisms in place in order to ensure efficient decision-making, e.g. by introducing a lead agency –

---

3. Jurisdictional issues are discussed in Chapter 5, section 2.
4. The EIA and SEA Directives are discussed in Chapter 7.

a prime responsible authority – as used in Denmark and the United States for offshore activities.[5]

## 2.3. Fundamental Rights

The ideals of democracy, the rule of law, respect for human rights and judicial review are cornerstones of the legal systems analysed. This book thus also includes a brief analysis of the constitutional set up and of substantive and procedural limitations on public decision-makers relating to certain fundamental rights such as private property rights, rights to a good environment, rights to public participation and access to justice.

In Denmark, Norway and the United States the ideals of democracy and fundamental rights have been laid down in written constitutions; in New Zealand these rights are rooted in constitutional practice, statutory law and common law. All countries apply the model of representative democracy as the basis for the legislative process. In Denmark, New Zealand and Norway the parliament consists of only one chamber, whereas the United States has a bicameral system.

In all the selected countries there is some decentralization, although there are considerable differences in the legislative and executive powers granted to the decentralized authorities. In the case of Denmark, New Zealand and Norway authority over energy and the environment is mainly vested in the state, but some powers have been decentralized to local authorities. In general, environmental law is more decentralized than energy law, with the development of energy law being entirely in the hands of the state. As far as the United States is concerned, the US Constitution recognizes that individual states have sovereign power over matters involving energy and the environment. State governments may delegate some of their authority to regional or local authorities. According to the US Constitution, the federal government has the power to regulate certain energy and environmental matters such as interstate movements of natural gas and electricity, nuclear safety and major hydropower projects. Since the 1970s an expansive programme of federal legislation on such topics as air and water pollution and species preservation has given the federal government a significant role. However, these programmes have often been structured as 'cooperative federalism', allowing for the implementation of national standards by the state authorities, and allowing the states to establish stricter rules for environmental protection under state authority.

---

5. The concept of a lead agency is discussed in Chapter 5, section 2.3.3.

The Norwegian Constitution establishes a more fundamental right to a good environment and thus provides a clear basis for safeguarding environmental interests. Neither in Denmark, New Zealand nor the United States do constitutional provisions provide a similarly explicit mandate for safeguarding environmental concerns. However the Norwegian constitutional provision stands as an ultimate guarantor and only in extreme cases may the courts find that there is non-compliance with the provision. So far it has only been used as a guide to the interpretation of legislation. In the United States, a right to a good environment is found in some state constitutions, but equally there has been little or no effort by private parties to assert this right.

Other constitutional provisions can influence how governments weigh environmental interests. In all the selected countries except New Zealand, basic constitutional protections of property rights can stand in the way of government intervention on behalf of environmental or energy interests, leading at least to the obligation to pay full compensation for breaches of property rights. In New Zealand the protection of property rights is derived from the common law tradition and is today incorporated in the Resource Management Act (RMA). In all countries land ownership rights have been progressively restricted by legislation and thus landowners are generally not entitled to compensation for economic loss from land use planning and general environmental regulations. In all countries, however, in specific circumstances public interference may amount to regulatory taking or expropriation resulting in entitlement to compensation. Property rights may also protect against interference by private or public parties which in Denmark and Norway is reflected in the concepts of neighbour law, and in the common law tradition in the doctrines of nuisance and trespass. In practice there is little difference between these two approaches, as discussed below; see section 2.7.

The rights to public participation and access to justice, as laid down in the Aarhus Convention, are part of all the legal systems analyzed, though in different ways. The EU, Denmark and Norway are all parties to the Aarhus Convention and have also, as part of their EU obligations, enacted legislation establishing these rights. Equally, in New Zealand and the United States the law conforms largely to the requirements of the Aarhus Convention. Public participation and access to justice in environmental and energy matters are thus clearly cornerstones of the legal systems considered.

Public participation is generally an important element of environmental legislation, in particular as part of planning and environmental impact assessment procedures. However, certain restrictions may be imposed on public participation in different systems. In New Zealand, public participation is dependent upon the notification of resource consents, but only a small proportion of resource consents are notified.[6]

In Denmark and Norway there is generally a broad right of administrative appeal, whereas New Zealand and the United States rely on appeals to courts. There are certain differences between the administrative appeal systems of Denmark and Norway. In Denmark specific administrative boards of appeal have been established in the fields of energy and the environment. The Danish administrative appeal boards generally operate independently as quasi-judicial bodies, thus fulfilling the criteria of the Aarhus Convention on access to justice. In Norway, there are no specialized administrative appeal bodies. The Norwegian courts only play a limited role in the enforcement and development of environmental law and energy law, whereas Danish courts are increasingly required to consider administrative decisions on the establishment of wind farms. Neither in Denmark nor in Norway are there special courts for environmental or energy issues.

The courts play a more important role in common law countries. In the United States, judicial review of administrative decisions in the field of environmental law and energy law is common. In contrast to Denmark and Norway, where – in simplified and general terms – the courts primarily review the legality of a decision by public authorities and not its appropriateness, the courts in the United States are more prominently engaged in the judicial review of government action. In New Zealand a special environment court has been established within the court system. The Environment Court has been constituted under the RMA, and most of the Court's work involves issues arising under the RMA. Appeals from the Environment Court can be made to the High Court, but only on a point of a law. The Court is not bound by strict rules of evidence and its proceedings are often less formal than those of the general courts. Any person who has submitted an objection to a project has the right to appeal to the Environment Court. In Denmark, Norway and the United States it is normally necessary to fulfil the traditional *locus standi* requirements before the courts.

Other important elements for ensuring access to justice are the remedies that are available to the courts and the extent to which such remedies are actually used. However, the costs of litigation may be significant and may effectively prevent access to the courts. Generally, it may be fair to conclude that, as in many other cases, ensuring a proper balance between all the inter-

---

6. See Chapter 6, section 7.5.

ests involved in wind energy development should not rely on the courts, but rather on an appropriate regulatory system.

### 2.4. Planning Law

An important instrument for ensuring an overall balance of land use interests is planning law.[7] Most countries apply some sort of planning system more or less closely related to land use control law. The extent to which such planning or land use control systems deal with wind energy development may vary.

Denmark is the only country in this comparative study that has explicit planning rules for wind energy development. Since 1999 the Danish planning rules for wind energy development have included a positive obligation to designate wind turbine areas on land. The designation of wind turbine areas used to be part of regional planning, but since the local government reform of 1 January 2007 it has become part of municipal planning. This shift from regional to municipal level has raised some concern that municipal authorities will be more reluctant to designate new wind turbine areas, due to local objections.

It appears that the fairly similar Norwegian planning system is moving in the opposite direction, towards the development of regional (county) plans for the location of wind turbines. This is reflected in the comprehensive guidelines for the planning and location of wind farms which were adopted in 2007. In Denmark and Norway the planning systems are generally confined to land areas, though in Norway they include internal waters. There is no coastal planning system that applies to offshore areas outside the baseline. However, in Denmark there is a practice for designating potential offshore wind turbine areas.

In the United States land use control and planning is a state matter and is only governed by federal laws to a very limited extent. This means that the extent of planning or zoning systems may vary from state to state. Furthermore, state regulation of land use is limited in many states so the focus is on regulation by local governments. Thus, there appears to be limited experience of how state planning or zoning systems deal with wind energy development. However, the federal Coastal Zone Management Act encourages the adoption of coastal zone management plans. Generally, land areas as well as parts of the territorial sea are included in the plans. Coastal zone management plans may specify guidelines for wind energy development.

---

7. The role of planning law is analysed in Chapter 6.

The New Zealand planning system is laid down in the Resource Management Act (RMA). The RMA generally calls for the overall balancing of interests and the sustainable management of natural and physical resources. Among other things, the Act specifically requires decision-makers to have regard to the efficient use of energy, the effects on climate change, and the benefits of the use and development of renewable energy.[8] However, there are no specific wind turbine planning requirements in the RMA. Authority over the land use aspects of a wind energy project rests with the district council or city council in whose territory the project is proposed. The project will be assessed in the light of the council's district plan. If a wind energy project is proposed for an area below the mean high water mark, it will be assessed under the regional coastal plan prepared by the regional council in accordance with the New Zealand Coastal Policy Statement under the RMA. Regional coastal plans do not include areas above the mean high water mark.

Given how often there are local objections to the establishment of wind turbines, it appears to be important for the legal framework to adequately address the overall balancing of interests. In particular, the positive effects of wind energy development are often outweighed in local decision-making. In New Zealand, the RMA explicitly gives a certain weighting to the benefits of renewable energy that should be taken into account in local decision-making. This reflects the integrated approach of the RMA. However, in countries with a more sectoral approach, explicit or positive planning obligations for wind turbines may facilitate the development of wind energy in other ways, as in the case of Denmark. The positive designation of wind turbines areas as part of the planning process provides a firm basis for subsequent local decision-making on the establishment of individual turbines in the designated area. It is likely that such an overall balancing of environmental interests is easier at the regional level than at the municipal level. It appears that Norway is on the way to adopting a similar approach.

### 2.5. Environmental Assessment

Environmental assessments are instruments for providing a better basis for decision-making. In general, the procedures do not set up any substantive requirements for the balancing of interests as such, but they are aimed at providing information on how different interests may be affected by a project or plan. The extent to which an environmental impact assessment (EIA) of pro-

---

8.   The Resource Management Act S. 7; see further Chapter 6, section 7.2.

ject, or a strategic environmental assessment (SEA) of a plan or programme applies to wind energy development may, however, vary.

EIA procedures have been recognized in international law as being important measures, in particular in the 1991 Convention on Environmental Impact Assessment in a Transboundary Context (the Espoo Convention).[9] The Convention addresses the assessment of transboundary effects, including notification and consultation procedures. In a 2004 amendment, wind farms were included in the Annex I list of mandatory EIA projects.[10] Furthermore, in 2003 a Protocol on Strategic Environmental Assessment was adopted requiring an SEA to be carried out for certain plans and programmes. Plans or programmes for wind farms are in Annex II of the Protocol, requiring an SEA if an EIA is required under national legislation.

At EU level the 1985 EIA Directive and the 2001 SEA Directive lay down comprehensive procedures for EIA and SEA. However, wind power installations are not mandatory Annex I projects under the EIA Directive, but must be subject to an EIA if they are likely to have a significant effect. An SEA is, however, needed for plans or programmes relating to wind power installations according to the SEA Directive. The EIA and SEA Directives do not distinguish between onshore and offshore activities.

Denmark has adopted stricter rules for wind turbines, since an EIA is mandatory for wind turbines more than 80 metres high and for groups of more than three turbines. The Danish EIA procedure is fairly complicated, involving the drawing up of municipal planning guidelines for the project. For larger turbines the EIA is carried out by state authorities rather than by municipal authorities. Specific EIA rules apply for offshore projects. The Danish SEA rules apply to both onshore and offshore activities.

Norway has adopted a more integrated approach to EIA and SEA, implementing both EU Directives in a single set of rules. Furthermore, the Norwegian EIA and SEA procedure is integrated with the permit procedure, in particular for projects that do not require a land use plan. This is the case for wind turbines. However, an impact assessment is only mandatory for wind turbines with an effect of more than 10 MW. Smaller wind farms or turbines are subject to a case-by-case assessment of whether they are likely to have a significant effect on the environment. There are today no specific rules for EIA/SEA for offshore projects outside internal waters, but the necessary rules

---

9. The Espoo Convention was signed in 1991 under the auspices of the UN Economic Commission for Europe; for further information see Chapter 6, section 2.
10. The amendment is not yet in force, however.

will have to be adopted when plans for offshore wind farms are presented, possibly in the near future.

In the United States there is a clear distinction between federal actions and non-federal actions in relation to impact assessment requirements. Federal actions are governed by the National Environmental Policy Act (NEPA), whereas non-federal actions are governed by state rules. Federal actions include private projects that require federal approval of some sort, including offshore projects in areas under federal jurisdiction. Whether a federal action is likely to have a significant impact on the environment, and thus require a full environmental impact statement (EIS), is generally decided on a case-by-case basis. At state level there is a certain variety ranging from states with no EIS rules (most states) to states with comprehensive EIS rules.

In New Zealand a project-specific assessment of environmental effects (AEE) is integrated in the resource consent process under the RMA. However, it appears that statutory requirements and guidance are kept to a minimum. There are no special rules that apply to AEE for wind farms. An evaluation of the appropriateness for sustainable development, i.e. a broad strategic assessment, is required for plans and programmes, including those related to the use of energy sources and energy developments.

Even though there appears to be some variation between the four countries there seems to be some common issues. The first relates to when an EIA or SEA is required. It appears that only Denmark and Norway have mandatory EIA requirements for wind turbines of a certain size. However, there is a large discrepancy regarding the threshold levels. Otherwise the case-by-case determination of the probability of significant effect appears to be the decisive criterion. The second issue relates to the integrated character of the EIA or SEA procedure. In this respect, New Zealand clearly has a very high degree of integration with the resource consent process. However, there are limited specific requirements for the assessment. Norway also appears to have adopted a somewhat integrated approach, even integrating EIAs and SEAs into one process.

## 2.6. Nature Protection Issues

A major issue related to the establishment of wind farms or turbines is the negative effects on nature and landscape. Nature protection interests may to some extent be safeguarded by land use planning or zoning. This is particularly relevant for landscape interests in general, including coastal areas. In addition, specific highly valued elements of nature or landscape, such as wetlands, special habitats and species, may be safeguarded by nature protection laws in the more traditional sense.

International nature protection law has a long history and includes several legal instruments ranging from the general protection of biodiversity in the Biodiversity Convention, to the protection of specific habitats or species in the Ramsar Convention on wetlands, and the Bonn Convention on migratory species. At EU level the Birds Directive and the Habitats Directive establish a strict protection scheme, in particular for areas designated as bird protection or habitat areas (Natura 2000). It is generally not possible to establish wind farms or turbines that may negatively affect Natura 2000 areas.[11] The directives also include strict species protection schemes.

Danish nature protection law seeks to implement the strict protection of Natura 2000 areas. However, there have been some failures of implementation, particular in relation to offshore areas since the implementing laws were primarily focused on land-based activities. It has now been explicitly stated that permits for offshore wind energy projects cannot be granted if a project will adversely affect the integrity of a site. In addition to the Natura 2000 areas, the Danish Nature Protection Act includes general protection for certain habitats and landscape elements, including a 300 metre prohibition zone along the coast and individual conservation areas.

Nature protection is also an important element in Norwegian environmental law. The Norwegian Nature Conservation Act operates with different classes of protected areas, including protected landscapes. However, the Act does not in itself protect anything, it gives the government the authority to protect areas and species as it deems necessary.

In the United States there is a complex interplay between federal laws and state laws to preserve land or protect particular species. The states are free to give greater protection to endangered species and ecosystems, but they cannot authorize breaches of federal standards. Wetlands are protected by federal legislation, in particular the Clean Water Act and the Rivers and Harbors Act. The establishment of wind turbines in a wetland is likely to require a federal permit. The Endangered Species Act provides a strict protection regime for the species listed in the Act, including protection of their habitats.

The New Zealand Resource Management Act integrates nature protection interests into the general legal framework of the Act. In addition, specific legislation provides for protection of designated areas. If an energy development project is proposed on conservation land (or waters) the state authority may

---

11. Areas that are not but should have been designated as bird protection areas are also subject to strict requirements; see Chapter 8, section 3.1.

refuse permission for the project. The Wildlife Act includes protected areas for wildlife as well as specific protection for listed species.

While nature protection law appear to be potential barriers to wind energy development in most countries there may be differences as to precisely what natural elements are protected and how. In particular, the protection of landscape values appears to vary from one country to another, i.e. whether there is a more general protection of landscape or more specific protection of designated landscapes. It is important that landscape and nature protection concerns are integrated into decision-making, as seems to be the case in most countries. Countries like Denmark, with a generally sectoral approach to offshore activities, should ensure proper integration of landscape and nature protection concerns in offshore development projects.

As for the protection of designated areas or listed species, there appear to be some difference from country to country with respect to the strict character of the rules. Of course, this also depends on the different categories of protected areas or species. Generally, strong nature protection interests would outweigh the positive benefits of wind energy development, but the situation may be somewhat more difficult in valuable coastal areas, since coastal areas are often the best wind areas. This emphasizes the importance of ensuring an in-depth assessment and balancing of the interests involved in each case.

### 2.7. Environmental Protection Issues

The environmental protection issues relevant to wind energy development are first and foremost noise and other negative effects such as vibration, shadows and reflection or flickering. Such negative effects may to varying degrees affect the health and life of humans, primarily those of neighbours. In most countries the regulation of noise and related negative effects is regulated through public law as well as private law (neighbour law or nuisance). There is a complex interplay between these two areas of law and a key question is to what extent wind energy projects may be prohibited or face claims for compensation based on neighbour law or nuisance.

Noise is regulated at international as well as EU level, primarily through different types of standardization. This also applies to noise from wind turbines, though only to a limited extent. The national level is the most important regulatory level as regards noise and similar effects.

In Denmark there are specific public law rules that regulate noise from wind turbines as well as the siting of the turbines. The noise standards are issued under the Environmental Protection Act, and specific rules for wind turbines under the Planning Act determine requirements for distance from neighbours etc. The latter may safeguard against disturbing effects other than noise, such as visual interference. The general neighbour law rules may apply to disturbance from wind turbines, even though public law standards are complied with. However, no compensation claims based on neighbour law have so far been successful in relation to wind turbines in Denmark. An explanation could be that the specific wind turbine standards in public law generally ensure that the establishment of wind turbines takes account of neighbour interests. However, it is possible that in exceptional cases the tolerance limit may be exceeded even though the public law standards are complied with. Nevertheless, a general compensation scheme for neighbours to wind turbines has been proposed as part of the political 2008 Energy Agreement. Such a compensation scheme would, however, be problematic from a legal point of view.

Norwegian law is also characterized by the interplay between public law and private law. Public law regulation of pollution, including noise, is regulated by the Pollution Control Act, and there are recommended maximum noise limits as guidelines for land use planning. If the maximum level is not complied with, a permit under the Pollution Control Act is required. Even though the noise levels are complied with or a permit may have been granted, it is still possible to claim compensation under the Norwegian Neighbour Act. The Norwegian courts have granted restrictions or compensation in wind turbine cases.[12]

In the United States public control of noise is primarily a matter of state and local, rather than federal, control. Federal law applies if a wind farm is located on federally managed lands or in offshore areas and an EIS may be required under the National Environmental Policy Act. At state level there is a certain variation from state to state. Noise standards may be established in state law or at local level. As federal and state regulatory control of noise emissions from wind turbines is limited, nuisance litigation is likely to be an important enforcement mechanism in cases of excessive noise or vibration. In several cases the US courts have held that a wind turbine was a nuisance, in particular in residential areas. Also, a permit does not pre-empt a nuisance claim.[13]

New Zealand regulates noise and vibration through the Resource Management Act. Specific noise limits are generally included in the district plans made by district councils and city councils under the Act. However, the environmental benefits of wind energy may outweigh the disadvantage of intru-

---

12. See Chapter 9, section 5.1.
13. See further on nuisance in the United States, Chapter 9, section 6.1.

sive noise in a resource consent decision. Where a resource consent is necessary, stringent noise measurement and auditing requirements will usually be laid down. A nuisance claim is not excluded even if a permit has been granted or the project is authorized under relevant planning legislation. However, an activity is generally considered immune from an action in nuisance if it is conducted within the conditions imposed and does not breach any other legal requirements or obligations.[14]

It appears that in practice there is little difference between the role of nuisance and the role of neighbour law. In Norway, the Neighbour Act lays down general conditions, whereas in Denmark neighbour law is based on court rulings, as in New Zealand and the United States. It is a common characteristic that compliance with public law standards does not exclude the possibility of a claim under nuisance or neighbour law. The differences as to whether a nuisance or neighbour law claim is likely to succeed appear to be based more on the extent to which public law specifically safeguards neighbour concerns related to wind turbines. Rather than noise limits, it appears that specific distance requirements or permits in particular may hamper successful nuisance or neighbour claims.

### 2.8. Energy Law Issues

Development of wind energy raises many different legal questions, and many of these are related to access to wind resources, to exploration, development and production, to sites and to the grid. Long-range planning, licensing requirements and award procedures are important in this connection. Electricity is bound to networks of cables and wires which require legal measures for central coordination of electricity flows in order to maintain a physical balance between production and consumption in the system, and for the control of monopoly power, including the regulation of prices. There are technical challenges connected with an intermittent and variable power source like wind energy. Some grid reinforcement and back up systems using conventional energy are therefore increasingly required as the proportion of wind generation increases.

The further development of renewable energy sources has increasingly become a topic in the international community in connection with the principle of sustainable development. However, in this field international law is primarily non-binding, with two major exceptions: the legal regime governing the rights of coastal states to exploit their adjacent seas and the air above

---

14. See further on New Zealand, Chapter 9, section 7.

them, and the Climate Change Convention with its Kyoto Protocol. The UN Convention on the Law of the Sea (UNCLOS) recognizes the sovereign rights of nation states to the economic exploitation and exploration of the natural resources within the exclusive zones off their coasts. This includes the production of energy from wind and the right to construct wind turbines, subject to the obligation to respect the rights of other states. The Kyoto Protocol includes commitments to adopt effective legislation and programmes to mitigate climate change and to specific individual targets for reducing greenhouse gas emissions.

In EU law there is an increasing emphasis on the need to increase the share of renewables in energy consumption, coupled with climate change measures and the need to reduce dependence on oil from unstable regions. Today, the core objectives of EU energy policy are thus threefold: sustainable development, competitiveness, and security of supply. In this connection energy security is strengthened by the use of renewable energy, both due to increased fuel flexibility and to the fact that renewables are local resources. At the same time it is recognized that these developments will not happen without support in terms of State aid, priority access to the grid, strengthening the grid and increasing resources devoted to research and technological development.

In the de-regulatory era of the 1980s and 1990s, most states de-coupled the ownership and the regulation of power generation facilities from the ownership and regulation of distribution systems. Competition was introduced in power generation and supply, and consumers were given freedom of choice of supply. In the four countries analysed in this study the electricity supply market has been fully liberalized, and this is a general trend in many parts of the world. From the start of the liberalization process in the EU, the option was included of giving priority to power generation using renewable sources. Moreover, the EU electricity market directives of 1996 and 2003 included the possibility of raising a levy for public service obligations on electricity providers in order to provide for energy security or environmental protection. These obligations cover the use of renewables and in 2001 were combined with setting indicative targets for each Member State for the share of renewables in their electricity production. While the EU abstains from dictating the energy mix as such, and the renewable source more specifically, the most recent proposals for new directives of 2008 include binding national targets for renewables – both for the Community as a whole, and as individual obligations for each Member State. The new proposals are under negotiation, but the framework for the future has been indicated and is politically agreed. It could be said that this development is the culmination of a step-by-step process by which the requirements for the use of renewables have been tightened gradually.

The legal, institutional and commercial arrangements for the supply of energy vary considerably between the countries considered in this book. EU law affects the national legislation of Denmark and Norway but long before the EU initiatives in this field Denmark had adopted a comprehensive legal framework for the promotion of renewables and in particular the use of wind energy. For the last 25 years, wind energy has constituted a far bigger proportion of energy supply in Denmark than in New Zealand, Norway or the United States. However, electricity based on hydropower plays a significant role in both New Zealand and Norway. In all countries, however, there are indications that the role of renewables in general, and of wind energy particular, will increase in the future national energy mix. Moreover, as it has become harder to find suitable sites on land, offshore areas are attracting more attention. Of the four countries considered in this book only Denmark has so far constructed wind turbines offshore and has developed the planning process and legal framework for this. Projects are planned in the United States and there is an ongoing political debate in Norway, whereas no such steps are envisaged for the time being in New Zealand.

The regulatory systems of Denmark and Norway strongly resemble each another. This has been highlighted in several of the sections above but it also applies to their energy legislation. Their regulatory regimes are quite similar, other than that Norway has not yet adopted legislation for developing wind energy offshore. To some extent these similarities follow from their membership of or affiliation to the EU, but this is only part of the answer. Often EU legislation is not exhaustive but only sets some minimum criteria and the framework for national implementation. This means that the Member States still have wide discretionary power to design the detailed regulatory system. Furthermore, as mentioned above, some initiatives at state level (including in Denmark and Norway) have anticipated those at EU level.

Denmark and Norway use sophisticated and detailed planning systems, both with respect to the need to build power plants and their location; see above under section 2.4. At the political level central energy plans are prepared and agreed, setting the long term targets and prioritizing the steps to be taken to ensure developments. Pursuant to the electricity legislation all licensees must carry out energy planning and coordinate their planning with other licensees. In New Zealand and the United States developments are more or less left to private initiative, and there is no central energy planning. However, in the United States some states do have modest planning mechanisms. It is nevertheless a system based on case-by-case development rather than general policy and activity planning. This does not mean that regulations do not exist, but that their focus is on environmental issues rather than energy matters. Thus environmental impacts assessments have to be made in all four countries; see above in section 2.5.

In both Denmark and Norway licensing systems have been set up for building, generation and supply activities. A licence is thus needed in order to construct a wind turbine above a certain size, and to produce and sell the electricity. For its offshore areas Denmark has developed a licensing system in which the essential stages of operations require separate public permits – construction, production and the use of the wind resource. Applications may be submitted in accordance with a tendering system and the procedures are thus competitive. None of the other three countries have implemented such a system. In both Denmark and Norway licences are issued for periods of between 20 and 25 years, and special conditions may be attached to a licence. Some conditions are specific to the project, but many of the conditions are standard terms which means that the content of the licences are similar. Among other things, the aim is to make sure that certain standards are followed. The licence award has to be based on objective, transparent and non-discriminatory criteria. In contrast to this, New Zealand and the United States do not require any licences to initiate activities. In the Western states of the United States, however, a lot of the land is owned by the federal government so that it has control over and issues permits for rights of way for energy distribution facilities such as electricity transmission lines.

In Denmark and Norway network companies need licences for distribution activities, and they have an obligation to connect new end-consumers to the network against payment. In the United States, 20 states have adopted Renewable Portfolio Standards (RPS) which require energy distributors to obtain and distribute renewably generated electricity. In New Zealand there are no specific or preferential provisions for market access or connection to the transmission network for wind energy.

Different forms of direct subsidies, regulatory incentives and tax exemptions have been implemented to develop the technology and expand the use of wind turbines. Guaranteed grid access and purchase obligations have been important to the success in Denmark, combined with tax exemptions and heavy state funding for research. Along with the increased focus on market liberalization and competition, market based instruments have also been introduced for renewable energy in the form of open tendering. Today, wind power in Denmark is sold on the market and the producer receives a bonus in addition to the market price. The system is combined with a quota emission system which gives wind energy a competitive advantage over installations producing electricity using fossil fuels, due to wind energy's exemption from $CO_2$ tax. In New Zealand such an emissions quota and trading system has been proposed in a bill before parliament, but at present there are no subsidies, preferential tariffs or green certificates to support renewables. There is only the recognition in the Resource Management Act of the role of renewables, and most recently the announcement of a moratorium on the construction of fossil fuel baseload electricity generation plants. In Norway the distribution network companies are obliged to add an extra charge to the tariff and to transfer the extra charge to the Energy Fund which provides financial support for renewable energy production, including wind power. In the United States, many states have adopted the system of minimum renewable energy requirements (RPS), usually coupled with a system of renewable energy credits, in which the producers of renewable energy can sell a credit for each kilowatt hour they provide. To promote the development of wind energy etc. in 1992 Congress adopted a federal Renewable Energy Production Tax Credit (PTC). The PTC seeks to make the price of wind-generated energy competitive. There is a comparable incentive system, called the Renewable Energy Production Incentive, for public power generating bodies which do not generate business income and therefore do not benefit from the income tax credit.

In both Denmark and Norway there is a tradition for involving the public, not only as regulators and as participants in decision-making, but also as owners of energy-generating activities. The extent of this has varied over the years, but in relation to electricity the important function of coordination and system operation, and thus the responsibility for integrating wind energy into the power system, is vested with a 100 per cent state-owned company. This is also the case in New Zealand, but in the United States the federal and state authorities are not directly involved in electricity supply at all. This does not mean that there is no intervention in energy activities in the United States. In all four countries the conditions and prices related to monopoly activities – meaning network activities – are controlled by a public authority. In addition, in Denmark and in the United States lead agencies have been appointed for offshore developments (see above in section 2.2) in order to coordinate the often opposing interests connected to the establishment of offshore wind power projects.

## 3. Conclusions

Despite the differences between the civil law and common law systems, there are a large number of similarities in the laws governing wind turbines in the

313

four countries analysed. This is the case with regard to jurisdictional issues, environmental impact assessment, nature protection law, noise regulation and to some extent also energy law. Even where real differences exist, the significance of these differences is reduced by the use of statutory law and administrative law in common law countries. The legal challenges thus appear to be fairly similar in civil law and common law countries, at least when it comes to wind energy development.

The promotion of wind energy is highly dependent upon the legal framework. The legal framework is important in ensuring not only favourable market conditions, but also in ensuring an adequate balancing of the different interests related to wind energy development – considering both the positive and the negative effects. It is necessary to address the opportunities and constraints in the laws governing wind energy development.

Because national sovereignty is still a key parameter with respect to rights to natural resources, and because of different mixes of sources of energy, renewable energy development is largely country-specific and very much related to physical circumstances, in other words the availability of natural resources and geographic criteria.

Moreover, there is an observable difference in regulatory philosophy – concerning the degree of state involvement, and the extent to which developments should be left to the market and private initiative. Increasingly, however, it is recognized that there is an important role for the state to play in removing barriers and promoting further development of renewables and, in this context, wind energy.

The main regulatory challenges identified in this comparative study are:

1) Avoidance of *regulatory gaps* and ensuring coordination between *overlapping jurisdictions*/competences
2) Ensuring that the legal framework adequately provides for *balancing the positive against the negative effects* of wind energy projects, and
3) Ensuring energy market conditions which allow the integration of wind energy into the electricity system.

*Regulatory gaps* and *overlapping jurisdiction* are particularly relevant in relation to offshore wind energy development. In many countries there is a regulatory divide either delimited by the shoreline, the baseline or the limit of the territorial sea. Such regulatory divides should be properly addressed in the legal system, ensuring that fundamental requirements, such as impact assessment, apply equally under different regimes. Furthermore, coordination between different authorities with overlapping competencies should be addressed in the legal framework, for example by using a lead agency to provide for coherent decision-making.

However, such initiatives alone will not ensure the *adequate balancing of the positive effects against the negative effects* of wind energy projects. The negative effects of wind energy projects are primarily related to environmental concerns ranging from overall landscape and nature values to more individual neighbour concerns – often referred to under the heading of NIMBY-ism (Not In My Back Yard). In most cases such interests are safeguarded by environmental legislation.[15] While these interests may imply certain restrictions on wind energy development, the more positive environmental effects of wind energy in reducing $CO_2$ emissions have not always been reflected in the different measures of environmental legislation specifically aimed at regulating the negative effects. This raises the question of whether and how a better balance of the negative and positive environmental effects of wind energy installations could be ensured.

On the basis of the four countries studied in this book, there appear to be at least two different regulatory strategies that may facilitate a balance between the positive and negative effects of wind energy. *The first strategy* is the integrated management approach which is clearly expressed in the New Zealand Resource Management Act (RMA). The Act uses sustainable management as a core unifying principle by which all environmental and resource management policy-making, planning and decision-making is to be guided. The RMA explicitly requires decision-makers to have particular regard to the efficient use of natural and physical resources and to the efficiency of the end-use of energy, the effects on climate change, and the benefits to be derived from the use and development of renewable energy. It has been demonstrated in New Zealand court cases that these provisions have been applied so as to favour wind energy projects over other land use interests.

*The other strategy* is the use of physical or land use planning as an active measure in the promotion of wind energy, as is the case in Denmark. The positive designation of wind turbine areas provides an opportunity to balance the positive and negative effects at an earlier stage than at the decision-making stage for individual projects. Further, impact assessment procedures at plan as well as project level are an important element in ensuring a proper balance between the positive and negative effects of wind energy, in particu-

15.  The environmental interests in relation to wind energy are primarily confined to land use and landscape, nature protection (including the protection of wetlands) environmental protection (in particular noise), visual interference and other types of disturbance related to wind turbines.

lar providing more factual information on the potential negative effects. Even though impact assessment procedures may be time-consuming they may also reduce controversy by providing a better informed decision-making basis.

Even though the negative effects of wind energy projects should be balanced against their positive effects, it must be recognized that certain interests need to be specifically addressed as part of the regulatory process. This includes the protection of valuable landscapes as well as valuable habitats and species. In particular habitats and species are often subject to strict nature protection legislation. The legal protection of landscape interests as such may be less apparent. Furthermore, there should be a special emphasis on ensuring an appropriate balancing in coastal landscapes where many wind energy projects are likely to be constructed.

Another conflicting interest that has to be addressed in the legal framework is that of neighbours. In all four countries *neighbour concerns* are subject to a complex interplay between public law and private law. Private law, in the form of neighbour law or nuisance, can give rise to claims for prohibitions or compensation. It appears that the role of neighbour law or nuisance may be reduced to the extent that public law explicitly addresses neighbour concerns, e.g. through noise limits, distance requirements etc. However, it is a delicate balance and should be carefully considered as part of the legal framework.

*Energy markets* are equally of great importance to the development of wind energy. There is a need to make sure that the use of wind energy is not unfavourably treated compared to traditional fuels and that producers can sell the wind power into the electricity grid efficiently. These developments will not happen without the involvement of national governments. In many ways the EU is now leading the way globally by its latest proposal to set binding targets for the use of renewable energy for each Member State. Moreover, well designed subsidies will be necessary – at least until the new technology has reached maturity. Not much experience has yet been gained about offshore wind farms further from land and in deeper waters. There is no doubt that this will be an area where there will be new developments in terms of technology and the legislative framework.

# Developing a Wind Farm
# – Case Scenarios and Questions

This Chapter outlines three scenarios for the development of a wind farm. The three scenarios are intended to form a basis for further discussions regarding the legal frameworks in Denmark, New Zealand, Norway and the United States.

Renewable energy has become an important issue for several reasons. Fossil fuels are a finite resource, and wind energy is now at a technical level where its contribution to energy supply is increasingly interesting. Furthermore, wind energy is non-polluting, at least in the traditional sense of polluting air or water, or generating waste. Nevertheless, landscape and wildlife may be affected by wind farms, while noise, shadows and other effects may cause inconvenience to neighbours.

The broad question is how wind energy development is regulated in different legal systems.

**Wind Farm Scenarios**

A new wind farm with a planned capacity of 50 MW from 25 turbines is to be established by a private energy company. The turbines will be approximately 70 metres high, including a base but excluding the blades. When a blade is at its highest point, the total height of the turbine will be about 110 metres. An area of approximately 5 km$^2$ is needed for the establishment of the wind farm.

There are three possible scenarios:

Scenario 1: Placing the wind farm *on land* between 500 and 1,000 metres from the shoreline.

The area in question is primarily designated as agricultural land. The wind farm will be located only 200 metres from a nature protection area designated for the protection of valuable coastal meadows (within the EU designated as a Natura 2000/habitat area). The nature protection area also has certain recreational interests. The wind farm will be located primarily on privately owned agricultural land. The owner of the agricultural land on which the main part of the turbines will be placed has his own residence 300 metres from the nearest turbine. This landowner agrees with the project. The other closest neighbour (private home) lives 500 metres from the nearest turbine. One kilometre from the nearest turbine there is a village. Five residents in the village are very active in the local organization: *Citizens against wind turbines*. One of the members of the organization owns a piece of land where it is planned to build one of the turbines, but this landowner is not willing to accept any wind turbines on his land.

Scenario 2: Placing the wind farm in shallow waters, partly in a sensitive wetland area.
   The wind farm area will stretch from the shoreline to approximately 500 metres (0.27 nautical miles) seawards from the shoreline. The wind farm area is located within the baseline, i.e. in internal waters. 10 of the 25 turbines will be located within a designated wetland protection area. The area is designated as valuable habitat for two rare bird species (bird protection area). A transformer and other ancillary installations will be located on land.

Scenario 3: Placing the wind farm in an offshore area in relatively shallow water, 30 kilometres (about 16 nautical miles) from the shoreline.
   The wind farm will be placed next to an existing wind farm already connected to the transmission grids on land. The existing wind farm has an offshore platform on which a transformer is placed close to the projected new wind farm. The offshore platform is large enough for a new transformer for the projected wind farm. In addition, the existing transformer plant can rebuilt for a third of the cost of a new plant to serve both the existing and the projected wind farms.

These scenarios should be analysed in relation to three different topics:

1) jurisdictional and planning matters,
2) EIA/SEA and environmental permits, and
3) energy permits/regulation.

For each scenario you may compare a selection of the regulatory aspects in Denmark with Norway, the United States and/or New Zealand.

**Topic 1**

Jurisdictional matters and planning requirements

– Please identify the relevant jurisdictional issues:
  – What level of regulation (international/national – or in federal systems federal/state) is relevant?
  – What is the competent level of administrative authority?
– Please identify the necessary planning requirements and the relevant planning authorities.

**Topic 2**

EIA/SEA and environmental permits

– Please identify which EIA/SEA and environmental permit requirements apply to the establishment of the wind farm.
– What are the possibilities for participation, objection or appeal for neighbours and others involved?
– Can neighbours or others request an injunction or claim compensation?

**Topic 3**

Energy permits/regulation
Please describe the relevant energy permit or tender requirements.

– Please describe the relevant energy permit or tender requirements
– Please identify the relevant authorities.
– How is access to and use of the grid regulated?

# Wind Power Development in a Small State: The Case of Maine

*By Donald N. Zillman*

## 1. Introduction

This article will provide a case study of wind power development in a low-profile state of the United States – the State of Maine. Some features of wind power development in Maine are unique to the state. Other features provide bases for the study of other US states and territories. The article examines the State of Maine and its wind profile. It then looks at several of Maine's commercial wind projects over the last decade. The article concludes by looking at a non-commercial wind power venture – the University of Maine at Presque Isle's proposal to install a 600 kilowatt wind turbine on campus.

## 2. Maine

Maine is the most north-eastern state in the United States. Uniquely among American states it is bordered by only by one other US state (New Hampshire) and by the Canadian provinces of New Brunswick and Quebec. Maine's current population is 1.3 million. It has no city with a population of over 100,000. Maine is famed for its multitude of towns, villages and small cities. Most are fiercely proud of their local history and traditions of local governance. Local governance sentiment also supports a 180 member State Legislature that preserves the reality of close citizen contact with the members of the Legislature and low-budget, door-to-door election campaigns.

Maine's economy has struggled for much of the last century. Traditional industries like fishing, agriculture, timber products, and shoe-making have declined in the face of national and foreign competition. Only two decades ago, there was a widespread belief that a high-school diploma was sufficient education to provide for a well-paid career in some aspect of industry or agriculture. The decline of these industries emphasizes that Maine now needs to develop new ways of making a living and that education beyond high school level is virtually essential for the state's young people.

Maine's geography and climate also play a role in the future of wind power. Maine's best known image is its 3,000 mile rocky coast dotted with iconic lighthouses and with fishing and lobster-catching villages. The waters are prone to storms. Offshore, Maine has attractive wind potential but the installation of wind turbines faces the challenge of waters that are often rough and winter temperatures that are well below freezing.

Inland Maine also has spectacular scenery. It features woods and lakes, the spurs of some of the northernmost mountains and high hills in the eastern United States, and the broad vistas of northern Maine which are of a similar scale to those in the western United States. Unlike in the western United States, most of the land is in private ownership (often owned by major timber companies). Many Mainers regard access to outdoor activities (hunting, fishing, snowmobiling, skiing, river tripping) as their birthright and would hesitate to accept any project that would intrude on such activities.

Maine also prides itself on the protection of its environment. Percival Baxter helped preserve the land surrounding Mount Katahdin (beloved of Henry David Thoreau) as permanent parkland. More recently, Governor Edmund Muskie, later Senator and US Secretary of State, began a clean-up of the polluted rivers of Maine. Muskie carried that passion to the United States Congress where he was one of the leading legislative sponsors of the remarkable set of environmental protection laws of the 1970s.

Of the 50 United States, Maine ranks 19th for wind energy potential. In 1991, a survey by the Pacific Northwest Laboratory estimated that Maine has the potential to generate 56 billion kWh from lands with a wind potential of class three or higher. By contrast, North Dakota has an estimated potential of 1,210 billion kWh and Texas a potential of 1,190 billion kWh. Maine ranks 5th among states east of the Mississippi River.[1]

### 3. Legal Perspectives

Sandy Gaines has ably reviewed the law of wind energy nationally and in selected US states; see above Chapter 10, section 6. As he notes, the United States lacks many of the elements of a legally prescribed energy policy. The federal government defers to state and local legislation on many aspects of energy. Land use laws may have the largest impact on the development of wind energy projects. These are primarily matters of state and local law.

---

1. See the American Wind Energy Association website, www.awea.org.

In Maine, a general state statute sets the outline of zoning and land use regulation for local government bodies.[2] The state enabling act authorizes, but does not require there to be local land use controls. If a local community wishes to exercise land use control, it can define the terms of its land use regulation, so long as it complies with the state enabling act. Part time local elected officials write the local law and designate local government officials to enforce its provisions.

Many parts of Maine do not fall within organized local governmental areas. A separate Maine statute provides for planning and zoning regulations for these unincorporated territories. A body with state-wide jurisdiction, the Land Use Regulation Commission (LURC) is charged with land use responsibilities for these territories.[3] LURC has often been involved in Maine wind power projects.

The zoning and planning laws are written and enforced by local government officers. Citizens or corporations may lobby for or against the legislation. They may also encourage or discourage enforcement actions. Courts play a role in land use decisions by interpreting the provisions of statutes or regulations or by determining whether government officers have reached correct decisions on particular projects. But, local legislators have the controlling hand.

Private citizens may also resort to the courts to challenge wind power projects on the basis of a variety of common law doctrines. These doctrines include nuisance law, negligence and strict liability for certain activities that may have an adverse impact on uses of land. Such disputes can lead to private civil actions in tort to be decided by a trial court and subject to appeal.

Maine has not enacted a comprehensive statute governing the construction and licensing of wind power projects.[4] Maine has encouraged wind power

2. Maine zoning law is spelled out in the multiple sections of Title 30-A Maine Revised Statutes Annotated surrounding and including section 4352.
3. Title 12 Maine Revised Statutes Annotated 683 and following sections detail the Land Use Regulation Commission's powers.
4. The Maine Wind Energy Act, Public Law 2003, chapter 665 encourages wind generation with a strong emphasis on the integration of wind generated electricity into the electrical grid. Section 3404 reflects the policy of the State for local governmental bodies to 'take every reasonable action to encourage the attraction of appropriately sited wind-energy-related development consistent with all state and federal environmental standards…'

development in its public utility statutes through provisions requiring or encouraging the use of renewable energy resources.[5]

Wind power development has also been influenced by the 1997 decision of the Maine Legislature to deregulate the electric power industry in the state. The Legislature faced an industry structure in which one investor-owned private corporation provided power generation, transmission and distribution to all the customers in its geographic service area. Three investor-owned businesses, Central Maine Power Company, Bangor Hydroelectric and Maine Public Service produced, distributed and sold power in Maine.

This system emerged in the early years of the 20th century. Maine, in common with many other states, compromised between state ownership of the electricity industry and unregulated competition between private businesses. The consequence was the investor-owned, commercial electricity company subject to considerable government control over the essentials of the business operation. The most notable regulation was the control of prices (tariffs) charged to customers. The prices charged to customers could be no more than what was 'just and reasonable' to pay for the utility company's costs of providing the service and to provide a reasonable return on investment. Government officials enforced the 'just and reasonable' standard through administrative and judicial proceedings.

A significant factor explaining the regulatory structure was that it was unlikely that there would be successful competition in certain parts of the electricity business, particularly distribution networks. Theories about natural monopolies suggested that a single company would be the most efficient way of providing electricity services with the necessary and expensive infrastructure. Any new entrant to the market would find it difficult to displace an established electricity network company.

In the last decades of the 20th century, the increased costs of electricity generation encouraged customers (particularly large industrial users) to look for less expensive ways of securing their electric power. Advocates of deregulation focused on that part of the utility business that did appear susceptible to effective competition – the generation of power. The Maine Legislature and other legislatures opened up power generation to competition and required network companies to transmit to their customers power purchased from other generators.[6]

---

5. See, 35-A Maine Revised Statutes Annotated S. 3210 (encouraging renewable generation of electric power).
6. 35-A Maine Revised Statutes Annotated S. 3202 and following sections.

Maine went so far as to force its integrated utilities to divest themselves of their power generation businesses. Central Maine Power, Bangor Hydro and Maine Public Service became network companies, in the business of transmitting and distributing power generated by other companies to their customers.

### 4. Maine Case Studies

Maine has been the location for a variety of proposed wind power projects over the last decade. All have been located on land. One proposal failed to reach operational status. One is currently in operation. Still others are in progress. A report on several of the more significant projects follows.

*4.1. Kenetech Windpower*

The most ambitious project was the first of the modern era. San Francisco based Kenetech Windpower, Inc. proposed the construction of 639 wind turbines at a cost of about $200 million dollars.[7] The total proposed generating capacity was 210 MW. The location was a 26 mile stretch of mountain ridges near the town of Stratton in western Maine near the New Hampshire border. The area was outside any organized unit of local government (in unincorporated territory). Therefore, LURC had regulatory jurisdiction over its licensing. The goal of the Kenetech project was to supply power to the New England Electric System and Central Maine Power.

The project demonstrated that the environmental attraction of renewable energy would not automatically overcome other environmental concerns about a wind energy project. Opponents of the project, including the National Audubon Society and the Sierra Club, felt that damage to fragile and attractive mountain highlands outweighed the advantages of renewable energy. They and others also expressed concerns about damage to bird life from collisions with turbines. A final concern was that efforts to reduce power usage would be undermined by any new sources of electricity.

---

7.  Information is drawn from: 'Wind power company willing to modify project', Bangor Daily News, 21 November 1994, B1; 'High-altitude wind farms may be back on permit track', Maine Times, 5 May 1995, at 7; 'Governor leaves fingerprints all over', Bangor Daily News, 1 July 1995, 1; 'Wilderness board elects new leader – Chairman named after turmoil over major wind-power project', Bangor Daily News, 17 June 1995, 1; 'Land-use report calls for OK of major wind-power project', Bangor Daily News, 15 July 1995, 1; 'LURC gives cautious nod to wind power project', Bangor Daily News, 18 August 1995, 1; and 'Commission halts plan for wind power', Portland Press Herald, 28 February 1997, 14.

Other environmental groups gave cautious approval to the project. Even before global warming concerns had become the focus of popular attention, the reduction of fossil fuel pollutants had an appeal. The Kenetech project also benefited from safety concerns about Maine's single nuclear power plant, Maine Yankee. The prospect of closing down the Maine Yankee plant (which eventually took place) increased the attraction of new sources of electricity.

Maine's newly elected independent Governor Angus King was a visible supporter of the project. In fact, King was subject to political criticism for favouring friends and campaign supporters who were advocates of the Kenetech project by attempting to influence the LURC regulators who had to decide on the project's future.

In July 1995 LURC staff recommended that the LURC Commissioners should approve the Kenetech project. The LURC Director spoke of the importance of promoting low-cost renewable energy and providing jobs in a depressed economy. One month later four of the six LURC Commissioners voted to approve the project. They approved the zoning change needed to build the project and also approved the company's development plan. The Commission did require Kenetech to address concerns about bird fatalities, road access, soil stability, and the demand for the power. Kenetech expressed the hope that further permit procedures could be completed by November 1995 and that initial generation could begin by autumn 1996, with completion of the entire project by 2000.

This marked the high water mark for the Kenetech project. On 28 February 1997 the Portland Press Herald reported that LURC had refused to extend permit deadlines for Kenetech. Kenetech's inactivity reflected a serious downturn in the fortunes of the company. The turbines which had been planned for use in Maine had failed at other Kenetech installations. In May 1996 Kenetech filed for bankruptcy protection. Efforts by Kenetech to sell its permit rights for the Maine project failed to find a buyer. Not surprisingly, LURC concluded that Kenetech did not have the finances to advance the project.

*4.2. Redington-Black Nubble*
A decade later, wind power development returned to the mountains of western Maine. During the decade, the terrorist attacks of 11 September 2001 had taken place, the Bush Administration had begun its 'war on terrorism', and global warming had achieved popular awareness in the United States. Endless Energy Corporation, based in Yarmouth, Maine, filed applications for permits

with LURC and the State Department of Environmental Protection for a 30 turbine, 90 MW, $130 million project located at two neighbouring sites.[8]

By 2005, wind had moved prominently into the discussion of energy in Maine. In May 2006, a report on a recent meeting of the LURC leadership noted that several commercial wind-power locations were under consideration around the state. Revisions of LURC's comprehensive plan were ready to give wind power serious consideration. Several participants suggested that LURC should pro-actively identify suitable and unsuitable wind-power sites in areas under its jurisdiction. This certainty could encourage wind companies and investors. State officials, including Governor John Baldacci and Public Utility Commissioner Kurt Adams, broadly endorsed greater use of renewable energy and specifically endorsed Maine's potential for wind power. Wind power technology had improved considerably since 1996. Sharp increases in fossil fuel prices (particularly natural gas) made wind more competitive. Global warming fears about the impact on the environment of fossil fuel combustion added to wind's attraction.

Yet, the Redington-Black Nubble proposal posed an even sharper set of environmental challenges than the Kenetech proposal. The Redington site was located within one mile of the legendary Appalachian Trail, the 2000 mile foot trail that follows the eastern mountains from Georgia to Maine. Redington was within three miles of one of Maine's two largest ski resorts. The attraction of the site as a location for wind power turbines was matched by its attraction as a highly visible recreational area. The Redington development also threatened forest vegetation and indigenous species.

The division of the views of environmentalists was reflected in a public hearing held by LURC in August 2006. Local testimony mostly opposed construction, emphasizing the destruction of rare and sensitive mountain areas. State-wide environmental groups strongly opposed the Redington site, but in-

8.  Information is drawn from: 'Wind power firm files with LURC', Bangor Daily News, 20 December 2005, 1; 'LURC debates rising interest in wind power', Bangor Daily News, 4 May 2006, 1; 'Wind power fans controversy', Kennebec Journal, 23 July 2006; 'NRCM Supports Scaled-down Version of Redington Wind Power Project', Natural Resources Council of Maine, 26 July 2006, www.nrcm.org/news; 'Effort to Block Wind Farm Culminated in Public Hearing', Appalachian Trail Conservancy, www.appalachiantrail.org/site; 'Maine Audubon Leading Process to Speed Approval of Wind-power Projects in Maine', www.maineaudubon.org/news; 26 July 2006; 'Panel rejects power project', Portland Press Herald, 25 January 2007, A1; 'Wind farm plan revised', Bangor Daily News, 10 May 2007; 'Regulations to weigh two wind farm projects', Bangor Daily News, 14 January 2008; and 'Two wind projects but only one winner', Bangor Daily News, 15 January 2008.

dicated support for other, both actual and hypothetical, wind power sites. Opponents of Redington also volunteered their services to assist with site selection that would allow the development of a healthy wind power industry in Maine without damaging unique and sensitive geographic areas.

In January 2007, LURC rejected the plan for the combined Redington-Black Nubble development. By a 6 to 1 majority the Commissioners took the unusual step of overriding a recommendation from LURC staff that had endorsed the proposal. The Commissioners criticized the staff for ignoring LURC standards that support natural resource preservation and encouraging the location of energy developments that threaten the environmental values of their locations.

The proponents of the Redington-Black Nubble project returned to LURC with a proposal that it should approve only the less visually offensive Black Nubble portion of the project. The project's opponents and the regulators were not in a mood for compromise. In January 2008, LURC also turned down the Black Nubble proposal by a 4 to 2 majority. The developer left the proceedings suggesting that a state agency which was more sensitive to the need for developing alternative energy resources should take over the licensing role from LURC.

At the same time, LURC did approve a 44 turbine project close to the Canadian border. The Kibby project, sponsored by the Canadian energy company TransCanada, was seen as being less threatening to sensitive environmental areas than Redington-Black Nubble.

*4.3. Mars Hill*
The Kenetech and Redington-Black Nubble experiences were discouraging for wind power advocates. Farther north in Maine, commercial wind power developments have had a better reception. Since January 2007 a project consisting of 28 wind turbines with 42 MW capacity has been operating on Mars Hill in central Aroostook County. Evergreen Wind Power, LLC is the developer-operator.[9]

Aroostook County is Maine's agricultural heartland. In contrast to Maine's western mountain regions, Aroostook's beauty arises from its expansive rolling fields laced with lakes and rivers. While there are forested areas, Aroostook's agricultural tradition provides ample open spaces that have wind

---

9. 'In upstate Maine, a wind-power project gathers momentum', Boston Globe, 7 August 2006; 'Mars Hill wind farm attracts tourists', Portland Press Herald, 1 August 2007.

power potential and where well-organized defenders of natural beauty or isolated areas immediately spring up.

Mars Hill is the most visible elevation in Central Aroostook County. The
Hill is located close to the town of the same name. The Hill had already been
developed with a small ski area, several communications towers, and access
roads. In mid-2006 the Mars Hill town manager estimated that 80-90 per cent
of the town's residents supported the development of the Evergreen Wind
project. These citizens were probably persuaded by an estimated half million
dollars in new tax revenues that were to accrue annually over the 20 year life
of the project. Town officials, who played the same role as LURC played in
relation to the Kenetech and Redington projects, approved the planning and
zoning work. Construction moved quickly and by January 2007 a commercial
scale wind project was in operation at Mars Hill.

While Mars Hill lacked some of the environmental sensitivities of the projects in the western mountains, it has not been without controversy. The project continues to divide local residents between those who live within sight of
the very visible project and those who do not. Opponents have focused their
objections on the damage to the aesthetics of the Hill and the noise from the
turbines. Some of the disputes are ones that no amount of scientific or economic data can resolve. Clearly, the 28 turbines have changed the view of
Mars Hill. Some long-time residents feel that a unique site has been dese-
crated. Other long-time residents believe that individually and collectively the
turbines are aesthetically attractive and symbolic of both development and
environmental values. Controversy over noise leads to the taking up of similarly polarised positions.

*4.4. Stetson Mountain*
Evergreen Wind Power's success at Mars Hill prompted it to move forward
with a 38 turbine, 57 MW, $100 million project on Stetson Mountain in far
eastern Maine in remote Washington County.[10] Company officials promoted
the site as being sufficiently removed both from environmentally spectacular

10. 'Wind farm would be N.E.'s largest', Bangor Daily News, 14 March 2007; 'Com-
    pany seeks approval for second wind farm', Portland Press Herald, 15 March 2007;
    'LURC approves wind farm application', Bangor Daily News, 30 April 2007; 'East-
    ern Maine residents give wind farm plan mixed reviews', Portland Press Herald, 9
    August 2007; 'LURC staff endorses wind farm', Bangor Daily News, 1 November
    2007; 'LURC OKs wind farm', Bangor Daily News, 8 November 2007; and 'TIF ap-
    proved for Stetson Mountain project', Bangor Daily News, 21 November 2007.

areas of the state and from populated areas. In short, Stetson Mountain avoided the drawbacks of both Redington and Mars Hill.

The Stetson proposal passed its first administrative hurdle in April 2007, when LURC accepted the application for review. The acceptance set the stage for public hearings. The Chairman of the Washington County Commission also indicated support for the project, noting its potential to bring jobs to an economically depressed part of Maine. The public hearing in August 2007 was attended by both supporters and opponents of the project. Opponents referred to the disadvantages of visual pollution, effects on wildlife, damage caused during construction and fire risks from the turbines.

At the final LURC hearing the benefits of new construction jobs, added tax revenue and pollution-free power generation won the argument. LURC approved the project. Construction began spring 2008.

*4.5. The University of Maine at Presque Isle*
The University of Maine at Presque Isle (UMPI) plans to install a single 600 KW turbine on campus property. The project is unlike Mars Hill and Stetson which are commercial ventures designed to sell power to others. The power from the UMPI project will be used on campus to help reduce an electricity bill for the campus that is expected to approach $350,000 for this calendar year.

The University of Maine at Presque Isle (UMPI) is 104 years old. It is one of seven universities in the state-wide University of Maine System – providing public higher education in the state. The campus had its origins as a teacher training college. In recent decades it has also developed into four year liberal arts college. It also offers a set of professional programmes in such fields as education, social work, business, criminal justice, athletic training and medical technology. Average enrolment is 1500 students and 170 faculty and staff.

The campus is located on a rolling hill on the south side of the community of Presque Isle, a city of 10,000. Other cities and towns within 20 miles (including Mars Hill) make Presque Isle the population, government, business, and cultural centre of sprawling Aroostook County. The County is geographically the largest county east of the Mississippi River. The University is also one of the largest businesses in the County.

University interest in renewable energy has been high for several years. Two active proponents of renewable energy are the Chief Financial Officer and the Director of Physical Facilities. In a world where green energy projects on campus are often driven by environmentally passionate faculty or student groups, there is an advantage in having primary advocates for renewable energy who understand money and facilities operations.

The construction of the handsome new Gentile Hall physical education and recreational facility in 2005 provided a first opportunity to explore the use of renewable energy at UMPI. The choice was geothermal energy and considerable investment went into exploring its possibilities. In the end, the geothermal resource was not good enough to justify a commitment and the Hall reverted to the use of power from conventional fuels.

Attention then turned to wind power. The highest part of campus sits astride the University athletic fields. Simple observation indicated that considerable wind power crossed campus on most days.

The geothermal adventure prompted a careful study of wind energy prospects. At first, UMPI officials hoped that the site would have the same commercial wind potential as Mars Hill. This raised the prospect of generating much of the campus's need for electricity as well as being able to supply power for sister public higher education institutions – Northern Maine Community College and the University of Maine at Fort Kent. Any additional power could be supplied to the grid and sold to other buyers.

The University commissioned a wind data study from the Renewable Energy Research Laboratory at the University of Massachusetts at Amherst. It also hired the firm of Woodard and Curran to assist with all aspects of project development.

The wind data study results dampened hopes that the quantity of wind power might attract commercial investors. The UMPI site was not Mars Hill. The wind rating of 'fair' and the evidence of 1700 hours of usable wind annually indicated to the consultants that the project 'may be viable as a break-even venture if federal and state grants can be secured and the University System is willing to undertake the project without private investment partners.'

That was sufficient to persuade UMPI to move forward. There were two driving factors. The first was a 40 per cent increase in the campus electricity bill in January 2007. This reflected the deregulation of electric power in Maine described earlier. Aroostook County was particularly burdened because only a single generator of electricity chose to serve the County market. The benefits of competition were hardly likely to work in a market with only one supplier. Second, from the beginning the University had expressed its desire to provide educational leadership benefits from a wind power project, not just cost savings. University leaders made clear their willingness to open the books to any responsible parties seeking information on the project. The University would risk making mistakes so that others could avoid them. The

330

University leadership also wanted to incorporate wind energy into teaching on campus and beyond.

In April 2007 UMPI officials determined to move from study to commitment. At a well-attended press conference they announced that the University was going ahead with the construction of a wind turbine. The announcement emphasized that the University had the funding to support the venture, although it would also seek 'free dollars' from a variety of funding sources in order to reduce its financial burden. The plan was that wind power generation would be up and running by the start of 2009. The press conference and subsequent public discussions emphasized both the cost savings to the University and the educational benefits of the programme. Officials made it clear that there were many further steps to be taken before the turbine would be installed and generating. But, a commitment to wind had been made.

What remained to be done? A next step was to obtain the approval of the governing authority, the Board of Trustees of the University of Maine System. The Board is the governing authority for the entire seven campus System. Preliminary and informal discussions with the System Chancellor and members of the Board were favourable. The new System Chancellor had stressed environmental values in his statement of System objectives. A generally enthusiastic response to the press conference announcement helped build System support. UMPI officials had prepared lengthy presentations and were prepared for probing questions at the September 2007 meeting of the System Board. Instead, Board members took turns to express their excitement over the wind project which was unanimously approved.

Finances are a second concern. UMPI is prepared to fund the entire project by borrowing money on its own credit and from the System if necessary. UMPI credit is solid and the prospects for payback are solid, if not commercially ideal. However, financial difficulties on other System campuses have reduced System flexibility.

More attractive sources are grants from state and federal government funds. UMPI submitted an application for $50,000 to the Maine Public Utilities Commission's renewable energy grants programme. UMPI was awarded the highest amount granted in the state for the project. This provided the opportunity for another press conference which broadened the exposure of the project.

Potentially greater financial support could come from the United States Government. The campuses' federal legislative delegation submitted proposals for congressional earmark funding in the 2006-07 session of Congress. The request was turned down. With the change of political control in the Congress in November 2006, earmarking has become unpredictable. However, UMPI officials believe the campus wind power project presents an attractive and uncontroversial case for federal support. The search goes on.

As this article goes to print, the major concern is the selection of the appropriate wind turbine. Woodard and Curran and the University of Maine System Office have been assisted by an expert on the Mars Hill project. UMPI officials have visited comparable wind power sites in New England and engaged in discussions with their operators about lessons learned. The project has encountered a very volatile market. Many manufacturers are moving to the production of turbines for commercial generation that are larger than can be used at the UMPI site.

A contractual commitment to a specific generating unit will focus attention on the grant of a permit. The Woodard and Curran report to UMPI examined a variety of environmental impacts of a hypothetical wind power project sited on the open area of the campus. A considerable portion of the assessment reviewed possible harm to birds and bats. It concluded that there would be no 'significant risk of mortality to birds and bats.' Likewise, construction impacts would be minimal given the small footprint of the project and its closeness to access roads on the campus. The operation of the project was also predicted to give rise to few ecological impacts.

Northern Maine's cold climate presents another risk. The report explains: 'Ice can form on wind turbines during certain conditions, as has been documented at existing wind facilities. The ice forms a thin "skin," then detaches from the turbine blade and falls to the ground, potentially injuring people below the wind turbine or damaging property.' While not overly concerned about the risk, the consultant recommended raising the issue with the equipment manufacturer.

The report also summarized the permits needed to implement the project. The State of Maine and the United States Government have no general wind permit requirements for small projects. State and federal wetlands regulations require permits from the respective environmental regulators. The project's location in the incorporated City of Presque Isle means that it is not under LURC's jurisdiction. The Presque Isle zoning board will be the primary licensing authority. So far discussions with City officials have been wholly supportive. The tower height might be one issue that would require approval. The tower height would also be likely to involve discussions with federal aviation authorities, given the proximity of the tower to a small commercial airport three miles from the site.

## 5. Conclusions

The various Maine wind projects have each had lives (and deaths) of their own. There is no uniform regulatory scheme governing their development. The various regulators have been initially receptive to wind projects because of their economic and environmental benefits. However, the devil has been in the detail.

Maine is a state of great scenic beauty. To both natives and regular visitors 'from away' Maine preserves the beauty and lifestyle of earlier times. Anything that threatens those values is taken seriously. Even at its best, wind power poses visual and operational challenges. The Maine experiences, successful and unsuccessful, have demonstrated this.

Shrewd wind developers have learned lessons from working with local citizens. They have also benefited from the increasing difficulties of the carbon economy – volatile costs, potential supply shortages, security issues and global warming. Wind power is becoming a significant contributor to American electricity generation. Maine plans to be a modest and innovative part of that development.

# Case Law

**1. New Zealand – by *Barry Barton***
***1.1. Decisions of the NZ Environment Court on Wind Energy Development***
*Genesis Power Ltd* v *Franklin District Council* [2005] NZRMA 541
The case before the Environment Court concerned a wind farm project on the west coast, not far south of Auckland. The project was for 18 turbines probably to be of 1 MW capacity. Franklin District Council had refused the application. The site was on the Awhitu Peninsula which lies between Manukau Harbour and the Tasman Sea, on a plateau above and behind the coastal cliffs. The area was farmed. The wind farm was a discretionary activity under the district plan.

The Court followed the ruling in *NZ Rail Ltd* v *Marlborough District Council* [1994] NZRMA 70 (HC) to the effect that the protection granted by Section 6(b) of the Resource Management Act 1991 is not to be achieved at all costs, but is subordinate to the purpose of the Act of promoting the sustainable management of natural and physical resources.

The Court moved directly to consider the likely effects of the project on the environment, beginning with the positive effects of a wind farm. It listed the benefits of further electricity supply, and wind energy in particular: security of supply, reduction of greenhouse gas emissions, reduction of dependence on the national grid, reduction of transmission losses, reliability, development benefits, and contribution to the national renewable energy target. These, the Court said, were all matters that needed to be put into the crucible containing the evidential material to be weighed against the alleged and more site-specific potential effects.

The negative environmental effects also had to go into the crucible. The first and foremost of these were the effects of the project on the visual amenity of the area, including effects on landscape and on the natural character of the coastal environment. Evidence was heard from landscape experts. The New Zealand Coastal Policy Statement was considered, and so were the relevant provisions of the regional policy statement, regional plan, and district plan. The Court concluded that the scale of the turbines was such that they would have a significant adverse effect on the visual integrity of the surrounding area, and that this effect could not be adequately mitigated.

Noise was another adverse effect. There were a number of farms, houses and workplaces in the vicinity. But the Court concluded that the effects would, at most, be minor. The effect of noise on horses required special consideration because there was an equestrian centre nearby. A great deal of evidence was heard from experts from various countries about the effect of wind turbine noise, movement, and flickering shadows. The Court decided that the witnesses for the equestrian centre were overstating the risks, and noted that the applicant had removed one turbine and relocated two others, significantly reducing their visibility.

Maori affiliations with the site were closely examined. The Court considered Maori evidence and archaeological evidence and concluded that, although the Awhitu Peninsula generally was of great importance to Maori, there was nothing very special about the particular site. It is interesting to note the evidence from Maori on Maori issues produced by the applicant as well as by Maori intervenors, and carefully tested by cross-examination by lawyers on both sides who are themselves Maori. New Zealand environmental law is changing.

The Court brought these factors together by applying Part 2 of the Act. Section 7 deals with matters to which the Court had to have particular regard, or into which it had to enquire. They concern the efficient use and development of natural and physical resources, the efficiency of the end use of energy, the maintenance and enhancement of amenity values, the maintenance and enhancement of the quality of the environment, the effects of climate change, and the benefits to be derived from the use and development of renewable energy. The matters relating to energy were new; they were inserted by an amendment to the Act in 2004. The amendment was 'a clear recognition by Parliament of both the importance of the use and development of renewable energy and the need to address climate change, both of which are key elements in the proposed wind farm.' [220] Counsel for the equestrian centre attempted to minimize the effect of these considerations by arguing that the contribution of the proposed wind farm to the global reduction of greenhouse gas emissions would be a minimal percentage. This argument was rejected; total emissions are made up of numerous small ones, and a small proportion multiplied by a vast total of harmful cases can be very large. There was no place for a *de minimis* argument (*de minimis non curat lex*). The ultimate question was whether the purpose of the Act would be better served by granting the consent or refusing it. The Court decided that the proposal met the sustainable management purpose of the Act. Notwithstanding the effects of the proposal on the coastal environment, consent was appropriate in the circumstances of the case. The benefits of the proposal in the national context outweighed the site-specific effects and the effects on the local surrounding area.

### 1.2. Unison Networks Ltd v Hastings District Council

(Environment Court W58/2006, Judge Thompson, Comsrs Howie & Edmonds, 17 July 2006)

The case before the Environment Court concerned two wind farm projects in hill country farmland in the Hawke's Bay area in the east of North Island. The first project was proposed by Unison Networks Ltd, for 15 turbines of 3 MW each. It is striking that this would require 550,000 $m^3$ of earthworks; like many of the wind farms under development in New Zealand, it was located in hill country at the crest of a range of hills. The second project was by Hawkes Bay Wind Farm Ltd, for 75 turbines of a similar size, and earthworks of 1.3 million $m^3$. Its site adjoined that of Unison. Both applicants were successful before the District Council, but they both appealed to the Environment Court against the conditions imposed and about issues between themselves. Other landowners took part in the appeal, making submissions on the effect of the wind turbines on landscape and visual values. The wind farm sites were on high ground and would be visible from much of the district. The Energy Efficiency and Conservation Authority also made submissions, in order to make sure that the big picture of the desirability of renewable energy was not lost sight of in the debate about local visual effects.

Under the Hastings District Plan, turbines were classified as non-complying activities in the use of land. That made Section 104D of the Resource Management Act 1991 (RMA) relevant; because the effects of the wind farms were plainly more than minor, the applicants had to show that the wind farms were not contrary to the objectives and policies of the Plan. But the Plan was silent on wind farms, because when it was being prepared they were not foreseen in the district. So the Court had to evaluate the objectives and policies concerning the use of rural land for industrial and energy purposes, as well as considering landscape issues. The Court found that neither wind farm proposal would be contrary to the objectives and policies of the Plan. This satisfied one of the two threshold tests in Section 104D of the RMA, so the Court could proceed to deal with the merits of the proposals under Section 104.

The first aspect of the merits was the actual and potential effects of the proposals, above all on landscape and visual amenity. (The site was too distant from other settlements for there to be any concern about noise, shadow flicker, impact on farm stock or traffic safety.) Four landscape architects gave evidence. They all eventually agreed that part of the sites was an outstanding natural landscape under Section 6(b). This meant that its protection from inappropriate development was a matter of national importance. The turbines would be prominent in the landscape, and would change its character. It was agreed that how a viewer relates to the landscape is important, and that there are differences in predisposition to power generation projects. The Court did not agree that the developments' effects would be minor; it found that they would be significant, and that the significant effects would have to be balanced against the other factors to which the Act directed its attention.

These factors were the purpose of the Act in Section 5, and the principles in Sections 6, 7, and 8 which required specific consideration. Aspects of the environment which are of concern to Maori are dealt with under Sections 6(e), 7(a), and 8. Evidence was heard from Mr Frederick Reti, speaking as representative of the *tangata whenua* – the Maori tribes with *mana whenua* (customary authority) over the area. He explained the myths that associate these ranges with the people, and the special significance that they hold that would be affected by the development. While this evidence was heard in the context of how people relate to the landscape in question, it could not be considered further without prejudice to the interests of the other parties, because it had not been raised as a ground of appeal and had been received late.

The Court then turned to Section 7. It is not necessary to review its consideration of all paragraphs. On paragraph (i), 'the effects of climate change' it noted that the parties agreed that the cost of doing nothing about climate change could be severe. On paragraph (j), 'the benefits to be derived from the use and development of renewable energy' the Court considered that there were agreed facts to the effect that the two wind farms would produce about 937 GWh per year with virtually no $CO_2$ emissions. Compared with coal-fired generation, this would save 571,000 tonnes of $CO_2$ per year. No one argued that this was so minute in relation to global totals that it should be ignored; that argument had been roundly rejected by the Court in *Genesis Power Ltd* v *Franklin District Council* [2005] NZRMA 541, paras [222]-[226]. The Court noted that the National Energy Efficiency and Conservation Strategy (under the Energy and Efficiency Conservation Act 2000) identified a policy of moving towards renewable energy, with a target of an additional 30 PJ per year of consumer energy from renewables by 2012.

The only part of Section 6 that required consideration was paragraph (b), 'the protection of outstanding natural features and landscapes from inappropriate subdivision, use, and development'. Being in Section 6, this is identified as a matter of national importance, and the decision-maker 'shall recognise and provide for' it – no small burden. But 'inappropriate' is an important qualifier. The Court followed *Genesis Power Ltd* v *Franklin District Council* and *NZ Rail Ltd* v *Marlborough District Council*, on the subordination of Section 6(b) to the purpose of the Act. The Court decided that the proposed developments were appropriate within the sense of Section 6(b). 'The generation of a substantial output of electricity from a perpetually renewable source which emits no pollution, particularly in the form of greenhouse gases, is of such national importance and benefit that it clearly outweighs such site-specific adverse effects as there will be.' [79]

Finally, as to the purpose of the Act in Section 5, the Court held that an overall balancing of the competing factors led to the conclusion that the purpose of sustainable management would best be promoted by granting these consents. It warned that the decision was site-specific; renewable energy would not always prevail.

Bringing these two projects before the Court raised a question of priority between them; they were close enough to have the potential to interfere with each other. The Court applied the principle that the Act's intention is for priority to be given to applications according to the date of application, under *Fleetwing Farms*, as considered by the High Court in *Geotherm Group Ltd* v *Waikato Regional Council* [2004] NZRMA 1. It also referred to a recent Court of Appeal decision, *Queenstown Lakes District Council* v *Hawthorn Estate Ltd* (CA45/05, 12 June 2006), which held that the 'environment' should be considered as it might be modified by resource consents that have been granted and are likely to be implemented [84]. Here Unison was first, so its application should be considered independently of Hawke's Bay's, and then Hawkes Bay's should be considered in the light of the effects of Unison's application. Unison's application was therefore granted. Its project became part of the environment against which the Hawkes Bay's proposal was to be considered, so that the Hawkes Bay's proposal could be granted but had to be modified so as to avoid wake turbulence effects on Unison's turbines which had priority: para [84].

## 2. Denmark – by *Helle Tegner Anker*
*2.1. Eastern High Court Ruling, B-1853-06, Kyndby Huse wind turbines – planning and EIA decisions*
A Nature Protection Appeal Board decision accepting the planning documents and an EIA permit for two 150 metre high demonstration wind turbines, with a capacity of 3.5 to 4.5 MW each, was challenged before the Eastern High Court by a citizens' action group (Citizens for Offshore Wind Turbines at Sea).

The two wind turbines were planned to be established in connection with an old power station situated on the coast. 24 existing wind turbines would be dismantled before the construction of the two new turbines. The distance from the wind turbines to the nearest dwellings would be 600 metres. The dwellings were located in a residential area with 161 houses built in the 1940s and 1950s for the workers at the power station. The houses had been sold to the previous tenants by the energy company, E2, in 2002.

In November 2004 the regional council adopted an amendment to the regional plan including an environmental impact assessment (EIA). The assessment concluded that the general requirements, e.g. in the wind turbine circular, would be complied with and that there would be no significant effects from noise, shadows or flickering. Nor would there be any significant adverse effects on a nearby EU habitat area (SAC). In April 2005 the regional council issued an EIA permit in accordance with the Planning Act.

The decisions of the regional council were appealed to the Nature Protection Appeal Board. The Nature Protection Appeal Board examined the legal merits with respect to the amendment of the regional plan and the EIA. The Appeal Board (8 of 9 members) found that a sufficient assessment had been carried out and that sufficient functional arguments, in particular the wind situation, justified placing the wind turbines within the coastal planning zone. Regarding the EIA permit, the Planning Act does not restrict appeals to legal merits. However, after an overall balancing of the interests involved, the Nature Protection Appeal Board (8 of 9 members) did not find that there were reasons for overturning the decision made by the regional council.

The Nature Protection Appeal Board's decision was then challenged before the Eastern High Court by the citizens' action group acting on behalf of individual members. The Eastern High Court gave a fairly short ruling without going into a detailed examination of the many arguments raised by the citizens' group. According to the Court it had not been shown that the decision of the Nature Protection Appeal Board suffered from any legal defects that could result in a finding that the decision was invalid. The decision of the Nature Protection Appeal Board was thus upheld.

*2.2. Eastern High Court Ruling B-1854-06, Kyndby Huse wind turbines –
prohibition and compensation claim*
In this case the citizens' action group claimed, on behalf of the individual members, that the energy company, E2, responsible for the planned construction of the two 150 metre demonstration turbines should not be allowed to construct the wind turbines or in the alternative should pay compensation to the landowners affected, primarily on the basis of neighbour law. The Eastern High Court decided, again in a very short ruling, that it had not been shown that it would be possible to prohibit the construction of the wind turbines on

the basis of neighbour law, private law or public law. The Court emphasized that an assumption had been made that the wind turbines would comply with the general requirements, including noise and distance requirements, and with the nature values in the area. The claim for compensation was not examined by the Court in this ruling. It appears from the wording of the Court's ruling that the Court would be unlikely to accept a claim for compensation based on the anticipated nuisance of a planned development.

# Country Facts

## Denmark

The Kingdom of Denmark comprises of the territories of Denmark, the Faroe Islands and Greenland.[1] The country consists of a main peninsula, Jutland, which borders northern Germany, and about 400 islands, of which only about 100 are inhabited. The major islands are Zealand and Fünen. The national capital, Copenhagen, is on Zealand.

The population of Denmark is 5.5 million. The population density is 122.4 per sq km. About 85 % of the Danes live in towns and about one third of the Danish population lives in the Copenhagen area.

Denmark covers an area of 43,093 sq km (16,632 sq miles). The Danish marine waters cover an area 2.5 times that of the land mass. Of the marine waters about half constitutes the Danish part of the North Sea, the Kattegat and the belt seas account for 15 %, and the Danish parts of the Skagerrak and of the Baltic Sea each account for 10 %. The coastline is 7,314 km long and thus forms an important element of the landscape. The country is largely flat with gently rolling hills. The highest point in Jutland is 173 metres high (567 feet). It is a distinctly agricultural country where 67 % of the land area is cultivated. Around 10 % of the area of Denmark is built-up (towns, roads and other infrastructure), and only 23 % remains forest and natural countryside. This makes Denmark one of the countries with the most intensive land use in the world.

Within the last 15 years Denmark has invested more in wind energy than any other European country and has become European leader in the area of renewable energy. In 2005 energy from renewable sources, including waste, constituted 28.5 % of national electricity consumption. Wind energy accounted for most of this with 18.5 %. Renewable sources contributed 15.5 %

1. See the website Denmark.dk; *European Environment Agency*, The European environment – State and outlook 2005, State of Environment report No 1/2005; *Ditlev Tamm, Torben Melchior & Børge Dahl (eds.)*: Danish Law in a European perspective, 2nd ed., 2002; *J. Holten-Andersen et al.*: The State of the Environment in Denmark, 1997; and *Ellen Margrethe Basse:* Environmental in Law Denmark, 2nd, 2004.

of total energy consumption, including 3 % from wind energy. The major energy sources in Denmark are coal, natural gas and oil.

Denmark is a constitutional monarchy and joined the European Economic Community (now the European Union) in 1973. Greenland and the Faroe Islands were granted home rule in 1979 and 1948 respectively. Neither of the two territories is part of the EU.

## Norway

Norway covers the western part of the Scandinavian peninsula and borders Sweden, Denmark and Russia. Its mainland area is 324,000 sq km. In addition, Svalbard (often called Spitzbergen) in the Barents Sea (61,000 sq km), and the Jan Mayen Island in the North Atlantic belong to Norway.[2] Norway is surrounded by sea in the south (Skagerrak), in the west (the North Sea and the Norwegian Sea) and in the north (the Barents Sea). Its coastline is marked by numerous islands and fjords. The mainland coastline alone is 25,000 km long, and the distance between the northernmost and southernmost points on the mainland is 1,750 km.

The population of Norway is 4.6 million, with a population density of 14 per sq km (Svalbard not included). About 80 % of Norwegians live in towns. The capital, Oslo, has a population of 500,000.

More than 60 % of Norway's mainland (and the whole Svalbard) is covered by mountains and glaciers, 24 % by forest, and 10 % by lakes, rivers and wetlands. Only 3 % of the land is arable land, while 1.2 % is built-up.

Norway has an extensive continental shelf, rich in hydrocarbon resources, and has established a 200 mile Exclusive Economic Zone (EEZ). Its marine waters, including the EEZ, cover nearly 1 million sq km.[3] The main economic and export activities are oil production, fisheries including fish farming, forestry, and heavy industry based on hydroelectric power. Norway is rich in energy resources. Since the start of oil exploration activities in the late 1960s, by 2005 the country had become the world's fifth largest net exporter of oil and the world's third largest exporter of natural gas. It also has a very important hydropower sector. Nearly 100 % of the country's electricity is produced by hydropower. Having been self-sufficient in power for a long time, the country is becoming increasingly dependent on imported electricity, in particular in years with less than average rainfall. Largely due to its rich

2.  Svalbard has a special status in international law under the 1920 Svalbard Treaty.
3.  This does not include the Fisheries protection zone of 800,000 sq km around Svalbard which is disputed internationally, and the 300,000 sq km fishery zone around Jan Mayen.

resources of hydropower, Norway has been late in developing the use of wind power, biofuels and other renewable alternatives. Due to the increasing dependency of imports, and the need to limit $CO_2$ emissions, Norway has now adopted active renewable energy and energy efficiency policies, and has started to establish wind farms along the western and northern coasts.

Norway is a constitutional monarchy. It is not a member of EU but has close ties with the EU through the 1992 European Economic Area (EEA) Agreement. This makes Norway a party to the EU internal market, and all the EU legislation related to the four EC Treaty freedoms apply fully to Norway. This includes most regulations and directives in the fields of energy and the environment. Fishery and agriculture, however, remain outside the scope of the EEA Agreement.

## The United States

The United States of America is a federal republic comprising 50 states and the District of Columbia (the seat of federal government). The original 13 states gained their independence from Great Britain by the Treaty of Paris in 1783; the current Constitution came into effect in 1789. The remainder of the United States territory was acquired through claims inherited from Great Britain, by purchase (the Louisiana Purchase from France and the purchase of Alaska from Russia), by absorbing an independent state (Texas, which had made itself independent of Mexico in 1836), or by treaty (notably the Treaty of Guadalupe Hidalgo in 1848, in which Mexico ceded most of the Southwestern USA and California). Various island territories are also affiliated to the USA, including Puerto Rico, the US Virgin Islands, Guam, the North Marianas and American Samoa. Numerous tribes of American Indians occupy sovereign self-governing reservations, mostly in the Western states.

The land area of the USA is 3,537,438 sq miles (9,161,964 sq km), with marine areas in the Atlantic, the Pacific and the Gulf of Mexico encompassing a further 256,645 sq miles (664,711 sq km). Excluding Alaska and Hawaii, the 48 continental United States cover about 2,960,000 sq miles. The USA has over 12,000 miles of coastline, about half of which is in Alaska. This does not include the shores of the Great Lakes.

Geographically, the continental USA is remarkably diverse. It has the only fjord in North America (the Hudson River, from New York City northward), broad coastal plains on the southern Atlantic and Gulf of Mexico coasts; three major mountain chains (the Appalachian Mountains in the east, the Rocky Mountains from Montana to New Mexico, and the Cascades (volcanic) and Sierra Nevada in the west); subtropical (Florida and southern Texas) and rainforest (Pacific Northwest) regions; rich flat rain-fed farmlands extending from the Great Lakes through the Midwest growing maize, wheat and soya beans, which give way to the semi-arid Great Plains that extend from Canada to Mexico, the primary region for beef cattle; extensive deserts in the Great Basin between the Rockies and the Sierra Nevada; and the Mediterranean climate of California, which is the major growing area for fruits, nuts and vegetables. The lowest point, in Death Valley, California, is 86 m below sea level; not far away, the highest point in the 48 states is Mt. Whitney (4,418 m). Mt. McKinley in Alaska rises to 6,194 m.

The USA is rich in natural resources of all kinds, including minerals, forests and fisheries. It is also rich in all types of energy resources. It has extensive coal reserves in the Appalachian and Rocky Mountain regions, numerous fields of oil and natural gas, including offshore regions in the Gulf of Mexico and the Pacific; hydropower, especially in the west; and enormous potential for renewable energy, including biofuels, wind power and solar power. Wind power production has grown rapidly in recent years; at the end of 2006, the USA had 11,603 MW of installed capacity that was generating an estimated 31 billion kWh of electricity. This is still less than 1% of US electricity usage.

The US population is just over 300 million. This gives an average population density of 100 people per sq mile, or about 38.5 per sq km. But this average masks great differences; New York City has a population density of about 10,000 people per sq km, while densities in large areas of Western states are less than 2 people per sq km (and in Alaska just 1 person per sq mile). Nearly 80 % of the population lives in urban areas; nearly one-half of that 'urban' population lives in suburban communities.

In 1994, the United States joined with Canada and Mexico in the North American Free Trade Agreement (NAFTA), which abolished most tariffs on trade between the three countries. There is, however, no free movement of workers under NAFTA. The NAFTA countries have also created a North American Commission for Environmental Cooperation.

### New Zealand

New Zealand comprises two main islands, North Island and South Island, and a number of other smaller islands in the South West Pacific Ocean.[4] The main land mass extends between the latitudes of approximately 34.00°S and 47.00°S. The indigenous Maori, who arrived in New Zealand around 1,000

4. The information in this country description was gathered primarily from: Statistics New Zealand, www.stats.govt.nz/Wikipedia;
www.en.wikipedia.org/wiki/New_Zealand; and the CIA World Factbook:
www.cia.gov/library/publications/the-world-factbook/geos/nz.html.

years ago, called the country Aotearoa, meaning the Land of the Long White Cloud. New Zealand also includes the self-governing dependencies of the Cook Islands, Niue, Tokelau and the Ross Dependency in Antarctica.

The national capital, Wellington, is situated at the southernmost extremity of North Island. New Zealand is a unicameral parliamentary democracy based on the Westminster system of government. The Parliament of New Zealand is democratically elected, and holds political power under the leadership of the Prime Minister, who is the Head of Executive Government.

The population of New Zealand is approximately 4.2 million, being predominantly of European descent (70 %), with around 15 % identifying themselves as Maori, 9 % as Asian and 7 % as Pacific Islander, although around 10 % of the people identify themselves with more than one ethnic group.

New Zealand is geographically isolated, being completely surrounded by ocean, and situated 2000 km to the east of Australia. It covers an area of 268,680 sq km (103,738 sq miles), with approximately 15,134 km of coastline and a 200 nautical mile Exclusive Economic Zone (EEZ) covering an area of over 4 million sq km (1.5 million sq miles), making it the seventh largest EEZ in the world.

The country has varied terrain ranging from coastal lowland areas, rainforests, and mountain ranges with glaciers and fiords. There are eighteen mountain peaks over 3000 metres (9800 ft) on South Island, the highest being Aoraki/Mount Cook at 3,754 metres (12,316 ft). The climate ranges from sub-tropical in the north to temperate in the south. Although temperatures are relatively mild, seldom averaging below 0°C (32°F) or rising above 30°C (86°F), some high country areas in the south can experience very cold winter temperatures. Much of the original forest cover was cleared first by the Polynesian and then by European settlers, with around only 23 % of the land remaining covered by indigenous forest. Now the land primarily sustains agriculture and forestry, which make up most of New Zealand's exports.

New Zealand has a high level of self-sufficiency in the production of primary energy, with hydropower producing 64 % of its electricity, gas and coal 25 %, geothermal energy 6.5 % and wind energy 2 %. In just the last two years however, there has been a logarithmic increase in wind energy developments and applications for consents for wind farms. According to the New Zealand Wind Energy Association, installed capacity has now reached 321 MW, almost double the capacity of 2006, which in turn was a dramatic increase over 2005. A further 46.5 MW is approved and under construction, and consents are being sought for a further 1,700 MW.[5] On the other hand, New Zealand is still highly dependent on imported hydrocarbons for industrial energy, with imported oil accounting for 15-20 % of industrial/commercial energy, and 85 % of transport energy.

5.  See: http://www.windenergy.org.nz/

# Bibliography

*Alter, Karen J.:* Establishing the Supremacy of European Law – The Making of an International Rule of Law in Europe, Oxford University Press, 2003.

*Anker, Helle T.:* Planlovgivning, in *Basse, Ellen Margrethe* (ed.): Miljøretten, Vol.2, DJØF, 2006 pp. 175-335.

*Anker, Helle Tegner & Basse, Ellen Margrethe:* Rationality, Environmental Law, and Biodiversity, in *Beckmann, Suzanne C. & Madsen, Erik Kloppenborg* (eds.): Environmental Regulation and Rationality, Aarhus University Press, 2001 pp. 163-192.

*Archer, Jack:* Evolution of Major 1990 CZMA Amendments: Restoring Federal Consistency and Protection of Coastal Water Quality, in Territorial Sea Journal, Vol.1, 1991 pp. 191-222.

*Barton, Barry:* Renewable Energy in New Zealand, in Journal of Energy and Natural Resources Law, Vol.23, 2005 pp. 141-155.

*Barton, Barry; Barrera-Hernández, Lila K.; Lucas, Alastair R. & Rønne, Anita* (eds.): Regulating Energy and Natural Resources, Oxford University Press, 2006.

*Barton, Barry; Redgwell, Catherine; Rønne, Anita & Zillman, Don* (eds.): Energy Security: Managing Risk in a Dynamic Legal and Regulatory Environment, Oxford University Press, 2004.

*Basse, Ellen Margrethe:* Environmental Law – Denmark, 2nd ed., DJØF/Kluwer, 2004.

*Basse, Ellen Margrethe:* Environmental law. Denmark, 2nd ed., Kluwer Law International, 2004.

*Basse, Ellen Margrethe:* Regulatory Chain – Results of an International Development, in *Basse, E.M.* (ed.): Environmental Law: From International to National Law, GadJura, 1997 pp. 9-52.

*Basse, Ellen Margrethe:* Sagsbehandling og beslutningsprocesser, in *Basse, Ellen Margrethe:* Miljøretten, Vol.1, DJØF, 2006.

*Basse, Ellen Margrethe:* The Ombudsman as Protector of Environmental Rights, in *Ármann, Snævarr; Erlendsdottir, Gudrun; Þórmundsson, Jónatan; Sigurdsson, Páll & Örlygsson, Þorgeir* (eds.): Afmælisrit Til Heiduira Gunnari G. Schram, Almenna bókafélagið, 2002 pp. 57-76.

*Bellingham, Mark:* Sustainability and biodiversity in law, in *Harris, Rob* (ed.): Handbook of Environmental Law, Royal Forest and Bird Protection Society of New Zealand, 2004 Ch. 15.

*Bellingham, Mark:* The law relating to forestry, in *Harris, Rob* (ed.): Handbook of Environmental Law, Royal Forest and Bird Protection Society of New Zealand, 2004 Ch. 9.

*Bermann, George A.:* Subsidiarity and the European Community, in Hastings International and Comparative Law Review, Vol.17, 1993 pp. 89-99.

*Berry, Simon & Hamling, Hannah:* Hazardous Substances, in *Nolan, Derek* (ed.): Environmental and Resource Management Law, Lexis Nexis, 2005 Ch. 11.

*Birne, Gregory H.:* Tower or Antenna as Constituting Nuisance, American Law Reports 5th, Vol.88, 2006 p. 641.

*Birnie, Patricia & Boyle, Alan:* International Law and the Environment, Oxford University Press, 2nd ed., 2002.

*Blackstone, William:* Commentaries on the Laws of England, Book I, 1765. Available at: http://www.lonang.com/exlibris/blackstone/.

*Bosselman, Fred:* Limitations Inherent in the Title to Wetlands at Common Law, in Stanford Environmental Law Journal, Vol.15, 1996 pp. 247-337.

*Bradbrook, Adrian J.:* The Development of Renewable Energy Technologies and Energy Efficiency Measures Through Public International Law, in *Zillman, Don; Redgwell, Catherine; Omorogbe, Yinka & Barrera-Hernández, Lila K.* (eds.): Beyond the Carbon Economy – Energy Law in Transition, Oxford University Press, 2008 Ch. 6.

*Brisman, Avi:* The Aesthetics of Wind Energy Systems, in New York University Environmental Law Journal, Vol.13, 2005 pp. 1-133.

*Brownlie, Ian:* Principles of International Law, 5th ed., Oxford University Press, 1998 pp. 31-33.

*Bruckerhoff, Joshua:* Giving Nature Constitutional Protection: A Less Anthropocentric Interpretation of Environmental Rights, in Texas Law Review, Vol.86, 2008 pp. 615-646.

*Bugge, Hans Christian:* General Principles of International Law and Environmental Protection- An Overview, in *Basse, Ellen Margrethe* (ed.): Environmental Law: From International to National Law, GadJura, 1997 pp. 53-72.

*Bugge, Hans Christian:* Legal issues in Land Use and Nature Protection, in *Anker, Helle Tegner & Basse, Ellen Margrethe* (eds.): Land Use and Nature Protection. Emerging Legal Aspects, DJØF, 2000.

*Campbell, Janette:* Statutory remedies: the enforcement provisions of the RMA, in *Nolan, Derek* (ed.): Environmental and Resource Management Law, 3rd ed., Lexis Nexis, 2005 Ch. 18.

*Carlman, I.:* The Resource Management Act – RMA – Through External Eyes, unpublished paper, Mid Sweden University, Östersund, 2006.

*Christensen, Mark:* New Organisms, in *Nolan, Derek* (ed.): Environmental and Resource Management Law, Lexis Nexis, 2005 Ch. 12.

*Craig, Paul & de Búrca, Gráinne:* EU Law, 4th ed., Oxford University Press, 2008.

*Craig, Paul:* The Jurisdiction of the Community Courts Reconsidered, in *de Búrca, Gráinne & Weiler, J.H.H.* (eds.): The European Court of Justice, Oxford University Press, 2001 pp. 177-214.

*Crawford, Jen & Mora, Natasha:* Law relating to hazardous substances and new organisms, in *Harris, Rob* (ed.): Handbook of Environmental Law, Royal Forest and Bird Protection Society of New Zealand, 2004 Ch. 13.

*Dawson, Alexandra D.:* Wetlands Regulation, Part I, in Zoning And Planning Law Report, Vol.6(9), 1983 p. 153.

*Dawson, Alexandra D.:* Wetlands Regulation, Part II, in Zoning And Planning Law Report, Vol.6(10), 1983 p. 161.

*de Sadeleer, Nicolas:* Environmental Principles, Oxford University Press, 2005.

*de Sadeleer, Nicolas:* Habitats Conservation in EC Law – From Nature Sanctuaries to Ecological Networks, in Yearbook of Environmental Law, Vol.5, 2005 pp. 215-252.

*Deans, Neil:* Freshwater issues and mechanisms for protecting water related values, in *Harris, Rob* (ed.): Handbook of Environmental Law, Royal Forest and Bird Protection Society of New Zealand, 2004 Ch. 7.

*Denza, Eileen:* The Relationship between International and National Law, in *Evans, Malcolm D.:* International Law, 2nd ed., Oxford University Press, 2006 pp. 423-450.

*Due, Ole:* Danish Law in a European Context, in *Børge Dahl, Torben Melchior & Ditlev Tamm* (eds.): Danish Law in a European Perspective, 2002 pp. 18-19.

*Duff, John A.:* The Coastal Zone Management Act: Reverse Pre-emption or Contractual Federalism?, in Ocean and Coastal Law Journal, Vol.6(1), 2001 pp. 109-118.

*Ebbesson, Jonas* (ed.): Access to Justice in Environmental Matters in the EU, Kluwer Law International, 2002.

*Edwards, Vanessa:* European Court of Justice – Significant environmental cases 2004, in Journal of Environmental Law, Vol.17(1), 2005 pp. 129-136.

*Elder, P.S.:* Environmental and Sustainability Assessment, in Journal of Environmental Law & Policy, Vol.2, 1992 p. 125.

*Findlay, Claire:* Protecting landscape values, in *Harris, Rob* (ed.): Handbook of Environmental Law, Royal Forest and Bird Protection Society of New Zealand, 2004 Ch. 20.

*Flannery, Timothy:* The Weather Makers: The History and Future Impact of Climate Change, Allen Lane, 2005.

*Garthwaite, Rachel & Crawford, Jen:* Law relating to Biosecurity, in *Harris, Rob* (ed.): Handbook of Environmental Law, Royal Forest and Bird Protection Society of New Zealand, 2004 Ch. 14.

*Gibson, John:* Integrated Coastal Zone Management Law in the European Union, in Coastal Management, Vol.31(2), 2003 pp. 127-136.

*Glendon, Mary Ann*; *Gordon, Michael & Carozza, Paolo G.:* Comparative Legal Traditions, 2$^{nd}$ ed., West Group, 1999.

*Goodman, Emily Hartshorne:* Defining Wetlands for Regulatory Purposes: A Case Study in the Role of Science in Policymaking, in Buffalo Environmental Law Journal, Vol.2, 1994 pp. 135-159.

*Grinlinton, David:* Access to Environmental Justice in New Zealand, in Acta Juridica, 1999 pp. 80-96.

*Grinlinton, David:* Contemporary Environmental Law in New Zealand, in *Bosselmann, Klaus & Grinlinton, David* (eds.): Environmental Law for a Sustainable Society, New Zealand Centre for Environmental Law, 2002 pp. 19-46.

*Grinlinton, David:* Integrated Environmental Assessment in New Zealand, in Environmental and Planning Law Journal, Vol.17(3), 2000 pp. 176-198.

*Grinlinton, David:* Natural Resources Law Reform in New Zealand – Integrating Law, Policy and Sustainability, in Australasian Journal of Natural Resources Law and Policy, Vol.2, 1995 pp. 1-37.

*Gross, Alois Valerian:* Windmill as Nuisance, in American Law Reports 4th, Vol.36, 1985 p. 1159.

*Grossman, Margaret Rosso:* Genetically Modified Crops in the United States: Federal Regulation and State Tort Liability, in Environmental Law Review, Vol.5, 2003 pp. 86-108.

*Haar, Charles M.:* The Master Plan: An Impermanent Constitution, in Law and Contemporary Problems, Vol.20(3), 1955 pp. 353-418.

*Halper, Louise A.:* Untangling the Nuisance Knot, in Boston College Environmental Affairs Law Review, Vol.26, 1998 pp. 89-130.

*Hammer, Ulf:* From self-regulation to public regulation, in *Barton, Barry;*
*Barrera-Hernández, Lila K.; Lucas, Alastair R. & Rønne, Anita* (eds.):
Regulating Energy and Natural Resources, Oxford University Press, 2006
pp. 171-183.

*Hammer, Ulf:* Norway: Security of Supply in Liberalized Energy Sectors: A
New Role for Regulation, in *Barton, Barry; Redgwell, Catherine; Rønne,*
*Anita & Zillman, Don* (eds.): Energy Security: Managing Risk in a Dy-
namic Legal and Regulatory Environment, Oxford University Press, 2004
Ch. 12.

*Hammer, Ulf:* Tilrettelegging av kraftmarkedet: en studie i reguleringen av
nettets koordinerende funksjoner, Cappelen Akademisk Forlag, 1999.

*Hanebury, J.B.:* Environmental Assessment as Applied to Policies, Plans and
Programs, in *Kennett, S.A.* (ed.): Law and Process in Environmental Management, Canadian Institute of Resources Law, 1993 pp. 103-126.

*Harris, Rob:* Protected public lands, in *Harris, Rob* (ed.): Handbook of Environmental Law, Royal Forest and Bird Protection Society of New Zealand, 2004 Ch. 18.

*Harris, Rob:* The coastal and marine environment, in *Harris, Rob* (ed.):
Handbook of Environmental Law, Royal Forest and Bird Protection Society of New Zealand, 2004 Ch. 8.

*Haynes II, William J. & Gardner, Royal C.:* The Value of Wetlands as Wetlands: The Case for Mitigation Banking, in Environmental Law Reporter,
Vol. 23(5), 1993 p. 10261.

*Hayward, Tim:* Constitutional Environmental Rights, Oxford University
Press, 2005.

*Heather, Claire & Baumann, Geraldine:* Historic heritage, in *Harris, Rob*
(ed.): Handbook of Environmental Law, Royal Forest and Bird Protection
Society of New Zealand, 2004 Ch. 21.

*Herlin-Karnell, Ester:* Commission v Council: Some Reflections on Criminal
Law in the First Pillar, in European Public Law, Vol.13(1), 2007 pp. 69-
85.

*Holmes Jr., Oliver Wendell:* The Common Law, Dover Publications, reprinted 1991.

*Jensen, Friis Orla:* Ejendomsret og miljøret, in *Basse, Ellen Margrethe* (ed.):
Miljøretten, Vol.1, DJØF, 2006 pp. 49-112.

*Jensen, Orla Friis:* The Role of Property Rights: Danish Perspective, in *An-*
*ker, Helle Tegner & Basse, Ellen Margrethe* (eds.): Land Use and Nature
Protection. Emerging Legal Aspects, DJØF, 2000.

*Jessen, Pernille Wegener:* Subsidies, in *Sørensen, Karsten Engsig; Egelund Olsen, Birgitte & Steinicke, Michael:* WTO law from a European perspective, Thomson, 2006 pp. 419-443.

*Jones, Elise:* The Coastal Barrier Resources Act: A Common Cents Approach to Coastal Protection, in Environmental Law, Vol.21(3), 1991 pp. 1015-1080.

*Juergensmeyer, Julian C. & Roberts, Thomas E.:* Land Use Planning and Development Regulation Law, West Publishing Company, 2003.

*Karia, Anil S.:* A Right to a Clean and Healthy Environment: A Proposed Amendment to Oregon's Constitution, in University of Baltimore Journal of Environmental Law, Vol.14, 2006 pp. 37-79.

*Keiter, Robert B.:* Taking Account of the Ecosystem on the Public Domain: Law and Ecology in the Greater Yellowstone Region, in University of Colorado Law Review, Vol.60, 1989 pp. 923-1007.

*Kirman, Claire & Whata, Christian:* Environmental Litigation and Dispute Resolution, in *Nolan, Derek* (ed.): Environmental and Resource Management Law, Lexis Nexis, 2005 Ch. 17.

*Knaap, Gerrit & Nelson, Arthur C.:* The Regulated Landscape: Lessons on State Land Use Planning from Oregon, Lincoln Institute of Land Policy, 1992.

*Koen, Lenaerts:* The Principle of Subsidiarity and the Environment in the European Union: Keeping the Balance of Federalism, in Fordham International Law Journal, Vol.17(4), 1994 pp. 846-895.

*Krämer, Ludwig:* EC Environmental Law, Thomson/Sweet & Maxwell, 2003.

*Lambers, Kees; Boerema, Luuk; Holsink, Marja; Nienhuys, Klarissa; Veltman, Jan & Zwiep, Karel van der* (eds.): Trilateral or European Protection of the Wadden Sea?, Sdu Uitgivers, 2003.

*Larsen, Hans & Petersen, Leif Sønderberg* (eds.): The Future Energy System – Distributed Production and Use, Risø Energy Report 4, 2005.

*Lile, William M., et al.:* Brief Making and the Use of Law Books, 3rd ed., 1914.

*Lowe, V.:* Jurisdiction, in *Evans, Malcolm D.* (ed.): International Law, 2nd ed., Oxford University Press, 2006 pp. 335-360.

*Lowell, Randy:* Private Actions and Marine and Water Resources: Protection, Recovery and Remediation, in South Carolina Environmental Law Journal, Vol.8(2), 2000 pp. 143-206.

*Lyster, Rosemary & Bradbrook, Adrian:* Energy Law and the Environment, Cambridge University Press, 2006.

*Malone, Linda A.:* Environmental Regulation of Land Use, Thomson, 2006.

*Malone, Linda A.:* The Coastal Zone Management Act and the Takings Clause in the 1990's: Making the Case for Federal Land Use to Preserve Coastal Areas, in University of Colorado Law Review, Vol.60, 1991 pp. 711-773.

*Mann, Howard:* Comment on the Paper by Philippe Sands, in *Lang, Winfried* (ed.): Sustainable Development and International Law, Graham & Trotman Ltd., 1995 pp. 67-74.

*McHarg, Aileen & Rønne, Anita:* Reducing Carbon-based Electricity Generation: Is the Answer Blowing in the Wind?, in *Zillman, Don; Redgwell, Catherine; Omorogbe, Yinka & Barrera-Hernández, Lila K.* (eds.): Beyond the Carbon Economy – Energy Law in Transition, Oxford University Press, 2008 pp. 287-317.

*McPherson, Michael:* Vanishing Sands: Comprehensive Planning and The Public Interest In Hawaii, in Ecology Law Quarterly, Vol.18(4), 1991 pp. 779-844.

*Merryman, John Henry; Clark, David S. & Haley, John O.* (eds.): The Civil Law Tradition: Europe, Latin America, and East Asia, Matthew Bender, 1994.

*Nicholas, J.; Juergensmeyer, J. & Basse, E.:* Perspectives Concerning the Use of Environmental Mitigation Fees as Incentives In Environmental Protection, Part I, in Environmental Liability, Vol.7(2), 1999 pp. 27-43.

*Nicholas, J.; Juergensmeyer, J. & Basse, E.:* Perspectives Concerning the Use of Environmental Mitigation Fees as Incentives In Environmental Protection, Part II, in Environmental Liability, Vol.7(3), 1999 pp. 71-79.

*Nolan, Derek & Kirman, Claire:* The Coastal Environment, in *Nolan, Derek* (ed.): Environmental and Resource Management Law, Lexis Nexis, 2005 Ch. 5.

*Olsen, Birgitte Egelund & Steinicke, Michael:* The WTO and the EU, in *Olsen, B. Egelund; Steinicke, M. & Sørensen, K. Engsig* (eds.): WTO law from a European perspective, Thomson, 2006 pp. 91-129.

*Olsen, Birgitte Egelund:* The principle of subsidiarity and its impact on regulation, in *Olsen, Birgitte Egelund & Sørensen, Karsten Engsig* (eds.): Regulation in the EU, Thomson, 2006 pp. 35-81.

*Olsen, Birgitte Egelund:* Trade and the environment, in *Egelund Olsen, Birgitte, Steinicke, Michael & Sørensen, Karsten Engsig:* WTO law from a European perspective, Thomson, 2006 pp. 233-278.

*Oppenheim, L.; Jennings, R. & Watts, A.* (eds.): Oppenheim's International Law, 9th ed., Longman, 1992.

*Orfield, Lester Bernhard:* The Growth of Scandinavian Law, University of Pennsylvania Press, 1953.

*Ortiz, Francesca:* Candidate Conservation Agreements as a Devolutionary Response to Extinction, in Georgia Law Review, Vol.33, 1999 pp. 413-512.

*Ottinger, Richard; Mathews, Lily & Czachor, Nadia Elizabeth:* Renewable energy in national legislation: challenges and opportunities, in *Zillman, Don; Redgwell, Catherine; Omorogbe, Yinka & Barrera-Hernández, Lila K.* (eds.): Beyond the Carbon Economy – Energy Law in Transition, Oxford University Press, 2008 Ch. 9.

*Palmer, Kenneth:* Compulsory Acquisition and Compensation, in *Bennion, Tom; Brown, David; Thomas, Rod & Toomey, Elizabeth* (eds.): Land Law in New Zealand, Thomson/Brookers, 2005 pp. 1139-1192.

*Palmer, Kenneth:* Heritage, in *Nolan, Derek* (ed.): Environmental and Resource Management Law, Lexis Nexis, 2005 Ch. 15.

*Palmer, Kenneth:* Local Government Law in New Zealand, Butterworths, 1993.

*Palmer, Kenneth:* Resource Management Act 1991, in *Nolan, Derek* (ed.): Environmental and Resource Management Law, Lexis Nexis, 2005 Ch. 3.

*Pereira, Ricardo:* Environmental criminal law in the first pillar: a positive development for environmental protection in the European Union?, in European Environmental Law Review, Vol.13(10), 2007 pp. 254-269.

*Pettersson, Maria:* Legal Preconditions for Wind Power Implementation in Sweden and Denmark, Luleå University of Technology, 2006.

*Plater, Zygmunt J.B.* (ed.); *Abrams, Robert; Goldfarb, William; Graham, Robert; Heinzerling, Lisa & Wirth, David:* Environmental Law and Policy: Nature, Law, and Society, 3rd ed., Aspen Publishers, 2004.

*Rasmussen, Hjalte:* Remedying the Crumbling EC Judicial System, in Common Market Law Review, Vol.37(5), 2000 pp. 1071-1112.

*Redgwell, Catherine:* International Regulation of Energy Activities, in *Roggenkamp, Martha M.; Redgwell, Catherine, del Guayo, Iñigo & Rønne, Anita* (eds.): Energy Law in Europe: National, EU and International Regulation, 2nd ed., Oxford University Press, 2007 Ch. 2.

*Redgwell, Catherine:* International Responses to the Challenges of a Lower Carbon Future: Climate Change, Carbon Capture and Storage, and Biofuels, in *Zillman, Don; Redgwell, Catherine; Omorogbe, Yinka & Barrera-Hernández, Lila K.* (eds.): Beyond the Carbon Economy – Energy Law in Transition, Oxford University Press, 2008 Ch. 5.

*Rive, Vernon:* Environmental Assessment, in *Nolan, Derek* (ed.): Environmental and Resource Management Law, Lexis Nexis, 2005 Ch. 16.

*Rive, Veron:* Forests, trees and native plants, in *Nolan, Derek* (ed.): Environmental and Resource Management Law, Lexis Nexis, 2005 Ch. 6.

*Roberts, Paul:* The End of Oil: The Decline of the Petroleum Economy and the Rise of a New Energy Order, Houghton Mifflin, 2004.

*Rodgers, William:* Hornbook on Environmental Law, 2nd ed., West Publishing Company, 1994.

*Rogers, Anthony L.; Manwell, James F. & Wright, Sally:* Wind Turbine Acoustic Noise, 2002 (amended 2006). Available at: http://www.wind-watch.org/documents/wp-content/uploads/rogers-windturbinenoise_rev2006.pdf.

*Roggenkamp, Martha M.; Redgwell, Catherine, del Guayo, Iñigo & Rønne, Anita* (eds.): Energy Law in Europe: National, EU and International Regulation, 2nd ed., Oxford University Press, 2007.

*Rønne, Anita:* Renewable Energy on the Market – a Danish Perspective, in Journal of Energy & Natural Resources Law, Vol.23(2), 2005 pp. 156-172.

*Rønne, Anita:* The Danish Way of Combating Greenhouse Gas Emissions, in *Cameron, Peter D. & Zillman, Don* (eds.): Kyoto: From Principles to Practice, Kluwer Law International, 2002 pp. 125-159.

*Ruhl, J.B. & Salzman, James:* The Effects of Wetland Mitigation Banking on People, in National Wetlands Newsletter, Vol. 28(2), 2006 pp. 9-14.

*Ruhl, J.B.:* How to Kill Endangered Species, Legally: The Nuts and Bolts of Endangered Species Act HCP Permits for Real Estate Development, in Environmental Lawyer, Vol.5(2), 1999 pp. 345-405.

*Sagemüller, Imke:* Legislative and Policy Regime Governing the Generation of Wind Energy in New Zealand, in Journal of Energy and Natural Resources Law, Vol.24, 2006 pp. 165-208.

*Salmon, Guy; Sundström, Matilda & Zilliacus, Kim:* Environmental Management and Natural Resource Allocation Frameworks of New Zealand, Sweden and Finland: A Comparative Description, Ecologic Foundation Research Report No. 1, 2005. Available at: www.ecologic.org.nz.

*San José, Daniel Garcia:* Environmental Protection and the European Convention on Human Rights, Council of Europe, 2005.

*Schütz, Sigrid Eskeland:* Miljøkonsekvensutgreiing av planar og tiltak, Faculty of Law, University of Bergen, 2007.

*Scott, Karen N.:* Tilting at Offshore Windmills: Regulating Wind Farm Development within the Renewable Energy Zone, in Journal of Environmental Law, Vol.18(1), 2006 pp. 89-118.

*Sheate, William:* Environmental Impact Assessment: Law and Policy-Making an Impact II, Cameron May, 1996.

*Shoemaker, Jessica A., Farmers' Legal Action Group, Inc.:* Farmers' Guide to Wind Energy: Legal Issues in Farming the Wind, 2007. Available at:

www.flaginc.org/topics/pubs/wind/FGWEcomplete.pdf.

*Siderius, Kees & van der Zwiep, Karel:* Memorandum. Towards a Trilateral Wadden Sea Convention, The Wadden Society, 1997.

*Sullivan, Edward:* Recent Developments in Comprehensive Planning Law, in Urban Lawyer, Vol.38, 2006 pp. 685-700.

*Sundberg, Jacob W.F.:* Civil Law, Common Law and the Scandinavians, in Scandinavian Studies in Law, Vol.13, 1969 pp. 179-205.

*Tamm, Ditlev:* The Danes and Their Heritage, in *Dahl, Børge*; *Melchior, Torben & Tamm, Ditlev* (eds.): Danish Law in a European Perspective, 2ⁿᵈ ed., Thomson, 2002 pp. 41-59.

*Taylor, Prue:* International law and the environment, in *Rob Harris* (ed.): Handbook of Environmental Law, The Royal Forest and Bird Protection Society of New Zealand, 2004 Ch. 23.

The World Commission on Environment and Development: Our Common Future, Oxford University Press, 1987.

*Titus, James G.:* Rising Seas, Coastal Erosion, and the Takings Clause: How to Save Wetlands and Beaches without Hurting Property Owners, in Maryland Law Review, Vol.57, 1998 pp. 1279-1399.

*Uerpmann, Robert:* International Law as an Element of European Constitutional Law: International Supplementary Constitutions, in Jean Monnet Working Papers No 9/2003.

*Verschuuren, Jonathan:* Effectiveness of Nature Protection Legislation in the EU and the US: The Birds and Habitats Directives and the Endangered Species Act, in Yearbook of Environmental Law, Vol.3, 2004 pp. 305-328.

*Villareal, Gavin R.:* Note. One Leg to Stand On: The Treaty Power and Congressional Authority for the Endangered Species Act after United States v. Lopez, in Texas Law Review, Vol.76(5), 1998 pp. 1125-1262.

*von Eyben, Bo:* Danish Property Law, in *Dahl, Børge; Melchior, Torben & Tamm, Ditlev* (eds.): Danish Law in a European Perspective, 2ⁿᵈ ed., Thomson – GadJura, 2002 pp. 209-236.

*Weiler, J.H.H.:* The Transformation of Europe, in Yale Law Journal, Vol.100, 1991 pp. 2403-2483.

*White, Omar N.:* The Endangered Species Act's Precarious Perch: A Constitutional Analysis under the Commerce Clause and the Treaty Power, in Ecology Law Quarterly, Vol.27, 2000 pp. 215-256.

*Wilde, Mark:* Civil liability for Environmental Damage. A Comparative Analysis of Law and Policy in Europe and the United States, Kluwer Law International, 2002.

*William Sheate:* Environmental Impact Assessment: Law and Policy-Making an Impact II, 1996 pp. 18-22.

*Zeigler Jr., Edward H.:* Rathkopf's The Law of Zoning and Planning, 4th ed., Thompson/West, 2006.